T0253512

Lecture Notes in Artificial Intelligence (LNAI)

Other volumes of the Lecture Notes in Computer Science relevant to Artificial Intelligence:

Lecture Notes in Artificial Intelligence

Subseries of Lecture Notes in Computer Science
Edited by J. Siekmann

Lecture Notes in Computer Science

Edited by G. Goos and J. Hartmanis

Editorial

Artificial Intelligence has become a major discipline under the roof of Computer Science. This is also reflected by a growing number of titles devoted to this fast developing field to be published in our Lecture Notes in Computer Science. To make these volumes immediately visible we have decided to distinguish them by a special cover as Lecture Notes in Artificial Intelligence, constituting a subseries of the Lecture Notes in Computer Science. This subseries is edited by an Editorial Board of experts from all areas of AI, chaired by Jörg Siekmann, who are looking forward to consider further AI monographs and proceedings of high scientific quality for publication.

We hope that the constitution of this subseries will be well accepted by the audience of the Lecture Notes in Computer Science, and we feel confident that the subseries will be recognized as an outstanding opportunity for publication by authors and editors of the AI community.

Editors and publisher

Lecture Notes in Artificial Intelligence

Edited by J. Siekmann

Subseries of Lecture Notes in Computer Science

353

Steffen Hölldobler

Foundations of Equational Logic Programming

Springer-Verlag

Berlin Heidelberg New York London Paris Tokyo Hong Kong

Editor

Steffen Hölldobler
Fachgebiet Intellektik, Fachbereich Informatik
Alexanderstr. 10, D-6100 Darmstadt, FRG

CR Subject Classification (1987): F.4.1, I.2.3

ISBN 3-540-51533-X Springer-Verlag Berlin Heidelberg New York
ISBN 0-387-51533-X Springer-Verlag New York Berlin Heidelberg

© Springer-Verlag Berlin Heidelberg 1989
Printed in Germany

Printing and binding: Druckhaus Beltz, Hemsbach/Bergstr.
2145/3140-543210 – Printed on acid-free paper

Preface

Logic programming languages were successfully applied to a variety of problems within automatic theorem proving, deductive databases, natural language processing, expert systems, knowledge representation, abstract interpretation, and meta-programming. There are many reasons for this success. Logic languages admit a simple, yet powerful semantics. They are declarative specification languages which are also directly executable. Control can be exercised over a program after its logic was specified. Powerful implementations were developed which allow the experienced user to write efficient programs. Because of their declarative nature and inherent parallelism they are good candidates for parallel implementations.

One of the main reasons for the efficiency of languages like Prolog was the decision to avoid equality like a plague. However, in many areas of mathematics, computer science, artificial intelligence, and operations research equations play a vital role. For example, equation solving is one of the main issues of computer algebra and automatic programming systems depend heavily on special equational theories.

In recent years many proposals for handling equational theories were drafted by researchers coming from logic programming, term rewriting, or unification theory. Though these fields emerged from symbolic logic and mechanical theorem proving, these proposals are often difficult to comprehend, because the authors use different concepts, notions, and notations. Many results were rediscovered. It is often not obvious how various calculi are related and many questions are still unanswered.

To overcome these problems we define a general framework for equational logic programming in this book. Besides presenting well-known concepts within this framework, we generalize many results, solve open problems, and develop new techniques.

After introducing the subject and stating some preliminary notions and results in chapters 1 and 2, equational logic programs are formally defined as (Horn clause) logic programs augmented with conditional equational theories. These programs admit least model and fixpoint semantics as shown in chapter 3.

In the sequel we rigorously develop various proof techniques. Basic results from unification theory are reviewed in chapter 4. These results are applied in chapter 5 to prove the soundness and strong completeness of SLDE-resolution, i.e. SLD-resolution, where the traditional unification algorithm is replaced by a sound and complete unification procedure under the equational theory in consideration.

In chapter 6 we develop such a universal unification procedure based on linear para-modulation. We demonstrate how certain conditions imposed one-by-one on a conditional equational theory restrict the search space and lead to special forms of paramodulation such as directed paramodulation, rewriting, and (basic) narrowing. At the end of this chapter we prove that the unification as well as the matching problem for canonical theories is undecidable.

In chapter 7 we extend the transformation rules which were first defined by Herbrand and later used by Martelli & Montanari to compute the most general unifier of two expressions in order to deal with conditional equational theories. This has the advantage that only the initial symbol of the left-hand and right-hand side of an equation trigger the application of the transformation rules. The completeness is proved by transforming refutations with respect to paramodulation into refutations with respect to the transformation rules. Applying this technique we can easily restrict our set of transformations if the conditional equational theory satisfies the conditions that allow to apply special forms of paramodulation.

Since unification problems under equational theories may have infinitely many different solutions or may be undecidable, a call of a universal unification procedure may result in infinitely many resolvents or may run forever without producing a single solution. These problems can be overcome if a unification procedure is defined by a sound and strongly complete set of inference rules. If we apply a so-called lazy resolution rule, where the corresponding arguments of the selected literals are added as equations to the new goal clause, then resolution and the inference rules for computing the unifiers under an equational theory can be treated on the same level. In chapter 8 we prove this result rigorously.

Finally, in chapter 9 we summarize our results, compare them with other approaches, and outline some open problems.

Several topics are not within the scope of this book. We do not consider representation and implementation issues with the exception of narrowing. Nor do we develop certain heuristics for the application of a selection function. We also do not take into account the problem of solving inequations or disequations. But we believe that these topics can be elaborated within the framework defined herein.

The book addresses students as well as scientists. It is self-contained, nevertheless some familiarity with predicate logic makes it easier to comprehend.

I owe Wolfgang Niegel a debt of gratitude for supporting me during the last eigth years. I also wish to thank Jörg Siekmann for his kind interest in my work. He gave many valuable hints for the final preparation of this thesis. J. Alan Robinson arose my interest in functional

and logic programming and inspired me to work in this area, for which I am most grateful. I learned a lot about proofs from discussions with Stephan Heilbrunner. The collaboration with Joachim Schreiber greatly improved my understanding of linear paramodulation. Last but not least I would like to thank Ulrich Furbach for being available whenever I needed help. Without his assistance work would have been much more difficult.

Sections 6.1 and 6.2 are based on joint work with Ulrich Furbach and Joachim Schreiber (Furbach et al. 1989). The results of sections 6.3 - 6.5 were presented in Hölldobler (1988a). Section 6.6 was done in collaboration with Stephan Heilbrunner (Heilbrunner & Hölldobler 1987). Special versions of chapters 3 and 7 were published in Hölldobler (1987a,b) and the results of chapter 7 were presented in Hölldobler (1988b). This thesis was written while I was at the University of the Federal Armed Forces, Munich.

Darmstadt, August 1989   Steffen Hölldobler

Contents

X

1 Introduction

Predicate logic was derived from efforts to analyze and formalize the properties of pure human thought. It was Leibniz's idea to have a universal language (*lingua characteristica*), in which every possible form of truth can be expressed, and a calculus (*calculus ratiocanator*), in which reasoning can be mechanized in a systematic and mathematically precise way (see Davis 1973, Siekmann 1987). But it took more than 200 years until Frege (1879) - in his famous *Begriffsschrift* - formally developed the main concepts of modern mathematical logic. Herbrand, Skolem, and Gödel showed in 1930 that the predicate calculus is a complete system, which provides a formal and constructive proof of every logically valid sentence in the language of the predicate calculus. To mechanize reasoning within the predicate calculus they proved that it suffices to consider only interpretations over the so-called Herbrand universe. In other words, the truth of a sentence in the language of the predicate calculus can be determined solely by the structure of its components (see e.g. Robinson 1979). It also turned out that the clausal form of logic is very helpful in order to let a machine perform the reasoning.

Right from the beginning, automatic theorem proving has also been the problem of how to prune the tremendous search space without affecting the completeness of the system. Robinson's (1965) resolution principle, in which the unification concept was placed at the heart of the proof system, has been the basis to impose a goal directedness on the search process. In the following years many efforts have been undertaken to increase the efficiency of resolution, for example a strategy has been developed such that resolution proofs become linear (see e.g. Loveland 1978).

In 1971 Colmerauer invented SYSTEM Q for natural language processing, which was later renamed to PROLOG. It was a linear resolution system in which the clauses involved were restricted to Horn clauses (see Cohen 1988, Kowalski 1988). Kowalski (1974) has given a procedural interpretation for PROLOG, which brings together the notions of deduction and computation. A PROLOG program like

   prefix([],z) ⇐
   prefix(x:y,x:z) ⇐ prefix(y,z)

is interpreted as a set of procedure declarations for *prefix*. The conclusion of a clause is interpreted as procedure head and the hypotheses of a clause are interpreted as procedure body containing procedure calls. A PROLOG program is called by a goal clause like

   ⇐ prefix(v, a:b:[])

which consists of procedure calls. A procedure like

   prefix(x:y,x:z) ⇐ prefix(y,z)

is invoked by applying the resolution rule to a procedure call in the goal clause and the program clause. The parameters are passed by the unification algorithm binding - in our example - v to the list $a{:}y$, x to a, and to the list $b{:}[]$. We obtain the new goal clause

$\Leftarrow$ prefix(y,b:[])

which may call the procedure

prefix([],z') $\Leftarrow$

resulting in the empty clause, which is interpreted as a halt statement. By combining the substitutions computed in the resolution steps, we find that v was bound to $a{:}[]$, which is interpreted as the answer to our initial question that states $a{:}[]$ is a prefix of the list $a{:}b{:}[]$.

Already we can see from this simple example some of the special features of programming in Horn logic. The language is essentially non-deterministic: we may choose an arbitrary procedure call in a goal clause as the next and only subgoal to perform resolution upon. Furthermore, there is in general more than one procedure declaration whose head unifies with the selected procedure call. The latter non-determinism differs from the former in that we have to consider all the choices to preserve the completeness of our system. These non-determinisms allow the separation of the logic needed to describe the problem from the control needed to exercise over the program in order to compute answers to queries; in Kowalski's (1979a) celebrated quotation:

Algorithm = Logic + Control.

Parameters are passed not only from the procedure call to the procedure body, but also from the procedure head to the goal clause. This is due to the unification algorithm, which is essentially an algorithm that computes the most general substitution - if it exists - such that the procedure call and the procedure head become syntactically identical. As a consequence, selector functions operating on data structures such as *car* and *cdr* are no longer needed and data structures may be only partially determined.

The theoretical foundations for computing in Horn logic laid down by Hill (1974) show that linear resolution with unrestricted selection functions for Horn clauses (LUSH-) resolution (or linear resolution with selection function for definite clauses (SLD-resolution)) is complete. Van Emden & Kowalski (1976), Clark(1979), and Apt & van Emden (1982) further developed the principal semantic properties of Horn logic which are

-     the existence of a canonical domain of computation,
-     the existence of a least and greatest model semantics,
-     the existence of a least and greatest fixpoint semantics,

- soundness and strong completeness results for successful and finitely failed derivations of the underlying implementation model, and
- soundness and completeness results for negation-as-failure.

(For an overview see Lloyd 1984.)

As logic programming is based on the notion of a relation, functional programming is based on the notion of a function. Functions have always been one of the basic concepts of mathematics. Based on the SKI-calculus (Schönfinkel 1924) and the λ-calculus (Church 1941) several programming languages have been developed, notably LISP (McCarthy et al. 1969) and, more recently languages like HOPE (Burstall et al. 1980), KRC (Turner 1981), or ML (Milner 1984). A functional program consists of a set of function definitions like

map(f,[]) → []

map(f,x:y) → f(x):map(f,y)

and is called by an expression like

map(add1,1:2:[]).

A computation step is performed by searching the expression for a subterm which is syntactically equal to an instance of the left-hand side of a function definition and, if such a redex exists, by replacing the subterm by the respective right-hand side of the function definition. In our example,

map(add1,1:2:[])

is syntactically equal to the left-hand side of

map(f,x:y) → f(x):map(f,y),

if f is bound to *add1*, x is bound to *1*, and y is bound to 2:[]. Hence, map(add1,1:2:[]) can be rewritten (or reduced) to

add1(1):map(add1,2:[]).

These rewriting steps can be repeated until the expression does not contain any redex. In our example, add1(1):map(add1,2:[]) can successively be rewritten as

add1(1):add1(2):[],

and, if *add1* is defined as the function that adds *1* to a given number, then

2:3:[]

can be regarded as the value of the initial expression.

Functional programming is non-deterministic, since in general more than one redex occurs in an expression. It is deterministic, since there is at most one function definition that can be applied to a single redex. Control knowledge is implicitly contained in nested function applications, higher-order functions - like *map* - are available, and the lazy evaluation of terms allows the handling of streams and infinite data objects. (For an overview see Henderson 1980.)

Functional and logic programming are quite similar. In both approaches sequences of symbols are replaced by others until a canonical or normal form has been reached. In a functional program this is indicated by an expression that does not contain a redex, whereas in logic programming the derivation of the empty clause signals the termination of the computation. The computation performed is totally syntactical. In the computation of a function, terms are replaced by their equals and, hence, the value of an expression must denote the same as the expression itself. In the computation of a goal clause, goals are successively replaced by semantically equivalent ones. As a set containing the empty clause is always unsatisfiable, so is the set containing the logic program and the initial goal clause from which the empty goal clause can be derived.

It is remarkable that one reason for getting interested in Horn clauses was that recursive function definitions can be much more naturally expressed in Horn than in non-Horn clauses (Kowalski 1979b, Cohen 1988). Consequently, Kowalski (1983) regards functions to be good for notation and complains that "*computation by means of rewrite rules is less versatile than backward chaining*". Thus, he prefers to use functional notation, but to transform a functional program into a logic one by replacing nested functional expressions by the logical *and* and intermediate variables.

Robinson (1983) argued against Kowalski's point of view: "*Relations have a very important role, of course, but they are not everything. It sometimes seems to me that we have returned to the earliest days in computing, when in expressing the evaluation of an expression, one had to introduce names for intermediate values and store them in cells with those names: finally there would be a cell with one's answer in it. Of course, the intermediate naming of steps in a successive evaluation is something that we really don't want to have to do. ... If you look at some PROLOG programs where deeply nested expressions are involved, you suddenly find yourself back in those days, having to name intermediate stages of a successive nested evaluation in order to come out at the end with a value*". In a more general setting Bobrow (1984) pointed out that "*no single paradigm is appropriate to all problems and powerful systems must allow multiple styles*".

There is another problem: the flattening of a program makes it difficult to apply rewrite rules. One has to define a complex control strategy and variables have to be annotated as those that may produce values and others that may receive values (for example see LEAF (Barbuti et al. 1986)). However, as we will see later, reducing goal clauses may cut an infinite search space into a finite one.

In addition, functional languages admit powerful features such as higher-order functions, lazy evaluation, the handling of streams, types, and polymorphism. These features can be achieved in logic languages only by means of extralogical constructions such as the *cut* (see Clocksin & Mellish 1981) or input-output patterns (Clark & Gregory 1981). These extralogical constructions are used by the programmer to make the computation behave deterministically and very often a logic program is used to compute a function. Why should we not use a functional language as well, if it has a clear semantics and, beyond that, powerful environments and widespread programming expertise are available for it?

Robinson & Sibert (1982) were the first to develop a language, called LOGLISP, in which a logic language, called LOGIC, is mutually embedded within the functional language LISP. Their basic idea was to define LOGIC as a set of LISP-functions which can be called from within LISP and to LISP-simplify goal clauses within the deduction cycle and, thus, to call LISP from within LOGIC. It turned out that the communication interfaces between LOGIC and LISP are quite complex. Therfore, a combined functional and logic programming language should be built upon the same data objects. In the sequel several proposals have been made to combine existing functional and logic languages (e.g. QUTE (Sato & Sakurai 1983) and APPLOG (Cohen 1986)).

Based on the idea of reducing expressions within the deduction cycle Subrahmanyam & You (1984, 1986) developed the language FUNLOG. There, expressions which cannot be unified are reduced once and then are again submitted to the unification algorithm. As a consequence, FUNLOG is "lazy" in the sense that expressions are only reduced if they are not unifiable.

Robinson & Greene (1987) designed the successor of LOGLISP, SUPER, a language which is based on Greene's (1985) LNF calculus. LNF is a functional language with lazy reduction semantics. Function expressions are compiled to combinatory terms and lazy normal order reduction is applied to the compiled expressions. Relations are introduced via set abstractions and are computed using additional reduction rules for the logical connectives and the existential quantifiers.

The disadvantage of all these proposals is that the system is in general not complete. It should be noted that completeness was never a goal in the development of these combined languages, rather they should provide a natural means to compute functions as well as relations.

A different approach has been taken by Miller & Nadathur (1987). They propose to base a combined function and logic language on a higher-order logic calculus and to use Huet's (1975) unification algorithm to unify typed lambda expressions. But this algorithm computes only an initial segment common to all unifiers of two expressions and the search space increases dramatically if one asks for a complete set of solutions.

Several authors incorporated logic features into functional languages by introducing the concept of a "logical variable" (e.g. Lindstrom 1985, Darlington et al. 1986). Their basic idea is to replace the matching algorithm used in a rewriting step by the unification algorithm and, thus, parameters are passed from the goal to the procedure and vice versa.

Another approach is to augment logic programs with a first-order equality theory. Kornfeld (1983), for example, suggests to add an *Equals* predicate to PROLOG such that, whenever the unification of two terms *s* and *t* fails, an attempt is made to solve the goal *Equals(s,t)*. The clauses for *Equals* have to be submitted by the user and, hence, Kornfeld's PROLOG-with-equality is in general incomplete. H. Gallaire (1985) pointed out that "*when dealing with full integration* (of functional and relational languages) *allowing the introduction of functions as terms in clause heads as well as in clause bodies, the tricks to handle functions through an Equal predicate do not work anymore. If functions are allowed in predicate heads, we directly come to the need of handling sets of equations*."

Several methods can be applied to logic languages with equality. Of course, we can add the axioms of equality (reflexivity, symmetry, transitivity, and substitution axioms) to our program and use resolution to compute answers to queries posed to the program (see e.g. Chang & Lee 1973). But, obviously, this is hopelessly inefficient as a basis for mechanizing equational reasoning.

Robinson & Wos (1969) proposed to use an additional rule of inference such as para-modulation which allows to replace terms within a clause by equal ones. This rule applied together with resolution is proven to be complete if the axiom of reflexivity and the so-called *functional reflexive axioms* are added to the set of clauses. Robinson & Wos were not sure whether they really needed the functional reflexive axioms and they conjectured that their calculus was complete even without these axioms. Several refinements of paramodulation have been formulated. Slagle (1974) showed that hyperresolution and a directed form of paramodulation (called *narrowing*) is complete if the equational theory in consideration is a *set of simplifiers* and each clause is replaced by its *collapse*. A set of simplifiers is nothing else as a complete set of reductions (Knuth & Bendix 1970) or a canonical and unconditional term rewriting system (Huet & Oppen 1980) and the collapse of a clause is nothing else but the normal form of the clause with respect to the set of simplifiers. It should be noted that Slagle's narrowing rule is defined to be applicable only to terms that are neither a constant nor a variable. Lankford (1975) proved that resolution and *special paramodulation*, i.e. para-modulation which is not applied to variables, is complete if the equational theory is a set of equations. Furthermore, he showed that clauses can be replaced by their normal form and equations can be directed if the set of equations is a canonical term rewriting system. Thus, by Lankford's results, the functional reflexive axioms are not needed if the equational theory is a set of equations. Brand (1975), Peterson (1983) and, more recently, Hsiang & Rusino-witch (1987) demonstrated that the functional reflexive axioms are not needed in general to prove the completeness of unrestricted paramodulation.

One of the disadvantages of paramodulation is that there are in general many terms in a clause to which paramodulation can be applied. E-resolution was introduced by Morris (1969) in order to give paramodulation goal directedness: paramodulation can only be applied to the selected literals. The completeness of E-resolution was shown by Anderson (1970). However, E-resolution inherits the difficult problem to find appropriate para-modulation steps such that the selected literals can be unified. This problem is in general un-decidable and various techniques have been proposed to overcome it. In Digricoli's (1979) RUE-resolution rule only a partial unifier between the selected literals is computed and the remaining disagreement pairs are added as *constraints* to the derived clause. Bläsius (1987) and Bläsius & Siekmann (1988) refined the paramodulated connection graph proof procedure (Siekmann & Wrightson 1980) for similar reasons. Their idea can best be explained by an example. To show that the terms h(b,x) and f(e) can be made equal under an equational theory which contains the equations EQ(h(b,a),f(b)) and EQ(b,e) it is necessary to transform the initial symbol "h" of h(x,b) to "f" or vice versa. This can only be done by using the equa-tion EQ(h(b,a),f(b)), which generates the subproblems that b must be equal to b, x must be equal to a, and b must be equal to e. The first two problems can be solved by the usual unifi-cation algorithm, whereas the last problem can be solved using the equation EQ(b,e).

A similar technique is based on the transformation rules given by Herbrand (1930) and Martelli & Montanari (1982) to compute the most general unifier of two expressions. Kirch-ner (1984), Martelli et al. (1986), Gallier & Snyder (1987a,b), and Hölldobler (1987a) ex-tended the original set of transformation rules to cope with equational theories.

We already mentioned the flattening of clauses obtained by replacing nested functional ex-pressions by the logical *and*. The flat clauses can then be handled by an SLD-refutation pro-cedure, e.g. Cox & Pietrzykowsky (1985), Bosco et al. (1986) or Togushi & Nogushi (1987).

An entirely different technique to handle troublesome equational axioms was proposed by Plotkin (1972). His idea was to build special equational axioms such as commutativity, asso-ciativity, etc. into the unification procedure and use such a unification procedure within a re-solution step (see Siekmann 1984, 1986, or 1989 for a survey).

Whereas unification procedures for different theories are usually based on entirely differ-ent techniques, universal unification procedures for a class of theories take as input an equa-tional theory of the respective class and the unification problem and generate as output a set of solutions for the unification problem under the equational theory. Such universal unification procedures were developed for example by Fay (1979), Hullot (1980), Réty et al. (1985) or Reddy (1985) for the class of canonical and unconditional term rewriting systems. In fact, any method developed for equational reasoning such as paramodulation, E-resolution, RUE-resolution, or sets of transformations can be seen as a universal unification procedure.

In this thesis we are concerned with equational logic programs, i.e. logic programs (in the sense of Lloyd 1984) augmented with Horn equational theories. Why are we interested in this class? As we laid down at the beginning we want to integrate functional and logic programming. However, at least for the moment we do not want to deal with higher-order unification. Thus, functions are viewed as equations. Furthermore, Jaffar et al. (1984, 1986) showed that the main semantic properties of logic programs hold also for equational logic programs. But they "*do not address the issue of corresponding computational methods*" (Jaffar et al. 1984). Last but not least we want to give a general framework for "corresponding computational methods" and, as we will see later, Horn equational theories are the largest class that admits least model semantics.

Before we desribe the organization of this thesis let us clarify some notions. Since we are interested in equational logic programming all inference rules will be linearly applied to goal clauses only (see e.g. Chang & Lee 1973). Completeness always means that whenever a substitution is a correct answer for an equational logic program and a goal clause, then we can compute an eventually more general answer substitution. This can be rephrased as follows. Whenever there exists a substitution σ such that the respective instance of a set S of Horn clauses is unsatisfiable, then the empty clause can be derived from this set of Horn clauses. Furthermore, the restriction of the composed substitutions used in the derivation steps to the variables occurring in S is more general than σ. Moreover, we always show strong completeness results, i.e. refutations will be independent of a selection function. In other words, in each step it suffices to select a single subgoal from the goal and to apply the respective inference rules only upon this subgoal.

Figure 1.1 gives an overview of this thesis.

In section 2 we present some basic notions concerning alphabets, terms, atoms, equations, and substitutions. It should be noted that we strictly distinguish between an atom and an equation.

In section 3 we formally introduce equational logic programs. An equational logic program generally consists of two sets of definite clauses: the logic part contains only clauses whose head is an atom and whose body may contain atoms as well as equations, whereas the equational part contains only clauses built entirely from equations. Since the

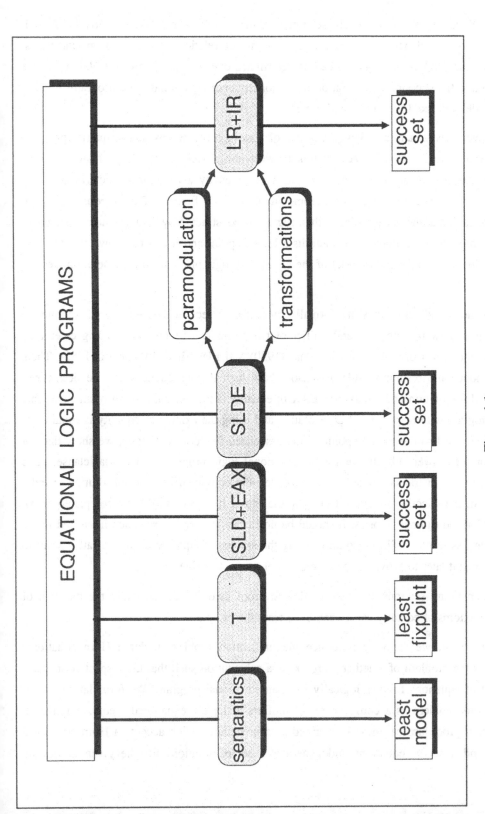

Figure 1.1

equational part is also a Horn clause program, the model-intersection property holds and, thus, the equational part generates a finest congruence relation on the set of ground terms. We show that logical consequence can be determined over the quotient of the Herbrand base modulo this finest congruence relation. As a consequence equational logic programs admit a least model and fixed functional assignment.

However, this semantics gives us no idea of how to compute answers to queries posed to an equational logic program. A first link between the model theory of an equational logic program and the respective proof theory can be given by a fixpoint characterization of a program. The idea is to assign a monotonic and continuous function T to an equational logic program such that the least model of the program is constructed by T in a bottom-up manner. T being monotonic and continuous admits a least fixpoint and it can be shown that this fixpoint is identical to the least model of the equational logic program in consideration (section 3.2).

Derivations and refutations are formally presented in section 3.4. As a first example we demonstrate how the most general unifier of two terms can be computed using essentially the inference rules presented by Herbrand (1930) and Martelli & Montanari (1982). Then, we introduce the resolution rule and show how logical consequences can be determined using SLD-resolution and the axioms EAX of equality. Thus, the success set of an equational logic program with respect to SLD-resolution and using the axioms of equality is equal to its least model and to the least fixpoint of the associated function T. Finally, we show that for each correct answer substitution for an equational logic program and a goal clause, there exists a more general computed one. Moreover, the computed answer substitution is independent of the selection function. Hence, at the end of this section we have completely introduced Horn equational theories. It should be noted that we are not so much interested in the completeness result of SLD-resolution using the axioms of equality itself, we rather want to use this result later to prove the completeness of more attractive systems.

The remaining sections are concerned with proof theory and, especially the question of how the axioms of equality can be removed from the program.

In section 4, we formally introduce the unification problem under a Horn equational theory as the problem of whether there exists a substitution such that the respective instance of a set of equations follows logically from an equational program. We formulate the solution to this problem as a complete set of unifiers under the equational theory. A universal unification procedure can now be defined as a procedure which accepts a Horn equational theory and a set of equations and generates a set of solutions for the given unification problem.

In 1972 G. D. Plotkin proposed to handle unconditional equational theories through appropriate complete unification procedures. In section 5 we show that SLDE-resolution, i.e. SLD-resolution where the notion of a most general unifier has been replaced by the notion of a unifier under a Horn equational theory is nothing else but a certain strategy to select subgoals from a goal clause provided that the equational logic program contains the axioms of equality. This is not really what we want. However, this result is used to prove that SLD-resolution, where the traditional unification algorithm has been replaced by a complete unification procedure under a Horn equational theory, is complete and independent of the selection function.

We are left with the problem of finding universal unification procedures for Horn equational theories. One way to handle equality is to give a substitution rule, which states that *two equal terms remain equal if in one term a subterm has been replaced by a term which is equal to it*. This concept leads to the introduction of the paramodulation rule in section 6. To be precise, whenever we use "paramodulation" in this thesis without further comments, we refer to "linear paramodulation".

But why are we interested in such an old method as paramodulation (Robinson & Wos 1969)? There are several reasons. We were unaware of a completeness result for linear paramodulation for Horn equational theories. If paramodulation is complete, do we need a factoring rule or the functional reflexive axioms? If we need the functional reflexive axioms, what is the reason for it and under which conditions can these axioms be removed? There were other reasons as well. We have defined a universal unification procedure for confluent theories (Hölldobler 1987a), but in the proofs we could not find the place where we have used the fact that the theory is confluent. We only had the intuitive argument that equations were only applied in one direction. Therefore, one question was where precisely had we used the confluency of the equational theory. In the literature we can find several universal unification procedures for term rewriting systems. In some cases a rewrite rule l→r is defined such that the variables occurring in the term r also have to occur in the term l (e.g. Hullot 1980), whereas sometimes "extra" variables are allowed to occur in r (e.g. Hussmann 1985). Can we generalize the former procedures or is there a failure in the completeness proofs of the latter ones? How can we define the notion of a "basic" occurrence (see Hullot 1980) such that it is more intelligible? How must we define rewriting such that it can be used as a simplification rule in refutations with respect to "basic" narrowing? Recently, there were many proposals for universal unification procedures based on paramodulation. Most of these proposals were for unconditional equational theories and, thus, two more questions arose. Can these procedures be generalized such that they handle conditional equational theories as well? How are these procedures related to each other?

Therefore, the goal is to give a general framework for universal unification procedures for Horn equational theories based on paramodulation such that we can answer all the given questions, but the methods are as general as possible.

We start by giving a rigorous proof of the completeness of paramodulation without factoring for Horn equational theories using well-known techniques from logic programming. Furthermore, we show in detail why the functional reflexive axioms are needed even in the case, where we only want to know whether a set of ground equations is a logical consequence of an equational logic program. Of course, paramodulation is far from being practical, since it generates many redundant and irrelevant inferences. In the sequel we impose certain conditions on an equational program such that paramodulation can be restricted.

In section 6.3 we show how the ground confluence of an equational logic program affects the search space: it suffices to use the equations of the head of an equational clause only in one direction. We demonstrate that the notion of a term rewriting system can easily be derived from equational programs by restricting the variables that occur in the body and in the right hand side of the head of an equational clause such that these variables have to occur in the left hand side of the head of the equational clause. Such equational clauses will be called rewrite rule. The main effect of this variable condition is that the functional reflexive axioms are no longer needed if we want to know whether a set of ground equations is a logical consequence of a set of rewrite rules (section 6.4). One should observe, that a term rewriting system generally contains conditional rules.

An immediate consequence of this observation is that for ground confluent term rewriting systems narrowing, a restricted form of paramodulation which is applicable only if the selected term is not a variable, can be used to solve the unification problem provided that no left hand side of a rewrite rule is a variable and that answer substitutions are normalizable (section 6.5). This demonstrates that the commonly used techniques for doing logic programming within term rewriting systems can easily be derived from equational programs and paramodulation. Furthermore, if the term rewriting system is canonical, then innermost narrowing can be applied. We show that an adaptation of Boyer & Moore's (1972) idea of structure sharing that splits clauses into a skeleton and an environment part achieves the same effect as basic narrowing without introducing Hullot's notion of a "basic occurrence". Furthermore, we easily derive Fribourg's (1985) completeness result for innermost narrowing if the canonical term rewriting system is completely defined and we consider only ground substitutions.

In section 6.6 we show that the unification and matching problem for the class of equational theories that can be defined by a canonical and unconditional term rewriting system is undecidable. This is achieved by reducing it to the problem of whether the language generated by two context free grammers is disjoint. Moreover, since also the matching problem is undecidable, we conclude that the class of canonical theories with a decidable matching problem is a proper subset of the set of canonical theories.

As we mentioned already paramodulation has the disadvantage that a given subgoal generally contains many subterms which are candidates for applying paramodulation to and we have to investigate all of them to ensure the completeness of the system. To overcome this problem we can use complete sets of transformations. The basic idea is as follows. If we want to unify two expressions, we look only at the initial symbols of these expressions and let the initial symbols drive the decision of which transformation should be applied. This idea can already be found by Herbrand (1930). In his thesis he proposed essentially the transformation rules that can be used to compute the most general unifier of two terms (see Martelli & Montanari 1982). In section 7 we extend these transformations to handle Horn equational theories as well. The completeness of the set of transformations is given by transforming refutations with respect to paramodulation into refutations with respect to the transformation rules. Hence, the refinements of paramodulation developed in chapter 6 carry over to the set of transformations.

Thus we develop two classes of universal unification procedures for Horn equational theories which are based on paramodulation and complete sets of transformations respectively. Using the strong completeness result of EP-resolution from chapter 5, we can build any one of the procedures into EP-resolution. However, EP-resolution inherits a principal problem. Since a unification problem under a Horn equational theory may be infinitary or undecidable, a unification procedure may return infinitely many solutions or may not terminate even without producing a single solution. To overcome this problem we make use of a *lazy resolution* rule (LR). If we want to resolve upon the selected literals P(a) and P(b), then, traditionally, we unify a and b and apply the unifying substitution to the remaining literals. However, in a lazy resolution step we do not unify a and b immediately, rather we will add the *constraint* EQ(a,b) to the new clause. This technique seems to have first been used by Huet (1972) in the context of resolution and higher-order unification. Now assume a universal unification procedure for Horn equational theories is defined by a sound and strongly complete set of inference rules (IR). Examples for such sets of inference rules are paramodulation or complete sets of transformations. From the completeness of EP-resolution follows immediately that lazy resolution together with this set of inference rules is complete. In section 8 we show the independence of a selection function for refutations with respect to lazy resolution and such sets of inference rules by using a simple switching lemma. As a consequence, the user can decide via the selection function which parts of the unification problem should be solved immediately after a lazy resolution step and which parts of it should be delayed until more information will eventually be available. Thus we give a general result which can be instantiated to strong completeness results for e.g. lazy E-resolution (Bürckert 1986, 1987) or EQLOG (Goguen & Meseguer 1984, 1986).

Finally, in section 9 we summarize the results obtained in this thesis and we finish by comparing our approaches with other techniques and by pointing out some open problems and future developments.

2 Preliminaries

A **first order theory** is defined by a first order language built over some alphabet, a set of axioms, and a set of inference rules (e.g. Mendelson 1979). The language consists of the well-formed formulas of the first order theory. The axioms are a designated subset of the well-formed formulas. The axioms and rules of inference are used to derive the theorems of the first order theory. We start with defining alphabets.

Definition:

An **alphabet** is the union of seven disjoint sets of symbols:

(1) the set of **variables,**

(2) the set of **function symbols,**

(3) the set of **predicate symbols,**

(4) the set {EQ},

(5) the set of **connectives** $\{\neg, \vee, \wedge, \Rightarrow, \Leftrightarrow\}$

(6) the set of **quantifiers** $\{\forall, \exists\}$, and

(7) the set of **punctuation symbols** $\{(, \{, , , \},)\}$.

The sets (4)-(7) are the same for each alphabet, whereas the countably infinite sets (1)-(3) may vary from alphabet to alphabet.

We assume that an **arity** was assigned to each function and predicate symbol and a function or predicate symbol is said to be **n-ary** iff its arity is n.

The set of function symbols must contain at least one 0-ary element and is partitioned into two disjoint subsets, the set of **defined function symbols** and the set of **constructors**. 0-ary constructors are often called **constants**. Constructors are used to build structured data objects. Defined function symbols are names for functions which perform computations on data objects.

As an example consider the variable x, the function symbols f, c, a, the predicate symbol Q with the arities 0 assigned to a, 1 assigned to c and f, and 2 assigned to Q. Let f be the only defined function symbol. Then c and a are constructors and, since a has arity 0, it is a constant.

If not indicated otherwise we make use of the notational conventions depicted in table 2.1 in the sense that whenever we refer to x we implicitly assume that x is a variable (see also Notations).

A	atom	Q	predicate symbol
B	finite multiset of atoms	R	term rewriting system
C	atom or equation	S	set of Horn clauses
D	finite multiset of atoms and equations	V	finite set of variables
E	equation	a,b,...	constructors
EP	equational program	f,g,...	defined function symbols
F	finite multiset of equations	i,j,...	natural numbers
I	E-interpretation	r,s,...	terms
LP	logic program	x,y,...	variables
P	program clause	$\sigma,\theta,...$	substitutions

Table 2.1: Notational Conventions

Sometimes we use multisets in this thesis. **Multisets** are like sets, but allow multiple occurrences of identical elements. Set operators are applied to multisets as well with their obvious meaning. For example, if D and D' are multisets, the **equality** D=D' means that any element occurring n-times in D, also occurs n-times in D', and vice versa. The **union** D∪D' is a multiset containing m+n occurrences of any element occurring m-times in D and n-times in D'. The **difference** D\D' is a multiset containing m-n occurrences of any element occurring m-times in D and n-times in D'.

2.1 Terms, Atoms, and Equations

Now we turn to the definition of the constituents of our first order language over an alphabet.

Definition:

A variable is a **term**. If f is an n-ary function symbol, $n \geq 0$, and t_i, $1 \leq i \leq n$, are terms, then $f(t_1, \ldots, t_n)$ is a **term**.

If f is an n-ary defined function symbol then $f(t_1, \ldots, t_n)$ is called a **functional term**, otherwise $f(t_1, \ldots, t_n)$ is called a **construction**.

Definition:

If Q is an n-ary predicate symbol, $n \geq 0$, and t_i, $1 \leq i \leq n$, are terms, then $Q(t_1, \ldots, t_n)$ is an **atom**.

If X is a 0-ary function or predicate symbol we abbreviate X() to X.

Definition:

An **equation** has the form EQ(s,t). s and t are said to be the **elements** of EQ(s,t).

If s=t (resp. s≠t) then EQ(s,t) is said to be **trivial** (resp. **non-trivial**).

Due to our notational conventions, f(c(x)) is a functional term, c(a) is a construction, Q(f(c(x)),c(a)) is an atom, and EQ(f(c(x)),c(a)) is a non-trivial equation with elements f(c(x)) and c(a). We already mentioned in the introduction that we strictly distinguish between atoms and equations. An atom is always of the form $P(t_1, \ldots, t_n)$ with $P \neq EQ$, whereas an equation is always of the form EQ(s,t). The reason is that we intend to treat atoms and equations differently.

Definition:

A variable x has the **initial symbol** x. A term, an equation, or an atom of the form $X(t_1, \ldots, t_n)$ has the **initial symbol** X.

For example, the atom Q(f(a),x) has the initial symbol Q.

In order to have a formal way to deal with a subterm of an atom, equation, or term X we define the notion of an occurrence (or a position) in X.

Definition:

Let X be an atom, an equation, or a term. The set of **occurrences in X**, Occ(X), is inductively defined as follows:

(1) $\Lambda \in \mathrm{Occ}(X)$, and

(2) $\pi \in \mathrm{Occ}(t_i)$ implies $i \cdot \pi \in \mathrm{Occ}(Y(t_1,\ldots,t_n))$, $1 \le i \le n$, where Y is "EQ", a function, or a predicate symbol.

Let $\pi, \pi_1, \pi_2 \in \mathrm{Occ}(X)$, the set of occurrences is partially ordered by the prefix ordering $\pi_1 \le \pi_2$ iff there exists a π such that $\pi_1 = \pi_2 \cdot \pi$. If neither $\pi_1 \le \pi_2$ nor $\pi_2 \le \pi_1$ we say π_1 and π_2 are **disjoint**, in symbols $\pi_1 \ne \pi_2$, and $\pi_1 < \pi_2$ iff $\pi_1 \le \pi_2$ and $\pi_1 \ne \pi_2$.

Hence, an occurrence in X is a finite word over a representation of the natural numbers, where Λ denotes the empty word and • denotes concatenation. An occurrence can be seen as an access path in an atom or a term. Consider, for example, the atom $Q(f(c),x)$, then

$$\mathrm{Occ}(Q(f(c),x)) = \{\Lambda, 1, 1 \cdot 1, 2\},$$

$1 \cdot 1 < 1 < \Lambda$, and $1 \ne 2$. Figure 2.1.1 illustrates the notion of an occurrence, where the atom $Q(f(b),x)$ is depicted as a labelled tree.

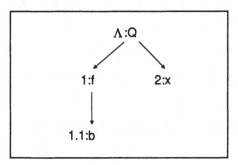

Figure 2.1.1

Definition:

Let s be a term. For all $\pi \in \mathrm{Occ}(s)$ and an arbitrary term t we define **the subterm of s at π, $s|\pi|$**, and **the replacement of t in s at π, $s|\pi \leftarrow t|$**, inductively as follows:

(1) $s|\Lambda| = s$,

(2) $f(s_1,\ldots,s_i,\ldots,s_n)|i \cdot \pi| = s_i|\pi|$,

(3) $s|\Lambda \leftarrow t| = t$, and

(4) $f(s_1,\ldots,s_i,\ldots,s_n)|i \cdot \pi \leftarrow t| = f(s_1,\ldots,s_i|\pi \leftarrow t|,\ldots,s_n)$.

If $\pi \ne \Lambda$, then $s|\pi|$ is said to be a **proper subterm** of s.

If t is the subterm of s at π then we also say that s **contains** t at π or t **occurs** in s at π. We will omit "at π" if it can be determined from the context. Furthermore, we may qualify the term t by saying that it is a variable, not a variable, a functional term, or a construction and therefore, we will call π a **variable, non-variable, functional term, or construction occur-**

rence, respectively. Observe that $\pi_1 \leq \pi_2$ iff $s|\pi_1|$ is a subterm of $s|\pi_2|$. In the sequel we will also make use of the obvious extensions of the above definitions to atoms and equations.

As an example let f be a defined function symbol, b be a constant and consider the atom A $= Q(f(b),x)$, then $f(b)$ is a functional term occurring in A at 1, b is a construction occurring in A at $1\bullet 1$, and x is a variable occurring in A at 2. Λ, 1, and $1\bullet 1$ are non-variable occurrences, whereas 2 is a variable occurrence. Further, $Q(x,x)|1 \leftarrow f(b)| = Q(f(b),x)$.

Notation:

Let X be a term, an equation, or an atom,

$\mathbf{Var(X)} = \{ x \mid \exists \pi \in Occ(X): X|\pi| = x \text{ and x is a variable } \}$

           is the **set of variables occurring in** X,

$\mathbf{Con(X)} = \{ t \mid \exists \pi \in Occ(X): X|\pi| = t \text{ and t is a construction } \}$

           is the **set of constructions occurring in** X, and

$\mathbf{Fun(X)} = \{ t \mid \exists \pi \in Occ(X): X|\pi| = t \text{ and t is a functional term } \}$

           is the **set of functional terms occurring in** X.

For example, $Var(Q(f(a),x)) = \{x\}$ and $Fun(Q(f(a),x)) = \{f(a)\}$.

Definition:

     A term, an atom, or an equation is said to be **ground** if it does not contain a variable.

For example, $f(c(a))$ is a ground term, whereas $Q(a,x)$ is not a ground atom.

We extend the previous definitions in the obvious way to hold also for (multi-) sets of terms, atoms, or equations.

2.2 Substitutions

Definition:

A **substitution** is a mapping σ from the set of variables into the set of terms which is equal to the identity mapping almost everywhere. Hence, it can be represented as the finite set of pairs

$$\sigma = \{\ x_1 \leftarrow t_1, \ldots, x_n \leftarrow t_n\ \},$$

where $x_i \neq t_i$ for all i, $1 \leq i \leq n$. The identity mapping, i.e. the **empty substitution**, is denoted by ε. Let V be a set of variables. The **restriction of σ to V** is defined as

$$\sigma|_V = \{\ x \leftarrow t \in \sigma \mid x \in V\ \}.$$

For example, the restriction of $\{x \leftarrow f(y),\ z \leftarrow b\}$ to $\{x\}$ is the substitution $\{x \leftarrow f(y)\}$.

Definition:

If σ is a substitution, then the **domain** of σ is defined as

Dom$(\sigma) = \{\ x \mid x$ is a variable and $\sigma x \neq x\ \}$

and the **codomain** of σ is defined as

Cod$(\sigma) = \{\ \sigma x \mid x \in$ Dom$(\sigma)\ \}.$

The set of variables occurring in the codomain of σ is denoted by **VCod**(σ).

Let $\sigma = \{x \leftarrow f(y),\ z \leftarrow b\}$, then Dom$(\sigma) = \{x,z\}$, Cod$(\sigma) = \{f(y),b\}$, and VCod$(\sigma) = \{y\}$.

Definition:

The **composition** $\theta\sigma$ of the substitutions σ and θ is the substitution

$$\{\ x \leftarrow t \in \theta \mid x \notin \text{Dom}(\sigma)\ \} \cup \{\ x \leftarrow \theta t \mid x \leftarrow t \in \sigma \wedge x \neq \theta t\ \}.$$

As an example consider the substitutions $\sigma = \{x \leftarrow y,\ z \leftarrow f(y)\}$ and $\theta = \{y \leftarrow x,\ x \leftarrow a\}$, then $\theta\sigma = \{y \leftarrow x,\ z \leftarrow f(x)\}$.

Definition:

A substitution σ is **idempotent** iff $\sigma\sigma = \sigma$.

Observe that a substitution σ is idempotent iff Dom(σ) and VCod(σ) are disjoint (see Herold 1983). For example, $\{x \leftarrow f(y),\ z \leftarrow b\}$ is idempotent, but $\sigma = \{x \leftarrow f(x)\}$ is not idempotent, since $\sigma\sigma = \{x \leftarrow f(f(x))\} \neq \sigma$.

We do not want to restrict ourselves to idempotent substitutions, since we are interested, for example, in the question of whether there exists a substitution λ such that $(\lambda\{x \leftarrow f(y)\})|_{\{x\}} = \{x \leftarrow f(f(y))\}$. We can find such a λ, namely $\lambda = \{y \leftarrow f(y)\}$, but λ is not idempotent. Moreover, the composition of idempotent substitutions is not necessarily idempotent. For example, consider the substitutions $\sigma = \{y \leftarrow a\}$ and $\theta = \{x \leftarrow y\}$. Then, $\theta\sigma = \{x \leftarrow y,\ y \leftarrow a\}$, which is obviously not idempotent.

We now extend substitutions as morphisms on the set of terms, atoms, and equations:

Definition:

Let X be a term, an atom, or an equation, Y be "EQ", a function, or a predicate
symbol, and σ be a substitution, then σX, the **instance** of X by σ, is inductively
defined as follows:

$$\sigma X = \begin{cases} t & \text{if } X \leftarrow t \in \sigma \\ X & \text{if } Var(X) \cap Dom(\sigma) = \varnothing \\ Y(\sigma t_1,...,\sigma t_n) & \text{if } X = Y(t_1,...,t_n) \end{cases}$$

If σX is a ground term, atom, or equation, then σX is called a **ground instance**
of X.

As an example consider the equation $E = EQ(x,g(z))$ and the substitution $\sigma = \{x \leftarrow f(y),$
$z \leftarrow b\}$. Then, $\sigma E = EQ(f(y),g(b))$. $EQ(f(y),g(b))$ is not a ground instance of E since it contains the variable y.

For simplicity of notation we assume to have at our disposal a set of variables, GENSYM,
out of which we can take an unlimited number of "new" variables. More formally, let the set
of variables $V = V_0 \cup GENSYM$ such that V_0 and GENSYM are disjoint. We will adopt the
computational proviso that whenever GENSYM is referenced by $x \in GENSYM$, GENSYM
and V_0 are subsequently "updated" by $GENSYM' = GENSYM \setminus \{x\}$ and $V_0' = V_0 \cup \{x\}$.
Since $V = V_0 \cup GENSYM = V_0' \cup GENSYM'$ we will not always keep track of the '-s. In
practice the problem of finding new variables is simplified by a subscript for the variables or
in LISP by using the GENSYM-operator, for example.

Proposition 2.2.1 (Lloyd 1984):

Let θ, σ, and γ be substitutions and X be a term, atom or equation, then

(1) $\theta\varepsilon = \varepsilon\theta = \theta$,

(2) $\sigma(\theta X) = (\sigma\theta)X$, and

(3) $\gamma(\sigma\theta) = (\gamma\sigma)\theta$.

Using (3) we can omit parentheses when writing compositions of substitutions. Furthermore, to avoid unnecessary parentheses when writing restrictions of compositions of substitutions we assume that composition precedes restriction.

Definition:

A substitution ρ is a **renaming substitution** for a term, an atom, or an equation
X iff

(1) $Dom(\rho) \subseteq Var(X)$,

(2) $Cod(\rho)$ contains only variables,

(3) $\forall x,y \in Dom(\rho): x \neq y \Rightarrow \rho x \neq \rho y$, and

(4) $(Var(X) \backslash Dom(\rho)) \cap VCod(\rho) = \emptyset$.

Conditions (1) and (2) state what is sometimes called a **variable-pure** substitution, whereas the remaining conditions ensure that different variables remain different after a renaming substitution has been applied.

As an example consider the atom $A = Q(x,y)$; here $\{x \leftarrow z\}$ is a renaming substitution for A, whereas $\{x \leftarrow y\}$ violates condition (4).

Definition:

> Let X and Y be terms, atoms or equations. X and Y are **variants** iff there exist renaming substitutions σ and θ such that $X = \sigma Y$ and $Y = \theta X$. We also say that **X is a variant of** Y and **Y is a variant of** X.

If X and Y are variants, $X = \sigma Y$, and the variables in the codomain of σ "have not occurred before", then X is said to be a **new variant** of Y. Note, in this case Y cannot be a new variant of X.

As an example consider the terms $s = f(x,y)$ and $t = f(y,x)$. s and t are variants, but neither is s a new variant of t, nor is t a new variant of s. However, $f(z,z')$ is a new variant of both s and t.

Proposition 2.2.2 (Lloyd 1984):

> *If X and Y be variants, then there exist substitutions σ and θ such that $X = \sigma Y$ and $Y = \theta X$, where σ is a renaming substitution for Y and θ is a renaming substitution for X.*

Proposition 2.2.3:

> *Let V be a set of variables and θ, σ, and γ be substitutions, then*
>
> *(1) $\theta(\sigma|_V)|_V = \theta\sigma|_V$,*
>
> *(2) $\pi \in Occ(s)$ implies $(\sigma s)|_\pi| = \sigma(s|_\pi|)$,*
>
> *(3) $\pi \in Occ(s)$ implies $(\sigma s)|_{\pi \leftarrow \sigma t|} = \sigma(s|_{\pi \leftarrow t|})$.*

Proof:

(1)   Let θ and σ be substitutions and V be a finite set of variables. Note, $Dom(\sigma|_V) = V \cap Dom(\sigma)$.

$$
\begin{aligned}
\theta(\sigma|_V)|_V \quad &= \quad \{x \leftarrow t \in \theta(\sigma|_V) \mid x \in V\} &\text{(restriction)}\\
&= \quad \{x \leftarrow t \in \theta \mid x \notin Dom(\sigma|_V) \wedge x \in V\}\\
&\quad \cup \{x \leftarrow \theta t \mid x \leftarrow t \in \sigma|_V \wedge x \neq \theta t \wedge x \in V\} &\text{(composition)}\\
&= \quad \{x \leftarrow t \in \theta \mid x \notin Dom(\sigma) \wedge x \in V\}\\
&\quad \cup \{x \leftarrow \theta t \mid x \leftarrow t \in \sigma \wedge x \neq \theta t \wedge x \in V\} &\text{(restriction)}
\end{aligned}
$$

$$= (\{x\leftarrow t{\in}\,\theta \mid x{\notin}\,\text{Dom}(\sigma)\} \cup \{x\leftarrow\theta t \mid x\leftarrow t{\in}\,\sigma \wedge x{\neq}\theta t\})$$
$$\cap \{x\leftarrow t \mid x{\in}\,V \wedge t \text{ is a term}\}$$
$$= \theta\sigma|_V. \qquad\qquad\qquad\qquad\qquad\qquad\text{(composition)}$$

(2)   The proof is by induction on the occurrence of the subterm $s|\pi|$ in s. The case $\pi{=}\Lambda$ being trivial we turn to the induction step and assume that $i{\bullet}\pi \in \text{Occ}(s)$. Hence, there exists a term of the form $f(t_1,\ldots,t_n)$ such that

$$s|\pi| = f(t_1,\ldots,t_n) \qquad\qquad\qquad\qquad\qquad\qquad (*)$$

and $1{\leq}i{\leq}n$. Now,

$\sigma(s|i{\bullet}\pi|)$	$= \sigma((s|\pi|)|i|)$	(definition of occurrences)
	$= \sigma(f(t_1,\ldots,t_n)|i|)$	(*)
	$= \sigma t_i$	(definition of occurrences)
	$= f(\sigma t_1,\ldots,\sigma t_n)|i|$	(definition of occurrences)
	$= (\sigma f(t_1,\ldots,t_n))|i|$	(definition of instances)
	$= (\sigma(s|\pi|))|i|$	(*)
	$= ((\sigma s)|\pi|)|i|$	(induction hypothesis)
	$= (\sigma s)|i{\bullet}\pi|.$	(definition of occurrences)

(3).   The proof is by induction similar to (2).   qed

3 Equational Logic Programming

Throughout this thesis we only consider the clausal form of logic. This form has the advantage that reasoning can be performed in the purely syntactic context of a Herbrand universe, base, and model. We have a canonical syntactic domain and functional assignment and resolution can be used to compute logical consequences.

As we are not really interested in full first order theories, we only investigate first order theories which are restricted to Horn clauses and include the equality relation. This loss of expressive power is acceptable (at least for the moment) since for Horn theories we have a sufficiently efficient derivation rule, namely the LUSH-resolution rule (Hill 1974), as a basis for the implementation. Furthermore, logical consequences can be determined by a single model, since the model intersection property holds for Horn clauses.

Work is going on to extend the expressive power of Horn clauses without loosing the desired efficiency properties of Horn clauses: For example, under the closed world assumption negation by failure was introduced by Clark (1977), Reiter (1978), and Sheperdson (1984) and was used to allow full first order logic expressions in the body of a Horn clause (Lloyd & Topor 1984, 1985, 1986).

In this chapter we define equational logic programs as logic programs which are augmented by Horn equational theories. We give two semantics for these programs. The first one is given as the least Herbrand E-model for equational logic programs. From the proof theoretic point of view this semantics corresponds to deductions with respect to resolution and taking into account the axioms of equality. Unfortunately, this semantics does not preserve a principal semantic property of logic programming: It does not admit a canonical domain of computation and a fixed functional assignment.

To overcome these problems we develop a second semantics. Since the equational theory added to a logic program is a Horn theory, it defines a finest congruence relation on the set of ground terms. Therefore, we may consider Herbrand universes, bases, interpretations, and models modulo this finest congruence relation. Because the model-intersection property holds also for these models, the semantics of an equational logic program can be defined as the least Herbrand model modulo the finest congruence relation defined by the equational part of the program. From the proof theoretic point of view this semantics corresponds to deductions with respect to a resolution rule where the unification algorithm has been replaced by a unification procedure under a Horn equational theory.

Having developed a model theory for equational logic programs we will then briefly recall the fixpoint theory and its adaptation to logic programming. Finally, we will show that LUSH- (or SLD-) resolution is a complete inference rule that can be used to demonstrate that a set of clauses consisting of an equational logic program, the axioms of equality, and a goal clause is unsatisfiable.

3.1 Equational Logic Programs

We already defined an alphabet and the constituents of a language of a first order theory. Now we turn to the definition of the language itself which consists of all Horn clauses constructed from the symbols in the alphabet. Horn clauses arise in three species, program clauses, equational clauses, and goal clauses. Recall, A denotes an atom, E denotes an equation, D denotes a finite multiset of atoms and equations, and F denotes a finite multiset of equations (see table 2.1, p. 16).

Definition:

> A **program clause** is of the form $A \Leftarrow D$ and an **equational clause** is of the form $E \Leftarrow F$. D (resp. F) is called the **body**, A (resp. E) is called the **head**, and the initial symbol of A (resp. E) is called the **name** of the program (resp. equational) clause.
>
> A **goal clause** is of the form $\Leftarrow D$. The elements of D are called **subgoals**. If $D = \emptyset$ then the goal clause is said to be **empty** and will be denoted by ▢.
>
> An **input clause** is either a program or an equational clause and a **Horn clause** is either an input or a goal clause.

Program clauses may contain atoms as well as equations in their bodies. Similarly, subgoals may be atoms or equations. However, the body of an equational clause consists only of equations. For notational convenience, we often omit curly brackets when writing clauses. For example, we abbreviate the program clause $Q(a) \Leftarrow \{EQ(a,b)\}$ to $Q(a) \Leftarrow EQ(a,b)$.

In first order logic (e.g. Mendelson 1979) the program clause $A \Leftarrow C_1, \ldots, C_n$ is the universally closed formula $\forall (A \vee \neg C_1 \ldots \vee \neg C_n)$ or, equivalently, $\forall (A \Leftarrow C_1 \wedge \ldots \wedge C_n)$. Furthermore, the goal clause $\Leftarrow C_1, \ldots, C_n$ is the universally closed formula $\forall (\neg C_1 \vee \ldots \vee \neg C_n)$ or, equivalently, $\neg \exists (C_1 \wedge \ldots \wedge C_n)$. The multiset notation reflects that $\vee$ and $\wedge$ are commutative and that we do not intend to include an inference rule (sometimes called *factoring*; e.g. Chang & Lee 1973) that allows to infer C from $C \wedge C$ (resp. $C \vee C$). Furthermore, the order in which the subgoals are investigated is irrelevant for proof theoretic arguments. Note, in contrast to our clauses an ordering from left to right is imposed on the subgoals of PROLOG-program (e.g. Clocksin & Mellish 1981).

Remark:

A goal clause as well as the body of a program clause consists of a multiset of atoms and equations. In section 3.4 we will use a lifting lemma (lemma 3.4.2.6) which preserves the length of the refutations. However, this lifting lemma does not hold if we assume that the body of a program clause is a set. As an example consider the set $X = \{P(a), P(x)\}$ and the substitution $\sigma = \{x \leftarrow a\}$. Then, $\sigma X = \{P(a)\}$. If the logic program consists only of the program clause $P(a) \Leftarrow$ then there exists a refutation of $\Leftarrow \sigma X$ with respect to the resolution rule of lenght 1. However, the refutation of $\Leftarrow X$ with respect to the resolution rule has length 2. (We will not consider factoring of program or goal clauses). Furthermore, in an implementation the test of whether two atoms or equations are identical is in general a very costly operation as the clauses are stored implicitly by separating the "skeleton part" and the "environment part" (e.g. Boyer & Moore 1972).

Since we consider only first order Horn theories the well-formed formulas of our theories are Horn clauses and sets of Horn clauses.

The following definition of the homogeneous form of a set of program clauses are essentially those given by van Emden & Lloyd (1984) and Hoddinott & Elcock (1986).

Definition:

The **homogeneous form** of a program clause $Q(t_1,\ldots,t_n) \Leftarrow D$ is the program clause

$Q(x_1,\ldots,x_n) \Leftarrow D \cup \{ EQ(x_i,t_i) \mid 1 \leq i \leq n \}$,

where x_i, $1 \leq i \leq n$, are new variables. The **homogeneous form** H(S) of a finite set of program and equational clauses S, is the set of clauses containing just the homogeneous form of each program clause in S.

As an example consider the program clause

$Q(a) \Leftarrow EQ(a,b)$.

Its homogeneous form is the clause

$Q(x) \Leftarrow EQ(a,b), EQ(x,a)$.

We now proceed to define the set of axioms of a first order Horn theory. Since we are interested in logic programming only input clauses can be axioms. We call such a set of input clauses a logic program.

Definition:

Let S be a finite set of program and equational clauses. The set of all clauses in S with the same name Q is called the **definition** of Q. S is called an **equational logic program** and is written in the form <EP,LP>, where LP = $\{ Q(t_1,\ldots,t_n) \Leftarrow D \in S \mid Q$ is a predicate symbol $\}$ and EP = $S \setminus$ LP. A **logic program** is an equational logic program <EP,LP>, where EP = $\{EQ(x,x) \Leftarrow \}$. An **equational program** is an equational logic program <EP,LP> where LP=$\emptyset$.

The axiom of reflexivity, $EQ(x,x)\Leftarrow$, is needed in a logic program, since the body of a program clause may contain equations. This is in contrast to Jaffar et al. (1984, 1986), who assumed that the symbol "EQ" does not occur in a program clause.

When writing logic (resp. equational) programs we often omit the EP (resp. LP) part and simply write LP (resp. EP) instead of $\langle\{EQ(x,x)\Leftarrow\},LP\rangle$ (resp. $\langle EP,\varnothing\rangle$). Furthermore, we often omit curly brackets.

One should observe that an equational logic program is a set of program and equational clauses and that the order in which the program clauses are written is irrelevant. This is in contrast to PROLOG (e.g. Clocksin & Mellish 1981), where an ordering is imposed on a logic program in the way the clauses are written down.

As an example consider the equational logic program
$$ELP = \langle EQ(a,b)\Leftarrow, Q(a)\Leftarrow \rangle.$$
$Q(a)\Leftarrow$ is the definition of Q and $EQ(a,b)\Leftarrow$ is the definition of EQ. ELP is not an equational program since it contains a definition for the predicate symbol Q. Another example is the equational program **EAX($\langle$EP,LP$\rangle$)** which contains the **axioms of equality** for an equational program $\langle$EP,LP$\rangle$, namely the axiom of **reflexivity** (r), **symmetry** (s), **transitivity** (t), and the set of axioms of **f-substitutivity** (sf) and **p-substitutivity** (sp).

EAX($\langle$EP,LP$\rangle$):

$EQ(x,x) \Leftarrow$	(r)
$EQ(x,y) \Leftarrow EQ(y,x)$	(s)
$EQ(x,z) \Leftarrow EQ(x,y), EQ(y,z)$	(t)
$EQ(f(x_1,\ldots,x_n),f(y_1,\ldots,y_n)) \Leftarrow \{ EQ(x_i,y_i) \mid 1\leq i\leq n \}$	
$\quad$ for each n-ary function symbol occurring in the alphabet	(sf)
$Q(x_1,\ldots,x_n) \Leftarrow Q(y_1,\ldots,y_n) \cup \{ EQ(x_i,y_i) \mid 1\leq i\leq n \}$	
$\quad$ for each n-ary predicate symbol occurring in the alphabet	(sp)

We have not included the axiom of p-substitutivity for equations since this axiom is subsumed by the axioms (r), (t), and (sf) (e.g. Loveland 1978). As a consequence, the set of p-substitutivity axioms is empty if $\langle$EP,LP$\rangle$ does not contain a predicate symbol.

Remark:

Whenever we give an equational logic program $\langle$EP,LP$\rangle$ in the sequel we implicitly define an alphabet by the convention that the set of variables (resp. function and predicate symbols) contains the variables (resp. function and predicate symbols) occurring in $\langle$EP,LP$\rangle$. With this understanding we can say that a term, atom, equation, or clause X is **based on** $\langle$EP,LP$\rangle$ iff X is built of symbols occurring in the corresponding alphabet.

3.2 Model Theory

In order to be able to discuss the truth or falsehood of a set of clauses S we must give a meaning to the symbols occurring in that set. This can be done by an interpretation of S which assigns truth-values to the ground atoms and equations arising from S. Recall that S is based on an alphabet. Hence, an interpretation is a function from the set of ground terms, ground atoms, and ground equations into the union of a non-empty domain of discourse and the set of truth-values such that an element of the domain is assigned to each constant, a mapping on the domain is assigned to each function symbol, and a relation on the domain is assigned to each predicate symbol.

Definition:

Let S be a finite set of clauses, DEF be the set of ground terms, ground atoms, and ground equations based on S, and U be a non-empty set. An **interpretation of S over** U is a function

$$I: DEF \rightarrow U \cup \{true, false\}$$

with the following properties:

(0)   Each ground term is mapped to an element of U; each ground atom or equation is mapped to *true* or *false*.

(1)   If f is an n-ary function symbol, $n \geq 0$, and t_i, $1 \leq i \leq n$, are ground terms, then $I(f(t_1,...,t_n)) = f'(I(t_1),...,I(t_2))$, where f' is a mapping from U^n to U.

(2)   If Q is an n-ary predicate symbol, $n \geq 0$, and t_i, $1 \leq i \leq n$, are ground terms, then $I(Q(t_1,...,t_n)) = Q'(I(t_1),...,I(t_n))$, where Q' is a mapping from U^n to $\{true, false\}$.

An **E-interpretation** is an interpretation with the additional properties:

(3)   If X is an n-ary function or predicate symbol, s_i and t_i, $1 \leq i \leq n$, are ground terms, and $I(s_i) = I(t_i)$, $1 \leq i \leq n$, then

$$I(X(s_1,...,s_n)) = I(X(t_1,...,t_n)).$$

(4)   If s and t are ground terms, then

$$I(EQ(s,t)) = true \text{ iff } I(s) = I(t).$$

The function I is also to be referred to as an **assignment (function)**, and I(x) is termed the **value** of x. The non-empty set U is often called **universe** (or **domain**) of I.

Property (3) comprises the substitutivity axioms of equality and (4) ensures that statements about equality have their intended meaning. It should be noticed that no E-interpretation I can assign *true* to Q(a) and EQ(a,b) and *false* to Q(b) since from $I(EQ(a,b)) = true$ and (4) we have $I(a) = I(b)$ and with (3) we can infer that $I(Q(a)) = I(Q(b))$ which contradicts the assumption that $I(Q(a)) = $ *true* and $I(Q(b)) = $ *false*. Furthermore, note that no E-interpretation assigns a value to terms, atoms, or equations containing variables.

Proposition 3.2.1:

> *Let U be a non-empty set, S be a finite set of clauses, and I be an E-interpreta-tion over U of S. I defines a congruence relation $\equiv$ on the set of ground terms by $s \equiv t$ iff I(EQ(s,t)) = true.*

Proof:

Let $s \equiv t$ iff $I(EQ(s,t)) = $ *true*. With part (4) of the definition of I we can derive that $s \equiv t$ iff $I(s) = I(t)$. We have to show that $\equiv$ is a congruence relation, i.e. that $\equiv$ is reflexive, symmetric, transitive, and that the axiom of substitutivity holds for it:

(1)   reflexivity:
Since I is a function, $I(t) = I(t)$, and hence $t \equiv t$.

(2)   symmetry:
If $s \equiv t$, then $I(s) = I(t)$ by the definition of $\equiv$. But now $I(t) = I(s)$ and by the definition of $\equiv$ we obtain $t \equiv s$.

(3)   transitivity:
If $s \equiv t$ and $t \equiv u$, then $I(s) = I(t)$ and $I(t) = I(u)$ and it follows immediately that $I(s) = I(u)$. By the definition of $\equiv$ we obtain $s \equiv u$.

(4)   substitutivity:
If $s_i \equiv t_i$ for $1 \leq i \leq n$, then $I(s_i) = I(t_i)$. Now let f by an n-ary function symbol. By part (3) of the definition of I we learn that $I(f(s_1,...,s_n)) = I(f(t_1,...,t_n))$. Hence, by the definition of $\equiv$, $f(s_1,...,s_n) \equiv f(t_1,...,t_n)$, which completes the proof.   qed

Having interpreted the terms, atoms, and equations of a first order theory we can now give meaning to the remaining formulas of our first order language.

Remark:

The following definitions and theorems are generalizations of definitions and theorems well known in logic programming (e.g. Lloyd 1984); the latter can be obtained by omitting the prefix "E-" at each occurrence.

Definition:

> An E-interpretation I is said to **E-satisfy** a ground Horn clause $C \Leftarrow D$ iff C has the value *true* under I or at least one $C' \in D$ has the value *false* under I; otherwise I is said to **E-falsify** $C \Leftarrow D$. I is said to **E-satisfy** a set S of Horn clauses iff I E-satisfies each ground instance of a clause in S. If there exists an I which E-satis-

fies S, then S is said to be **E-satisfiable**. S is said to be **E-valid** iff every E-interpretation E-satisfies S. S is **E-unsatisfiable** iff there exists no interpretation that E-satisfies S.

A ground goal clause has the value *true* under I iff at least one of its subgoals has the value *false* under I, or, conversely, a ground goal clause is *false* under I iff all of its subgoals have the value *true* under I. Hence, the empty clause ⃞ has the value *false* under all interpretations. On the other hand, the empty set of clauses has the value *true* under all interpretations.

For example, there is no E-interpretation that E-satisfies
$$S = \{ Q(a){\Leftarrow}, EQ(a,b){\Leftarrow}, {\Leftarrow}Q(b) \},$$
since such an E-interpretation must assign *true* to Q(a) and EQ(a,b), and *false* to Q(b). As shown above such an E-interpretation does not exist. This implies that S is E-unsatisfiable.

We are particularily interested in E-interpretations under which formulas express *true* statements.

Definition:

An E-interpretation I is said to be an **E-model** for S iff I E-satisfies S.

Now we can introduce the important notion of a logical consequence.

Definition:

Let S and S' be two sets of Horn clauses. S' is a **logical E-consequence** of S iff for every E-interpretation I of S, I is an E-model for S implies that I is an E-model for S'.

As an example consider
$$S = \{ Q(a){\Leftarrow}, EQ(a,b){\Leftarrow} \}.$$
Any E-model I for S must assign *true* to the atom Q(a) and the equation EQ(a,b). Since I is an E-interpretation it follows that I(a) = I(b) and, therefore, I(Q(a)) = I(Q(b)). Hence, I must also assign *true* to Q(b), which shows that S' = {Q(b)⇐} is a logical E-consequence of S.

Notation:

If { C⇐ | C∈D } is a logical E-consequence of a set of clauses S, we say that D is a logical E-consequence of S. Furthermore, if D contains only one element, say C, then we say that C is a logical E-consequence of S instead of {C} is a logical E-consequence of S.

To ease our notation in case an equation is a logical E-consequence of an equational logic program <EP,LP>, we introduce the relation $=_{EP}$ on the set of terms.

Definition:

s =EP t iff EQ(s,t) is a logical E-consequence of <EP,LP>.

Clearly, =EP is a congruence relation.

In a first order theory the axioms and rules of inference are used to derive the logical consequences of the theory. Such a system is organized around the concepts of validity and proof. However, "machine-oriented" formalisms such as J. A. Robinson's resolution rule are based on the concepts of unsatisfiability and refutation. These two approaches are connected by proposition 3.2.2.

Proposition 3.2.2:

Given an equational logic program <EP,LP> and a goal clause ⇐D, then <EP,LP>∪{⇐D} is E-unsatisfiable iff D is a logical E-consequence of <EP,LP>.

Proof:

Suppose that <EP,LP>∪{⇐D} is E-unsatisfiable. Let I be any E-interpretation of <EP,LP>. Suppose I is an E-model of <EP,LP>. Since <EP,LP>∪{⇐D} is E-unsatisfiable, I cannot be an E-model for ⇐D. Hence, each element C of D has the value *true* under I. Thus, I is an E-model for { C⇐ | C∈D } and, therefore, D is a logical E-consequence of <EP,LP>.

Conversely, suppose D is a logical E-consequence of <EP,LP>. Let I be an E-interpretation of <EP,LP> and suppose I is an E-model for <EP,LP>. Then I is also an E-model for { C⇐ | C∈D }. Thus, each element C of D has the value *true* under I. Hence, I is not an E-model for ⇐D and we conclude that <EP,LP>∪{⇐D} is E-unsatisfiable.   qed

For example, if the equational logic program

ELP = < EQ(a,b)⇐, Q(a)⇐ >

and the goal clause ⇐Q(b) are E-unsatisfiable, then proposition 3.2.2 tells us that Q(b) is a logical E-consequence of ELP.

Thus the main problem is to determine whether an equational logic program <EP,LP> and a goal clause ⇐D are E-unsatisfiable. In other words, we have to show that ⇐D is *false* under all E-interpretations of <EP,LP>. It is well known that it suffices to investigate only E-interpretations over a fixed domain, the so-called Herbrand E-interpretations. Recall, a set of function symbols contains at least one constant.

Definition:

Let S be a finite set of clauses and I be an E-interpretation of S. I is a **Herbrand E-interpretation** if the following conditions are satisfied:

(1)   The domain of the E-interpretation is the set of ground terms.

(2)   If f is an n-ary function symbol, $n \geq 0$, and t_i, $1 \leq i \leq n$, are ground terms, then
$I(f(t_1,\ldots,t_n)) = f(I(t_1),\ldots,I(t_n))$.

Because of property (2) Herbrand E-interpretations are restricted in assigning values to function symbols. However, there is no restriction concerning the assignment of predicate symbols and of "EQ". Observe, trivial equations are always *true*. Therefore, a Herbrand E-interpretation can conveniently be represented by a set I of ground atoms and ground non-trivial equations with the understanding that C is assigned to *true* iff $C \in I$ or C is a ground trivial equation.

As an example consider the set of clauses
$$S = \{ Q(a) \Leftarrow, EQ(a,b) \Leftarrow, \Leftarrow Q(b) \}.$$
There are six Herbrand E-interpretations:

$I_1 = \{ Q(a), Q(b), EQ(a,b) \}$

$I_2 = \{ Q(a), Q(b) \}$

$I_3 = \{ Q(b) \}$

$I_4 = \{ Q(a) \}$

$I_5 = \{ EQ(a,b) \}$

$I_6 = \varnothing$

If I does not contain an equation, like I_2, I_3, I_5, and I_6 in the example above, then I is just an interpretation where equality denotes syntactic equality.

Definition:

A **Herbrand E-model** for a finite set of clauses S is a Herbrand E-interpretation for S, which is an E-model for S.

Theorem 3.2.3:

Let S be a finite set of clauses. S is E-unsatisfiable iff S has no Herbrand E-models.

Proof:

The only-if half of the theorem is obvious since, by the definition, S is E-unsatisfiable iff S is *false* under all the E-interpretations over any domain. Conversely, assume that S is *false* under all Herbrand E-interpretations. If S is not E-unsatisfiable, then we find an E-interpretation I over some domain U such that S is *true* under I. We define I* as follows:

$I^* = \{ X(t_1,\ldots,t_n) \mid X(t_1,\ldots,t_n)$ is *true* under I $\}$.

Clearly, I* is a Herbrand E-interpretation. Now, suppose I is an E-model for S. We prove by induction on the structure of S that I* is an E-model for S. If I assigns *true* (resp. *false*) to the ground equation or atom C, then, by definition, C is *true* (resp. *false*) under I*. Next, if I E-satisfies a ground Horn clause C⇐D, then either C is *true* under I or we find a C'∈ D such that C' is *false* under I. It follows immediately, that either C is *true* under I* or C' is *false* under I*. Hence, I* E-satisfies C⇐D. Similarily, if I E-satisfies S, then I* E-satisfies S. Hence, I* is a Herbrand E-model for S, contradicting the assumption that S has no Herbrand E-models.   qed

This proposition shows that it is sufficient to investigate Herbrand E-interpretations in order to show that an equational logic program and a goal clause are E-unsatisfiable. But we can do even better: Herbrand E-interpretations for equational logic programs meet the model intersection property.

Proposition 3.2.4 (E-model Intersection Property):

Let Mod(<EP,LP>) be a non-empty set of Herbrand E-models for <EP,LP>.
Then ∩Mod(<EP,LP>) is a Herbrand E-model for <EP,LP>.

Proof:

Suppose that I is the intersection of all models in Mod(<EP,LP>). We have to show that I is an E-interpretation. Clearly, conditions (0)-(2) are fulfilled by I. Now suppose condition (3) is not fulfilled. Without loss of generality we may assume that X is an unary function or predicate symbol occurring in EP. Then we find ground terms s and t such that I(s) = I(t) but I(X(s)) ≠ I(X(t)). Therefore, for some I' ∈ Mod(<EP,LP>) we find I'(s) = I'(t) and I'(X(s)) ≠ I'(X(t)) contradicting the fact that Mod(<EP,LP>) contains only E-models. Condition (4) holds analogously.

It remains to be shown that I is an E-model for <EP,LP>. If I is not an E-model for <EP,LP>, then some ground instance C⇐D of a clause in <EP,LP> is *false* under I. This means that C is not in I whereas D is a subset of I. Hence, for some I' ∈ Mod(<EP,LP>) we find that C is not in I' whereas D is a subset of I' contradicting the fact that I' is an E-model for <EP,LP>.   qed

This coincides with a result obtained by Mahr & Markowski (1983): Horn equality theories admit initial semantics (see Goguen et al. 1977). In fact, Mahr & Markowski proved a stronger result, namely that Horn equality theories are the largest class of equational theories that admit initial semantics.

Since every equational logic program <EP,LP> has the set of all ground atoms and equations based on <EP,LP> as an E-model, the set of all Herbrand E-models for <EP,LP> is non-empty. Thus, the intersection of all Herbrand E-models for <EP,LP> is again an E-model, called the **least Herbrand E-model**, for <EP,LP>.

Notation:

Let M_E**(EP,LP)** denote the least Herbrand E-model for <EP,LP>.

In order to show that an equational logic program <EP,LP> and a goal clause are E-unsatisfiable, we have to investigate only the least Herbrand E-model for <EP,LP>. However, the domain of Herbrand interpretations is the set of ground terms, the so-called **Herbrand universe**. Unfortunately, Herbrand universes support only the notion of syntactic equality, but we would like to have a richer equational theory. In proposition 3.2.1 we have shown that each E-interpretation I for a set of clauses admits a congruence relation $\equiv$ on the set of ground terms by $s \equiv t$ iff $EQ(s,t) \in I$. Hence, for a given equational logic program <EP,LP> we could consider quotient universes of the set of ground terms modulo $\equiv$, where $\equiv$ is the congruence relation defined by an E-model for EP. In general there is an infinite number of such E-models for EP and hence an infinite number of congruence relations $\equiv$. We desire, however, the existence of a canonical E-model for the equational theory, i.e. a fixed domain and functional assignment. Fortunately, proposition 3.2.4 ensures that equational programs admit such a finest congruence relation.

Corollary 3.2.5:

There exists a finest congruence on the set of ground terms generated by each equational program.

Proof:

It follows immediately from proposition 3.2.4 that the least Herbrand E-model of EP is an E-model for EP. Hence, the finest congruence on the set of ground terms generated by EP is given by the least Herbrand E-model for EP.   qed

Jaffar et al. (1984) obtained a similar result, however, they considered only Herbrand interpretations.

Notation:

Let $\equiv_{EP}$ be the finest congruence on the set of ground terms generated by an equational program EP. Further, let [t] denote the congruence class defined by $\equiv_{EP}$ and containing t. The functional assignment is obtained as $f([t_1],\ldots,[t_n]) = [f(t_1,\ldots,t_n)]$ for all n-ary function symbols. We abbreviate $Q([t_1],\ldots,[t_n])$ to $[Q(t_1,\ldots,t_n)]$, where Q is an n-ary predicate symbol, and { [A] | A $\in$ B } to [B]. Furthermore, $[P(s_1,\ldots,s_m)] = [Q(t_1,\ldots,t_n)]$ iff P=Q, m=n, and for all $1 \leq i \leq n$ we find $[s_i] = [t_i]$.

Throughout the remaining part of this section we use the equational logic program

CATS: EQ(0+y, y) $\Leftarrow$ (+1)

EQ(s(x)+y, s(x+y)) $\Leftarrow$ (+2)

EQ(0*y, 0) $\Leftarrow$ (*1)

EQ(s(x)*y, y+x*y) $\Leftarrow$ (*2)

cats(x,y,x+y,4*x+2*y) $\Leftarrow$ (c)

for demonstrations. Informally, + and * are addition and multiplication on natural numbers, and *true* is assigned to *cats(c,b,h,l)* iff *c* cats and *b* birds have together $h = c+b$ heads and $l = 4*c+2*b$ legs. For notational convenience we often abbreviate $s^n(0)$ to n.

Definition:

The **Herbrand $\equiv$-universe U$_\equiv$(<EP,LP>)** of <EP,LP> is the quotient of the set of ground terms modulo $\equiv_{EP}$.

As an example consider the equational logic program CATS, then

U$_\equiv$(CATS) = { [0], [s(0)], [s(s(0))], … },

where for example [0] = { 0, 0+0, 0*0, 0*s(0), s(0)*0, … }.

Definition:

The **Herbrand $\equiv$-base B$_\equiv$(<EP,LP>)** of <EP,LP> is defined as

B$_\equiv$(<EP,LP>) = { [Q(t$_1$,…,t$_n$)] | Q is EQ, in which case n=2, or Q is an n-ary pre-
dicate symbol occurring in LP and t$_i$ $\in$ U$_\equiv$(<EP,LP>), $1 \leq i \leq n$ }

As an example consider again the equational logic program CATS, then

B$_\equiv$(CATS) = { [cats(0,0,0,0)], [cats(1,0,0,0)], [cats(0,1,0,0)],… }
$\cup$ { [EQ(s,t)] | s,t $\in$ U$_\equiv$(<EP,LP>) } .

Definition:

An E-interpretation I of <EP,LP> is a **Herbrand $\equiv$-interpretation** if the following conditions are E-satisfied:

(1)   The domain of the E-interpretation is the Herbrand $\equiv$-universe.

(2)   If f is an n-ary function symbol, n$\geq$0, and t$_i$, $1 \leq i \leq n$, are ground terms, then
I(f(t$_1$,…,t$_n$)) = [f(I(t$_1$),…,I(t$_n$))].

Hence, Herbrand $\equiv$-interpretations have a fixed domain, namely U$_\equiv$(<EP,LP>), and if f is an n-ary function symbol, the mapping from U$_\equiv$(<EP,LP>)^n into U$_\equiv$(<EP,LP>) defined by [t$_1$],…,[t$_n$] $\rightarrow$ [f(t$_1$,…,t$_n$)] is assigned to f. Therefore, Herbrand $\equiv$-interpretations have a fixed assignment of function symbols. Different Herbrand $\equiv$-interpretations arise by assigning different predicates to predicate symbols. Hence, we can represent a Herbrand $\equiv$-interpretation

of <EP,LP> by a subset I of the Herbrand ≡-base with the understanding that *true* is assigned to the atom A iff [A] ∈ I and *true* is assigned to the equation EQ(s,t) iff s ≡$_{EP}$ t (or, equivalently, [s] = [t]).

As in the standard case we are interested in those Herbrand ≡-interpretations which assign *true* to an equational logic program. Such Herbrand ≡-interpretations are called Herbrand ≡-models.

Definition:

A **Herbrand ≡-model** for <EP,LP> is a Herbrand ≡-interpretation for <EP,LP> which is an E-model for <EP,LP>.

As an example consider again the program CATS, where the Herbrand ≡-interpretation

{ [cats(0,0,0,0)], [cats(1,0,1,4)], [cats(0,1,1,2)], ... }

∪ { [EQ(t,t)] | t ∈ U$_≡$(<EP,LP>) }

is a Herbrand ≡-model. In other words, if we can count *n* cats and *m* birds, then the number of heads must be the sum of *n* and *m* and the number of legs must be the sum of four times *n* and twice *m*.

Recall that we are interested in the logical E-consequences of an equational logic program <EP,LP>. From proposition 3.2.4 we know that it suffices to investigate only the least Herbrand E-model of <EP,LP>. However, Herbrand E-interpretations support only syntactic equality, whereas Herbrand ≡-interpretations support equational theories defined by EP. Hence, we would like to have a result that allows us to investigate only Herbrand ≡-interpretations in order to determine the logical E-consequences of <EP,LP>.

Theorem 3.2.6:

<EP,LP> ∪ {⇐C} *has no Herbrand ≡-models iff* <EP,LP> ∪ {⇐C} *has no Herbrand E-models.*

Proof:

The only-if part is trivial since each Herbrand ≡-model is a Herbrand E-model. We turn to the other part and show by contradiction that the theorem holds. If I is a Herbrand E-model for <EP,LP> ∪ {⇐C}, then I(C) = *false*. Furthermore, let ≡ be the congruence relation defined by I according to proposition 3.2.1 and ≡$_{EP}$ be the finest congruence relation defined by EP. We define a Herbrand ≡-interpretation I$_≡$ over U$_≡$(<EP,LP>), i.e. the quotient of the set of ground terms modulo ≡$_{EP}$, as follows:

I$_≡$ = { [A]∈ B$_≡$(<EP,LP>) | A∈ I }.

This is well defined since ≡$_{EP}$ is finer than ≡. Obviously, I$_≡$(C) = *false* and it remains to show that I$_≡$ is a E-model for <EP,LP>. To prove this claim we distinguish two cases:

(1)   assume $I(A) = true$: then by the definition of $I_\equiv$, $[A] \in I_\equiv$ and hence $I_\equiv(A) = true$.

(2)   assume $I(EQ(s,t)) = true$: then we have $s \equiv t$. Since $\equiv_{EP}$ is finer than $\equiv$ (corollary 3.2.5) we obtain $s \equiv_{EP} t$ and hence $I_\equiv(EQ(s,t)) = true$.

It follows immediately that $I_\equiv$ is an E-model for <EP,LP>.   qed

   This theorem was first proved by Jaffar et al. (1984) in the context of interpretations. It gives us the justification that we are working on a fixed domain and functional assignment defined by the least $\equiv$-model for an equational logic program. Moreover, as in logic programming we can show that the model-intersection property holds also for Herbrand $\equiv$-models. In other words, logical E-consequence can be determined by a single model, namely the least Herbrand $\equiv$-model. Let $Mod_\equiv(<EP,LP>)$ denote the set of all Herbrand $\equiv$-models for <EP,LP>. Observe, if there exists an $I \in Mod_\equiv(<EP,LP>)$ such that $I(EQ(s,t)) = true$ then for all $I' \in Mod_\equiv(<EP,LP>)$ we have $I'(EQ(s,t)) = true$.

Proposition 3.2.7:

   $\cap Mod_\equiv(<EP,LP>) \in Mod_\equiv(<EP,LP>)$

Proof:

   If $\cap Mod_\equiv(<EP,LP>)$ is not a Herbrand $\equiv$-model for <EP,LP>, then $\cap Mod_\equiv(<EP,LP>)$ E-falsifies some ground instance $C \Leftarrow D$ of a clause of <EP,LP>, i.e. *false* is assigned to C and *true* is assgined to each element of D. Therefore, for some $I \in Mod_\equiv(<EP,LP>)$ we find that *false* is assigned to C and *true* is assigned to each element of D contradicting the assumption that $I \in Mod_\equiv(<EP,LP>)$.   qed

Notation:

   Let $M_\equiv(<EP,LP>)$ denote the least Herbrand $\equiv$-model of <EP,LP>.

   The following theorem shows that the elements of the least Herbrand $\equiv$-model for an equational logic program <EP,LP> are precisely the logical E-consequences of <EP,LP>. Recall, each logic program implicitly contains the axiom of reflexivity.

Theorem 3.2.8:

   $M_\equiv(<EP,LP>)$
   $= \{ [C] \in B_\equiv(<EP,LP>) \mid C \text{ is a logical E-consequence of } <EP,LP> \}$

Proof:

   The proof is an extension of the respective theorem in logic programming first shown by van Emden & Kowalski (1976):

C is a logical E-consequence of <EP,LP>

iff <EP,LP> ∪ {C⇐} is E-unsatisfiable   (proposition 3.2.2)

iff <EP,LP> ∪ {C⇐} has no Herbrand E-models   (theorem 3.2.3)

iff <EP,LP> ∪ {C⇐} has no Herbrand ≡-models   (theorem 3.2.6)

iff ⇐C is *false* under all Herbrand ≡-models for <EP,LP>

iff C is *true* under all Herbrand ≡-models for <EP,LP>

iff [C] ∈ M≡(<EP,LP>)   (proposition 3.2.7).

                                                                        qed

Therefore, the meaning of an equational logic program <EP,LP> is its least Herbrand ≡-model, which consists of the set of ground atoms that are logical E-consequences of <EP,LP> and the set of ground equations EQ(s,t) such that s $\equiv_{EP}$ t. Before turning to the question of how to determine whether an atom or an equation is a logical E-consequence of an equational logic program we introduce the notion of an answer substitution.

Definition:

An **answer substitution** for ⇐D and <EP,LP> is a substitution for the variables in D.

It should be observed, that we do not require that an answer substitution is ground or that each variable occurring in D is an element of the domain of the answer substitution.

Definition:

Let σ be an answer substitution for ⇐D and <EP,LP>. We say that σ is a **correct answer substitution** for ⇐D and <EP,LP> iff σD is a logical E-consequence of <EP,LP>.

This is a purely semantic definition of a correct answer. Unfortunately, the least Herbrand ≡-model of an equational logic program gives us no idea of how to determine whether a given goal clause is a logical E-consequence of that program. A first link between the model theory of an equational logic program and the respective proof theory can be given by a fixpoint characterization of a program.

3.3 Fixpoint Theory

The reason for giving a fixpoint characterization for a logic program is to define a method that constructs the least model of the program in a bottom-up manner. This is done by associating a monotonic and continuous function T with a logic program and showing that the least fixpoint of T is equal to the least model of the program. Furthermore, the function T is designed such that an application of T corresponds one-to-one to an application of the inference rule in the first-order theory in consideration. But whereas the function T constructs the least model of the program in a bottom-up manner, the inference rule tests whether an atom is in the least model of the program in a top-down manner (see Apt & van Emden 1982).

Why do we introduce the fixpoint characterization of a logic program at all? For example, an anonymous referee of the paper (Furbach et al. 1988) claims that the use of fixpoint theory "*is an unnecessary complicated way of bringing together model- and proof-theoretical issues of logic programming.*" Then the referee continues: "*The alternative way is to describe the step from an argument to a value of T_{EP}* (see section 6.1) *by an inference rule and to show that the corresponding calculus leads to the same results as paramodulation and reflection* (see section 6.2)". But this is precisely the role the fixpoint characterization plays in logic programming. It is used as a tool to prove in an elegant way the soundness and completeness of the corresponding first order theory.

Before we recast the model theoretic semantics of an equational logic program in fixpoint theory (Scott 1970) we briefly summarize the principal concepts of the fixpoint approach.

Definition:

> A **complete lattice** is a set U over which there is a reflexive, antisymmetric, and transitive order relation $\leq$. For each subset X of U there is a least upper bound, **lub(X)**, and a greatest lower bound, **glb(X)**, in U with respect to $\leq$.
>
> A function T over a complete lattice U is **monotonic** if $T(x) \leq T(y)$, whenever $x \leq y$.
>
> A **directed** set is a set which contains an upper bound for each of its finite subsets.
>
> A function T over a complete lattice U is **continuous** if for each directed subset X of U we find $T(\text{lub}(X)) = \text{lub}(\{T(Y) \mid Y \in X\})$.

It should be noted that if T is continuous then it is also monotonic.

Now consider an equational logic program ELP. The powerset of $B_\equiv(ELP)$ and set inclusion forms a complete lattice with bottom element $\emptyset$ and top element $B_\equiv(ELP)$. For example, let

$< EQ(a,b){\Leftarrow}, Q(a){\Leftarrow}, Q(b){\Leftarrow}, Q(c){\Leftarrow} >$

be the equational logic program. The corresponding complete lattice is depicted in figure 3.3.1.

Proposition 3.3.1 (Tarski 1955):

Let U be a complete lattice and T be a monotonic function over U. Then T has a least fixpoint, lfp(T). Furthermore,

$lfp(T) = glb\{x \mid T(x){=}x\} = glb\{x \mid T(x){\leq}x\}.$

A second identification of the least fixpoint has been given by Kleene.

Notation:

Let U be a complete lattice, T be a monotonic function over U, and ω be the first infinite ordinal. Then,

$T{\uparrow}0 = glb(U),$

$T{\uparrow}n = T(T{\uparrow}(n{-}1))$ if n is a successor ordinal

Proposition 3.3.2 (Stoy 1977):

Let U be a complete lattice and T be a continuous function over U. Then,

$lfp(T) = T{\uparrow}\omega.$

We now come back to equational logic programs $<EP,LP>$. To apply the results of fixpoint theory we make use of a function $T_{<EP,LP>}$ which maps $\equiv$-interpretations into $\equiv$-interpretations (Jaffar et al. 1984, 1986).

Definition:

Let I be an $\equiv$-interpretation of $<EP,LP>$.

$T_{<EP,LP>}(I) = \quad \{ [EQ(t,t)] \mid t$ is a ground term $\}$

$\cup \quad \{ [A] \mid$ there exists a ground instance $A'{\Leftarrow}D$ of a clause in LP

such that $[A] = [A']$ and $[D] \subseteq I \}$.

Intuitively, this definition characterizes the semantics of an equational logic program in a bottom up way. $T_{<EP,LP>}(I)$ is the union of the set of all ground equations $EQ(s,t)$ such that $[s] = [t]$ and the set of ground atoms is deducible in one step from the elements in I using program clauses in LP. Therefore, the set of ground atoms deducible from LP is $T_{<EP,LP>}{\uparrow}\omega$. This result was already stated by Jaffar et al. (1984, 1986), in the context of Herbrand interpretations, but the formal proofs were omitted.

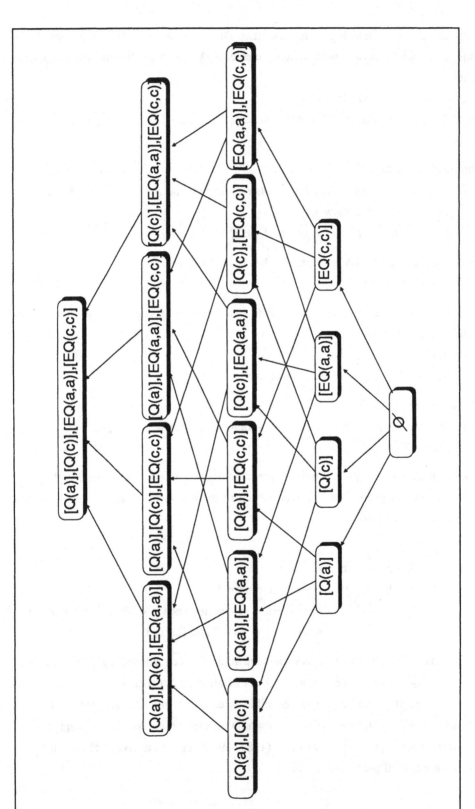

Figure 3.3.1

Proposition 3.3.3:

   $T_{<EP,LP>}$ *is continuous.*

Proof:

   Let X be a directed subset of the powerset of the Herbrand $\equiv$-base $B_{\equiv}(<EP,LP>)$. $T_{<EP,LP>}$ is continuous iff $lub(\{T_{<EP,LP>}(Y) \mid Y \in X\}) = T_{<EP,LP>}(lub\ (X))$. Note first that $[\{C_1,...,C_n\}] \subseteq lub(X)$ iff $[\{A_1,...,A_n\}] \subseteq Z$ for some $Z \in X$.

$[C] \in T_{<EP,LP>}(lub(X))$

iff $[C] = [EQ(t,t)]$, for some ground term t, or there exists a ground instance $A \Leftarrow D$ of a clause in LP such that $[C] = [A]$ and $[D] \subseteq lub(X)$

iff $[C] = [EQ(t,t)]$, for some ground term t, or there exists a ground instance $A \Leftarrow D$ of a clause in LP such that $[C] = [A]$ and $[D] \subseteq Z$, for some $Z \in X$

iff $[C] \in T_{<EP,LP>}(Z)$, for some $Z \in X$

iff $[C] \in lub(\{T_{<EP,LP>}(Y) \mid Y \in X\})$.   qed

   Since the lattice obtained from the powerset of $B_{\equiv}(<EP,LP>)$ and set inclusion among subsets of $B_{\equiv}(<EP,LP>)$ is complete and $T_{<EP,LP>}$ is continuous over this lattice, by propositions 3.3.1 and 3.3.2 we can characterize the least fixpoint of $T_{<EP,LP>}$ as $T_{<EP,LP>}\uparrow\omega$ and as $glb \{ I \mid T_{<EP,LP>}(I) \subseteq I \}$.

Theorem 3.3.4:

   $lfp(T_{<EP,LP>}) = T_{<EP,LP>}\uparrow\omega = glb \{ I \mid T_{<EP,LP>}(I) \subseteq I \}$

Proof:

   The proof of this theorem follows immediately from the propositions 3.3.1 - 3.3.3.   qed

Lemma 3.3.5:

   Let I be a Herbrand $\equiv$-interpretation of $<EP,LP>$. Then I is an $\equiv$-model for $<EP,LP>$ iff $T_{<EP,LP>}(I) \subseteq I$.

Proof:

I is a Herbrand $\equiv$-model for $<EP,LP>$

iff $\{ [EQ(t,t)] \mid t$ is a ground term $\} \subseteq I$ and for each ground instance $A \Leftarrow D$ of a program clause in LP, we have that $[D] \subseteq I$ implies $[A] \in I$

iff $T_{<EP,LP>}(I) \subseteq I$.   qed

   Finally, we state that the least Herbrand $\equiv$-model and the least fixpoint of an equational logic program $<EP,LP>$ are equivalent.

Theorem 3.3.6:

   $M_{\equiv}(<EP,LP>) = lfp(T_{<EP,LP>})$

Proof:

$M_\equiv(<EP,LP>)$ $=$ glb { I | I is a Herbrand $\equiv$-model for $<EP,LP>$ }

$=$ glb { I | $T_{<EP,LP>}(I) \subseteq I$ } $\hspace{2cm}$ (lemma 3.3.5)

$=$ lfp($T_{<EP,LP>}$) $\hspace{3cm}$ (theorem 3.3.4)

$\hspace{12cm}$ qed

Coming back to the CATS-example, the least fixpoint of T_{CATS} can be obtained by one application of T_{CATS} upon $\emptyset$ as

$\hspace{1cm}$ { [cats(0,0,0,0)], [cats(1,0,1,4)], [cats(0,1,1,2)], ... }

$\hspace{1cm}$ $\cup$ { [EQ(t,t)] | t is a ground term }.

Given the goal clause

$\hspace{1cm}$ $\Leftarrow$cats(x,y,4,12)

we have to check whether there exist ground terms s and t for x and y such that cats(s,t,4,12) is an element of $T_{CATS}\uparrow\omega$. For example, s=2 and t=2 are such terms.

The obvious problems are that we have to investigate the search space in a bottom-up manner and that we have to determine whether two congruence classes are identical, in other words we have to decide whether for some s and t the equation EQ(s,t) is a logical E-consequence of EP.

3.4 Proof Theory

In this section we are mainly concerned with the problem of how to compute correct and complete answers to queries posed to an equational logic program. More formally, we want to solve the problem of how to determine the E-unsatisfiability of an equational logic program together with a goal clause. From theorems 3.2.3 and 3.2.6 we know that an equational logic program <EP,LP> and a goal clause ⇐D are E-unsatisfiable iff <EP,LP>∪{⇐D} has no Herbrand ≡-models. In order to prove that <EP,LP> and ⇐D are E-unsatisfiable we have to show that ⇐D is *false* under all Herbrand ≡-models for <EP,LP>. Theorem 3.2.8 ensures that it suffices to show that ⇐D is *false* under the least Herbrand ≡-model for <EP,LP>. Recall, the empty clause is *false* under all interpretations. Hence, each set of clauses containing ▢ is unsatisfiable. Furthermore, if the empty clause is a logical consequence of ⇐D, then ⇐D must be *false* under all interpretations. Therefore, we are looking for inference rules which can be used to derive the empty clause from a goal clause and an equational logic program.

As we will see later, it suffices to apply an inference rule in each step only to a single subgoal in a goal clause. The strategy to select a certain subgoal can be separated from the equational logic program and can be defined by a selection function. This is one of the advantages of logic programming: An algorithm can be divided into the specification of the problem in the form of a logic program and the control over the application of the program clauses and the selection of subgoals (Kowalski 1979).

Definition:

> A **selection function** is a function from a set of goal clauses into a set of atoms and equations, such that the value of the function for a non-empty goal clause is always a subgoal, called the **selected subgoal**, in that goal clause.

Notation:

In the sequel we assume that **SEL** denotes a selection function.

Definition:

> An **inference rule** is a function → which maps a goal clause ⇐D, a subgoal C ∈ D, a substitution σ, and eventually an input clause P into a new goal clause ⇐D'.

Notation:

In case → does not require an input clause we write # instead of P to maintain a uniform notation. If → maps ⇐D, C, P, and σ into ⇐D' then we write

> ⇐D →(C, P, σ) ⇐D'.

If C, P, or σ can be determined by the context we omit them and write $\rightarrow$, or $\rightarrow(\sigma)$, etc. instead of $\rightarrow(C, P, \sigma)$. Furthermore, we write the selected subgoal in bold face.

Next we define the notions derivation and refutation. Since we intend to introduce several new inference rules we define these notions with respect to a set of inference rules. Throughout this thesis we assume that a program clause and a goal clause have no variables in common. This can be achieved by renaming the program clause.

Definition:

Let $<EP,LP>$ be an equational logic program, $\Leftarrow D_0$ be a goal clause, and RULES be a set of inference rules. A **derivation from** $<EP,LP> \cup \{\Leftarrow D_0\}$ **wrt** RULES is either the empty sequence or a (possibly infinite) sequence ($<D_j, P_j, C_j, \sigma_j, \rightarrow_j>$: $1 \leq j$) such that for $1 \leq j$

$$\Leftarrow D_{j-1} \rightarrow_j (P_j, C_j, \sigma_j) \Leftarrow D_j$$

where $\rightarrow_j$ is an element of RULES and P_j is a new variant of a clause from $<EP,LP> \cup \{\#\}$. A **derivation from** $\Leftarrow D_0$ **to** $\Leftarrow D_n$ **wrt** $<EP,LP>$ **and** RULES is a derivation ($<D_j, P_j, C_j, \sigma_j, \rightarrow_j>$: $1 \leq j \leq n$) from $<EP,LP> \cup \{\Leftarrow D_0\}$ wrt RULES. We also say that this derivation has **length** n. A **refutation from** $<EP,LP> \cup \{\Leftarrow D_0\}$ **wrt** RULES is a derivation from $\Leftarrow D_0$ to the empty clause wrt $<EP,LP>$ and RULES.

For notational convenience we omit the P_j, C_j, σ_j, or $\rightarrow_j$ in a derivation if they can be determined from the context.

Derivations can be finite or infinite. A finite derivation can be successful or failed. A derivation has **failed** if it ends with a non-empty goal clause having the property that the equational logic program contains no clause whose head unifies with the selected subgoal of the goal clause. Such a goal clause is often called a **failure**. A derivation is **successful** if it ends with the empty clause, i.e. if it is a refutation.

Definition:

Let ($<D_j, P_j, C_j, \sigma_j, \rightarrow_j>$: $1 \leq j \leq n$) be a refutation from $<EP,LP> \cup \{\Leftarrow D_0\}$ wrt a set of inference rules and let $V = Var(D_0)$. Then $\sigma_n \sigma_{n-1} \ldots \sigma_1 |_V$ is called the **computed answer substitution**.

To make the selection function which has been used in a refutation explicit, we say that there exists a refutation **via SEL** and, if σ is the computed answer substitution in that refutation, we say σ is an **SEL-computed answer substitution**.

All derivations from an equational logic program and a goal clause can be depicted graphically in a derivation tree.

Definition:

Let <EP,LP> be an equational logic program, $\Leftarrow$D be a goal clause and RULES be a set of inference rules. The **derivation tree** for <EP,LP> and $\Leftarrow$D wrt RULES is defined as follows:

(1)   Each node of the tree is a goal clause.

(2)   The root node is $\Leftarrow$D.

(3)   Let $\Leftarrow$D' be a node in the derivation tree, $\rightarrow_x \in$ RULES, $C \in$ D', P be a new variant of a clause in <EP,LP>$\cup$\{#\}, and σ be a substitution. If $\Leftarrow$D' $\rightarrow_x$(C, P, σ) $\Leftarrow$D*, then $\Leftarrow$D* is a descendant of $\Leftarrow$D' and the arc leading from $\Leftarrow$D' to $\Leftarrow$D* is labelled x(C, P, σ).

(4)   The empty node has no descendants.

Each branch of the derivation for <EP,LP> and $\Leftarrow$D wrt RULES corresponds to a derivation of <EP,LP> and $\Leftarrow$D wrt RULES. Branches corresponding to refutations are called **success branches,** branches corresponding to infinite derivations are called **infinite branches,** and branches corresponding to failed derivations are called **failure branches.**

3.4.1 Unification

As first examples for inference rules we consider the rules defined by Herbrand (1930) and later used by Martelli & Montanari (1982) to compute the "most general unifier" of two atoms, terms, or equations. Informally, a unifier is a substitution such that the instances of two terms, atoms, or equations under this substitution are syntactically identical. Hence, in this section we consider a fixed equational program EP = {EQ(x,x)⇐}. For notational convenience we omit the equational logic program in the remaining part of this section. Recall that F denotes a multiset of equations.

Definition:

σ is said to be a **unifier** for ⇐F iff σ is a correct answer substitution for ⇐F. σ is said to be a **most general unifier (mgu)** for ⇐F iff for any unifier θ for ⇐F there exists a substitution γ such that θ = γσ. If there exists a unifier for ⇐F then ⇐F is said to be **unifiable**.

This is a purely semantic definition of a (most general) unifier. But recall that σ is a correct answer substitution for ⇐F iff F is a logical E-consequence of the equational program that contains only the axiom of reflexivity. The only equality defined by such a program is the syntactic equality. Hence, σ is a unifier for ⇐{EQ(s_i,t_i) | 1≤i≤n} iff for all i, 1≤i≤n, we find $\sigma s_i = \sigma t_i$.

As an example consider the terms s = f(x,y,g(b)) and t = f(a,z,g(b)). θ = {x←a, y←a, z←a} is a unifier for ⇐EQ(s,t), since θs = f(a,a,g(b)) = θt. However, θ is not a most general unifier, since σ = {x←a, y←z} is also a unifier for ⇐EQ(s,t) and we have θ = {z←a}σ. It can be shown that σ is a most general unifier for s and t. Therefore we define the following inference rules.

Definition (Term Decomposition →d):

⇐ D∪{EQ(f(s_1,...,s_n), f(t_1,...,t_n))} →d ⇐ D∪{EQ(s_i,t_i) | 1≤i≤n}.

Hence, this rule decomposes an equation if the elements of this equation have the same initial symbol and forces the comparison of corresponding arguments. In figure 3.4.1.1 we depict the term decomposition rule.

Coming back to our example,

⇐ **EQ(f(x,y,g(b)), f(a,z,g(b)))** →d ⇐ EQ(x,a), EQ(y,z), EQ(g(b), g(b))

Definition (Variable Elimination →v):

If x ∉ Var(t), then

⇐ D∪{EQ(x,t)} (resp. ⇐ D∪{EQ(t,x)}) →v({x←t}) ⇐ {x←t}D.

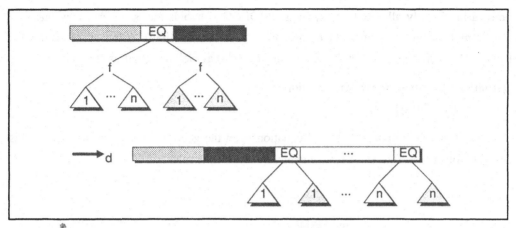

Figure 3.4.1.1: Term Decomposition

Hence, this rule eliminates a variable x by replacing each of its occurrences by the corresponding term t and removing the trivial equation EQ(t,t) provided that x does not occur in t. In figure 3.4.1.2 we depict the variable elimination rule. This rule is applicable to selected equations of the form EQ(x,t) as well as EQ(t,x). The reason is, that the ordering of the elements of an equation is immaterial.

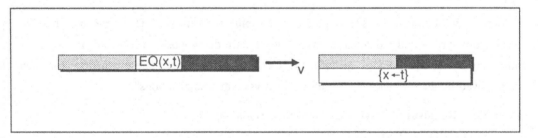

Figure 3.4.1.2: Variable Elimination

In our example,

$\Leftarrow$ **EQ(x,a)**, EQ(y,z), EQ(g(b), g(b)) $\rightarrow_{v(\{x\leftarrow a\})}$ $\Leftarrow$ EQ(y,z), EQ(g(b), g(b))

and

$\Leftarrow$**EQ(y,z)**, EQ(g(b), g(b)) $\rightarrow_{v(\{y\leftarrow z\})}$ $\Leftarrow$ EQ(g(b), g(b)).

The condition x $\notin$ Var(t) in the definition of the variable elimination rule is called **occur check**. This condition ensures that substitutions obtained by the variable elimination rule are idempotent. Unfortunately, performing the occur check is very time consuming and, hence, omitted in virtually all PROLOG-systems. PROLOG II avoids the occur check by interpreting formulas over the domain of rational trees (Colmerauer 1984). A logical semantics for PROLOG II was given by van Emden & Lloyd (1984) as well as by Jaffar et al. (1985).

Definition (Removal of Trivial Equations →$_t$):

$\Leftarrow D \cup \{EQ(t,t)\}$ →$_t$ $\Leftarrow D$.

Hence, this rule eliminates a trivial equation from the goal clause, i.e. an equation that is already "solved". In figure 3.4.1.3 we depict this inference rule.

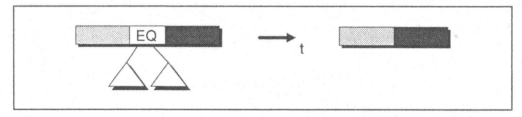

Figure 3.4.1.3: Removal of Trivial Equations

In our example,

$\Leftarrow EQ(g(b), g(b))$ →$_t$ □.

Martelli & Montanari (1982) defined this rule only for variables. Therefore, they have to decompose syntactically identical terms using the term decomposition rule until a set containing only trivial equations of the form $EQ(x,x)$ has been reached. These equations can then be removed by the inference rule "removal of trivial variable equations":

Definition (Removal of Trivial Variable Equations →$_{tv}$}:

$\Leftarrow D \cup \{EQ(x,x)\}$ →$_{tv}$ $\Leftarrow D$

We can now combine the derivation steps of our example into a refutation of the goal clause $\Leftarrow EQ(f(x,y,g(b)), f(a,z,g(b)))$ with respect to term decomposition, variable elimination, and removal of trivial equations of length 4:

$\Leftarrow EQ(f(x,y,g(b)), f(a,z,g(b)))$

→$_d$ $\Leftarrow EQ(x,a), EQ(y,z), EQ(g(b), g(b))$

→$_{v(\{x \leftarrow a\})}$ $\Leftarrow \{x \leftarrow a\}(EQ(y,z), EQ(g(b), g(b)))$

→$_{v(\{y \leftarrow z\})}$ $\Leftarrow \{y \leftarrow z\}EQ(g(b), g(b))$

→$_t$ □.

In this example we used the most general unifiers $\sigma_1 = \varepsilon$, $\sigma_2 = \{x \leftarrow a\}$, $\sigma_3 = \{y \leftarrow z\}$, and $\sigma_4 = \varepsilon$. Hence, $\sigma_4\sigma_3\sigma_2\sigma_1 = \{x \leftarrow a, y \leftarrow z\}$, which is also the computed answer substitution of the refutation of $\Leftarrow EQ(f(x,y,g(b)), f(a,z,g(b)))$ wrt $\{\rightarrow_d, \rightarrow_v, \rightarrow_t\}$, since x as well as y occur in the initial goal clause.

Proposition 3.4.1.1:

   Each derivation of $\Leftarrow F$ wrt $\{\rightarrow_d, \rightarrow_v, \rightarrow_t\}$ is finite.

Proof:

   To each goal clause $\Leftarrow F$ assign a tuple $\langle \#v, \#s \rangle$, where $\#v$ is the number of variables and $\#s$ is the number of symbols occurring in F. $\langle \#v, \#s \rangle$ is **smaller** than $\langle \#v', \#s' \rangle$ iff $\#v < \#v'$ or if $\#v = \#v'$ then $\#s < \#s'$. With this ordering, N^2 becomes a well-founded set. Observe, $\rightarrow_d$ decreases $\#s$ and leaves $\#v$ unchanged, $\rightarrow_v$ decreases $\#v$, and $\rightarrow_t$ decreases $\#s$ and possibly $\#v$.   qed

   If in a derivation with respect to term decomposition, variable elimination, and removal of trivial equations the selected subgoal is of the form $EQ(f(t_1,...,t_n), g(s_1,...,s_m))$ and $f \neq g$ or of the form $EQ(x,t)$ and $x \in Var(t)$, then the derivation will fail.

Theorem 3.4.1.2 (Unification Theorem, Martelli & Montanari 1982)**:**

   Let SEL be a selection function that selects an arbitrary subgoal. If the derivation of $\Leftarrow F$ wrt $\{\rightarrow_d, \rightarrow_v, \rightarrow_t\}$ via SEL terminates with a failure, then $\Leftarrow F$ has no unifier. Otherwise, $\Leftarrow F$ is unifiable. Furthermore, if σ is the SEL-computed answer substitution of the refutation wrt $\{\rightarrow_d, \rightarrow_v, \rightarrow_t\}$ then σ is an mgu for $\Leftarrow F$.

Thus we have a non-deterministic unification algorithm. Robinson's (1965) original unification algorithm can be derived from the above one by considering the multiset of equations as a stack. In section 6.2 we define an inference rule called reflection, which is essentially an abbreviation of the inference rules presented in this section, since it allows to infer $\Leftarrow \sigma D$ from $\Leftarrow D \cup \{EQ(s,t)\}$ iff s and t are unifiable with most general unifier σ. Clearly, such a reflection step can be performed by the inference rules presented in this section.

The unification algorithm presented herein is not minimal in time or space. Better unification algorithms (in this sense) can be obtained by choosing certain data structures to represent the equations (see e.g. Robinson 1971, Martelli & Montanari 1982, Corbin & Bidoit 1983). Paterson & Wegman (1978) gave a unification algorithm linear in time and space.

Fages & Huet (1983, 1986) showed that most general unifiers are unique modulo variable renaming. Hence, by abuse of notation we will refer to a most general unifier as **the** most general unifier.

Since variable elimination is only applied to equations of the form $EQ(x,t)$ (resp. $EQ(t,x)$) if x does not occur in t and, then, each occurrence of x is replaced by t, we find that the most general unifier σ of two terms s and t is idempotent or, equivalently, $Dom(\sigma) \cap VCod(\sigma) = \varnothing$ (see Herold 1983). Hence, if θ is a unifier for s and t, then we find a substitution γ such that $\gamma\sigma = \theta$ and $Dom(\gamma) \cap Dom(\sigma) = \varnothing$.

In the sequel we need a slightly more general definition of a most general unifier, since we want to unify atoms and equations as well.

Definition:

Let X be an n-ary predicate symbol or the symbol "EQ", in which case n=2. $X(s_1,...s_n)$ and $X(t_1,...,t_n)$ are **unifiable** with **mgu** σ iff σ is the mgu of $\Leftarrow \{EQ(s_i,t_i) \mid 1 \leq i \leq n\}$.

Clearly, proposition 3.4.1.1 and theorem 3.4.1.2 carry over to atoms and equations.

3.4.2 SLD-Resolution

We turn our attention again to Horn theories. Having defined an alphabet, the well-formed formulas, and the axioms of our theory, we now define the inference rule which completes our theory, namely the resolution rule.

Definition:

Let $P = C' \Leftarrow D'$ be a new variant of an input clause and $G = \Leftarrow D \cup \{C\}$ be a goal clause. If C' and C are unifiable with mgu σ then $G' = \Leftarrow \sigma(D \cup D')$ is called **(SLD or LUSH)-resolvent** of P and G, in symbols $G \rightarrow_r G'$. We also say that G has been **resolved against P at C with** σ.

In figure 3.4.2.1 we depict the resolution rule.

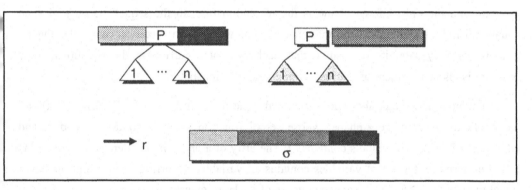

Figure 3.4.2.1: Resolution

As an example consider the equational program $\{ EQ(a,b) \Leftarrow, Q(a) \Leftarrow \}$ together with its equational axioms and the goal clause $\Leftarrow Q(b)$. $Q(b)$ and the head $Q(x)$ of the axiom (sp)

$$Q(x) \Leftarrow Q(y), EQ(x,y)$$

of p-substitutivity are unifiable with most general unifiers $\{x \leftarrow b\}$ and, therefore,

$$\Leftarrow Q(y), EQ(b,y)$$

is a resolvent of (sp) and $\Leftarrow Q(b)$.

SLD-resolution stands for linear resolution with selection function on **definite** clauses (Kowalski & Kuehner 1971). Originally, Hill (1974) coined the name LUSH-resolution as an abbreviation for linear resolution with unrestricted selection function on Horn clauses. In the literature, the term **SLD-resolution** is often used instead of LUSH-resolution. (For a discussion of appropriate acronyms see Ringwood (1988).)

For notational convenience we call derivations (resp. refutations) with respect to SLD-resolution **SLD-derivation** (resp. **SLD-refutation**).

Remark:

Let σ be the most general unifier of the selected subgoal and the head of a program clause. Clearly, σ is idempotent. Furthermore, since σ is applied to the goal clause and program clauses contain only new variables we find that no variable from the domain of σ occurs in the newly generated goal clause. As a consequence, the computed answer substitution of a refutation with respect to resolution must be idempotent. As we will see, this holds for all refutations we give in this thesis.

We now completely defined a first order Horn theory. Given an alphabet, the language consists of Horn clauses and sets of Horn clauses, the set of axioms is an equational logic program and the only inference rule is the resolution rule. In the sequel we only give an equational logic program and the inference rules if we want to specify a first order theory. This is perfectly safe, if we assume that each symbol occurring in the equational logic program is also an element of the respective set in the alphabet.

For example, if we talk about the equational logic program ELP = { EQ(a,b)$\Leftarrow$, Q(a)$\Leftarrow$ } we implicitly assume the alphabet whose set of function symbols contains a and b, and whose set of predicate symbols contains Q. The arity of a and b is 0, whereas the arity of Q is 1. Furthermore, the set of variables contains all variables occurring in ELP and the equational axioms for ELP. The language consists of all Horn clauses and sets of clauses that can be built using these symbols.

So far the special properties of the equality relation were implicitly specified by an E-interpretation. However, to compute the E-unsatisfiablity of an equational logic program together with a goal clause using the resolution rule, we must explicitly define the special properies of the equality relation by means of the equality axioms and add these axioms to the program. Recall, the axioms of equality consist of the reflexivity, symmetry, transitivity, and substitutivity axioms (see section 3.1). It is a well-known result that a set S of clauses is E-unsatisfiable iff there exists a refutation of S with respect to the resolution rule (e.g. Chang & Lee 1973). Hill (1974) showed that for Horn clauses SLD-resolution is refutation complete. Hence, we obtain '

Theorem 3.4.2.1:

> Let $<EP,LP>$ be an equational logic program and $\Leftarrow D$ a goal clause. $<EP,LP>\cup\{\Leftarrow D\}$ is E-unsatisfiable iff there exists an SLD-refutation of $<EP,LP>\cup EAX(<EP,LP>)\cup\{\Leftarrow D\}$.

If an equational logic program does not contain the symbol "EQ", then we do not have to add the equality axioms and theorem 3.4.2.1 still remains valid (Hill 1974).

Obviously, the equality axioms lead to the generation of numerous useless resolvents. Hence, we would like to remove these axioms from the equational logic program. The following theorem shows that we may omit the p-substitutivity axioms if we consider the homogeneous form <EP,H(LP)> of the equational logic program <EP,LP> (see p. 27) .

Notation:

Let <EP,LP>$^+$ be the set <EP,LP>$\cup$EAX(<EP,LP>) without the p-substitutivity axioms. It should be observed that for an equational program EP we find EP$^+$ = EP$\cup$EAX(EP)

Theorem 3.4.2.2 (Hoddinott & Elcock 1986):

Let <EP,LP> be an equational logic program and $\Leftarrow$D be a goal clause. There exists an SLD-refutation of <EP,LP>$\cup$EAX(<EP,LP>)$\cup\{\Leftarrow$D} iff there exists an SLD-refutation of <EP,H(LP)>$^+\cup\{\Leftarrow$D}.

In the remaining part of this section we generalize various results from logic programming as presented by Lloyd (1984) to show that SLD-resolution is sound and complete if we add the axioms of equality to the equational logic program.

Definition:

The **success set** of an equational logic program <EP,LP>, **SS(<EP,LP>)**, is

{ [C] $\in$ B$_\equiv$(<EP,LP>) | there exists an SLD-refutation of <EP,H(LP)>$^+\cup\{\Leftarrow$C} }.

Of course it is desirable that for an equational logic program the success set, the least Herbrand $\equiv$-model, and the least fixpoint of T$_{<EP,LP>}$ are identical. In other words, the model-, fixpoint-, and proof-theoretic characterizations of an equational logic program coincide.

Theorem 3.4.2.3:

$$SS(<EP,LP>) = M_\equiv(<EP,LP>) = lfp(T_{<EP,LP>})$$

Proof:

From theorem 3.3.6 we know that M$_\equiv$(<EP,LP>) = lfp(T$_{<EP,LP>}$) and, hence, it suffices to show that SS(<EP,LP>) = M$_\equiv$(<EP,LP>).

[C] $\in$ SS(<EP,LP>)

iff   there exists an SLD-refutation of <EP,H(LP)>$^+\cup\{\Leftarrow$C}

iff   there exists an SLD-refutation of <EP,LP>$\cup$EAX(<EP,LP>)$\cup\{\Leftarrow$C}   (theorem 3.4.2.2)

iff   <EP,LP>$\cup\{\Leftarrow$C} is E-unsatisfiable   (theorem 3.4.2.1)

iff   C is a logical E-consequence of <EP,LP>   (proposition 3.2.2)

iff   [C] $\in$ M$_\equiv$(<EP,LP>)   (theorem 3.2.8)

                                                                              qed

Of course, this theorem can also be proved by showing that the success-set of <EP,LP> is equal to the least fixpoint of T_{<EP,LP>} by applying the techniques developed by van Emden & Kowalski (1976) and Apt & van Emden (1982). However, it is not that easy since an application of the function $T_{<EP,LP>}$ upon a set of atoms and equations does not directly correspond to an SLD-resolution step. The reason is that in the definition of $T_{<EP,LP>}$ the equality theory defined by EP is hidden in the finest congruence class defined by EP, whereas in an SLD-refutation the question whether two terms are in the same congruence class must be computed using the axioms of equality.

We now lift the results of theorem 3.4.2.3. Recall, that derivations may be empty. Thus, whenever we prove a result concerning a derivation by induction on the length of the derivation we will use the "meta-theorem"

$$[\Phi(0) \wedge \forall i \geq 0: \Phi(i) \Rightarrow \Phi(i+1)] \Rightarrow \forall i: \Phi(i),$$

where Φ is the predicate to show (see e.g. Manna 1974).

Theorem 3.4.2.4 (Soundness of SLD-resolution):

Every computed answer substitution for $<EP,H(LP)>^+ \cup \{\Leftarrow D\}$ wrt SLD-resolution is a correct answer substitution for $<EP,LP>$ and $\Leftarrow D$.

Proof:

Let $\sigma_1,\ldots,\sigma_n$ be the sequence of mgus used in the refutation of $<EP,H(LP)>^+ \cup \{\Leftarrow D\}$ and $\sigma = \sigma_n \ldots \sigma_1$. We have to show that σD is a logical E-consequence of $<EP,LP>$. The result is proved by induction on the length n of the refutation. The case n=0 being trivial (D=$\emptyset$ and $\sigma=\varepsilon$) we turn to the induction step and assume that the result holds for n. Let $C \in D'$ and $P = C^* \Leftarrow D^*$ be a new variant of a clause in $<EP,H(LP)>^+$. Suppose that

$$\Leftarrow D' \rightarrow_r(C, P, \sigma 0) \Leftarrow D$$

and that there exists a refutation of $<EP,H(LP)>^+ \cup \{\Leftarrow D\}$ with mgus $\sigma_1,\ldots,\sigma_n$. Let $\sigma = \sigma_n \ldots \sigma_1$ and $\sigma' = \sigma \sigma_0$. Hence, $D = \sigma_0((D' \backslash \{C\}) \cup D^*)$. By the induction hypothesis,

$$\sigma D \text{ is a logical E-consequence of } <EP,LP> \tag{1}$$

and, thus,

$$\sigma'D^* \text{ is a logical E-consequence of } <EP,LP> \tag{2}$$

From (1) we learn that $\sigma'(D' \backslash \{C\})$ is also a logical E-consequence of $<EP,LP>$. It remains to be shown that $\sigma'C$ is a logical E-consequence of $<EP,LP>$. We distinguish five cases with respect to the program clause P:

(1)   Suppose P is a new variant of a clause in $<EP,H(LP)>$. It follows immediately from (2) that $\sigma'C = \sigma'C^*$ is a logical E-consequence of $<EP,LP>$.

(2)   Suppose P is a new variant of the axiom of reflexivity. Hence, $C^* = EQ(x,x)$, C is of
       the form $EQ(s,t)$, and $\sigma_0 s = \sigma_0 t$. Thus, $\sigma'C$ is a trivial equation and the result follows
       immediately since any trivial equation is a logical E-consequence of $<EP,LP>$.

(3)   Suppose P is a new variant of the axiom of symmetry. Hence, $C^* = EQ(x,y)$, C is of
       the form $EQ(s,t)$, and $D^* = \{EQ(y,x)\}$. From (2) we learn that $\sigma'EQ(t,s) = \sigma'EQ(y,x)$
       is a logical E-consequence of $<EP,LP>$. Since each E-interpretation satisfies the axiom
       of symmetry we conclude that $\sigma'C = \sigma'C^*$ is a logical E-consequence of $<EP,LP>$.

(4)   Suppose P is a new variant of the axiom of transitivity. Hence, $C^* = EQ(x,z)$, C is of
       the form $EQ(s,t)$, and $D^* = \{EQ(x,y), EQ(y,z)\}$. From (2) we learn that $\{\sigma'EQ(s,y),$
       $\sigma'EQ(y,t)\} = \sigma'D^*$ is a logical E-consequence of $<EP,LP>$. Since each E-interpretation
       satisfies the axiom of transitivity we conclude that $\sigma'C = \sigma'C^*$ is a logical E-conse-
       quence of $<EP,LP>$.

(5)   Suppose P is a new variant of a substitutivity axiom for function symbols. Hence, $C^* =$
       $EQ(f(x_1,...,x_m), f(y_1,...,y_m))$, $\sigma_0 C$ is of the form $EQ(f(s_1,...,s_m), f(t_1,...,t_m))$, and $D^* =$
       $\{EQ(x_i,y_i) \mid 1 \le i \le m\}$. From (2) we learn that $\{\sigma'EQ(s_i,t_i) \mid 1 \le i \le m\} = \sigma'D^*$ is a logical
       E-consequence of $<EP,LP>$. Since each E-interpretation satisfies the substitutivity
       axioms we conclude that $\sigma'C = \sigma'C^*$ is a logical E-consequence of $<EP,LP>$.   qed

We now turn to the completeness of our system, which is proved in two steps. First, we
show the completeness for the ground case and, then, we lift this result.

Lemma 3.4.2.5:

   If the atom or equation C is a logical E-consequence of the equational logic
   program $<EP,LP>$, then there exists an SLD-refutation of $<EP,H(LP)>^+ \cup$
   $\{\Leftarrow C\}$ with the identity substitution as computed answer substitution.

Proof:

   Suppose C is a logical E-consequence of $<EP,LP>$ and $Var(C) = \{x_i \mid 1 \le i \le n\}$. Let $a_1,...,a_n$
be n distinct constants not appearing in $<EP,LP>$ or C. Furthermore, let $\theta = \{x_i \leftarrow a_i \mid 1 \le i \le n\}$.
Clearly, θC is a logical E-consequence of $<EP,LP>$. Since θC is ground, theorem 3.4.2.3
shows that there exists an SLD-refutation of $<EP,H(LP)>^+ \cup \{\Leftarrow C\}$ with identity substitution
as computed answer substitution. Because the a_i, $1 \le i \le n$, do not appear in $<EP,LP>$ or in C,
by textual replacing of a_i by x_i, $1 \le i \le n$, in this refutation, we obtain an SLD-refutation of
$<EP,H(LP)>^+ \cup \{\Leftarrow C\}$ with the identity substitution as computed answer substitution.   qed

   The completeness can now be obtained by "lifting" this result.

Lemma 3.4.2.6 (Lifting Lemma for SLD-resolution, e.g. Lloyd 1984):

If there exists an SLD-refutation of $<EP,LP>\cup\{\Leftarrow\theta D\}$ with computed answer substitution γ and length k, then there exists an SLD-refutation of $<EP,LP>\cup\{\Leftarrow D\}$ with the same lenght. Furthermore, if σ is the computed answer substitution of the refutation of $<EP,LP>\cup\{\Leftarrow D\}$, then there exists a substitution λ such that $\gamma\theta = \lambda\sigma$.

Observe, the lifting lemma does not hold if the goal clause consists of a set of subgoals instead of a multiset of subgoals. Recall, $<EP,H(LP)>^+$ is also an equational logic program and, hence, lemma 3.4.2.6 holds also for $<EP,H(LP)>^+$.

Theorem 3.4.2.7 (Completeness of SLD-resolution):

For every correct answer substitution θ for $<EP,LP>$ and $\Leftarrow D$, there exists a computed answer substitution σ obtained by an SLD-refutation of $<EP,H(LP)>^+\cup\{\Leftarrow D\}$ and a substitution γ such that $\theta = \gamma\sigma$.

Proof:

Suppose θ is a correct answer substitution for $<EP,LP>$ and $\Leftarrow D$. Hence, θD is a logical E-consequence of $<EP,LP>$. By lemma 3.4.2.5, for all $C \in D$ we find an SLD-refutation of $<EP,H(LP)>^+\cup\{\Leftarrow\theta C\}$ with identity substitution as computed answer substitution. We can combine these refutations into an SLD-refutation of $<EP,H(LP)>^+\cup\{\Leftarrow\theta D\}$ with identity substitution as computed answer substitution. By an application of the lifting lemma for SLD-resolution we learn that there exists an SLD-refutation of $<EP,H(LP)>^+\cup\{\Leftarrow D\}$. Furthermore, if σ is the computed answer substitution of the refutation of $<EP,H(LP)>^+\cup\{\Leftarrow D\}$, then there exists a substitution γ such that $\theta = \gamma\sigma$.   qed

Theorem 3.4.2.7 shows that if $<EP,LP>$ and $\Leftarrow D$ are E-unsatisfiable, then there exists an SLD-refutation of $<EP,H(EP)>^+\cup\{\Leftarrow D\}$ with a fixed selection function. We now show that the completeness of SLD-resolution is "independent" of the selection function, i.e. that the selection function can be specified in advance before proving that an equational logic program and a goal clause are E-unsatisfiable.

Theorem 3.4.2.8 (Independence of the Selection Function, Lloyd 1984):

Let SEL' be selection function. If there exists an SLD-refutation of $<EP,LP>\cup\{\Leftarrow D\}$ via SEL, then there exists an SLD-refutation of $<EP,LP>\cup\{\Leftarrow D\}$ via SEL'. Furthermore, if σ and θ are the respective computed answer substitutions, then σD is a variant of θD.

Theorem 3.4.2.9 (Strong Completeness of SLD-resolution):

For every correct answer substitution θ *for* $<EP,LP>$ *and* $\Leftarrow D$, *there exists an SEL-computed answer substitution* σ *obtained by an SLD-refutation of* $<EP,H(LP)>^+\cup\{\Leftarrow D\}$ *and a substitution* γ *such that* $\theta = \gamma\sigma$.

Proof:

The theorem follows immediately from theorems 3.4.2.7 and 3.4.2.8.   qed

Thus we obtained a strong completeness result for SLD-resolution provided that the axioms of reflexivity, symmetry, transitivity, and f-substitutivity are added to the equational logic program. In sections 6 and 7 we define inference rules which subsume these equational axioms and replace the resolution rule. These new inference rules apply only if the selected subgoal is an equation. Hence, it is convenient to split the resolution rule in two new inference rules which apply if the selected subgoal is an equation or an atom, respectively. The first one is called "lazy resolution" and the second one "resolution restricted to equations".

Definition (Lazy Resolution $\rightarrow_{lr}$**):**

Let $Q(s_1,...,s_n)\Leftarrow D$ be a new variant of a program clause, then

$$\Leftarrow D'\cup\{Q(t_1,...,t_n)\} \quad \rightarrow_{lr} \quad \Leftarrow D\cup D'\cup\{EQ(s_i,t_i) \mid 1\leq i\leq n\}.$$

Hence, the lazy resolution rule compares the initial symbol of the selected atom with the name of the program clause and, if the symbols are identical, forces the comparison of corresponding arguments. In figure 3.4.2.2 we depict the lazy resolution rule.

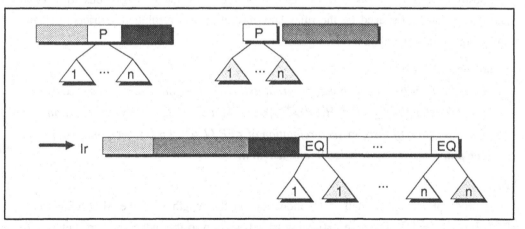

Figure 3.4.2.2: Lazy Resolution

Definition (Resolution Restricted to Equations →_{rr}):

Let EQ(s,t)⇐D be a new variant of an equational clause and σ be a most general unifier of EQ(s,t) and EQ(s',t'), then

$$\Leftarrow D' \cup \{EQ(s',t')\} \quad \rightarrow_{rr(\sigma)} \quad \Leftarrow \sigma(D \cup D')$$

In figure 3.4.2.3 we depict the restricted resolution rule.

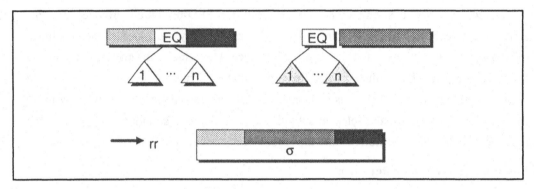

Figure 3.4.2.3: Resolution Restricted to Equations

As an example consider the program clauses Q(a)⇐. Now,

$$\Leftarrow Q(y) \quad \rightarrow_{lr(Q(a))} \quad \Leftarrow EQ(y,a) \quad \rightarrow_{rr(EQ(x,x)\Leftarrow,\ \sigma)} \quad \square$$

where σ = {y←a, x←a}.

Proposition 3.4.2.10 shows that the resolution rule using the homogeneous form of an input clause can be replaced by the rules lazy resolution and resolution restricted to equations using the original clause.

Proposition 3.4.2.10:

Let <EP,LP> be an equational program and ⇐D be a goal clause. There exists an SLD-refutation of <EP∪H(LP)>⁺∪{⇐D} with computed answer substitution θ and length n iff there exists a refutation of <EP,LP>⁺∪{⇐D} wrt {→_{lr}, →_{rr}}, computed answer substitution θ, and length n.

Proof:

The proof of the only-if-half is by induction on the length n of the SLD-refutation of <EP,H(LP)>⁺∪{⇐D}. The case n=0 being trivial we turn to the induction step. Let C ∈ D' and P be a new variant of a clause from <EP,H(LP)>. Suppose that

$$\Leftarrow D' \quad \rightarrow_{r(C, P, \sigma)} \quad \Leftarrow D \tag{1}$$

and that there exists a refutation of $\langle EP,H(LP)\rangle \cup \{\Leftarrow D\}$ with computed answer substitution θ and length n. Hence, $\theta' = \sigma\theta|_{Var(D')}$ is the computed answer substitution of the refutation of $\langle EP,H(LP)\rangle \cup \{\Leftarrow D'\}$. We distinguish two cases with respect to the selected subgoal C.

If C is an equation, then P must be an equational clause and it follows immediately from (1) that

$$\Leftarrow D' \rightarrow_{rr}(C, P, \sigma) \Leftarrow D.$$

The induction hypothesis ensures that the corollary holds in this case.

Ohterwise, if C is the atom $Q(t_1,\ldots,t_n)$, then P must be the homogeneous form of a program clause $P^* = Q(s_1,\ldots,s_n)\Leftarrow D^*$, i.e.

$$P = Q(x_1,\ldots,x_n) \Leftarrow D^* \cup \{EQ(x_i,s_i) \mid 1 \leq i \leq n\},$$

where x_i, $1 \leq i \leq n$, are new variables. Therefore, $\sigma = \{x_i \leftarrow t_i \mid 1 \leq i \leq n\}$ and $D = D' \cup D^* \cup \{EQ(t_i,s_i) \mid 1 \leq i \leq n\}\setminus\{C\}$, which is precisely the goal clause obtained by applying lazy resolution to $\Leftarrow D'$, C, and P^*. Hence,

$$\Leftarrow D \rightarrow_{lr}(C, P^*, \varepsilon) \Leftarrow D'.$$

Since the x_i, $1 \leq i \leq n$, are new variables, none of them occurs in D'. Hence, with proposition 2.2.3(1)

$$\theta' = \theta\sigma|_v = \theta(\sigma|_v)|_v = \theta\varepsilon|_v$$

and the induction hypothesis ensures that the proposition holds in this case.

The proof of the if-half is again by induction on the length n of the refutation of $\langle EP,LP\rangle^+ \cup \{\Leftarrow D\}$ wrt $\{\rightarrow_{lr}, \rightarrow_{rr}\}$. The case $n=0$ being trivial we turn to the induction step. Let $\rightarrow \in \{\rightarrow_{lr}, \rightarrow_{rr}\}$, $C \in D'$, and P be a new variant of a clause in $\langle EP,LP\rangle^+$. Suppose that

$$\Leftarrow D' \rightarrow(C, P, \sigma) \Leftarrow D \tag{2}$$

and that there exists a refutation of $\langle EP,LP\rangle^+ \cup \{\Leftarrow D\}$ wrt $\{\rightarrow_{lr}, \rightarrow_{rr}\}$, computed answer substitution θ, and lenght n. Hence, $\theta' = \theta\sigma|_{Var(D')}$ is the computed answer substitution of the refutation of $\langle EP,LP\rangle^+ \cup \{\Leftarrow D\}$ wrt $\{\rightarrow_{lr}, \rightarrow_{rr}\}$. We distinguish two cases with respect to the selected subgoal C.

If C is an equation, then P must be an equational clause and the inference rule applied in (2) must be resolution restricted to equations. It follows immediately that

$$\Leftarrow D' \rightarrow_r(C, P, \sigma) \Leftarrow D$$

and the induction hypothesis ensures that the corollary holds in this case.

Otherwise, if C is the atom $Q(t_1,\ldots,t_n)$, then P must be a program clause, say $P = Q(s_1,\ldots,s_n) \Leftarrow D^*$, the inference rule applied in (2) must be lazy resolution, and the substitution σ used in (2) must be the identity substitution. Therefore, $D = D' \cup D^* \cup \{EQ(t_i,s_i) \mid 1 \leq i \leq n\}$. Recall that the homogeneous form P' of P is $Q(x_1,\ldots,x_n) \Leftarrow D^* \cup \{EQ(x_i,s_i) \mid 1 \leq i \leq n\}$, where x_i, $1 \leq i \leq n$, are new variables. Hence,

$\Leftarrow D' \rightarrow_r(C, P', \sigma') \Leftarrow D,$

where $\sigma' = \{x_i \leftarrow t_i \mid 1 \le i \le n\}$. Since the x_i, $1 \le i \le n$, are new variables, none of them occurs in D' and with proposition 2.2.3(1) we obtain

$\theta' = \theta\epsilon|v = \theta(\sigma'|v)|v = \theta\sigma'|v.$

Finally, the induction hypothesis ensures that the corollary holds.   qed

Proposition 3.4.2.10 shows that there is a one-to-one correspondence between SLD-refutations taking into account the homogeneous form of an equational logic program and refutations with respect to lazy resolution and resolution restricted to equations. Hence, with theorems 3.4.2.4 and 3.4.2.9 we find that lazy resolution and resolution restricted to equations are sound and strongly complete.

Theorem 3.4.2.11 (Soundness and Strong Completeness of $\rightarrow_{lr}$ and $\rightarrow_{rr}$):

Let $<EP,LP>$ be an equational logic program.

(1)   *Every computed answer substitution of $<EP,LP>^+ \cup \{\Leftarrow D\}$ wrt $\{\rightarrow_{lr}, \rightarrow_{rr}\}$ is a correct answer substitution for $<EP,LP>$ and $\Leftarrow D$.*

(2)   *For every correct answer substitution θ for $<EP,LP>$ and $\Leftarrow D$, there exists an SEL-computed answer substitution σ obtained by a refutation of $<EP,LP>^+ \cup \{\Leftarrow D\}$ wrt $\{\rightarrow_{lr}, \rightarrow_{rr}\}$ and a substitution γ such that $\theta = \gamma\sigma$.*

We finish this section with a small example. Consider the logic program

ELEMENT: elem(x,x:z) $\Leftarrow$ (e1)

             elem(x,y:z) $\Leftarrow$ elem(x,z)   (e2)

where : denotes the list-constructor written in infix notation and *elem(a,l)* states that *a* is an element of the list *l*. We can now invoke the system by raising a question like "*Which elements are contained in the list a:b:[]?*". In our notation, this can be expressed by the initial goal clause

$\Leftarrow$ elem(v,a:b:[]).

In figure 3.4.2.4 we depict the derivation tree for this goal clause and ELEMENT with respect to lazy resolution and resolution restricted to equations. It is a finite tree with two success and two failure branches. The derivations corresponding to the success branches yield the answer substitutions $\{v \leftarrow a\}$ and $\{v \leftarrow b\}$. Hence, the system answers "*a and b are the elements of the list a:b:[].*"

The derivation tree is finite, since we selected the equation $EQ(y_2:z_2,[])$ in the last goal clause of the right-most branch. If the selection function would instead have selected the

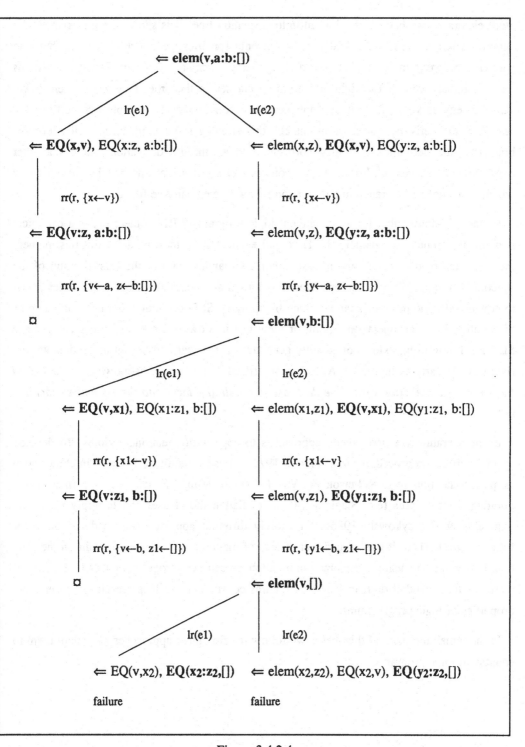

Figure 3.4.2.4

atom elem(x,z), we had obtained an infinite derivation tree. This shows the importance of a "good" search strategy, i.e. a strategy that not only specifies the selection function but also specifies the program clause that should be applied in each step. Standard PROLOG systems select subgoals from left-to-right and program clauses in the order they are written down. This strategy is very efficient to implement and corresponds to a depth-first left-to-right search of the derivation tree. Unfortunately, this strategy is incomplete, since the leftmost branch of the derivation tree may correspond to an infinite derivation whereas another branch may be successful. Naturally, we would prefer a **fair** search strategy, i.e. a strategy by which each successful branch in a derivation tree will eventually be found.

So far we showed that for an equational logic program <EP,LP> there exists a canonical domain of computation, namely the Herbrand ≡-universe, a least model semantics, namely the least Herbrand ≡-model, and a least fixpoint semantics, namely the least fixpoint of the function $T_{<EP,LP>}$. We also demonstrated that correct and complete answers to queries posed to equational logic programs can be given by applying SLD-resolution and using the axioms of equality. From an operational point of view this is, however, not very satisfactory, since SLD-resolution using axioms of equality generates far too many irrelevant and redundant derivations. As early as in 1967 J. A. Robinson argued that a *"new plateau would be achieved by removing these axioms from the database and building them into the deductive machinery"*.

In the literature we find several approaches to cope with equational axioms: To develop special unification procedures (e.g. Plotkin 1972), to use an additional rule of inference such as paramodulation (e.g. Robinson & Wos 1969), to define special inference rules incorporating these axioms (e.g. Slagle 1974), or to flatten the clauses and to apply resolution (e.g. Cox & Pietrzykowski 1986). An entirely different approach was made by Jaffar & Lassez (1987). There it was argued that instead of mapping the intended domain on the Herbrand universe and using specialized unification procedures, programming can be done directly in the intended domain using its natural constraints, while preserving the semantic properties of logic programming.

In the remaining parts of this theses we follow the first three approaches and adapt them to equational logic programs.

4 Universal Unification

In 1972 G. D. Plotkin showed that certain troublesome equational axioms can be removed from the database and be built into the unification procedure. Thus, unification becomes unification under an equational theory and the unification algorithm called within a resolution step is replaced by a unification procedure under an equational theory. In this thesis we are not mainly interested in a specific unification problem, rather we are concerned with unification problems for classes of equational theories such as Horn equational theories. These unification problems are often said to be universal ones.

In this chapter we fix the notation for universal unification and we recall some basic results from unification theory. For a more detailed discussion the reader is referred to Siekmann (1984, 1986, 1989). Throughout this section we only consider equational programs. Hence, we do not distinguish between resolution and resolution restricted to equations.

As an example consider the equational logic program

LENGTH:	EQ(length([]), 0) $\Leftarrow$	(11)
	EQ(length(x:y), 1+length(y)) $\Leftarrow$	(12)
	EQ(0+y, y) $\Leftarrow$	(+1)
	EQ(s(x)+y, s(x+y)) $\Leftarrow$	(+2)

which can be used to compute the length of a list. We can now ask, whether EQ(length(a:[]), 1) is a logical E-consequence of LENGTH. Using SLD-resolution and the axioms of equality we obtain the following refutation (recall that we use n as an abbreviation for $s^n(0)$):

$\Leftarrow$ **EQ(length(a:[]), 1)**	$\rightarrow_{r(t)}$	$\Leftarrow$ **EQ(length(a:[]), x), EQ(x,1)**
	$\rightarrow_{r(12)}$	$\Leftarrow$ **EQ(1+length([]), 1)**
	$\rightarrow_{r(t)}$	$\Leftarrow$ **EQ(1+length([]), y), EQ(y,1)**
	$\rightarrow_{r(+2)}$	$\Leftarrow$ **EQ(s(0+lenght([])), 1)**
	$\rightarrow_{r(sf)}$	$\Leftarrow$ **EQ(0+length([]), 0)**
	$\rightarrow_{r(t)}$	$\Leftarrow$ **EQ(0+length([]), z), EQ(z,0)**
	$\rightarrow_{r(+1)}$	$\Leftarrow$ **EQ(length([]), 0)**
	$\rightarrow_{r(11)}$	**□.**

In this refutation the axiom of transitivity was applied three times. This axiom, however, generates a new intermediary variable, which gives rise to several additional derivations. Unfortunately, there are many infinite and redundant derivations among them. For example, in step two of the previous refutation resolution using the axiom of reflexivity can also be applied to EQ(x,1), in which case the resolvent is the initial goal clause again.

On the other hand, if we had a unification procedure at our disposal, which would be applied to check that length(a:[]) and 1 denote the same under the equational theory defined by LENGTH, then we could apply resolution using the axiom of reflexivity upon ⇐EQ(length(a:[]), 1) to obtain the empty goal clause in a single step.

Definition:

> An **EP-unification problem** consists of a finite multiset F of equations and an equational program EP. The problem has a solution iff there exists a correct answer substitution for EP and ⇐F. If σ is a correct answer substitution for EP and ⇐F, then F is said to be **EP-unifiable** and σ is called an **EP-unifier** for F.

This definition generalizes the definition of a unifier given in section 3.4.1. We also want to remind the reader that an equational program is a conditional equational theory. If F contains only one equation, say EQ(s,t), then we denote the EP-unification problem by <s=t>EP. It should be observed, that

$$\sigma \text{ is a solution for } <s=t>_{EP}$$

$$\text{iff}$$

$$\sigma s =_{EP} \sigma t$$

$$\text{iff}$$

$$\sigma EQ(s,t) \text{ is a logical E-consequence of EP.}$$

As an example consider the unification problem <s(y)=length(x)>LENGTH. This problem has, for example, a solution {x←a:[], y←0} as we have seen in the previous refutation.

A set of EP-unifiers may contain zero, one, finitely, or infinitely many element(s):

- the unification problem <0=1>LENGTH has no solution.

- From theorem 3.4.1.2 we know that a unifiable set of equations has a single most general unifier modulo variable renaming.

- Consider now the equational program

    COM: EQ(f(x,y), f(y,x)) ⇐

    which specifies the commutativity of the function symbol f. The interested reader may verify that the solutions for <f(x,g(a,b))=f(g(y,b),x)>COM can be represented by finitely many unifiers.

- Finally, consider the equational program

    ASSOC: EQ(f(x,f(y,z)), f(f(x,y),z)) ⇐

which specifies the associativity of the function symbol f. The unification problem
$<f(x,g(a,b))=f(g(y,b),x)>$ASSOC has infinitely many solutions

　　$\{x\leftarrow g(a,b),\ y\leftarrow a\}$,
　　$\{x\leftarrow f(g(a,b),g(a,b)),\ y\leftarrow a\}$,
　　$\{x\leftarrow f(g(a,b),f(g(a,b),g(a,b))),\ y\leftarrow a\}$,

　　… .

It should be noted that the set of EP-unifiers is recursively enumerable: Since the set of
terms is recursively enumerable, so is the set of substitutions; now for each substitution
which is an EP-unifier for a given set F of equations, we find, by theorem 3.4.2.9, an SLD-
refutation of $EP^+\cup\{\Leftarrow F\}$. Recall, EP is an arbitrary Horn equational theory and not only a
decidable and unconditional theory as in Plotkin (1972) or Siekmann (1984, 1986, 1989).
The fact that each set of EP-unifiers is recursively enumerable seems to have been not
noticed by Gallier & Raatz (1986, 1989), who, subsequently, restrict their EP-unification
problems to unconditional equational programs EP.

Definition:

> The **universal unification problem** for a given class C of equational programs
> consists of finding an algorithm which for all EP $\in$ C and multisets F of equa-
> tions decides whether there exists a correct answer substitution for EP and $\Leftarrow F$.

The universal unification problem is decidable if we find an algorithm which for all EP $\in$
C and F decides whether the set of EP-unifiers for F is empty. Goldfarb (1981) and Huet
(1973) showed that the unification problems for second and third order logic are undecidable
by reducing it to Hilbert's Tenth Problem and to Post's Correspondence Problem, respectively. The unification problem for distributive and associative theories was proved to be undecidable by Szabo (1982) and Siekmann & Szabo (1989).

Definition:

> The **instantiation** (or **subsumption**) **preorder** $\leq_{EP}$ is defined over the set of
> terms as follows: s $\leq_{EP}$ t iff there exists a substitution σ such that s $=_{EP}$ σt. If s
> $\leq_{EP}$ t then s is said to be **more specific** than t wrt EP and t is said to be **more
> general** than s wrt EP.

As an example consider the equational program LENGTH and the terms length(a:[]) and
length(x). Then length(x) is more general than length(a:[]) since, for example,
EQ(length(a:[]), $\{x\leftarrow b:[]\}$length(x)) is a logical E-consequence of LENGTH.

As an immediate consequence of this definition, a variable is a most general term and a
ground term is a most specific term.

If $EQ(s,\sigma t)$ is a logical E-consequence of EP, then σ is often called **EP-matcher** for $EQ(s,t)$. Similarly, we can define an **EP-matching problem**.

Proposition 4.1:

   $\leq_{EP}$ *is a preorder.*

Proof:

   We have to show that $\leq_{EP}$ is reflexive and transitive. Clearly, $\leq_{EP}$ is reflexive. Suppose now that $s \leq_{EP} t$ and $t \leq_{EP} u$, i.e. there exist substitutions σ, θ, such that $s =_{EP} \sigma t$ and $t =_{EP} \theta u$. Hence, $\sigma t =_{EP} \sigma\theta u$ and we find that for each E-interpretation I of EP, I is a model for EP implies I is a model for $EQ(s,\sigma t)$ and $EQ(\sigma t,\sigma\theta u)$. Since E-interpretations are transitve we find $s =_{EP} \sigma\theta u$ and, hence, $s \leq_{EP} u$.   qed

   We can now generalize the notion of a variant to a variant under an equational theory EP or "EP-variant".

Definition:

   s and t are said to be **EP-variants**, in symbols $s \sim_{EP} t$, iff $s \leq_{EP} t$ and $t \leq_{EP} s$.
   We also say that s **is an EP-variant of** t and t **is an EP-variant of** s.

   Again, if $EP = \varnothing$ then we omit the symbol $\varnothing$ and write $s \sim t$ instead of $s \sim_{\varnothing} t$. From proposition 2.2.2 we know that, if $s \sim t$, then there exist substitutions σ and θ such that $s = \sigma t$ and $t = \theta s$, where σ is a renaming substitution for t and θ is a renaming substitution for s. It was shown that the quotient of the set of terms modulo $\sim$ is a complete lattice, called the **instantiation** (or **subsumption**) **lattice** (Reynolds 1970, Huet 1980). Observe, Proposition 2.2.2 cannot be extended to hold for arbitrary equational programs. As an example consider the equational program LENGTH and the equations $EQ(0+y, y)$. Obviously, $y \sim_{LENGTH} 0+y$, but no renaming substitution can identify y and $0+y$.

   We now extend $=_{EP}$, $\leq_{EP}$, and $\sim_{EP}$ to substitutions.

Definition:

   Let V be a finite set of variables. The relation $=_{EP}[V]$ is defined on substitutions by $\sigma =_{EP} \theta\ [V]$ iff for all x in V we find that $\sigma x =_{EP} \theta x$. The relation $\leq_{EP}[V]$ is defined on substitutions by $\sigma \leq_{EP} \theta\ [V]$ iff there exists a substitution λ such that $\sigma =_{EP} \lambda\theta\ [V]$. If $\sigma \leq_{EP} \theta\ [V]$ then σ is called an **EP-instance of** θ **wrt** V.

   As an example consider again the equational program COM. The substitution $\sigma = \{y\leftarrow f(a,g(a))\}$ is an EP-instance of $\theta = \{y\leftarrow f(x,a)\}$ wrt $\{y\}$ since for $\gamma = \{x\leftarrow g(a)\}$ we find that $\sigma y = f(a,g(a)) =_{CON} f(g(a),a)) = \gamma\theta y$.

The identity substitution ε is the most general substitution and a ground substitution is a most specific one. Ground substitutions are sometimes called **environments** (e.g. Reddy 1985).

Proposition 4.2:

Let V be a finite set of variables. $\leq_{EP}[V]$ is a preorder.

Proof:

We have to show that $\leq_{EP}[V]$ is reflexive and transitive. Clearly, $\leq_{EP}$ is reflexive. If $\sigma \leq_{EP} \gamma$ [V] and $\gamma \leq_{EP} \theta$ [V], then there exist substitutions λ and μ such that for all x in V we find that $\sigma x =_{EP} \lambda\gamma x$ and $\gamma x =_{EP} \mu\theta x$. The proposition follows in analogy to the proof of proposition 4.1.   qed

Definition:

Let V be a finite set of variables. σ and θ are said to be **EP-variants wrt V**, in symbols $\sigma \sim_{EP} \theta$ [V], iff $\sigma \leq_{EP} \theta$ [V] and $\theta \leq_{EP} \sigma$ [V]. We also say that σ is an **EP-variant of θ and θ is an EP-variant of σ.**

It is easy to see that $\sim_{EP}$ and $\sim_{EP}[V]$ are equivalence relations: By definition $\sim_{EP}$ and $\sim_{EP}[V]$ are symmetric and from propositions 4.1 and 4.2 we conclude that $\sim_{EP}$ and $\sim_{EP}[V]$ are reflexive and transitive.

$\sim_{EP}[V]$ and $=_{EP}[V]$ are different relations. For example consider the case that $EP=\emptyset$. Now, $\sigma\sim\theta[V]$ states that for all $x\in V$ we find that σx and θx are variants, whereas $\sigma=\theta[V]$ states that for all $x\in V$ we find that σx is identical to θx. In general, $\sigma =_{EP} \theta$ [V] implies $\sigma \sim_{EP} \theta$ [V], but the opposite does not hold in general.

For notational convenience we write $\sigma \leq_{EP} \theta$ instead of $\sigma \leq_{EP} \theta$ [V] iff Dom(θ) $\subseteq$ V and $\sigma =_{EP} \theta$ instead of $\sigma =_{EP} \theta$ [V] iff Dom(σ) = Dom(θ) $\subseteq$ V.

The following proposition states some frequently used facts.

Proposition 4.3:

If V and V' are finite sets of variables, then,

(1)	$\sigma \leq_{EP} \theta$ [V]	implies	$\sigma \leq_{EP} \theta$ [V∩V'],
(2)	$\sigma \leq \theta$ [V]	implies	$\sigma \leq_{EP} \theta$ [V],
(3)	$\sigma =_{EP} \theta$ [V]	implies	$\gamma\sigma =_{EP} \gamma\theta$ [V],

(4)	$Var(t) \subseteq V$	and $\sigma =_{EP} \theta$ [V]	imply	$\sigma t =_{EP} \theta t$,
(5)	$\sigma \leq_{EP} \theta$ [V]	and $\theta =_{EP} \gamma$ [V]	imply	$\sigma \leq_{EP} \gamma[V]$,
(6)	$VCod(\gamma) \subseteq V$	and $\sigma \leq_{EP} \theta$ [V]	imply	$\sigma\gamma \leq_{EP} \theta\gamma$ [V].
(7)	$VCod(\gamma) \subseteq V$	and $\sigma \sim_{EP} \theta$ [V]	imply	$\sigma\gamma \sim_{EP} \theta\gamma$ [V], and
(8)	$\sigma \sim_{EP} \theta$ [V]	and $\sigma \leq_{EP} \gamma$ [V]	imply	$\theta \leq_{EP} \gamma$ [V]

Proof:

(1) $\sigma \leq_{EP} \theta[V]$

    iff $\exists\lambda: \forall x\in V: \sigma x =_{EP} \lambda\theta x$

    only if $\exists\lambda: \forall x\in V\cap V': \sigma x =_{EP} \lambda\theta x$

    iff $\sigma \leq_{EP} \theta\ [V\cap V']$.

(2) $\sigma \leq \theta\ [V]$

    iff $\exists\lambda: \forall x\in V: \sigma x = \lambda\theta x$

    only if $\exists\lambda: \forall x\in V: \sigma x =_{EP} \lambda\theta x$, for any EP

    iff $\sigma \leq_{EP} \theta\ [V]$.

(3) $\sigma =_{EP} \theta\ [V]$

    iff $\forall x\in V: \sigma x =_{EP} \theta x$

    only if $\forall x\in V: \gamma\sigma x =_{EP} \gamma\theta x$

    iff $\gamma\sigma =_{EP} \gamma\theta\ [V]$.

(4)   Suppose $Var(t) \subseteq V$.

    $\sigma =_{EP} \theta\ [V]$

    iff $\forall x\in V: \sigma x =_{EP} \theta x$

    only if $\forall x\in Var(t): \sigma x =_{EP} \theta x$

    iff $\sigma t =_{EP} \theta t$.

(5) $\sigma \leq_{EP} \theta\ [V]$ and $\theta =_{EP} \gamma\ [V]$

    iff $\exists\lambda: \forall x\in V: \sigma x =_{EP} \lambda\theta x$ and $\theta x =_{EP} \gamma x$

    iff $\exists\lambda: \forall x\in V: \sigma x =_{EP}\lambda\theta x$ and $\lambda\theta x =_{EP} \lambda\gamma x$ (part 3)

    iff $\exists\lambda: \forall x\in V: \sigma x =_{EP} \lambda\gamma x$ (since $=_{EP}$ is transitive)

    iff $\sigma \leq_{EP} \gamma\ [V]$.

(6) $\sigma \leq_{EP} \theta\ [V]$ iff $\exists\lambda: \forall x\in V: \sigma x =_{EP} \lambda\theta x$.   (*)

Now let $x\in V$. We distinguish two cases wrt the domain of γ. Suppose first that $x \in Dom(\gamma)$ and $x\leftarrow t \in \gamma$. Then, $\sigma\gamma x = \sigma t$ and $\theta\gamma x = \theta t$. Since $Var(t) \subseteq VCod(\gamma) \subseteq V$ an application of part(4) to (*) shows that

    $\exists\lambda: \sigma\gamma x = \sigma t =_{EP} \lambda\theta t = \lambda\theta\gamma x$.

Now suppose that $x \notin Dom(\gamma)$. Then, $\sigma\gamma x = \sigma x$ and $\theta\gamma x = \theta x$ and it follows immediately from (*) that

    $\exists\lambda: \sigma\gamma x = \sigma x =_{EP} \lambda\theta x = \lambda\theta\gamma x$.

In any case we find that

    $\exists\lambda: \forall x\in V: \sigma\gamma x =_{EP} \lambda\theta\gamma x$. Hence, $\sigma\gamma \leq_{EP} \theta\gamma\ [V]$.

(7)   VCod(γ) $\subseteq$ V and σ ~$_{EP}$ θ [V]

    iff   VCod(γ) $\subseteq$ V and σ $\leq_{EP}$ θ [V] and θ $\leq_{EP}$ σ [V]

    only if $\sigma\gamma$ $\leq_{EP}$ $\theta\gamma$ [V] and $\theta\gamma$ $\leq_{EP}$ $\sigma\gamma$ [V]   (part 6)

    iff $\sigma\gamma$ ~$_{EP}$ $\theta\gamma$ [V].

(8) σ ~$_{EP}$ θ [V] implies θ $\leq_{EP}$ σ [V]. Hence, using the transitivity of $\leq_{EP}$[V] (proposition 4.2) we learn from θ $\leq_{EP}$ σ [V] and σ $\leq_{EP}$ γ [V] that θ $\leq_{EP}$ γ [V].   qed

It should be noted, that part (4) and as a consequence (6) and (7) do not hold if we drop the condition Var(t) $\subseteq$ V (resp. VCod(γ) $\subseteq$ V). As an example consider the term t = f(x,y) and the substitutions σ = {x$\leftarrow$a, y$\leftarrow$b} and θ = {x$\leftarrow$a, y$\leftarrow$c}. Now let EP = $\varnothing$ and V = {x}. Obviously, σ=θ[V]. But, σt = f(a,b) $\neq$ f(a,c) = θt.

Furthermore, σ $\leq_{EP}$ θ [V] does not imply $\gamma\sigma$ $\leq_{EP}$ $\gamma\theta$ [V]. As an example consider EP = {EQ(f(a),c)$\Leftarrow$}, σ = {y$\leftarrow$f(a)}, θ = {y$\leftarrow$f(x)}, and V = {y}. Now we have

    σy = f(a) $\leq_{EP}$ f(x) = θy,

since for λ = {x$\leftarrow$a} we find

    λf(x) = f(a).

However, for γ = {x$\leftarrow$b} we obtain

    $\gamma\sigma$y = {y$\leftarrow$f(a), x$\leftarrow$b}y = f(a),

    $\gamma\theta$y = {y$\leftarrow$f(b), x$\leftarrow$b}y = f(b),

and it follows immediately that

    $\neg\exists\lambda$: $\gamma\sigma$y =$_{EP}$ $\lambda\gamma\theta$y.

Proposition 4.4 shows that whenever a substitution σ is a matcher for s and t which only binds variables occurring in s, then this substitution σ is a most general unifier for s and t.

Proposition 4.4:

    Suppose Var(s)$\cap$Var(t) = $\varnothing$. If there exists a substitution σ such that Dom(σ) = Var(s) and σs = t then σ is the most general unifier of s and t.

Proof:

Let σ be a substitution such that σs = t and Dom(σ) = Var(s). Obviously, σ is a unifier for s and t. The proof is by contradiction. Assume that σ is not the mgu of s and t. Then we find substitutions λ and θ such that

    θs = θt and σ = $\lambda\theta$.   (1)

Since Dom(σ)$\cap$Var(t) = $\varnothing$ and σ = $\lambda\theta$ we find Dom(θ)$\cap$Var(t) = $\varnothing$ and thus θt = t. Hence, (1) reduces to

    θs = t and σ = $\lambda\theta$.   (2)

Because $Var(s) \cap Var(t) = \emptyset$ we find $Dom(\theta) = Var(s) = Dom(\sigma)$. We distinguish two cases wrt λ. Suppose first that $\lambda\theta = \theta$. Hence, $\theta = \sigma$ and σ is an mgu for s and t. Now suppose that $\lambda\theta \neq \theta$. But then, $Dom(\lambda) \cap VCod(\theta) \neq \emptyset$. Hence, $Var(s) \cap VCod(\theta) \neq \emptyset$ and, therefore, $\theta s \neq t$ contradicting the fact that θ is an mgu of s and t. Thus, λ must be the empty substitution and it follows immediately that $\sigma = \theta$.   qed

As in the case where EP is empty, we are not so much interested in the set of all EP-unifiers of two terms, rather in a set, which is as small as possible, but from which any EP-unifier for these terms can be obtained. A set obeying the last condition is called a **complete set of EP-unifiers**.

Definition:

Let EP be an equational program, F be a set of equations, and V be a finite set of variables such that $Var(F) \subseteq V$. A set Σ of substitutions is a **complete set of EP-unifiers for F away from V** iff

(1) $\forall \sigma \in \Sigma: Dom(\sigma) \subseteq Var(F)$ and $VCod(\sigma) \cap V = \emptyset$,

(2)   each substitution in Σ is an EP-unifier for F, and

(3)   for each EP-unifier for F we find a substitution σ in Σ such that $\sigma \leq_{EP} \theta$ [Var(F)].

The first condition is technical. The necessity of considering a set V stems from the fact that terms occurring in F may be subterms of larger terms containing variables not in Var(F) and we do not want to mix these with variables in VCod(σ). If we are only interested in solving the EP-unification problem the first condition may be omitted. The second condition concernes correctness and the last condition concernes completeness of a set of EP-unifiers (Plotkin 1972, Huet & Oppen 1980). It should be noted that we defined complete sets of EP-unifiers for Horn equational theories and not just for unconditional theories.

For a given equational program EP and set of equations F a complete set of EP-unifiers can always be found by taking all EP-unifiers and verifying condition (1). However, there may be no EP-unifier at all nor may there exist a finite complete set of EP-unifiers. As an example consider the equational program ASSOC and let $s = f(x,g(a,b))$ and $t = f(g(y,b),x)$. $\langle s=t \rangle_{ASSOC}$ has the solution

$\sigma = \{x \leftarrow g(a,b), y \leftarrow a\}$

since

$\sigma s = f(g(a,b),g(a,b)) = \sigma t$.

But

$\theta = \{x \leftarrow f(g(a,b),g(a,b)), y \leftarrow a\}$

is also an ASSOC-unifier for s and t and neither $\sigma \leq_{ASSOC} \theta$ [{x,y}] nor $\theta \leq_{ASSOC} \sigma$ [{x,y}]. It is easy to see that there are infinitely many ASSOC-unifiers having this property (Plotkin 1972).

Thus, it suffices to look for complete sets of EP-unifiers for a given unification problem, since any other EP-unifier can be obtained by instantiation. However, such a complete set of EP-unifiers may still contain many redundant elements.

Definition:

A complete set Σ of EP-unifiers for F away from V is said to be **minimal** iff

(4)   for all $\sigma, \theta \in \Sigma$ we find that $\sigma \leq_{EP} \theta$ [Var(F)] implies $\sigma = \theta$.

Whenever there exists a finite and complete set of EP-unifiers and the relation $\leq_{EP}[V]$ on substitutions is decidable, then there exists also a minimal one. This set can be obtained by removing from the complete set of EP-unifiers each EP-unifier for which a more general (modulo EP) one is contained in this set. However, this is not possible in general as the following theorem shows.

Theorem 4.5 (Fages & Huet 1983, 1986):

For some equational program EP there exist EP-unifiable terms for which there is no minimal complete set of EP-unifiers.

Fages & Huet proved this result by demonstrating that for the equational program {EQ(g(a,x),x)⇐, EQ(f(g(x,y)),f(y))⇐} and the terms f(x) and f(a), minimality is incompatible with completeness.

Notation:

If a minimal complete set of EP-unifiers for F away from V exists we call this set a **set of most general EP-unifiers for F away from V**.

Whenever a minimal complete set of EP-unifiers for s and t exists, it is unique modulo ~EP[Var(s,t)]:

Theorem 4.6 (Fages & Huet 1983, 1986):

Let Σ_1 and Σ_2 be two sets of most general EP-unifiers for F. There exists a bijection $\Phi: \Sigma_1 \to \Sigma_2$ such that

$$\forall \sigma \in \Sigma_1: \sigma \sim_{EP} \Phi(\sigma) \ [Var(F)].$$

In the sequel we always consider a set of most general EP-unifiers for F as some representative of the quotient of all sets of most general EP-unifiers for F modulo ~EP[Var(F)].

Definition:

    An **EP-unification procedure** UP_{EP} is a procedure which takes a set F of equations as input and generates a subset of the set of EP-unifiers for F. An EP-unification procedure is **complete** iff it generates a complete set of EP-unifiers for F. A complete EP-unification procedure is **minimal** iff it generates a most general set of EP-unifiers for F whenever this set exists.

Definition:

    A **universal unification procedure** UP_C for a class of equational programs C is a procedure which takes an equational program $EP \in C$ and a set of equations F as input and generates a subset of the set of EP-unifiers for F.

Remark:

Similarily to the standard case a minimal/complete universal unification procedure for a class of equational programs can be defined.

If $EP = \emptyset$ then for all F a minimal complete set of unifiers exists and has at most one element (Robinson 1965). To compute this set, the algorithm given in section 3.4.1 can be used.

EP-unification was first studied in (Plotkin 1972) for decidable equational theories which can be specified by a finite set of equations. Plotkin gives a minimal unification procedures for associative functions. In the sequel several unification procedures have been developed. (For a comprehensive overview see Siekmann 1984, 1986, 1988.)

For a given equational program EP or class of equational programs C we have to solve the following problems:

The Unification Problem:

    Is the (universal) unification problem decidable ?

The Existence Problem:

    Does a minimal complete set of EP-unifiers always exist ?

The Enumeration Problem:

    Is a minimal complete set of EP-unifiers recursively enumerable ?

Obviously, a desirable goal is to develop minimal unification procedures or at least those unification procedures who generate the set of most general unifiers if this set is infinite and a finite superset of the set of most general unifiers if this set is finite. Since in many cases this was not (cannot be?) achieved, Szabo (1984) gives a weaker criterion for unification procedures: Let Σ_i be the set of unifiers generated by UP_i. The goal is to generate unification procedures UP_i, $1 \leq i \leq n$, such that for $1 < i \leq n$ we find that the set of most general unifiers is a subset of Σ_n, $\Sigma_i \subseteq \Sigma_{i-1}$, and Σ_1 is a subset of the set of EP-unifiers.

As in the case where the equational program EP is empty we also want to EP-unify atoms and equations.

Definition:

    Let X be an n-ary predicate symbol or the symbol "EQ", in which case n=2. $X(s_1,...,s_n)$ and $X(t_1,...,t_n)$ are **EP-unifiable** with σ iff σ is an EP-unifier for $\Leftarrow \{EQ(s_i,t_i)|1 \leq i \leq n\}$.

Obviously, all definitions and theorems given in this section carry over to atoms and equations. By abuse of notation we sometimes write $\sigma C =_{EP} \sigma C'$ if C and C' are EP-unifiable with σ.

Using these basic notions and results concerning universal unification, we have the theoretical framework to remove equational axioms from the database and to build them into the unification procedure, however the difficult problem remains to actually find appropriate unification procedures for the special case at hand.

5 SLDE-Resolution

As we learned in the previous chapter the notion of a most general unifier of a set F of equations can be generalized to a complete set of EP-unifiers. This set can be used for a resolution based theorem prover. G. D. Plotkin's (1972) basic idea was to take each unifier of the set of EP-unifiers for the selected literals instead of the traditional most general unifier. With the strength and the weakness of PROLOG many researchers have applied Plotkin's idea to SLD-resolution. For example, Jaffar et al. (1984, 1986) showed that the least Herbrand ≡-model of an equational logic program <EP,LP> is precisely the success set of LP with respect to resolution using EP-unifiers. Gallier & Raatz (1986, 1989) proved the completeness of resolution using an EP-unification algorithm for unconditional equational programs EP.

In this section we give rigorous proofs for the soundness and completeness of resolution using EP-unifiers as well as using correct and complete EP-unification procedures. Moreover, we show that these resolution rules are independent of the selection function.

At first we demonstrate that resolution with EP-unifiers as defined by Jaffar et al. (1984, 1986) is nothing else but applying a certain selection function to refutations with respect to lazy resolution and resolution restricted to equations. Therefore, we define the notion of a **descendant** of a subgoal, which is roughly speaking an equation that should be solved before any other subgoal is selected.

Definition:

Suppose $\Leftarrow D \rightarrow(\sigma) \Leftarrow D'$ wrt $\{\rightarrow_{lr}, \rightarrow_{rr}\}$.

If the equation $E \in D$ is not the selected subgoal, then $\sigma E \in D'$ is an **immediate descendant** of E.

If $P(s_1,\ldots,s_m)$ is the selected subgoal and $P(t_1,\ldots,t_m) \Leftarrow D^*$ is the new variant of the program clause used, then each $E \in \{EQ(s_i,t_i) \mid 1 \leq i \leq m\}$ is an **immediate descendant** of $P(s_1,\ldots,s_m)$.

If $EQ(s,t)$ is the selected subgoal and $EQ(u,v) \Leftarrow F^*$ is the new variant of the equational clause used, then each $E \in \sigma F^*$ is an **immediate descendant** of $EQ(s,t)$.

C_n is called a **descendant** of C_1 iff there exists a sequence $(C_i : 1 \leq i \leq n)$ such that C_i is an immediate descendant of C_{i-1}, $1 < i \leq n$.

As an example consider the equational logic program

$$P(c) \Leftarrow Q(c) \tag{p}$$
$$Q(c) \Leftarrow \tag{q}$$

$$EQ(a,b) \Leftarrow \qquad\qquad (e1)$$
$$EQ(b,c) \Leftarrow \qquad\qquad (e2)$$

and the goal clause $\Leftarrow P(a)$. We obtain the following refutation with respect to lazy resolution and resolution restricted to equations:

$\Leftarrow P(a)$	$\rightarrow lr(p)$	$\Leftarrow Q(c), EQ(a,c)$
	$\rightarrow lr(q)$	$\Leftarrow EQ(c,c), EQ(a,c)$
	$\rightarrow rr(r)$	$\Leftarrow EQ(a,c)$
	$\rightarrow rr(t)$	$\Leftarrow EQ(a,x), EQ(x,c)$
	$\rightarrow rr(e1)$	$\Leftarrow EQ(b,c)$
	$\rightarrow rr(e2)$	$\Box$.

$Q(c)$ is not an immediate descendant of $P(a)$. In fact, an atom can never be a descendant. However, $EQ(a,c)$ is a descendant of $P(a)$, and so are $EQ(a,x)$, $EQ(x,c)$, and $EQ(b,c)$.

A special selection function, called **SLDE**, will now select descendants of primarily selected subgoals as long as such descendants exist.

Definition:

Let **SLDE** be the selection function that selects subgoals according to the following program:
(1) select an arbitrary subgoal C
(2) while $F(C) \neq \emptyset$ select an arbitrary subgoal from $F(C)$, where $F(C)$ is the set of descendants of C in the current goal clause.
(3) goto (1).
Selections in (1) will be called **arbitrary**, and selections in (2) will be called **constrained**.

SLDE selects an arbitrary subgoal of a goal clause $\Leftarrow D$ if D does not contain a descendant of C. Furthermore, a constrained selection selects an arbitrary subgoal among the descendants of C. The refutation depicted above is not an SLDE-refutation since the second selected subgoal, $Q(c)$, is not a descendant of $P(a)$. A corresponding SLDE-refutation is

$\Leftarrow P(a)$	$\rightarrow lr(p)$	$\Leftarrow Q(c), EQ(a,c)$
	$\rightarrow rr(t)$	$\Leftarrow Q(c), EQ(a,x), EQ(x,c)$
	$\rightarrow rr(e1)$	$\Leftarrow Q(c), EQ(b,c)$
	$\rightarrow rr(e2)$	$\Leftarrow Q(c)$
	$\rightarrow lr(q)$	$\Leftarrow EQ(c,c)$
	$\rightarrow rr(r)$	$\Box$,

where the elements of the set $F(C)$ used by the selection function SLDE are written in italics.

It should be noted that SLDE-resolution is in general defined as follows in the literature (e.g. Jaffar et al. 1984, 1986). Let $\Leftarrow D \cup \{C\}$ be a goal clause and C be the selected subgoal. Suppose first that C is the atom $P(s_1,...,s_n)$ and $P(t_1,...,t_n) \Leftarrow D^*$ is a new variant of a program clause. If σ is an EP-unifier for $\{EQ(s_i,t_i) \mid 1 \leq i \leq n\}$, then $\Leftarrow \sigma(D \cup D^*)$ is an SLDE-resolvent of $\Leftarrow D \cup \{C\}$. Suppose that C is the equation $EQ(s,t)$. If σ is an EP-unifier for $\{EQ(s,t)\}$, then $\Leftarrow \sigma D$ is an SLDE-resolvent of $\Leftarrow D \cup \{C\}$. It is easy to see that both definitions are related via theorem 3.4.2.11. The second definition is purely semantical, whereas the first one is based on a refutation complete system using lazy resolution, resolution restricted to equations, and the axioms of equality.

The following corollary is an immediate consequence of the soundness and strong completeness of lazy resolution and resolution restricted to equations (theorem 3.4.2.11).

Corollary 5.1 (Soundness and Strong Completeness of SLDE-resolution):

(1)   *Every SLDE-computed answer substitution for $<EP,LP>^+ \cup \{\Leftarrow D\}$ wrt $\{\rightarrow_{lr}, \rightarrow_{rr}\}$ is a correct answer substitution for $<EP,LP>$ and $\Leftarrow D$.*

(2)   *For every correct answer substitution θ for $<EP,LP>$ and $\Leftarrow D$, there exists an SLDE-computed answer substitution σ obtained by a refutation of $<EP,LP>^+ \cup \{\Leftarrow D\}$ wrt $\{\rightarrow_{lr}, \rightarrow_{rr}\}$ and a substitution γ such that $\theta = \gamma\sigma$.*

As we mentioned at the beginning of this section, we would like to build the axioms of equality into the unification procedure and, then, to apply resolution using such a tailored unification procedure. Therefore, whenever the selection function SLDE selects an arbitrary subgoal, then instead of using resolution and equational clauses from EP^+ we call a respective EP-unification procedure. Such a derivation is called EP-derivation. Recall that each logic program implicitely contains the axiom of reflexivity.

Definition:

Let UP$_{EP}$ be an EP-unification procedure, $P = C' \Leftarrow D'$ be a new variant of a program clause, and $G = \Leftarrow D \cup \{C\}$ be a goal clause. If C and C' are EP-unifiable with $\sigma \in UP_{EP}(C,C')$, then $G' = \Leftarrow \sigma(D \cup D')$ is called **EP-resolvent** of P and G, in symbols $G \rightarrow_{EP(C, P, \sigma)} G'$.

In our previous example, the goal clause $\Leftarrow Q(c)$ is an EP-resolvent of the program clause $P(c) \Leftarrow Q(c)$ and the goal clause $\Leftarrow P(a)$, since ϵ is an EP-unifier for $P(a)$ and $P(c)$.

The notions derivation and refutation can now be generalized to **EP-derivation** and **EP-refutation** in the obvious way. If we have a correct and complete EP-unification procedure, we can now prove the soundness and strong completeness of EP-resolution:

Theorem 5.2 (Soundness of EP-resolution):

> Let $<EP,LP>$ be an equational logic program and UP_{EP} be a correct EP-unification procedure. Every computed answer substitution of $LP \cup \{\Leftarrow D\}$ wrt EP-resolution is a correct answer substitution for $<EP,LP>$ and $\Leftarrow D$.

Proof:

Let $\sigma_1, ..., \sigma_n$ be the sequence of EP-unifiers used in the EP-refutation of $LP \cup \{\Leftarrow D\}$ and $\sigma = \sigma_n...\sigma_1$. We have to show that σD is a logical E-consequence of $<EP,LP>$. The result is proved by induction on the length n of the refutation. The case n=0 being trivial we turn to the induction step and assume that the result holds for n. Let $C' \in D'$ and $P = C^* \Leftarrow D^*$ be a new variant of a clause in LP. Suppose

$$\Leftarrow D' \quad \rightarrow_{EP}(C, P, \sigma_0) \quad \Leftarrow D$$

and there exists an EP-refutation of $LP \cup \{\Leftarrow D\}$ with EP-unifiers $\sigma_1, ..., \sigma_n$. Let $\sigma = \sigma_n...\sigma_1$ and $\sigma' = \sigma\sigma_0$. Hence, $D = \sigma_0((D' \backslash \{C'\}) \cup D^*)$. By the induction hypothesis,

$$\sigma D \text{ is a logical E-consequence of } <EP,LP> \tag{1}$$

and, thus,

$$\sigma'D^* \text{ is a logical E-consequence of } <EP,LP>. \tag{2}$$

From (1) we learn that $\sigma'(D' \backslash \{C'\})$ is also a logical E-consequence of $<EP,LP>$. It remains to be shown that $\sigma'C'$ is a logical E-consequence of $<EP,LP>$. Recall that P may be either a program clause or the axiom of reflexivity.

(1) If P is a program clause, then by (2) $\sigma'C^*$ is a logical E-consequence of $<EP,LP>$. Since UP_{EP} is correct and C^* and C' are EP-unifiable with σ_0 we find that $\sigma'C'$ is also a logical E-consequence of $<EP,LP>$.

(2) If P is the axiom of reflexivity, then C' must be of the form $EQ(s,t)$. Since UP_{EP} is correct we find $\sigma_0 s =_{EP} \sigma_0 t$ and, hence, $\sigma'C' = \sigma\sigma_0 EQ(s,t)$ is a logical E-consequence of $<EP,LP>$. qed

Before turning to the completeness of EP-resolution we show that EP-derivations can be lifted.

Lemma 5.3 (Lifting Lemma for EP-resolution):

> Let $<EP,LP>$ be an equational logic program, UP_{EP} be a complete unification procedure for EP, and $\sigma \leq_{EP} \theta$. If there exists an EP-refutation of $LP \cup \{\Leftarrow \sigma D\}$, then there exists an EP-refutation of $LP \cup \{\Leftarrow \theta D\}$ with the same length. Furthermore, if $\sigma_1, ..., \sigma_k$ are the EP-unifiers from the EP-refutation of $LP \cup \{\Leftarrow \sigma D\}$ and $\theta_1, ..., \theta_k$ are the EP-unifiers from the EP-refutation of $LP \cup \{\Leftarrow \theta D\}$, then $\theta_k...\theta_1\theta \geq_{EP} \sigma_k...\sigma_1\sigma$.

Proof:

The result is proved by induction on the length k of the EP-refutation of $LP \cup \{\Leftarrow \sigma D\}$. The case k=0 being trivial we turn to the induction step and assume that the result holds for k-1. Let $\theta' \geq_{EP} \sigma'$. Suppose there exists an EP-refutation of $LP \cup \{\Leftarrow \sigma' D'\}$ with length k using EP-unifiers $\sigma_1, \ldots, \sigma_k$. Now let $\sigma' C'$ be the selected subgoal and $C^* \Leftarrow D^*$ be the new variant of a program clause used in the first step. We may assume that σ' as well as θ' does not bind a variable occurring in $C^* \Leftarrow D^*$; especially $\sigma' C^* = \theta' C^* = C^*$. Furthermore, let $D = (D' \setminus \{C'\}) \cup D^*$ and $\sigma = \sigma_1 \sigma'$. Then,

$$\Leftarrow \sigma' D' \quad \rightarrow_{EP(\sigma1)} \quad \Leftarrow \sigma D$$

and

$$\Leftarrow \sigma D \quad \rightarrow_{EP}^{k-1} \quad \square. \tag{1}$$

Since $\theta' \geq_{EP} \sigma'$ we find a substitution μ such that $\mu \theta' =_{EP} \sigma'$ and, by proposition 4.3(3),

$$\sigma_1 \mu \theta' =_{EP} \sigma_1 \sigma'. \tag{2}$$

Because $\sigma_1 \sigma'$ is an EP-unifier for C' and C^* we find that $\sigma_1 \mu \theta'$ is also an EP-unifier for C' and C^* and, hence, $\sigma_1 \mu$ is an EP-unifier for $\theta' C'$ and $C^* = \theta' C^*$. Since UP_{EP} is complete we find a substitution θ_1 such that $\theta_1 \in UP_{EP}(\theta' C', C^*)$ and $\theta_1 \geq_{EP} \sigma_1 \mu$. By proposition 4.3(6) and (2) we learn that

$$\theta_1 \theta' \geq_{EP} \sigma_1 \mu \theta' =_{EP} \sigma_1 \sigma' = \sigma.$$

Therefore, with $\theta = \theta_1 \theta'$ we conclude that

$$\Leftarrow \theta' D' \quad \rightarrow_{EP} \quad \Leftarrow \theta D \tag{3}$$

and

$$\theta \geq_{EP} \sigma. \tag{4}$$

By an application of the induction hypothesis to (4) and (1) we find a refutation of $LP \cup \{\Leftarrow \theta D\}$ having length k-1. Furthermore, if $\sigma_2, \ldots, \sigma_k$ are the EP-unifiers from the EP-refutation of $LP \cup \{\Leftarrow \sigma D\}$ and $\theta_2, \ldots, \theta_k$ are the EP-unifiers from the EP-refutation of $LP \cup \{\Leftarrow \theta D\}$, then

$$\theta_k \ldots \theta_2 \theta \geq_{EP} \sigma_k \ldots \sigma_2 \sigma. \tag{5}$$

Clearly, there exists an EP-refutation of $LP \cup \{\Leftarrow \theta' D'\}$ using EP-unifiers $\theta_1, \ldots, \theta_k$. Finally, using (5) we find that

$$\theta_k \ldots \theta_1 \theta' = \theta_k \ldots \theta_2 \theta \geq_{EP} \sigma_k \ldots \sigma_2 \sigma = \sigma_k \ldots \sigma_1 \sigma'. \qquad \text{qed}$$

It should be observed that in the EP-refutation of $LP \cup \{\Leftarrow \theta D\}$ we applied the same selection function as in the EP-refutation of $LP \cup \{\Leftarrow \sigma D\}$.

Lemma 5.4:

Let <EP,LP> be an equational logic program and let UP_{EP} be a complete unification procedure for EP. If there exists an SLDE-refutation of $<EP,LP>^+ \cup \{\Leftarrow D\}$ wrt $\{\to_{lr}, \to_{rr}\}$ with k arbitrary selections, then there exists an EP-refutation of $LP \cup \{\Leftarrow D\}$ of length k. Furthermore, if $\sigma_1, ..., \sigma_n, n \geq k$ are the mgus from the SLDE-refutation and $\theta_1, ..., \theta_k$ are the EP-unifiers from the EP-refutation, then $\theta_k...\theta_1 \geq_{EP} \sigma_n...\sigma_1$.

Proof:

The proof is by induction on k. The case k=0 being trivial we turn to the induction step and assume that the result holds for k-1. Suppose there exists a refutation of $<EP,LP> \cup \{\Leftarrow D'\}$ with k arbitrary selections. Suppose $C' \in D'$ is the first selected subgoal. Let $C^* \Leftarrow D^*$ be the new variant of a program clause and σ_1 be the mgu used in the first step. We distinguish two cases.

Suppose first that C' is an atom, i.e. lazy resolution has been applied in the first step. Let $D = (D' \setminus \{C'\}) \cup D^*$ and F be the set of immediate descendants of C'. C' and C^* must be atoms with identical predicate symbol. Let $C' = Q(s_1,...,s_p)$, $C^* = Q(t_1,...,t_p)$, and $F = \{EQ(s_i,t_i) \mid 1 \leq i \leq p\}$.) Hence, we find an m and substitutions $\sigma_1, ..., \sigma_m$ such that

$$\Leftarrow D' \to_{lr(\epsilon)} \Leftarrow D \cup F \to_{rr}^m \Leftarrow \lambda D, \tag{1}$$

where $\lambda = \sigma_m...\sigma_1$ and $\sigma_1, ..., \sigma_m$ are the mgus used while solving F, and an SLDE-refutation of $<EP,LP> \cup \{\Leftarrow \lambda D\}$ with k-1 arbitrary selections. By an application of the induction hypothesis we find an EP-refutation of $LP \cup \{\Leftarrow \lambda D\}$ of length k-1. Furthermore, if $\sigma_{m+1}, ..., \sigma_n$ are the mgus from the SLDE-refutation and $\gamma_2, ..., \gamma_k$ are the EP-unifiers from the EP-refutation, then

$$\gamma_k...\gamma_2 \geq_{EP} \sigma_n...\sigma_{m+1}.$$

Hence, by proposition 4.3(6),

$$\gamma_k...\gamma_2\lambda \geq_{EP} \sigma_n...\sigma_{m+1}\lambda. \tag{2}$$

From (1) we learn that λ is an EP-unifier for F. Since UP_{EP} is complete we find a substitution θ_1 such that $\theta_1 \in UP_{EP}(C',C^*) = UP_{EP}(F)$ and $\theta_1 \geq_{EP} \lambda$. Since there exists an EP-refutation of $LP \cup \{\Leftarrow \lambda D\}$ we find an EP-refutation of $LP \cup \{\Leftarrow \theta_1 D\}$ of the same length (lemma 5.3). Furthermore, if $\theta_2, ..., \theta_k$ are the EP-unifiers from the EP-refutation of $LP \cup \{\Leftarrow \theta_1 D\}$, then

$$\theta_k...\theta_2\theta_1 \geq_{EP} \gamma_k...\gamma_2\lambda. \tag{3}$$

Clearly, there exists an EP-refutation of $LP \cup \{\Leftarrow D'\}$ using EP-unifiers $\theta_1, ..., \theta_k$ and from (3) and (2) we conclude that

$$\theta_k...\theta_1 \geq_{EP} \gamma_k...\gamma_2\lambda \geq_{EP} \sigma_n...\sigma_{m+1}\lambda = \sigma_n...\sigma_1.$$

If C' is the equation EQ(s,t), then the result holds in analogy to the previous case except that λ is an EP-unifier for EQ(s,t) and the first input clause in the EP-refutation of $LP\cup\{\Leftarrow D'\}$ is a new instance of the axiom of reflexivity.   qed

We can now prove the strong completeness of EP-resolution.

Theorem 5.5 (Strong Completeness of EP-resolution):

Let <EP,LP> be an equational logic program, UP_{EP} be a complete unification procedure for EP, and SEL be a selection function. For every correct answer substitution θ for <EP,LP> and $\Leftarrow D$ there exists an SEL-computed answer substitution σ obtained by an EP-refutation of $LP\cup\{\Leftarrow D\}$ such that $\sigma \geq_{EP} \theta$.

Proof:

Since θ is a correct answer substitution for <EP,LP> and $\Leftarrow D$, by corollary 5.1(2), there exists an SLDE-computed answer substitution γ for $<EP,LP>\cup\{\Leftarrow D\}$ wrt $\{\rightarrow_{lr}, \rightarrow_{rr}\}$ such that $\gamma \geq \theta$. By lemma 5.4 we find an EP-refutation of $LP\cup\{\Leftarrow D\}$. Furthermore, if $\gamma_1, ..., \gamma_n$ are the mgus from the SLDE-refutation and $\sigma_1, ..., \sigma_k$, $k\leq n$, are the EP-unifiers from the EP-refutation, then $\sigma_k...\sigma_1 \geq_{EP} \gamma_n...\gamma_1$. Hence,

$$\sigma = \sigma_k...\sigma_1|Var(D) \geq_{EP} \gamma_n...\gamma_1|Var(D) = \gamma \geq \theta.$$

The theorem follows immediately from the observation that there is a one-to-one correspondence between the arbitrary selections in the SLDE-refutation and the selections in the EP-refutation.   qed

We generalized results obtained by Jaffar et al. (1984, 1986) and Gallier & Raatz (1986, 1989). Jaffar et al. showed that the EP-success-set of LP is equal to the least Herbrand $\equiv$-model for <EP,LP>, whereas Gallier & Raatz gave a completeness result in case that EP only consists of unconditional equational clauses. Furthermore, we presented a rigorous proof of completeness results for EP-resolution in (Beierle & Pletat 1987), who state the completeness of EP-resolution, whose proofs, however, are based on results in yet unpublished papers. Moreover, we showed that EP-resolution is independent of the selection function, a result that was conjectured by Beierle & Pletat (1987).

Whereas SLDE-refutations compute a set of answer substitutions such that for each correct answer substitution we find a more general one in this set, EP-refutations compute a set of answer substitutions such that for each correct answer substitution we find a more general one under EP in this set. As an example consider the equational logic program

P-ASSOC:	$P(x',f(x',g(a,b))) \Leftarrow$	(p)
	$EQ(f(x,f(y,z)), f(f(x,y),z)) \Leftarrow$	(a)

and the goal clause $G = \Leftarrow P(x, f(g(y,b),x))$. The equational part of P-ASSOC is the equational program ASSOC. Let $P = \{(p)\}$. For ASSOC minimal and complete EP-unification procedures were invented by Plotkin (1972) and Siekmann (1975). Hence, we find an ASSOC-refutation of $P \cup \{G\}$ with length 1. The computed answer substitution, however, depends on UP_{ASSOC}. As UP_{ASSOC} is minimal and complete it returns the infinite set

$$\sigma_1 = \{x' \leftarrow g(a,b), \ x \leftarrow g(a,b), \ y \leftarrow a\},$$
$$\sigma_2 = \{x' \leftarrow f(g(a,b),g(a,b)), \ x \leftarrow f(g(a,b), g(a,b)), \ y \leftarrow a\},$$
$$\sigma_3 = \{x' \leftarrow f(g(a,b),f(g(a,b),g(a,b))), \ x \leftarrow f(g(a,b),f(g(a,b),g(a,b))), \ y \leftarrow a\},$$

...

of most general ASSOC-unifiers. Thus, we obtain an infinite set of computed answer substitutions by restricting σ_i, $1 \leq i$, to the variables x and y. Of course, these answer substitutions can be computed using SLDE-refutations for P-ASSOC$^+ \cup \{G\}$. However, there are more computed answer substitutions for these SLDE-refutations, for example $\{x \leftarrow f(f(g(a,b),g(a,b)),g(a,b)), \ y \leftarrow a\}$, and an answer substitution is in general computed more than once.

In this sense EP-resolution generates less derivations. But EP-resolution rests heavily on the EP-unification procedure that is built-in. In the worst case a call to such an EP-unification procedure is simply a call of the equational program EP$^+$.

Theorem 5.5 is fairly general, since the only assumption needed to establish the strong completeness of EP-resolution is the existence of a complete EP-unification procedure for a Horn equality theory EP. Thus, any known complete EP-unification procedure (for an overview see Siekmann 1989) can be built into a resolution-based theorem prover for first order Horn logic preserving strong completeness. For example, take Nipkow's (1987) unification algorithm for primal algebras or the boolean unification algorithm of Büttner & Simonis (1987). Unification in primal algebras or boolean rings is unitary, i.e. there is at most one most general unifier under these theories. It was shown by Büttner & Simonis that such an application has practical relevance for simulating and manipulating hardware designs. However, we must be careful. For example, boolean unification is unitary only if each function symbol occurring in the logic part occurs also in the equational part of a program. In other words, the logic part must not contain "free" function symbols (see Schmidt-Schauss 1988).

Nevertheless, EP-resolution inherits some problems. As we demonstrated in the P-ASSOC-example, a set of most general unifiers may be infinite. Thus, there may be infinitely many EP-resolvents of a goal and a program clause and none of them is subsumed by another one. Hence, to be refutation-complete we have to investigate all of them, which results in a derivation tree whose depth as well as breadth is infinite. Furthermore, an EP-unification problem is in general only semidecidable (see also theorem 6.6.2.7). Hence, if we call an EP-unification procedure with a certain set of equations we do not know whether or when this procedure stops.

Several proposals have been made to overcome these difficulties. One idea is to compute only those parts of an EP-unifier which are common to all EP-unifiers for the given set of equations thus obtaining a partial (or lazy) EP-unifier and a new set of yet unsolved equations (Huet 1972). These equations can now be added to the new goal clause and are then possible choices for the selection function, like for example in Hölldobler et al. (1985) and Furbach & Hölldobler (1986, 1988), or they can be delayed until all other subgoals are solved and will then be submitted to a complete EP-unification algorithm, like for example in Bürckert (1986, 1987).

In the following two chapters we develop correct and complete universal unification procedures for Horn equational theories that can be built into a theorem prover based on EP-resolution. These universal unification procedures are defined by sets of inference rules.

6 Paramodulation

We already presented two ways of handling equality within first order theories: First, by giving an explicit set of first-order axioms and, second, by replacing the unification algorithm by a complete EP-unification procedure in the resolution rule. The second method solves the problem only partially, since we have to find a universal unification procedure for Horn equational theories. In this chapter we define such a procedure using an idea of Robinson & Wos (1979): A substitution rule ("linear paramodulation") is supplied together with the axiom of reflexivity. The axiom of reflexivity states that

two terms are equal if they are syntactically equal,

whereas the substitution rule states that

two equal terms s and t remain equal if a subterm v of s is replaced by a term w which is equal to v.

For example consider the equational program

$$\text{NC:} \quad \text{EQ(a,b)} \Leftarrow \qquad\qquad\qquad\qquad\qquad (a1)$$
$$\text{EQ(a,c)} \Leftarrow \qquad\qquad\qquad\qquad\qquad (a2)$$

and the question whether the terms b and c are equal under NC. The answer is "yes" and can be found by replacing the "b" in

$$\Leftarrow \text{EQ(b,c)}$$

by "a" according to (a1) yielding

$$\Leftarrow \text{EQ(a,c)}$$

and, then, by replacing the "a" according to (a2) by "c" yielding

$$\Leftarrow \text{EQ(c,c)}.$$

Finally, by an application of the axiom of reflexivity we obtain the empty goal clause.

In this example we replaced the right-hand side of the head of (a1) by its left-hand side and the left-hand side of the head of (a2) by its right-hand side. For notational convenience we define the substitution rule such that it always replaces the left-hand side of the head of an equational clause by its right-hand side. To illustrate this use of an equational clause EQ(l,r)⇐F we write this clause in the form l→r⇐F. But as we demonstrated in the example such a substitution rule is incomplete. To overcome this problem we define the "inverse" of an equational program as follows.

Definition:

$$\text{EP}^{-1} = \{\ r\to l\Leftarrow F \mid l\to r\Leftarrow F \in \text{EP}\ \}.$$

The clauses from EP^{-1} are then added to the equational program EP. In our example, (a1) and (a2) will be written as

$$a{\to}b \Leftarrow,$$ (a1)

$$a{\to}c \Leftarrow,$$ (a2)

respectively. NC^{-1} contains the clauses

$$b{\to}a \Leftarrow$$ (a1')

$$c{\to}a \Leftarrow$$ (a2')

and our initial query

$$\Leftarrow EQ(b,c)$$

can now be answered by replacing the "b" by "a" according to (a1') and, then, the "a" by "c" according to (a2). In both cases always the left-hand side of the head of an equational clause was replaced by its right-hand side.

The "$\to$"-notation does not change the semantics of an equational logic program as, whenever an equation EQ(s,t) is in the least Herbrand E-model of an equational logic program, then EQ(t,s) is also in this model due to the fact that E-interpretations are symmtrical.

Notation:

If an equational clause is of the form $f(s_1,...,s_n){\to}t\Leftarrow F$, then f is said to be the **initial symbol** of this clause. If $F = \varnothing$ we write $f(s_1,...,s_n){\to}t$ instead of $f(s_1,...,s_n){\to}t\Leftarrow$.

We already motivated our interest in paramodulation in the introduction. Recall that paramodulation always means linear paramodulation. We want to show the completeness of paramodulation in the sense that whenever there exists a correct answer substitution for an equational program and a goal clause, then we can compute a more general answer substitution using paramodulation. Only recently, U. Furbach (1987) showed that for each E-unsatisfiable set of Horn clauses containing the reflexivity and functional reflexive axioms we find an input refutation with respect to paramodulation and reflection. However, since the author uses various results from the theorem proving literature, his proof gives us no understanding of why, for example, the functional reflexive axioms are needed. Moreover, we are interested in a strong completeness result for paramodulation, i.e. we want to prove that paramodulation is independent of a selection function.

However, the search space generated by paramodulation is far too large and many restrictions of paramodulation have been proposed. Mainly, these proposals were made in the context of canonical and unconditional term rewriting systems (e.g. Slagle 1974, Lankford 1975). For these systems a directed form of paramodulation is complete even if it is applied only to non-variable terms. But several questions remain. What condition is needed to use equational clauses only in one direction? Must all variables occurring in the right-hand side rule occur also in the left-hand side of this rule (see the definitions of a rewriting system in Hullot (1980) and Hussmann (1985))? Can we find a better definition for a "basic" occurrence (Hullot 1980)? How must we define "rewriting" such that it can be applied as a simplification rule to refutations with respect to "basic" narrowing (see Réty 1987)? Can we generalize the answers to the previous questions to hold also for Horn equational theories?

Our goal is to give a general framework for universal unification algorithms based on linear paramodulation. To prove the soundness and strong completeness of the various sets of inference rules we use well-known techniques from logic programming (Lloyd 1984).

In the following section we give a least fixpoint characterization for an equational program EP which coincides with the least Herbrand E-model for EP. This characterization is then used in section 6.2 to prove the soundness and strong completeness of paramodulation. Unfortunately, this result holds only in the presence of the functional reflexive axioms. We illustrate the necessity of these axioms in detail.

We show how certain restrictions imposed one-by-one on an equational logic program prune the search space. In section 6.3 we demonstrate that clauses from EP^{-1} are no longer needed if EP is ground confluent. But we still have to apply paramodulation to variable occurrences even if the initial goal clause is ground. This is due to the fact that in a paramodulation step using $l \rightarrow r \Leftarrow F$ new variables occurring in r or F but not in l are imported into the goal clause. Term rewriting systems (section 6.4) are equational logic programs with the additional property that for each clause $l \rightarrow r \Leftarrow F$ we find that the variables occurring in r and F also occur in l. In section 6.5 we show that paramodulation need not be applied to variable occurrences if the equational program is a confluent term rewriting system and the answer substitution is normalizable. Such a paramodulation step was often called a narrowing. Moreover, Boyer & Moore's (1972) idea of structure sharing that splits a clause into a skeleton and an environment part further reduces the search space if the term rewriting system is canonical. In fact, it achieves the same effect as "basic" narrowing (Hullot 1980) does, however, we need not introduce the clumsy notion of a "basic" occurrence. Finally, we show that rewriting can be used as a simplification rule for canonical term rewriting systems and that "innermost basic" narrowing is complete if, in addition, the term rewriting system is completely defined and we consider only ground answer substitutions.

In section 6.6 we prove that the unification and matching problem for canonical theories is undecidable. As a consequence, the class of canonical theories with decidable matching problem is a proper subset of the class of canonical theories, which solves an open problem posed by Szabo (1984) and Siekmann (1984).

Finally, we summarize our results in section 6.7.

6.1 Fixpoint Characterization

Let EP be an equational program and B(EP) its Herbrand basis, i.e. the set of all ground atoms. Then $2^{B(EP)}$, the set of all interpretations of EP, is a complete lattice under the partial order set inclusion (e.g. Lloyd 1984). The top element of this lattice is B(EP) and the bottom element is $\emptyset$. The least upper bound (lub) of any set of interpretations is the interpretation which is the union of all the interpretations in the set. The greatest lower bound (glb) is their intersection. Similar to logic programs we can associate a mapping T_{EP} with an equational program EP.

Definition:

Let I be an interpretation of EP. The mapping $T_{EP} : 2^{B(EP)} \to 2^{B(EP)}$ is defined as $T_{EP}(I) =$

$\{ EQ(t,t) \mid t \text{ is a ground term } \}$

$\cup \{ E \in B(EP) \mid \text{there exists a } \pi \in Occ(E) \text{ and a ground instance } v{\to}w{\Leftarrow}F$
  of a clause in EP such that $E|\pi| = v$ and $F \cup \{E|\pi{\leftarrow}w|\} \subseteq I \}.$

Informally, $T_{EP}(I)$ contains the set of all ground instances of the axiom of reflexivity and the set of ground equations that can be "constructed" from elements of I by replacing one occurrence of the right-hand side of $v{\to}w$ by its left-hand side (see figure 6.1.1).

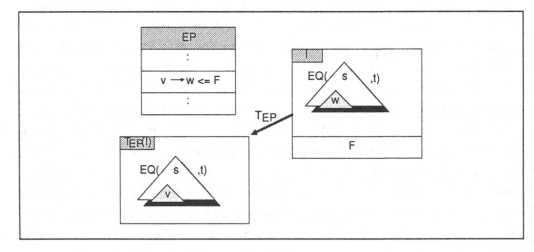

Figure 6.1.1

As an example consider the equational program

NC: $a \to b$

     $a \to c.$

Now,

$$T_{NC}\uparrow 1 = \{ \text{EQ}(a,a),\ \text{EQ}(b,b),\ \text{EQ}(c,c) \},$$

$$T_{NC}\uparrow 2 = T_{NC}\uparrow 1 \cup \{ \text{EQ}(a,b),\ \text{EQ}(b,a),\ \text{EQ}(a,c),\ \text{EQ}(c,a) \},$$

and

$$T_{NC}\uparrow 3 = T_{NC}\uparrow 2.$$

Note, neither EQ(c,b) nor EQ(c,b) occur in $T_{NC}\uparrow 2$. These elements are only obtained if we also use clauses from NC^{-1}. Let $N = NC \cup NC^{-1}$, then

$$T_N\uparrow 2 = T_{NC}\uparrow 2,$$

$$T_N\uparrow 3 = T_{NC}\uparrow 2 \cup \{ \text{EQ}(c,b),\ \text{EQ}(b,c) \},$$

and

$$T_N\uparrow 4 = T_N\uparrow 3.$$

To apply the results of fixpoint theory, we have to show that T_{EP} is monotonic and continuous.

Proposition 6.1.1:

T_{EP} is continuous and, hence, monotonic.

Proof:

Let X be a directed subset of $2^{B(EP)}$. Recall, $Y \subseteq lub(X)$ iff $Y \subseteq I$, for some $I \in X$. In order to prove that T_{EP} is continuous, we have to show $T_{EP}(lub(X)) = lub(\{T_{EP}(Y) \mid Y \in X\})$, for each directed subset X:

$E \in T_{EP}(lub(X))$

iff $E \in \{ \text{EQ}(t,t) \mid t \text{ is a ground term } \}$
  $\cup \{ E \mid \text{there exist a } \pi \in Occ(E) \text{ and a ground instance } v{\rightarrow}w{\Leftarrow}F \text{ of a clause in}$
  $\text{EP such that } E|\pi| = v \text{ and } F\cup\{E|\pi{\leftarrow}w|\} \subseteq lub(X) \}$

iff $E \in \{ \text{EQ}(t,t) \mid t \text{ is a ground term } \}$
  $\cup \{ E \mid \text{there exist a } \pi \in Occ(E) \text{ and a ground instance } v{\rightarrow}w{\Leftarrow}F \text{ of a clause in}$
  $\text{EP such that } E|\pi| = v \text{ and } F\cup\{E|\pi{\leftarrow}w|\} \subseteq I, \text{ for some } I \in X \}$

iff $E \in T_{EP}(I)$, for some $I \in X$

iff $E \in lub(\{T_{EP}(Y) \mid Y \in X\}).$ qed

Since T_{EP} is continuous, we can apply the results of fixpoint theory (see section 3.3) to obtain the least fixpoint of T_{EP}.

Proposition 6.1.2:

$$lfp(T_{EP}) = glb\{ I \mid T_{EP}(I) = I \} = glb\{ I \mid T_{EP}(I) \subseteq I \} = T_{EP}\uparrow\omega$$

Proof:

The result follows immediately from T_{EP} being continuous and, hence, monotonic using the propositions 3.3.1 and 3.3.2.   qed

Thus, we can characterize an equational program EP by the least fixpoint of T_{EP}. It is, of course, desirable that the declarative semantics and the fixpoint characterization of an equational program are identical. To prove this result we show first that the substitution rule applied to the elements of an E-interpretation yields only elements of that E-interpretation.

Proposition 6.1.3:

Let I be an E-interpretation. Suppose $\{EQ(v,w), EQ(s,t)\} \subseteq I$ and $EQ(s,t)|\pi| = v$.
Then $EQ(s,t)|\pi \leftarrow w| \in I$.

Proof:

The result is proved by induction on π. If $\pi = 1$, then $s = v$ and, since I is symmetric, it follows from $EQ(v,w) \in I$ that $EQ(w,v) \in I$. Further, because I is transitive it follows from $\{EQ(w,v), EQ(v,t)\} \subseteq I$ that $EQ(w,t) \in I$. If $\pi = 2$, then $t = v$ and the result follows by I being transitive.

Now suppose the result holds for π. If $EQ(s,t)|\pi \bullet i| = v$, then $EQ(s,t)|\pi|$ must be of the form $f(t_1, \ldots, t_n)$, $n \geq i$. Since I is reflexive we find $EQ(f(t_1, \ldots, t_n), f(t_1, \ldots, t_n)) \in I$ such that $t_i = v$. Furthermore, since $EQ(v,w) \in I$ and I satisfies the axioms of f-substitutivity, $EQ(f(t_1, \ldots, v, \ldots, t_n), f(t_1, \ldots, w, \ldots, t_n)) \in I$. The result holds by an application of the induction hypothesis.   qed

Theorem 6.1.4:

Let EP be an equational program. If I is an E-model for EP, then $T_{EP}(I) \subseteq I$.

Proof:

Suppose $E \in T_{EP}(I)$. We have to show that $E \in I$. By the definition of T_{EP} we distinguish two cases.

If E is a ground instance of the axiom of reflexivity, then E is of the form $EQ(t,t)$ and, since I is reflexive, we find $E \in I$.

Suppose now that there exists a $\pi \in Occ(E)$ and a ground instance $v \rightarrow w \Leftarrow F$ of a clause in EP such that $E|\pi| = v$ and $F \cup \{E|\pi \leftarrow w|\} \subseteq I$. Since I is an E-model for EP, we find $EQ(v,w) \in I$. Furthermore, I being symmetric implies $EQ(w,v) \in I$. Hence, by an application of proposition 6.1.3 we find $E|\pi \leftarrow w| \in I$.   qed

One should observe, that $T_{EP}(I) \subseteq I$ does not imply that I is an E-model for EP. As an example consider again the equational program

AB: a → c

               b → d.

Let N = AB∪AB^{-1} and

   I = { EQ(a,a), EQ(b,b), EQ(c,c), EQ(d,d), EQ(a,b), EQ(a,c),

          EQ(a,d), EQ(b,d), EQ(c,a), EQ(c,b), EQ(c,d), EQ(d,b) }.

Now,

   T_N(I) = { EQ(a,a), EQ(b,b), EQ(c,c), EQ(d,d), EQ(a,b), EQ(a,c),

          EQ(a,d), EQ(b,d), EQ(c,a), EQ(c,b), EQ(c,d), EQ(d,b) } ⊆ I.

However, I is not an E-model, since I does not contain the equations EQ(b,a), EQ(b,c), EQ(d,a), and EQ(d,c). The problem comes from equations like EQ(a,b) in I. That a and b denote the same thing is not implied by AB. In this sense EQ(a,b) is "junk" in a model for AB. I is an E-model for AB, however, it is not an E-model for the "junk" contained in I.

Corollary 6.1.5 shows that the least fixpoint of T_{EP} is contained in the least Herbrand E-model of EP, M_E(EP).

Corollary 6.1.5:

   lfp(T_{EP}) ⊆ M_E(EP)

Proof:

lfp(T_{EP})   =   glb { I | T_{EP}(I) ⊆ I }   proposition 6.1.2

               ⊆   glb { I | I is an E-model for EP }   theorem 6.1.4

               = M_{EP}.   qed

Corollary 6.1.5 holds for any equational program and, thus, also for an equational program EP∪EP^{-1}.

We cannot prove the opposite of corollary 6.1.5 due to the fact that $T_{EP∪EP-1}$(I) ⊆ I does not imply that I is an E-model for EP. However, we can show that the least fixpoint of $T_{EP∪EP-1}$ is an E-model for EP.

Theorem 6.1.6:

   lfp($T_{EP∪EP-1}$) is a Herbrand E-model for EP.

Proof:

Let T = $T_{EP∪EP-1}$. First, we show that lfp(T) is a model for EP. Therefore, we have to prove that for all ground instances s→t⇐F of program clauses in EP we find F ⊆ lfp(T) implies EQ(s,t) ∈ lfp(T). If F ⊆ lfp(T), then there exists an n such that F ⊆ T↑n. Clearly, EQ(t,t) ∈ T↑n and, hence, EQ(s,t) ∈ T↑(n+1) by replacing the t at occurrence 1 in EQ(t,t).

Second, we prove that lfp(T) is an E-model for EP. Clearly, lfp(T) contains all ground instances of the axiom of reflexivity. It remains to be shown that lfp(T) is symmetric, transitive, and obeys the f-substitutivity axioms.

If $EQ(s,t) \in lfp(T)$, then we find an n such that $EQ(s,t) \in T\!\uparrow\!n$. We show by induction on n that $EQ(t,s)$ is also an element of $T\!\uparrow\!n$. The case n=1 being trivial (s=t) we turn to the induction step and assume that the result holds for n-1. Suppose, $EQ(s,t) \in T\!\uparrow\!n$. Then we find $\pi \in Occ(EQ(s,t))$ and a ground instance $v{\rightarrow}w{\Leftarrow}F$ of a clause in $EP{\cup}EP^{-1}$ such that $EQ(s,t)|\pi| = v$ and $F{\cup}\{EQ(s,t)|\pi{\leftarrow}w|\} \subseteq T\!\uparrow\!(n-1)$. Without loss of generality we may assume that π is of the form $1{\bullet}\pi'$. From the induction hypothesis we learn that $EQ(t,s|2{\bullet}\pi'{\leftarrow}w|) \in T\!\uparrow\!(n-1)$ and, hence, $EQ(t,s) \in T\!\uparrow\!n$. Finally, since T is continuous, we conclude $EQ(t,s) \in lfp(T)$.

If $\{EQ(s,t), EQ(t,u)\} \subseteq lfp(T)$, then we find m and n such that $EQ(s,t) \in T\!\uparrow\!m$ and $EQ(t,u) \in T\!\uparrow\!n$. Clearly, $\{EQ(s,t), EQ(t,u)\} \subseteq T\!\uparrow\!(m+n)$. We show by induction on n that $EQ(s,u)$ is also an element of lfp(T). Suppose, $EQ(t,u) \in T\!\uparrow\!n$. The case n=1 being trivial (t=u) we turn to the induction step and assume the result holds for n-1. Hence, we find $\pi \in Occ(EQ(t,u))$ and a ground instance $v{\rightarrow}w{\Leftarrow}F$ of a clause in $EP{\cup}EP^{-1}$ such that $EQ(t,u)|\pi| = v$ and $F{\cup}\{EQ(t,u)|\pi{\leftarrow}w|\} \subseteq T\!\uparrow\!(n-1)$. Without loss of generality we may assume that $v{\rightarrow}w{\Leftarrow}F$ is the ground instance of a clause in EP. We distinguish two cases wrt π. If π is of the form $1{\bullet}\pi'$, then $EQ(s,t)|2{\bullet}\pi'| = v$ and $w{\rightarrow}v{\Leftarrow}F$ is a ground instance of a clause in EP^{-1}. Therefore, $EQ(s,t)|2{\bullet}\pi'{\leftarrow}w| \in T\!\uparrow\!(m+1)+(n-1)$ and from the induction hypothesis we learn that $EQ(s,u) \in lfp(T)$. If π is of the form $2{\bullet}\pi'$, then the induction hypothesis ensures that $EQ(s,u)|\pi{\leftarrow}w| \in lfp(T)$. Hence, we find a k such that $F{\cup}\{EQ(s,u)|\pi{\leftarrow}w|\} \subseteq T\!\uparrow\!k$ and, thus, $EQ(s,u) \in T\!\uparrow\!(k+1)$. Therefore, $EQ(s,u) \in lfp(T)$.

Finally, if $EQ(s_j,t_j) \in lfp(T)$, for all $1{\leq}j{\leq}m$, then we find an n such that $EQ(s_j,t_j) \in T\!\uparrow\!n$. We show by induction on n that $EQ(f(s_1,\ldots,s_m),f(t_1,\ldots,t_m)) \in lfp(T)$. The case n=1 being trivial ($s_j{=}t_j$) we turn to the induction step and assume that the result holds for n-1. Suppose, $EQ(s_j,t_j) \in T\!\uparrow\!n$, $1{\leq}j{\leq}m$. Hence, we find $\pi \in Occ(EQ(s_j,t_j))$ and a ground instance $v{\rightarrow}w{\Leftarrow}F$ of a clause in $EP{\cup}EP^{-1}$ such that $EQ(s_j,t_j)|\pi| = v$ and $F{\cup}\{EQ(s_j,t_j)|\pi{\leftarrow}w|\} \subseteq T\!\uparrow\!(n-1)$. Without loss of generality we may assume that π is of the form $1{\bullet}\pi'$. From the induction hypothesis we learn that

$$EQ(f(t_1,\ldots,s_j|\pi'{\leftarrow}w|,\ldots,t_m), f(t_1,\ldots,t_j,\ldots,t_m))$$
$$= EQ(f(t_1,\ldots,s_j,\ldots,t_m), f(t_1,\ldots,t_j,\ldots,t_m))|1{\bullet}j{\bullet}\pi'{\leftarrow}w| \in lfp(T).$$

Hence, there exists a k such that

$$F{\cup}\{EQ(f(t_1,\ldots,s_j,\ldots,t_m), f(t_1,\ldots,t_j,\ldots,t_m))|1{\bullet}j{\bullet}\pi''{\leftarrow}w|\} \subseteq T\!\uparrow\!k.$$

Thus,

$$EQ(f(t_1,\ldots,s_j,\ldots,t_m), f(t_1,\ldots,t_j,\ldots,t_m))|1{\bullet}j{\bullet}\pi''{\leftarrow}v| \in T\!\uparrow\!(k+1)$$

and, hence,

$$EQ(f(t_1,\ldots,s_j,\ldots,t_m), f(t_1,\ldots,t_j,\ldots,t_m)) \in lfp(T).$$ qed

As we demonstrated in the NC-example at the beginning of this section theorem 6.1.6 does not hold if we consider T_{EP} instead of $T_{EP \cup EP-1}$. In the proof of theorem 6.1.6 clauses from EP^{-1} are needed to show that $T_{EP \cup EP-1}$ is transitive.

Corollary 6.1.7:

$M_E(EP) \subseteq lfp(T_{EP \cup EP-1}).$

Proof:

From theorem 6.1.6 we learn that $lfp(T_{EP \cup EP-1})$ is a Herbrand E-model for EP. Hence, $lfp(T_{EP \cup EP-1})$ is an element of the set of all Herbrand E-models for EP, whose intersection is $M_E(EP)$. qed

Thus, the basic result of this section is the identity of the least Herbrand E-model of an equational logic program EP and the least fixpoint of T_{EP} (corollaries 6.1.5 and 6.1.7). We now use the fixpoint characterization of EP to prove the soundness and strong completeness of linear paramodulation.

6.2 Paramodulation

As Slagle (1972) pointed out, "*inference rules should be faster than resolution programs computing the corresponding axioms* (here: the axioms of equality) *by avoiding certain troublesome inferences made by resolution*". In this section we introduce the inference rules "paramodulation", defined to mechanize the substitution rule, and "reflection", defined to mechanize the axiom of reflexivity.

Definition:

Let G be the goal clause ⇐F∪{E}, P = v→w⇐F* be a new variant of a program clause, and π ∈ Occ(E). If E|π| and v are unifiable with mgu σ, then G' = ⇐σ(F∪{E|π←w|}∪F*) is called **paramodulant of G and P at π using σ**, in symbols G →p(E, π, P, σ) G'.

In figure 6.2.1 we depict the paramodulation rule.

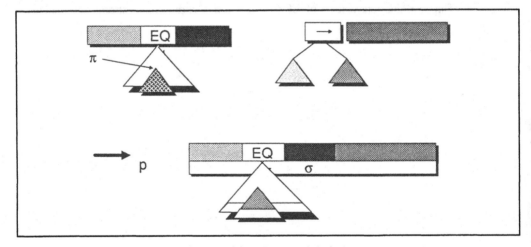

Figure 6.2.1: Paramodulation

As an example consider the equational program

FUN:	g → a	(g)
	f(c(g),c(a)) → d(c(g),c(a))	(f)

and the goal clause

G = ⇐ EQ(f(x,y), d(x,y)).

Then,

⇐ EQ(d(c(g)),c(a)),d(c(g)),c(a)))

is a paramodulant of G and (f) at 1 using the most general unifier $\{x \leftarrow c(g),\, y \leftarrow c(a)\}$. The equational clause (f) was used from left-to-right, in that an instance of the left-hand side of the head of (f) was replaced by its right-hand side. Hence, paramodulation is **directed**.

As with the resolution rule it is important that the substitution used in a paramodulation step is a most general unifier since, otherwise, the set of unifiers has to be investigated to ensure refutation-completeness (e.g. Gallier & Raatz 1986, 1989).

Though our paramodulation rule is applicable only from left-to-right, we can apply the paramodulation rule also from right-to-left by taking an equational clause from EP^{-1} as argument. There seems to be a flaw in the definition of paramodulation in (Chang & Lee 1973), where paramodulation is only applicable from left-to-right and we cannot derive that, for example, EQ(b,c) is a logical E-consequence of the equational program NC. In fact, in the proof of their lemma 8.2, Chang & Lee apply paramodulation from right-to-left thus violating their definition.

In the theorem proving literature (e.g. Chang & Lee 1973) the completeness of paramodulation is in general proved with respect to arbitrary clauses containing not only equations. Hence, the resolution rule is needed to resolve atoms and can also be applied to resolve equations. Since we intend to treat only Horn equational theories via paramodulation the only need for the resolution rule stems from the axiom of reflexivity. It should be noted that each resolution step using an equational clause from EP can be modelled by a paramodulation step using the same equational clause and applying resolution with the axiom of reflexivity afterwards. As an example consider the equational clause $g \rightarrow a$ and the goal clause $\Leftarrow EQ(g,y)$. Resolving $\Leftarrow EQ(g,y)$ against $g \rightarrow a$ yields the empty clause and the substitution $\{y \leftarrow a\}$. However, the paramodulant of $\Leftarrow EQ(g,y)$ and $g \rightarrow a$ at 1 using ε is the goal clause $\Leftarrow EQ(a,y)$, which can be resolved against the axiom of reflexivity yielding the empty clause and computed answer substitution $\{y \leftarrow a\}$. Hence, adding the resolution rule leads to the generation of many redundant goal clauses.

Keeping with Fribourg's (1984) approach we introduce a new inference rule called **reflection**.

Definition:

> Let G be the goal clause $\Leftarrow F \cup \{EQ(s,t)\}$. If s and t are unifiable with mgu σ, then $G' = \Leftarrow \sigma F$ is called **reflectant of G using** σ, in symbols $G \rightarrow_{f(EQ(s,t),\, \sigma)} G'$.

Hence, reflection essentially calls the unification algorithm presented in section 3.4.1 with the equation EQ(s,t). In figure 6.2.2 we depict the reflection rule.

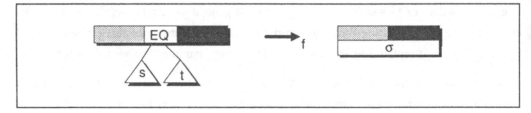

Figure 6.2.2: Reflection

For example, $f(c(g),c(a))$ and $f(c(g),c(a))$ are unifiable with ε. Hence, the empty clause is a reflectant of $\Leftarrow EQ(f(c(g),c(a)), f(c(g),c(a)))$. In contrast to the resolution rule using the axiom of reflexivity $EQ(x,x)\Leftarrow$ as input clause we are not introducing a new variable x, whose binding is in general neglected.

The last step in a refutation with respect to paramodulation and reflection must always be a reflection step since a paramodulation step never decreases the number of subgoals in a goal clause.

We can now define the success set of an equational program with respect to paramodulation and reflection.

Definition:
> The **p-success set** of an equational logic program EP is defined as
> $P\text{-}SS_{EP} = \{\ E\ |\ $ E is a ground equation and there exists a refutation of
> $EP\cup\{\Leftarrow E\}$ wrt $\{\rightarrow_p, \rightarrow_f\}\ \}$.

In order to show that an inference system based on paramodulation is sound and complete we have to prove that each computed answer substitution is correct and that for each correct answer substitution there exists a (eventually more general) computed one.

Theorem 6.2.1 (Soundness of Paramodulation and Reflection):
> *Every computed answer substitution for $EP\cup\{\Leftarrow F\}$ wrt $\{\rightarrow_p, \rightarrow_f\}$ is a correct answer substitution for EP and $\Leftarrow F$.*

Proof:
Let $\theta_1, \ldots, \theta_n$ be the sequence of mgus used in the refutation of $EP\cup\{\Leftarrow F\}$ wrt $\{\rightarrow_p, \rightarrow_f\}$. We have to show that $\theta_n\ldots\theta_1 F$ is a logical E-consequence of EP. The result is proved by induction on the length n of the refutation. The case n=0 being trivial we turn to the induction step and assume that the result holds for n-1. Let $\theta_1, \ldots, \theta_n$ be the sequence of mgus used in a refutation of $EP\cup\{\Leftarrow F'\}$ of length n. Furthermore, let $F' = F^+\cup\{EQ(s,t)\}$ and assume that

$$\Leftarrow F' = \Leftarrow F^+ \cup \{EQ(s,t)\} \rightarrow_{(\theta_1)} \Leftarrow F \tag{1}$$

We distinguish two cases:

If reflection was applied in (1) then, by the induction hypothesis, $\theta_n...\theta_1 F$ is a logical E-consequence of EP. Since θ_1 is a unifier for s and t, so is $\theta_n...\theta_1$. Hence, $\theta_n...\theta_1 EQ(s,t)$ is an instance of the axiom of reflexivity and it follows that $\theta_n...\theta_1 EQ(s,t)$ is a logical E-consequence of EP.

If paramodulation was applied to $\pi \in Occ(EQ(s,t))$, then let $u = EQ(s,t)|\pi|$ and $v \rightarrow w \Leftarrow F^*$ be the input clause used. By the induction hypothesis, $\theta_n...\theta_1(F \cup \{EQ(s,t)|\pi \leftarrow w|\} \cup F^*)\}$ is a logical E-consequence of EP. Consequently, $\theta_n...\theta_1 EQ(v,w) \Leftarrow$ is a logical E-consequence of EP and, hence, $\theta_n...\theta_1 EQ(w,v) \Leftarrow$ is a logical E-consequence of EP. Furthermore, since θ_1 is a unifier for u and v, we find $\theta_n...\theta_1 u = \theta_n...\theta_1 v$. Thus, by proposition 6.1.3, we learn that $\theta_n...\theta_1 EQ(s,t)$ is a logical E-consequence of EP.   qed

Since theorem 6.2.1 holds for arbitrary equational programs and, especially, for $EP \cup EP^{-1}$, it is an immediate consequence of theorem 6.2.1 that the p-success set of an equational program is contained in its least E-model.

Corollary 6.2.2:

$$P\text{-}SS_{EP} \subseteq M_E(EP)$$

Proof:

Let EQ(s,t) be a ground equation. If $EP \cup \{\Leftarrow EQ(s,t)\}$ has a refutation wrt $\{\rightarrow_p, \rightarrow_f\}$ then, by theorem 6.2.1, EQ(s,t) is a logical E-consequence of EP. Thus, by proposition 3.2.4, EQ(s,t) is in the least Herbrand E-model of EP.   qed

It is possible to be even more precise than corollary 6.2.2. We can show that if $EP \cup \{\Leftarrow EQ(s,t)\}$ has a refutation of length n, then $EQ(s,t) \in T_{EP} \uparrow n$, where s and t are ground terms.

Notation:

Let EP be an equational program. If E (resp. EQ(s,t)) is an equation, then E_g (resp. $EQ_g(s,t)$) denotes the set of all ground instances of E (resp. EQ(s,t)).

Theorem 6.2.3:

If $EP \cup \{\Leftarrow F\}$ has a refutation wrt $\{\rightarrow_p, \rightarrow_f\}$ of length n using mgus $\theta_1, ..., \theta_n$,
then for every equation E in $\theta_n...\theta_1 F$ we find that $E_g \subseteq T_{EP} \uparrow n$.

Proof:

The result is proved by induction on the length n of the refutation. The case n=0 being trivial we turn to the induction step and assume that the result holds for n-1. Suppose there exists a refutation of $EP \cup \{\Leftarrow F'\}$ of length n. Let F' be of the form $F \cup \{EQ(s,t)\}$.

If EQ(s,t) is not the first selected equation, then θ_1EQ(s,t) is an equation of the second goal clause in the refutation. The induction hypothesis implies that $\theta_n...\theta_1$EQ$_g$(s,t) $\subseteq$ TEP$\uparrow$(n-1) and, by the monotonicity of TEP, TEP$\uparrow$(n-1) $\subseteq$ TEP$\uparrow$n.

If EQ(s,t) is the first selected equation, then we distinquish two cases: If reflection was applied then, since θ_1 is a unifier for s and t, so is $\theta_n...\theta_1$. Clearly, $\theta_n...\theta_1$EQ$_g$(s,t) $\subseteq$ TEP$\uparrow$n. If paramodulation was applied to $\pi \in$ Occ(EQ(s,t)), then let u = EQ(s,t)$|\pi|$ and v$\rightarrow$w$\Leftarrow$F* be the first input clause. The induction hypothesis implies that $\theta_n...\theta_1$(EQ$_g$(s,t)$|\pi\leftarrow$w$|$) $\subseteq$ TEP$\uparrow$(n-1) and, if F*$\neq\emptyset$, for every equation E in F*, $\theta_n...\theta_1$E$_g$ $\subseteq$ TEP$\uparrow$(n-1). Hence, by the definition of TEP, $\theta_n...\theta_1$(EQ$_g$(s,t)$|\pi\leftarrow$v$|$) $\subseteq$ TEP$\uparrow$n. Since θ_1 is a unifier for v and u we find $\theta_n...\theta_1$EQ$_g$(s,t) $\subseteq$ TEP$\uparrow$n.   qed

To examplify theorem 6.2.3 and to emphasize the difference between the fixpoint characterization of an equational program and its characterization in terms of refutations with respect to paramodulation and reflection consider the equational program EP = { f $\rightarrow$ a }. There exists a refutation of EP$\cup\{\Leftarrow$EQ(f,a)$\}$ wrt {$\rightarrow_p$, $\rightarrow_f$} of length 2: First paramodulation can be applied to 1 using f$\rightarrow$a from left-to-right yielding the goal clause $\Leftarrow$EQ(a,a). Finally, the empty clause can be derived by a reflection. Obviously, EQ(a,a) $\in$ TEP$\uparrow$1. We can now replace the a at 1 in EQ(a,a) by f using the program clause f$\rightarrow$a from right-to-left. It follows that EQ(f,a) $\in$ TEP$\uparrow$2.

From theorem 6.2.3 follows that the p-success set of an equational program EP is contained in the least fixpoint of TEP.

Corollary 6.2.4:

   P-SSEP $\subseteq$ lfp(TEP)

Proof:

Let EQ(s,t) be a ground equation. If EP$\cup\{\Leftarrow$EQ(s,t)$\}$ has a refutation wrt {$\rightarrow_p$, $\rightarrow_f$} of length n then, by theorem 6.2.3, EQ(s,t) $\in$ TEP$\uparrow$n. It follows that EQ(s,t) $\in$ lfp(TEP).   qed

Recall, theorem 6.2.3 and corollary 6.2.4 hold for arbitrary equational programs. Especially, we find that the p-success set of EP$\cup$EP^{-1} is a subset of the least fixpoint of TEP$\cup$EP-1.

Next we would like to show that the least fixpoint of TEP is contained in the p-success set of EP. To prove such a result we need a lifting lemma for paramodulation and reflection. As we will see, to lift a refutation of σG to a refutation of G with respect to paramodulation and reflection we generally need the functional reflexive axioms of EP.

Definition:

The **functional reflexive axioms** of EP are defined as

   F(EP) = { f(x$_1$,...,x$_n$) $\rightarrow$ f(x$_1$,...,x$_n$) | f is an n-ary function symbol occurring in EP }.

One should observe that EP∪F(EP) is an equational program. Furthermore, F(EP^{-1}) = F(EP). Hence, corollaries 6.2.2 and 6.2.4 hold also for EP∪F(EP), i.e. the p-success set of EP∪F(EP) is contained in the least Herbrand E-model of EP∪F(EP) as well as in the least fixpoint of T$_{EP∪F(EP)}$.

Since each E-model I for EP contains all ground instances of the axiom of reflexivity, I is also an E-model for EP∪F(EP) and vice versa. Thus,

$$M_E(EP) = M_E(EP∪F(EP))$$

and, likewise,

$$lfp(T_{EP}) = lfp(T_{EP∪F(EP)}).$$

For reasons which become obvious later, we do not explicitly add the functional reflexive axioms to the equational program, but we define a new inference rule, "instantiation", which when applied to a goal clause has precisely the same effect as the application of para-modulation using a functional reflexive axiom. It should be observed that paramodulation using a functional reflexive axiom applied to a non-variable subterm in a goal clause yields the same goal clause again.

Definition:
> Let G be the goal clause ⇐F∪{E}, x be a variable in E, f be an n-ary function
> symbol, $x_1, ..., x_n$ be new variables, and σ = {x←f($x_1,...,x_n$)}. Then, G' = ⇐σG
> is called an **instance** of G, in symbols, G →$_{i(E, σ)}$ G'.

In figure 6.2.3 we depict the instantiation rule.

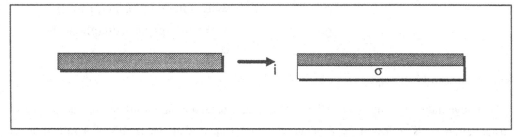

Figure 6.2.3: Instantiation

Now, if paramodulation was applied to an occurrence π in σE which is not an occurrence in E, then in order to lift this paramodulation step we instantiate the E to λE ≥ σE by repea-ted applications of instantiation until π ∈ Occ(λE) and, then, we apply paramodulation. We comprise such a sequence of instantiation steps followed by a single paramodulation step into an instantiation and paramodulation step.

Definition:

G' can be obtained from G by **instantiation and paramodulation using** σ, in symbols G →ip(σ) G' iff G' can be obtained from G by a (possible empty) finite sequence of instantiation steps followed by a single paramodulation step and, if σ1, ..., σn are the unifiers used in this derivation, then σ = σn...σ1.

We denote G →ip(E, π, P, σ) G' iff E is the selected equation to which all instantiation steps and the final paramodulation step are applied, π is the first selected occurrence, and P is the equational clause used in the paramodulation step.

As an example consider again the equational program

FUN:	g → a	(g)
	f(c(g),c(a)) → d(c(g),c(a))	(f)

and the goal clause ⇐EQ(f(x,x), d(x,x)). The derivation

⇐ EQ(f(x,x), d(x, x))	→i({x←c(y)})	⇐ EQ(f(c(y),c(y)), d(c(y),c(y)))
	→p(g, {y←g})	⇐ EQ(**f(c(g),c(a))**, d(c(g),c(g)))
	→p(f)	⇐ EQ(d(c(g),c(a)), d(c(g),c(g)))
	→p(g)	⇐ EQ(d(c(g),c(a)), d(c(g),c(a)))
	→f	▫

with respect to {→f, →i, →p} can now be transformed into the derivation

⇐ EQ(f(x,x), d(x, x))	→ip(g, {x←c(g)})	⇐ EQ(**f(c(g),c(a))**, d(c(g),c(g)))
	→ip(f)	⇐ EQ(d(c(g),c(a)), d(c(g),c(g)))
	→ip(g)	⇐ EQ(d(c(g),c(a)), d(c(g),c(a)))
	→f	▫

with respect to {→f, →ip}.

The advantage of using the rule instantiation and paramodulation instead of a sequence of instantiation steps followed by a paramodulation step is that the length of a refutation of EP∪{⇐σF} and its "lifted" counterpart, i.e. a refutation of EP∪{⇐F}, is the same. This property is important if we want to show that refutations with respect to paramodulation and reflection are independent of a selection function.

Some authors prefer to define paramodulation in the first place as instantiation and paramodulation and, thus, avoid an instantiation rule or, equivalently, the functional reflexive axioms completely (e.g. Gallier & Raatz 1986, 1989). However, our goal is to point out precisely, where the instantiation rule is needed to ensure the completeness of paramodulation and to use this knowledge later to impose conditions as weak as possible on an equational program such that the instantiation rule can be omitted.

Lemma 6.2.5 shows that if instantiation and paramodulation was applied to a goal clause σG containing σE at an occurrence of E, then instantiation and paramodulation can also be applied to G using the same program clause.

Lemma 6.2.5:

> *Let $G = \Leftarrow F \cup \{E\}$ be a goal clause, $\pi \in Occ(E)$, $P = v \rightarrow w \Leftarrow F^*$ be a new variant of a program clause, and σ be a substitution. If $\sigma G \rightarrow_{ip(E, \pi, P, \theta)} \theta\sigma G'$, then there exist substitutions γ and λ such that $G \rightarrow_{ip(E, \pi, P, \gamma)} \gamma G'$ and $\lambda\gamma = \theta\sigma$.*

Proof:

Without loss of generality we may assume that $Dom(\sigma) \cap Var(P) = \emptyset$. We distinguish two cases. If $\theta\sigma G'$ was obtained from σG by a parmodulation step, then $\sigma E|\pi|$ and $\sigma v = v$ are unifiable with mgu θ. Since $\theta\sigma$ is a unifier of u and v, we find an mgu γ of u and v and a substitution λ such that $\lambda\gamma = \theta\sigma$. The result follows immediately.

If $\theta\sigma G'$ was obtained from σG by a non-empty sequence of instantiation steps followed by a paramodulation step, then $\sigma E|\pi|$ must be a variable. Without loss of generality we may assume that $\sigma E|\pi| = E|\pi|$. Hence, $G \rightarrow_{ip(E, \pi, P, \gamma)} \gamma G'$, where $\gamma = \theta$. Since the x was not bound by σ we learn that $\gamma = \theta \leq \sigma\theta$. Hence, there exists a substitution λ such that $\lambda\gamma = \sigma\theta$, which completes the proof.   qed

In figure 6.2.4.a we depict the derivation from σG to $\theta\sigma G'$, whereas in figure 6.2.4.b we depict the corresponding derivation from G to $\gamma G'$.

We can now turn to the proof of the lifting lemma for reflection, instantiation and paramodulation.

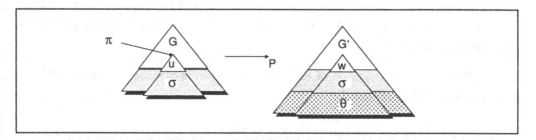

Figure 6.2.4.a

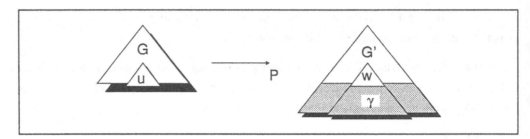

Figure 6.2.4.b

Lemma 6.2.6 (Lifting Lemma for Reflection, Instantiation and Paramodulation):

If there exists a refutation of $EP \cup \{\Leftarrow\delta F\}$ wrt $\{\rightarrow_f, \rightarrow_{ip}\}$, then there exists a refutation of $EP \cup \{\Leftarrow F\}$ wrt $\{\rightarrow_f, \rightarrow_{ip}\}$ of the same length. Furthermore, if $\theta_1,$ ..., θ_n are the unifiers used in the refutation of $EP \cup \{\Leftarrow\delta F\}$ and $\sigma_1, ..., \sigma_n$ are the unifiers used in the refutation of $EP \cup \{\Leftarrow F\}$, then $\theta_n...\theta_1\delta \leq \sigma_n...\sigma_1$.

Proof:

The proof is by induction on the length n of the refutation of $EP \cup \{\Leftarrow\delta F\}$. The case $n=0$ being trivial ($F=\varnothing$) we turn to the induction step and assume that the result holds for n. Suppose $EP \cup \{\Leftarrow\delta'F'\}$ has a refutation of length $n+1$ using unifiers $\theta_1, ..., \theta_{n+1}$. Let F' be of the form $F^+ \cup \{EQ(s,t)\}$ and suppose that $EQ(s,t)$ is the first selected equation. We distinguish two cases.

If the first step was a reflection step, then $\theta_1\delta'$ is a unifier for s and t. Hence, we find an mgu σ_1 of s and t and a substitution δ such that $\delta\sigma_1 = \theta_1\delta'$. Let $F = \sigma_1F^+$. Since there exists a refutation of $EP \cup \{\Leftarrow\delta F\}$ of length n using unifiers $\theta_2, ..., \theta_{n+1}$, by the induction hypothesis there exists a refutation of $EP \cup \{\Leftarrow F\}$ with the same length and, if mgus $\sigma_2, ...,\sigma_{n+1}$ are the unifiers of this refutation, then $\theta_{n+1}...\theta_2\delta \leq \sigma_{n+1}...\sigma_2$. Hence, we find a substitution γ such that $\theta_{n+1}...\theta_2\delta = \gamma\sigma_{n+1}...\sigma_2$. Clearly, there exists a refutation of $EP \cup \{\Leftarrow F'\}$ using unifiers $\sigma_1, ..., \sigma_{n+1}$ and $\theta_{n+1}...\theta_1\delta' = \theta_{n+1}...\theta_2\delta\sigma_1 = \gamma\sigma_{n+1}...\sigma_1$. It follows immediately that $\theta_{n+1}...\theta_1\delta' \leq \sigma_{n+1}...\sigma_1$.

If the first step in the refutation of $EP \cup \{\Leftarrow\delta'F'\}$ was an instantiation and paramodulation at π, then we find F* such that

$$\Leftarrow \delta'F' \rightarrow_{ip}(E, \pi, P, \theta_1) \Leftarrow \theta_1\delta'F^*,$$

where $E = EQ(s,t)$. If $\pi \in Occ(E)$, then by lemma 6.2.4, we find substitutions σ_1 and δ such that

$$\Leftarrow F' \rightarrow_{ip}(E, \pi, P, \sigma_1) \Leftarrow \sigma_1F^*$$

and $\delta\sigma_1 = \theta_1\delta'$. The result follows by the induction hypothesis in analogy to the first case. Otherwise, if $\pi \in Occ(\delta'E)\backslash Occ(E)$, then we find $\pi_1, \pi_2 \in Occ(\delta'E)$ such that $E|\pi_1|$ is a variable, say x, and $\pi = \pi_1 \cdot \pi_2$. Let $\mu = \delta'|\{x\}$. Obviously, there exists a derivation from $\Leftarrow F'$ to $\Leftarrow \mu F'$ using only instantiation and the lemma follows in analogy to the previous case.   qed

The instantiation rule is needed if in the refutation of $EP \cup \{\Leftarrow \delta F\}$ paramodulation was applied to an occurrence that is not an occurrence of F. As an example consider again the equational program

FUN: $g \to a$ (g)

         $f(c(g),c(a)) \to d(c(g),c(a))$ (f)

the substitution $\delta = \{x \leftarrow c(a)\}$ and the goal clause $\Leftarrow EQ(f(x,x),d(x,x))$. We obtain the refutation

$\Leftarrow EQ(f(c(g),c(g)), d(c(g),c(g)))$ $\to_{p(g)}$ $\Leftarrow EQ(f(c(g),c(a)), d(c(g),c(g)))$

                                         $\to_{p(g)}$ $\Leftarrow EQ(f(c(g),c(a)), d(c(g),c(a)))$

                                         $\to_{p(f)}$ $\Leftarrow EQ(d(c(g),c(a)), d(c(g),c(a)))$

                                         $\to_f$ $\square$.

The corresponding refutation using instantiation and paramodulation in the first step is

$\Leftarrow EQ(f(x,x), d(x, x))$ $\to_{ip(g, \{x \leftarrow c(g)\})}$ $\Leftarrow EQ(f(c(g),c(a)), d(c(g),c(g)))$

                             $\to_{ip(g)}$ $\Leftarrow EQ(f(c(g),c(a)), d(c(g),c(a)))$

                             $\to_{ip(g)}$ $\Leftarrow EQ(d(c(g),c(a)), d(c(g),c(a)))$

                             $\to_f$ $\square$.

It should be noted that there does not exist a refutation of $FUN \cup \{\Leftarrow EQ(f(x,x), d(x,x))\}$ with respect to paramodulation and reflection. In such a refutation the program clause (f) must be used at least once since, otherwise, reflection cannot be applied to a descendant of the equation $EQ(f(x,x), d(x,x))$. To use (f), x must be instantiated to c(g) and one "g" must be replaced by "a" using paramodulation and (g). However, there is no way to instantiate x to the terms c(g) and c(a) at the same time using paramodulation only. The reader may convince himself that this holds also if we consider clauses from $FUN \cup FUN^{-1}$.

The example (as well as the proof of lemma 6.2.6) requires the application of a sequence of instantiation steps followed by a paramodulation step. Padawitz (1988) achieved the same effect by using "prefixed" equational clauses. In our example, he would use the "prefixed" clause $c(g) \to c(a)$ obtained from (g) by adding the "prefix c( )". Thus,

     $\Leftarrow EQ(f(x,x), d(x,x))$ $\to_p$ $\Leftarrow EQ(f(c(g),c(a)), d(c(g),c(g)))$.

We can now define the success set of an equational program with respect to reflection, instantiation and paramodulation.

Definition:

The **ip-success set** of an equational program EP is defined as

IP-SS$_{EP}$ = { E | E is a ground equation and there exists a refutation of EP$\cup$$\{\Leftarrow E\}$
wrt $\{\rightarrow f, \rightarrow ip\}$ }.

Using the lifting lemma we can show that whenever an equation is in T$_{EP}\uparrow$n, it is also in the ip-success set of EP.

Theorem 6.2.7:

If E $\in$ T$_{EP}\uparrow$n then there exists a refutation of EP$\cup$$\{\Leftarrow E\}$ wrt $\{\rightarrow f, \rightarrow ip\}$.

Proof:

The result is proved by induction on n. If n=1, then E $\in$ T$_{EP}\uparrow$1 implies that E is a ground instance of the axiom of reflexivity. Clearly, EP$\cup$$\{\Leftarrow E\}$ has a refutation of length 1 applying reflection.

Now suppose that the result holds for n-1 and let E $\in$ T$_{EP}\uparrow$n. With respect to the definition of T$_{EP}$ we distinguish two cases. If E is a ground instance of the axiom of reflexivity, then EP$\cup$$\{\Leftarrow E\}$ has a refutation of length 1 applying reflection. If there exist a $\pi \in$ Occ(E) and a ground instance $\theta(v \rightarrow w \Leftarrow F)$ of a clause in EP such that E$|\pi|$ = θv and $\theta(F \cup \{E|\pi \leftarrow w|\}) \subseteq$ T$_{EP}\uparrow$(n-1) then, by the induction hypothesis there exists a refutation of EP$\cup$$\{\Leftarrow E'\}$ for each E' $\in$ $\theta(F \cup \{EQ|\pi \leftarrow w|\})$. Because each E' is ground, these refutations can be combined into a refutation of EP$\cup$ $\Leftarrow\theta(F \cup \{E|\pi \leftarrow w|)\}\}$ wrt $\{\rightarrow ip, \rightarrow f\}$. Since θ is a unifier of E$|\pi|$ and v, we find an mgu σ of E$|\pi|$ and v and a substitution γ such that $\gamma\sigma = \theta$. By the lifting lemma, there exists a refutation of EP$\cup$$\{\Leftarrow\sigma(F \cup \{E|\pi \leftarrow w|)\}\}$ wrt $\{\rightarrow ip, \rightarrow f\}$. Clearly, EP$\cup$$\{\Leftarrow E\}$ has a refutation.   qed

The lifting lemma must be applied to the proof of the previous theorem, since the substitution θ which "grounds" the input clause $v \rightarrow w \Leftarrow F$ is not necessarily the same as the most general unifier σ of E$|\pi|$ and v. This is due to the fact that w and F may contain variables that do not occur in v and, hence, will not be bound to a ground term by σ.

From theorem 6.2.7 follows that the least fixpoint of T$_{EP}$ is contained in the ip-success set of EP.

Corollary 6.2.8:

lfp(T$_{EP}$) $\subseteq$ IP-SS$_{EP}$

Proof:

If E ∈ lfp(T$_{EP}$), then by theorem 6.2.7 there exists a refutation of EP∪{⇐E} wrt {→$_{ip}$, →$_f$} and, hence, E ∈ IP-SS$_{EP}$.   qed

Obviously, the p-success set of EP is contained in the ip-success set of EP. The opposite, however, is not true. For example, consider the equational program

   FUN' = FUN ∪ { h→b ⇐ EQ(f(x,x), d(x,x)) }.

EQ(h,b) ∈ IP-SS$_{EP}$ since

   ⇐ EQ(h,b) →$_p$ ⇐ EQ(b,b), EQ(f(x,x), d(x,x)) →$_f$ ⇐ EQ(f(x,x), d(x,x)) →* □.

However, as we demonstrated above, there does not exist a refutation of EP∪{⇐EQ(f(x,x), d(x,x))} with respect to paramodulation and reflection. Hence, EQ(h,b) ∉ P-SS$_{EP}$. Likewise, EQ(h,b) ∉ P-SS$_{EP∪EP}$-1.

Corollary 6.2.9:

   (1)   P-SS$_{EP}$ ⊆ IP-SS$_{EP}$,

   (2)   IP-SS$_{EP}$ is not a subset of P-SS$_{EP}$,

   (3)   IP-SS$_{EP}$ ⊆ lfp(T$_{EP}$), and

   (4)   lfp(T$_{EP}$) is not a subset of P-SS$_{EP}$.

Proof:

(1) and (2) follow from the above remarks.

(3)   Obviously, IP-SS$_{EP}$ ⊆ P-SS$_{EP∪F(EP)}$ and, since P-SS$_{EP∪F(EP)}$ ⊆ lfp(T$_{EP∪F(EP)}$) = lfp(T$_{EP}$) (corollary 6.2.4) we find IP-SS$_{EP}$ ⊆ lfp(T$_{EP}$).

(4)   If lfp(T$_{EP}$) ⊆ P-SS$_{EP}$ then, by corollary 6.2.4, lfp(T$_{EP}$) = P-SS$_{EP}$. Since, by corollary 6.2.8 and part (3), lfp(T$_{EP}$) = IP-SS$_{EP}$ we find P-SS$_{EP}$ = IP-SS$_{EP}$, contradicting (2).

                                                                                     qed

As a consequence of (2) we find that the p-success set of EP is a proper subset of the p-success set of EP∪F(EP). Figure 6.2.5 gives an overview over the results obtained so far.

Now we turn our attention to correct answer substitutions.

Lemma 6.2.10:

   If E is a logical E-consequence of EP, then there exists a refutation of EP∪EP^{-1}∪{⇐E} wrt {→$_{ip}$, →$_f$} with the empty substitution as computed answer substitution.

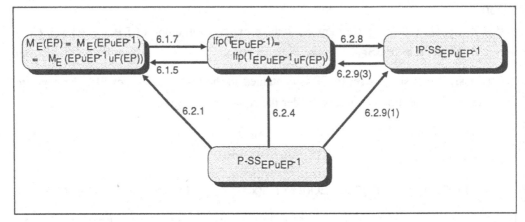

Figure 6.2.5

Proof:

Suppose E contains the variables $x_1, ..., x_n$. Let $a_1, ..., a_n$ be distinct constants not appearing in EP and E and let θ be the substitution $\{x_i \leftarrow a_i \mid 1 \leq i \leq n\}$. Clearly, θE is a logical E-consequence of EP. From corollary 6.1.7 we learn that $\theta E \in lfp(T_{EP \cup EP^{-1}})$. Hence, by corollary 6.2.8 we find a refutation of $EP \cup EP^{-1} \cup \{\Leftarrow \theta E\}$ wrt $\{\rightarrow_{ip}, \rightarrow_f\}$. Since the a_i do not appear in EP or E, by textually replacing a_i by x_i, $1 \leq i \leq n$, in this refutation, we obtain a refutation of $EP \cup EP^{-1} \cup \{\Leftarrow E\}$ wrt $\{\rightarrow_{ip}, \rightarrow_f\}$ and with computed answer substitution ε.   qed

Finally, we can prove that an inference system based on reflection, instantiation and paramodulation is complete.

Theorem 6.2.11 (Completeness of Reflection, Instantiation and Paramodulation):

For each correct answer substitution θ for EP and $\Leftarrow F$ there exists a computed answer substitution σ obtained by a refutation of $EP \cup EP^{-1} \cup \{\Leftarrow F\}$ wrt $\{\rightarrow_{ip}, \rightarrow_f\}$ such that $\theta \leq \sigma$.

Proof:

Since θ is correct, θF is a logical E-consequence of EP. By lemma 6.2.10, we find for all $E \in F$ a refutation of $EP \cup EP^{-1} \cup \{\Leftarrow \theta E\}$ wrt $\{\rightarrow_{ip}, \rightarrow_f\}$ and with the empty substitution as computed answer substitution. These refutations can be combined into a refutation of $EP \cup EP^{-1} \cup \{\Leftarrow \theta F\}$ using unifiers $\theta_1, ..., \theta_n$ such that the computed answer substitution is ε. By the lifting lemma, there exists a refutation of $EP \cup EP^{-1} \cup \{\Leftarrow F\}$ of the same length and, if $\sigma_1, ..., \sigma_n$ are the unifiers used in this refutation, then $\theta_n...\theta_1\theta \leq \sigma_n...\sigma_1$. Let σ be the restriction of $\sigma_n...\sigma_1$ to the variables in F. Then

$$\theta_n...\theta_1\theta|_{Var(F)} = \theta \leq \sigma = \sigma_n...\sigma_1|_{Var(F)},$$

which completes the proof.   qed

It should be noted that there is no need for factoring equational or goal clauses. The completeness of paramodulation and reflection without factoring was only recently shown by U. Furbach (1987). This was done by using the result from Henschen & Wos (1974), that whenever S is an E-unsatisfiable set of Horn clauses containing the axiom of reflexivity and the functional reflexive axioms, then there exists an input refutation and a unit refutation with respect to resolution, paramodulation, and factoring. (It is remarkable, that Henschen & Wos were mainly interested in unit refutations, because these provide a means for progressing rapidly towards shorter clauses, and used input refutations only as an intermediary result. To obtain a unit refutation, however, factoring is needed.) An input refutation with respect to resolution, paramodulation, and factoring was then transformed into a refutation where factoring was not employed. Hence, the result obtained by Furbach (1987) is based on various results from theorem-proving, and gives the reader no idea of various aspects about the completeness of paramodulation and reflection: e.g. Why must we include the functional reflexive axioms? Why are the functional reflexive axioms not needed if paramodulation is applied in a bottom-up manner? Why is the p-success set of EP not identical to the p-success set of $EP \cup F(EP)$?

A similar result has been obtained by Gallier & Raatz (1986, 1989). They introduce "SLDE-resolution" to compute answers to queries posed to equational logic programs. Each atom of the form $P(t_1,...,t_n)$ is transformed into the equation $EQ(P(t_1,...,t_n), true)$, where "true" is a new constant. Then, the authors use essentially the following inference rule: Let $\Leftarrow F \cup \{E\}$ be a goal clause, $v \rightarrow w \Leftarrow F^*$ be a new variant of an equational clause, σ and θ be substitutions, and $\pi \in Occ(\sigma E)$. If $\sigma E|\pi| = \theta v$, then infer $\Leftarrow \sigma F \cup \{\sigma E|\pi \leftarrow \theta w|\} \cup F^*$ from $\Leftarrow D \cup \{E\}$. This rule differs from the paramodulation rule defined herein as follows. Since σ and θ are arbitrary substitutions, σ can be used to instantiate variables in a program clause and θ can be used to instantiate variables in an equational clause that do not occur in the left-hand side of its head. Hence, these substitutions achieve the same effect as the functional reflexive axioms or the instantiation rule. Gallier & Raatz apply their inference rule successively to an equation $EQ(s,t)$ until s and t are syntactically unifiable. In other words, the subgoal $EQ(s,t)$ is "solved" before any other subgoal is considered as a candidate for the next inference step. This strategy corresponds to Morris (1969) and Anderson's (1970) E-resolution rule. As we will see in theorem 6.2.16 this is just the application of a special selection function.

To show the completeness of their system, Gallier & Raatz introduce the notion of "congruence closure" for Horn clauses which is equal to the least fixpoint of our mapping T_{EP}. However, the "congruence closure" is computed by interleaving steps in which congruence is propagated from "implicational reasoning", and steps in which congruence is propagated

from "equational reasoning". This technique can be examplified by the equational program
EP = { a→b, a→c⇐EQ(b,a) }. Starting with the empty set we obtain

{ EQ(a,b) }

by "implicational reasoning", since a→b occurs in EP. Using the axioms of equality we can
compute the "equational closure" of { EQ(a,b) }, i.e. the set

{ EQ(a,a), EQ(b,b), EQ(a,b), EQ(b,a) }.

Using a→c⇐EQ(b,a) we find

{ EQ(a,a), EQ(b,b), EQ(a,b), EQ(b,a), EQ(a,c) }

by "implicational reasoning" and, finally, by "equational reasoning" we obtain

{ EQ(a,a), EQ(b,b), EQ(c,c), EQ(a,b), EQ(b,a), EQ(a,c), EQ(c,a), EQ(b,c), EQ(c,b) }.

The interested reader may verify that this set is equal to the least fixpoint of T_{EP}. Finally,
Gallier & Raatz prove the competeness of their "SLDE-resolution" rule by relating the steps
of the construction of the "congruence closure" to "SLDE-resolution" steps.

Before we prove that refutations with respect to reflection, instantiation and paramodulation are independent of a selection function, we give two simple results, which are
used later. Obviously, each refutation with respect to $\{\to_f, \to_{ip}\}$ is a refutation with respect
to $\{\to_f, \to_i, \to_p\}$. The following proposition shows that for each refutation with respect to
$\{\to_f, \to_i, \to_p\}$ there exists a refutation with respect to $\{\to_f, \to_{ip}\}$ computing an eventually
more general answer substitution.

Proposition 6.2.12:

*If there exists a refutation of $EP \cup \{\Leftarrow F\}$ wrt $\{\to_i, \to_p, \to_f\}$ and computed
answer substitution θ, then there exists a refutation of $EP \cup \{\Leftarrow F\}$ wrt $\{\to_{ip},
\to_f\}$. Furthermore, if σ is the computed answer substitution of the refutation wrt
$\{\to_{ip}, \to_f\}$, then $\theta \leq \sigma$.*

Proof:

The proof is by induction on the length n of the refutation wrt $\{\to_i, \to_p, \to_f\}$. The case
n=0 being trivial we turn to the induction step and assume that the result holds for n. Let $\to$
$\in \{\to_i, \to_p, \to_f\}$. Suppose that

$\Leftarrow F' \to_{(\theta 0)} \Leftarrow F$ (1)

and that there exists a refutation of $EP \cup \{\Leftarrow F\}$ wrt $\{\to_i, \to_p, \to_f\}$ and computed answer sub-
stitution θ. Obviously, $\theta' = \theta\theta_0|_{Var(F')}$ is the computed answer substitition of the refutation of
$EP \cup \{\Leftarrow F'\}$ wrt $\{\to_i, \to_p, \to_f\}$. By the induction hypothesis we find a refutation of
$EP \cup \{\Leftarrow F\}$ wrt $\{\to_{ip}, \to_f\}$ and, if σ is the computed answer substitution of this refutation,
then $\theta \leq \sigma$. If in (1) paramodulation or reflection was applied then, obviously, there exists a
refutation of $EP \cup \{\Leftarrow F'\}$ wrt $\{\to_{ip}, \to_f\}$ with computed answer substitution $\sigma' = \sigma\theta_0|_{Var(F')}$
and, by proposition, 4.3(6) $\theta' \leq \sigma'$. Otherwise, if in (1) instantiation was applied, then the

result follows immediately by an application of the lifting lemma to the refutation of $EP \cup \{\Leftarrow F\}$ wrt $\{\rightarrow_{ip}, \rightarrow_f\}$.   qed

Proposition 6.2.13:

If there exists a refutation of $EP \cup \{\Leftarrow F\}$ wrt $\{\rightarrow_{ip}, \rightarrow_f\}$, computed answer sub-
stitution σ, and length n, then there exists a refutation of $EP \cup \{\Leftarrow \sigma F\}$ wrt $\{\rightarrow_{ip},$
$\rightarrow_f\}$, computed answer substitution ε, and length n.

Proof:

The proof is by induction on the length n of the refutation of $EP \cup \{\Leftarrow F\}$. The case n=0
being trivial we turn to the induction step and assume that the result holds for n. Suppose

$$\Leftarrow F' \rightarrow_{(\sigma 0)} \Leftarrow F \tag{1}$$

and there exists a refutation of $EP \cup \{\Leftarrow F\}$ wrt $\{\rightarrow_{ip}, \rightarrow_f\}$, computed answer substitution σ,
and length n. Obviously, $\sigma' = \sigma\sigma_0|_{Var(F')}$ is the computed answer substitution of the refuta-
tion of $EP \cup \{\Leftarrow F'\}$. We distinguish two cases:

If reflection was applied in (1) to $EQ(s,t) \in F'$, then σ_0 is the mgu of s and t. But then,

$$\sigma's = \sigma\sigma_0 s = \sigma\sigma_0 t = \sigma't.$$

It follows immediately that

$$\Leftarrow \sigma'F' \rightarrow_{f(\sigma'EQ(s,t), \varepsilon)} \Leftarrow \sigma\sigma_0(F'\setminus\{EQ(s,t)\}) = \Leftarrow\sigma F$$

and the induction hypothesis ensures that the result holds.

If in (1) instantiation and paramodulation was applied to $E \in F'$ at $\pi \in Occ(E)$ using $P = l\rightarrow r \Leftarrow F^*$, then we find substitutions μ, λ and an occurrence π' such that $\mu\lambda = \sigma_0$, $\pi' \in Occ(\lambda E)$, μ is the mgu of $(\lambda E)|\pi'|$ and l, and

$$\Leftarrow F' \qquad \rightarrow_i* \qquad \qquad \Leftarrow \lambda F'$$
$$\rightarrow_{p(\lambda E, \pi', P, \mu)} \quad \Leftarrow \mu\lambda(F'\setminus\{E\})\cup\mu\lambda F^*\cup\{\sigma_0 E|\pi'\leftarrow\mu\lambda r|\}$$
$$= \qquad\qquad\quad \Leftarrow \sigma_0(F'\setminus\{E\})\cup\sigma_0 F^*\cup\{\sigma_0 E|\pi'\leftarrow\sigma_0 r|\}$$
$$= \qquad\qquad\quad \Leftarrow F.$$

Since P is a new variant of an equational clause we find

$$(\sigma'E)|\pi'| = (\sigma\sigma_0 E)|\pi'| = (\sigma\mu\lambda E)|\pi'| = \sigma\mu l = \sigma\mu\lambda l = \sigma\sigma_0 l = \sigma'l.$$

Now let $\gamma = \sigma'|_{Var(l)}$ and $\gamma' = \sigma'\gamma$. Hence, $\gamma\cup\gamma' = \sigma'$. Furthermore, since σ' is idempotent we
learn that γ and γ' are also idempotent and, hence,

$$\gamma'\gamma = \gamma\cup\gamma' = \sigma'$$

and

$$\gamma'\sigma' = \sigma'.$$

Now,

$$\Leftarrow \sigma'F' \quad \rightarrow_{p(\sigma'E, \pi', P, \gamma)} \quad \Leftarrow \sigma'(F'\backslash\{E\})\cup\gamma F^*\cup\{(\sigma'E)|\pi'\leftarrow\gamma r|\}$$
$$= \quad \Leftarrow \sigma'(F'\backslash\{E\})\cup\sigma'F^*\cup\{(\sigma'E)|\pi'\leftarrow\sigma'r|\}$$
$$= \quad \Leftarrow \sigma\sigma_0(F'\backslash\{E\})\cup\sigma\sigma_0F^*\cup\{(\sigma\sigma_0E)|\pi'\leftarrow\sigma\sigma_0r|\}$$
$$= \quad \Leftarrow \sigma F.$$

By the induction hypothesis we find a refutation of $EP\cup\{\Leftarrow\sigma F\}$ wrt $\{\rightarrow_{ip}, \rightarrow_f\}$, computed answer substitution ε, and length n. The result follows immediately.   qed

From the proof of proposition 6.2.13 we learn that, if in the refutation of $EP\cup\{\Leftarrow F\}$ reflection was applied m times and instantiation and paramodulation was applied n times, then in the corresponding refutation of $EP\cup\{\Leftarrow\sigma F\}$ reflection was also applied m times and paramodulation was also applied n times. Furthermore, paramodulation was applied at the same occurrence and was using the same equational clause as in the refutation of $EP\cup\{\Leftarrow F\}$.

We now turn our attention to the selection function and the problem under which conditions derivations with respect to reflection, instantiation and paramodulation are independent of the selection function. It is easy to see that they are not independent of a **strong selection function,** i.e. a selection function that selects not only a subgoal but also a subterm in the selected subgoal if instantiation and paramodulation shall be applied. As an example consider the equational program

CYCLE: $f \rightarrow g \Leftarrow$ (f)

            $g \rightarrow h \Leftarrow$ (g)

            $h \rightarrow f \Leftarrow$ (h)

There exists a refutation of $CYCLE\cup\{\Leftarrow EQ(f,g)\}$ with respect to reflection, instantiation and paramodulation:

$$\Leftarrow EQ(f,g) \rightarrow_{p(f)} \Leftarrow EQ(g,g) \rightarrow_f \square.$$

However, if we choose a selection function that selects the subterms g, f, h, g, f, h, ... in this order, then the derivation will cycle:

$$\Leftarrow EQ(f,g) \rightarrow_{p(g)} \Leftarrow EQ(f,h) \rightarrow_{p(f)} \Leftarrow EQ(g,h) \rightarrow_{p(h)} \Leftarrow EQ(g,f) \rightarrow \dots .$$

But we show that reflection, instantiation and paramodulation are independent of the selection function. To prove this result we claim that refutations with respect to reflection, instantiation and paramodulation are independent of a selection function if they compute the identity as answer substitution. Since the lifting lemma 6.2.6 guarantees that the refutations of $EP\cup\{\Leftarrow\theta F\}$ and $EP\cup\{\Leftarrow F\}$ are via the same selection function, applying the lifting lemma to the claim yields the independence of a selection function. This use of the lifting lemma is the reason why we have not used the instantiation rule as an independent inference rule but as a rule which may be applied finitely many times before a single paramodulation step is performed.

Lemma 6.2.14 (Switching Lemma for $\rightarrow_{ip}$ and $\rightarrow_f$):

If there exists a refutation of $EP\cup\{\Leftarrow F\cup\{E_1, E_2\}\}$ wrt $\{\rightarrow_{ip}, \rightarrow_f\}$, length n, computed answer substitution ε, and via SEL, where SEL is a selection function that selects E_1 in the first and E_2 in the second step, then there exists a refutation of $EP\cup\{\Leftarrow F\cup\{E_1, E_2\}\}$ wrt $\{\rightarrow_{ip}, \rightarrow_f\}$, length n, computed answer substitution ε, and via SEL', which is the same as SEL except that the first two selections are reversed.

Proof:

It should be observed that an instantiation and paramodulation as well as a reflection step applied to E_1 or E_2 cannot instantiate a variable occurring in the initial goal clause. Hence, if reflection is applied to E_1 (resp. E_2), then E_1 (resp. E_2) must be a trivial equation. If instantiation and paramodulation is applied to E_1 (resp. E_2), then it must be a paramodulation step and the substitution used binds only variables occurring in the respective equational clause. Thus, if in the refutation via SEL either the first or the second step is a reflection, then these steps can be swapped. If the first step is a paramodulation step using σ and the second step is also a paramodulation step using θ, then $\sigma\theta = \theta\sigma$, since the program clauses used in the paramodulation steps have no variables in common. Therefore, these steps can also be swapped and the lemma follows immediately.   qed.

Theorem 6.2.15 (Independence of the Selection Function for $\rightarrow_{ip}$ and $\rightarrow_f$):

Let SEL and SEL' be two selection functions. If there exists a refutation of $EP\cup\{\Leftarrow F\}$ wrt $\{\rightarrow_{ip}, \rightarrow_f\}$, computed answer substitution ε, and via SEL, then there exists a refutation of $EP\cup\{\Leftarrow F\}$ wrt $\{\rightarrow_{ip}, \rightarrow_f\}$, computed answer substitution ε, and via SEL'.

Proof:

The proof is by induction on the length n of the refutation of $EP\cup\{\Leftarrow F\}$ via SEL. The case n=0 being trivial we turn to the induction step and assume that the result holds for n. We distinguish two cases.

Let P be a new variant of a program clause. Suppose

$$\Leftarrow F' \rightarrow_{ip(E, \pi, P, \theta)} \Leftarrow F \tag{1}$$

and there exists a refutation of $EP\cup\{\Leftarrow F\}$ wrt $\{\rightarrow_{ip}, \rightarrow_f\}$, length n, computed answer substitution σ, and via SEL such that $Dom(\sigma) \subseteq Var(P)$. Furthermore, suppose that $E' \in F'$ is the first selected equation by SEL'. By lemma 6.2.13, there exists a refutation of $EP\cup\{\Leftarrow\sigma F\}$ wrt $\{\rightarrow_{ip}, \rightarrow_f\}$, length n, computed answer substitution ε, and via SEL. An application of the induction hypothesis shows that there exists a refutation of $EP \cup \{\Leftarrow \sigma F\}$ wrt $\{\rightarrow_{ip}, \rightarrow_f\}$, length n, and computed answer substitution ε such that σ'E is the first selected equation. By the lifting lemma we find a refutation of $EP \cup \{\Leftarrow F\}$ wrt $\{\rightarrow_{ip}, \rightarrow_f\}$ and length n such that E' is the first selected equation and, if σ' is the computed answer substitution of the refutation of $EP \cup \{\Leftarrow F\}$, then $\sigma \leq \sigma$'. Hence, $Dom(\sigma') \subseteq Var(P)$. Clearly, there exists a refutation of $EP \cup \{\Leftarrow F'\}$ wrt $\{\rightarrow_{ip}, \rightarrow_f\}$, length n+1, and computed answer substitution ε such that E (resp. E') is the first (resp. second) selected equation. An application of the switching lemma 6.2.14 to this refutation yields a refutation of $EP \cup \{\Leftarrow F'\}$ wrt $\{\rightarrow_{ip}, \rightarrow_f\}$, length n+1, and computed answer substitution ε, such that E' (resp. E) is the first (resp. second) selected equation. If the first step in this refutation was a reflection, then the result follows immediately by the induction hypothesis. Otherwise, if the first step was an instantiation and paramodulation, say

$$\Leftarrow F' \rightarrow_{ip}(E', \pi', P', \theta') \Leftarrow F^*$$

then there exists a refutation of $EP \cup \{\Leftarrow F^*\}$ wrt $\{\rightarrow_{ip}, \rightarrow_f\}$, length n, computed answer substitution γ, such that $Dom(\gamma) \subseteq Var(P')$. By lemma 6.2.13, there exists a refutation of $EP \cup \{\Leftarrow \gamma F^*\}$ wrt $\{\rightarrow_{ip}, \rightarrow_f\}$, length n, and computed answer substitution ε. An application of the induction hypothesis shows that there exists a refutation of $EP \cup \{\Leftarrow \gamma F^*\}$ wrt $\{\rightarrow_{ip}, \rightarrow_f\}$, length n, computed answer substitution ε, and via SEL'. By the lifting lemma we find a refutation of $EP \cup \{\Leftarrow F^*\}$ wrt $\{\rightarrow_{ip}, \rightarrow_f\}$, length n, via SEL' and, if γ' is the computed answer substitution of the refutation of $EP \cup \{\Leftarrow F\}$, then $\gamma \leq \gamma$'. Hence, $Dom(\gamma') \subseteq Var(P')$. Clearly, there exists a refutation of $EP \cup \{\Leftarrow F^*\}$ wrt $\{\rightarrow_{ip}, \rightarrow_f\}$, length n+1, computed answer substitution ε, and via SEL'.

Suppose now that

$$\Leftarrow F' \rightarrow_f(E) \Leftarrow F$$

and there exists a refutation of $EP \cup \{\Leftarrow F\}$ wrt $\{\rightarrow_{ip}, \rightarrow_f\}$, computed answer substitution ε, and via SEL. Then the result follows in analogy to the previous case.   qed

We can now prove the strong completeness of reflection, instantiation and paramodulation:

Theorem 6.2.16 (Strong Completeness of $\rightarrow_{ip}$ and $\rightarrow_f$):

Let SEL be a selection function. For every correct answer substitution θ for EP and $\Leftarrow F$ there exists an SEL-computed answer substitution σ obtained by a refutation of $EP \cup EP^{-1} \cup \{\Leftarrow F\}$ wrt $\{\rightarrow_{ip}, \rightarrow_f\}$ such that $\theta \leq \sigma$.

Proof:

Since θ is a correct, θF is a logical E-consequence of EP. Hence, ε is a correct answer substitution for EP and $\Leftarrow \theta F$. By the completeness of $\rightarrow_{ip}$ and $\rightarrow_f$ we find a refutation of $EP \cup EP^{-1} \cup \{\Leftarrow \theta F\}$ wrt $\{\rightarrow_{ip}, \rightarrow_f\}$ and computed answer substitution ε. The independence of the selection function for $\rightarrow_{ip}$ and $\rightarrow_f$ ensures that there exists a refutation of $EP \cup EP^{-1} \cup \{\Leftarrow \theta F\}$ wrt $\{\rightarrow_{ip}, \rightarrow_f\}$, computed answer substitution ε, and via SEL. Finally, an application of the lifting lemma ensures that the result holds. qed

Hence, Morris' (1969) and Anderson's (1970) technique of applying paramodulation successively to an equation until it is completely "solved" is just the application of a special selection function. Similarly, Gallier & Raatz's (1986, 1988) result is just an instance of theorem 6.2.16.

At the end of this section we define two simplification rules for reflection, instantiation and paramodulation. The first one is concerned with those equations, whose elements have as initial symbol the same "decomposable" function symbol and the second simplification rule eliminates trivial equations.

Definition:

A function symbol f is said to be **decomposable** with respect to an equational program EP iff for every equation $EQ(f(s_1,...,s_n), f(t_1,...,t_n))$ that is a logical E-consequence of EP we find that $\{EQ(s_i,t_i) \mid 1 \leq i \leq n\}$ is a logical E-consequence of EP. If f is a decomposable function symbol, then an equation of the form $EQ(f(s_1,...,s_n), f(t_1,...,t_n))$ is said to be **decomposable**.

As an example consider the equational program

PLUS-MINUS:
$$0+y \rightarrow y \Leftarrow$$
$$s(x)+y \rightarrow s(x+y) \Leftarrow$$
$$-(-x) \rightarrow x \Leftarrow$$
$$-(x+y) \rightarrow (-x)+(-y) \Leftarrow$$

Obviously, "0" and "s" are decomposable. "+" is not decomposable, since $2+3 = 4+1$ and $2 \neq 4$ (resp. $3 \neq 1$). However, Kirchner (1984) showed that "-" is decomposable.

Lemma 6.2.17:

Let f be a decomposable function symbol. If there exists a refutation of $EP \cup \{EQ(f(s_1,...,s_n), f(t_1,...,t_n))\}$ wrt $\{\rightarrow_{ip}, \rightarrow_f\}$ and with computed answer substitution σ, then there exists a refutation of $EP \cup \{\Leftarrow F \cup \{EQ(s_i,t_i) \mid 1 \leq i \leq n\}\}$ wrt $\{\rightarrow_{ip}, \rightarrow_f\}$. Furthermore, if θ is the computed answer substitution of the refutation of $EP \cup \{\Leftarrow F \cup \{EQ(s_i,t_i) \mid 1 \leq i \leq n\}\}$, then $\theta \geq \sigma$.

Proof:

Let $F' = F \cup \{EQ(f(s_1,...,s_n), f(t_1,...,t_n))\}$. Since σ is the computed answer substitution of a refutation of $EP \cup \{\Leftarrow F'\}$ we find by theorem 6.2.1 that σ is a correct answer substitution for EP and $\Leftarrow F'$, i.e. σF is a logical E-consequence of EP. Now, let $F^* = F \cup \{EQ(s_i,t_i) \mid 1 \leq i \leq n\}$.

Since f is a decomposable function symbol, σF^* is also a logical E-consequence of EP and the result follows immediately by the completeness of $\to_{ip}$ and $\to_f$.   qed

Lemma 6.2.18:

> *IF there exists a refutation of $EP \cup \{\Leftarrow F \cup \{EQ(t,t)\}\}$ wrt $\{\to_{ip}, \to_f\}$ and with computed answer substitution σ, then there exists a refutation of $EP \cup \{\Leftarrow F\}$ wrt $\{\to_{ip}, \to_f\}$. Furthermore, if θ is the computed answer substitution of the refutation of $EP \cup \{\Leftarrow F\}$, then $\sigma \leq \theta$.*

Proof:

Since refutations wrt $\{\to_{ip}, \to_f\}$ are independent of the selection function, we may assume that the equation $EQ(t,t)$ is not selected as long as there are other alternatives, i.e. we find a derivation from $\Leftarrow F \cup \{EQ(t,t)\}$ to $\Leftarrow \theta_n \ldots \theta_1 EQ(t,t)$ using unifiers $\theta_1, \ldots, \theta_n$ and a refutation of $EP \cup \{\Leftarrow \theta_n \ldots \theta_1 EQ(t,t)\}$ using unifiers $\theta_{n+1}, \ldots, \theta_m$ such that $\sigma = \theta_m \ldots \theta_1 |_{\mathrm{Var}(F \cup \{EQ(t,t)\})}$. The lemma follows immediately with $\theta = \theta_n \ldots \theta_1 |_{\mathrm{Var}(F)}$.   qed.

It is easy to see that the inference rules "term decomposition" (applied only to decomposable equations) and "removal of trivial equations" can be applied as simplification rules in a refutation with respect to reflection, instantiation and paramodulation: From the proof of lemma 6.2.18 we learn that the removal of a trivial equation strictly decreases the length of the refutation. From lemma 6.2.17 we learn that paramodulation was not applied to the elements of a decomposable equation. Now, if we replace each reflection in a refutation with respect to reflection, instantiation and paramodulation by a sequence of applications of term decomposition, variable elimination, removal of trivial variable-equations (which can be done according to theorem 3.4.1.2), then the decomposition of a decomposable equation strictly decreases the length of such a refutation.

If the selection function selects a subgoal of the form $EQ(x,y)$, where x and y are different variables, then we cannot simply remove the variable x (or y) by applying reflection, but we also have to apply instantiation and paramodulation. However, since reflection, instantiation and paramodulation are independent of a selection function, we may choose a selection function which never selects an equation of the form $EQ(x,y)$ if it has another choice. Hence, in a refutation using such a selection function we eventually encounter a goal clause of the form

$$\Leftarrow \{ EQ(x_i,y_i) \mid 1 \leq i \leq n \},$$

where x_i, y_i, $1 \leq i \leq n$, are variables. The following proposition shows that it suffices to apply reflection to such a gaol clause.

Proposition 6.2.19:

> Let G be a gaol clause of the form $\Leftarrow\{EQ(x_i, y_i) \mid 1 \leq i \leq n\}$. For each correct
> answer substitution θ for EP and G there exists a computed answer substitution
> σ obtained by a refutation of $EP \cup \{G\}$ wrt reflection such that $\theta \leq_{EP} \sigma$.

Proof:

Before turning to the proof of the proposition we show that the following claim holds.

Claim: Suppose $x \notin Var(t)$. If δ is a correct answer substitution for EP and $\Leftarrow F \cup \{EQ(x,t)\}$,
then $\delta^*\{x \leftarrow t\}$ is also a correct answer substitution for EP and $\Leftarrow F \cup \{EQ(x,t)\}$ and $\delta =_{EP}$
$\delta^*\{x \leftarrow t\}$, where $\delta^* = \delta \backslash \{x \leftarrow \delta x\}$.

Proof of the claim: δ is a correct answer substitution for EP and $\Leftarrow F \cup \{EQ(x,t)\}$ iff each
ground instance $\mu\delta E$ of an equation $E \in F \cup \{EQ(x,t)\}$ is an element of $M_E(EP)$. Since

$$\delta^*\{x \leftarrow t\}EQ(x,t) = \delta^*EQ(t,t) = \delta EQ(x,t)$$

we find that each ground instance of $\delta^*\{x \leftarrow t\}EQ(x,t)$ is an element of $M_E(EP)$. Now, let E
$\in F$ and $\pi \in Occ(E)$ such that $E|\pi = x$. From proposition 6.1.3 we learn that $\mu\delta E|\pi \leftarrow \mu\delta x| =$
$\mu\delta E|\pi \leftarrow \delta^*\{x \leftarrow t\}x|$ is also an element of $M_E(EP)$. Since x occurs only finitely many times in
E, we conclude that each ground instance of $\delta^*\{x \leftarrow t\}E$ is an element of $M_E(EP)$. Hence,
$\delta^*\{x \leftarrow t\}$ is a correct answer substitution for EP and $\Leftarrow F \cup \{EQ(x,t)\}$. Finally, because

$$\delta^*\{x \leftarrow t\}x = \delta^*t = \delta t =_{EP} \delta x$$

and for all variables $y \neq x$ we find

$$\delta^*\{x \leftarrow t\}y = \delta y$$

we conclude that $\delta^*\{x \leftarrow t\} =_{EP} \delta$, which proves the claim.

Now, we show the proposition by induction on the number n of equations in G. The case
$n=0$ being trivial we turn to the induction step and assume that the result holds for n.
Suppose G' contains $n+1$ equations and suppose that θ' is a correct answer substitution for
EP and G. Let $G' = \Leftarrow F \cup \{EQ(x,y)\}$. If $x=y$, then the result follows immediately from lemma
6.2.18. Otherwise, if $x \neq y$, we learn from the claim that $\theta^*\{x \leftarrow y\}$ is also a correct answer
substitution for EP and G' and

$$\theta' =_{EP} \theta^*\{x \leftarrow y\}, \tag{1}$$

where $\theta^* = \theta' \backslash \{x \leftarrow \theta'x\}$. By lemma 6.2.10 we find a refutation of $EP \cup EP^{-1} \cup \{\theta^*\{x \leftarrow y\}G'\}$
wrt $\{\rightarrow_{ip}, \rightarrow_f\}$ and identity as computed answer substitution. Let $G = \Leftarrow \{x \leftarrow y\}F$. Since
$\theta^*\{x \leftarrow y\}EQ(x,y) = \theta^*EQ(y,y)$, lemma 6.2.18 ensures that we also find a refutation of
$EP \cup EP^{-1} \cup \{\theta^*G\}$ wrt $\{\rightarrow_{ip}, \rightarrow_f\}$ and identity as computed answer substitution. By an application of the lifting lemma 6.2.6 we find a refutation of $EP \cup EP^{-1} \cup \{\Leftarrow G\}$ wrt $\{\rightarrow_{ip}, \rightarrow_f\}$
and, if θ is the computed answer substitution of this refutation, then

$$\theta^* \leq \theta. \tag{2}$$

Hence, θ is a correct answer substitution for EP and G (theorem 6.2.1) and, since G contains only n equations of the form EQ(x',y'), we find a refutation of EP$\cup${G} wrt reflection by the induction hypothesis. Furthermore, if σ is the computed answer substitution of this refutation, then

$\theta \leq_{EP} \sigma.$ (3)

Clearly, there exists a refutation of G' wrt reflection with computed answer substitution

$\sigma' = \sigma\{x\leftarrow y\}.$

Finally,

$$
\begin{array}{llll}
\theta' & = & \theta*\{x\leftarrow y\} & \text{by (1)} \\
 & \leq & \theta\{x\leftarrow y\} & \text{by (2)} \\
 & \leq_{EP} & \sigma\{x\leftarrow y\} & \text{by (3)} \\
 & = & \sigma' & \text{qed}
\end{array}
$$

Remark:

In the sequel we may apply a selection function to derivations with respect to reflection, instantiation and paramodulation which never selects an equation of the form EQ(x,y) if it has another choice. Furthermore, if the goal clause contains only subgoals of the form EQ(x,y), then we may only apply reflection. The strong completeness of reflection, instantiation and paramodulation (theorem 6.2.16) and proposition 6.2.19 ensure the completeness of such a strategy.

From an operational point of view the strong completeness of reflection, instantiation and paramodulation is not very satisfactory since these inference rules generate far too many useless and redundant clauses. There are mainly three sources for these inefficiencies:

(1)   We have to use equational clauses from EP as well as from EP^{-1}.

(2)   If instantiation and paramodulation has to be applied to a variable occurrence, then we must guess the instantiation of this variable before the paramodulation step can be applied. Unfortunately, we have to investigate each of the infinitely many possibilities to ensure completeness.

(3)   If the selection function selects a certain equation E, then there are in general several occurrences in E to which paramodulation has to be applied.

In the following sections we impose certain restrictions on the equational program in order to overcome these inefficiencies.

6.3 Confluent Theories

We learned from the proof of theorem 6.1.6 and subsequent results that we have to take clauses from an equational program EP and its inverse program EP^{-1} to guarantee that its fixpoint characterization is identical to its least Herbrand E-model and, furthermore, that paramodulation is complete. To prune the search space we would like to restrict para-modulation in that it only uses clauses from EP as input clauses. By theorem 6.2.1, para-modulation and reflection using only clauses from EP are sound. However, they are not refu-tation-complete as can be seen by the equational program

NC: a → b

           a → c

and the equation EQ(b,c). Clearly, EQ(b,c) is a logical E-consequence of NC, yet there does not exist a refutation of NC∪{⇐EQ(b,c)} with respect to paramodulation and reflection.

The condition that has to be imposed on EP to retain completeness is ground confluency.

Definition:
> Let →* denote a derivation with respect to a set of inference rules using program clauses from EP. EP is said to be **ground confluent** iff for all ground goal clauses G, G_1, G_2 such that G →* G_1 and G →* G_2, there exists a goal clause G' such that G_1 →* G' and G_2 →* G'.

In the sequel we assume that ground confluence is defined with respect to reflection, in-stantiation and paramodulation. As a consequence, ground confluence is also given with respect to reflection, instantiation, and paramodulation.

In the proof of the completeness of reflection, instantiation and paramodulation we used theorem 6.2.7 in the form that $E \in T_{EP\cup EP-1}\uparrow n$ implies the existence of a refutation of $EP\cup EP^{-1}\cup\{\Leftarrow E\}$. However, EP being ground confluent we can now prove a result similar to theorem 6.2.7 except that paramodulation only has to use program clauses from EP. One should observe that the lifting lemma for reflection, instantiation and paramodulation holds for arbitrary equational programs.

Theorem 6.3.1:
> Let EP be a ground confluent equational program. If $E \in T_{EP\cup EP-1}\uparrow n$, then there exists a refutation of $EP\cup\{\Leftarrow E\}$ wrt $\{\rightarrow_{ip}, \rightarrow_f\}$.

Proof:
The result is proved by induction on n. The case n=1 being trivial (reflection was applied) we turn to the induction step and assume that the result holds for n-1. Let $E \in T_{EP\cup EP-1}\uparrow n$.

If E is a ground instance of the axiom of reflexivity, then $E\cup\{\Leftarrow EQ\}$ has a refutation of length 1 applying reflection.

Otherwise, there exist $\pi \in Occ(E)$ and a ground instance $\theta(v\rightarrow w\Leftarrow F)$ of a clause in $EP\cup EP^{-1}$ such that $E|\pi| = \theta v$ and $\theta F\cup\{E|\pi\leftarrow\theta w|\} \subseteq T_{EP\cup EP-1}\uparrow(n-1)$. By the induction hypothesis there exists a refutation of $EP\cup\{\Leftarrow E'\}$ wrt $\{\rightarrow_{ip}, \rightarrow_f\}$ for each $E' \in \theta(F\cup\{E|\pi\leftarrow w|\})$. Because each E' is ground, these refutations can be combined into a refutation of $EP\cup\{\Leftarrow\theta(F\cup\{E|\pi\leftarrow w|\})\}$. We distinguish two cases:

First suppose that $v\rightarrow w\Leftarrow F \in EP$. Since θ is a unifier of $E|\pi|$ and v, we find an mgu σ of $E|\pi|$ and v and a substitution γ such that $\gamma\sigma = \theta$. By the lifting lemma (lemma 6.2.6), there exists a refutation of $EP\cup\{\Leftarrow\sigma(F\cup\{E|\pi\leftarrow w|\})\}$ wrt $\{\rightarrow_{ip}, \rightarrow_f\}$ and, hence, we can find a refutation of $EP\cup\{\Leftarrow E\}$.

Otherwise, if $v\rightarrow w\Leftarrow F \in EP^{-1}$, then the induction hypothesis ensures that

$$\Leftarrow E|\pi\leftarrow\theta w| \rightarrow^* \square, \tag{1}$$

where $\rightarrow \in \{\rightarrow_{ip}, \rightarrow_f\}$. Since $w\rightarrow v\Leftarrow F \in EP$, there exist an mgu σ of θw and w, and a substitution γ such that $\theta = \gamma\sigma$ we find

$$\Leftarrow E|\pi\leftarrow\theta w| \rightarrow_{p(w\rightarrow v\Leftarrow F)} \Leftarrow \sigma(\{E|\pi\leftarrow v|\}\cup F). \tag{2}$$

By repeated applications of instantiation we obtain

$$\Leftarrow \sigma(\{E|\pi\leftarrow v|\}\cup F) \rightarrow_i^* \Leftarrow \gamma\sigma(\{E|\pi\leftarrow v|\}\cup F) = \Leftarrow \theta(\{E|\pi\leftarrow v|\}\cup F). \tag{3}$$

and from the induction hypothesis follows that

$$\Leftarrow \theta(\{E|\pi\leftarrow v|\}\cup F) \rightarrow^* \Leftarrow E|\pi\leftarrow\theta v| = \Leftarrow E. \tag{4}$$

Since EP is ground confluent we learn from (1), (2), (3) and (4) that there exists a refutation of $EP\cup\{\Leftarrow E\}$ wrt $\{\rightarrow_i, \rightarrow_p, \rightarrow_f\}$. An application of proposition 6.2.12 completes the proof.

qed

Figure 6.3.1 illustrates the last case of the proof. This is the case where we demonstrated that applications of paramodulation using program clauses from EP^{-1} can be omitted due to the fact that EP is ground confluent. It should be noted that the instantiation rule is only needed in the lifting lemma and to instantiate variables occurring in a goal clause by ground terms (see (3) in the above proof). These variables occur since for an equational clause $v\rightarrow w\Leftarrow F$ the condition $Var(v) \supseteq Var(w)\cup Var(F)$ may not be fulfilled.

Let EP be a ground confluent equational program. As an immediate consequence of theorem 6.3.1 we find that the least fixpoint of T_{EP} is identical with the least fixpoint of $T_{EP\cup EP-1}$.

Corollary 6.3.2:
  If EP be a ground confluent equational program, then $lfp(T_{EP}) = lfp(T_{EP\cup EP-1})$.

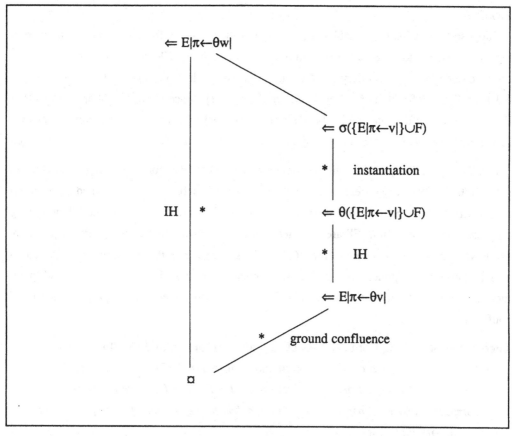

Figure 6.3.1

Proof:

Obviously, lfp(T_{EP}) ⊆ lfp($T_{EP∪EP-1}$). Now, if E ∈ lfp($T_{EP∪EP-1}$) then, by theorem 6.3.1, we find a refutation of EP∪{⇐E} wrt {→$_{ip}$, →$_f$}. Hence, E ∈ IP-SS$_{EP}$. From corollary 6.2.9(3) we learn that E ∈ lfp(T_{EP}) and, thus, lfp($T_{EP∪EP-1}$) ⊆ lfp(T_{EP}).   qed

In analogy to lemma 6.2.10 we can now show that E being a logical E-consequence of EP implies the existence of a refutation of EP∪{⇐E} with respect to reflection, instantiation and paramodulation with the empty computed answer substitution.

Lemma 6.3.3:

Let EP be a ground confluent equational program. If E is a logical E-conse-quence of EP, then there exists a refutation of EP∪{⇐E} wrt {→$_{ip}$, →$_f$} and with empty computed answer substitution.

Proof:

Suppose E contains the variables $x_1, ..., x_n$. Let $a_1, ..., a_n$ be distinct constants not appearing in EP and E and let θ be the substitution $\{x_i \leftarrow a_i \mid 1 \leq i \leq n\}$. Clearly, θE is a logical E-consequence of EP. From corollary 6.1.7 we learn that $\theta E \in \text{lfp}(T_{EP \cup EP}\text{-}1)$. Hence, by theorem 6.3.1 we find a refutation of $EP \cup \{\Leftarrow \theta E\}$ wrt $\{\rightarrow_{ip}, \rightarrow_f\}$. Since the a_i do not appear in EP or E we obtain a refutation of $EP \cup \{\Leftarrow E\}$ wrt $\{\rightarrow_{ip}, \rightarrow_f\}$ and with empty computed answer substitution by textually replacing a_i by x_i, $1 \leq i \leq n$, in this refutation.   qed

Finally, an application of the lifting lemma 6.2.6 ensures that for each correct answer substitution θ for $EP \cup \{\Leftarrow F\}$ there exists a computed answer substitution σ obtained by a refutation of $EP \cup \{\Leftarrow F\}$ such that $\theta \leq \sigma$. Hence, reflection, instantiation and paramodulation using only program clauses from EP are complete if EP is a ground confluent equational program. Moreover, since the switching lemma 6.2.14 does not reverse the direction in which equational clauses are applied, refutations with respect to reflection, instantiation and paramodulation are independent of a selection function even if the equational program is ground confluent.

Theorem 6.3.4 (Strong Completeness of $\rightarrow_{ip}$ and $\rightarrow_f$ for Ground Confluent EP):

Let EP be a ground confluent equational program and SEL be a selection function. For each correct answer substitution θ for $EP \cup \{\Leftarrow F\}$ there exists an SEL-computed answer substitution σ obtained by the refutation of $EP \cup \{\Leftarrow F\}$ wrt $\{\rightarrow_{ip}, \rightarrow_f\}$ such that $\theta \leq \sigma$.

Proof:

Since θ is correct we conclude that θF is a logical E-consequence of EP. By lemma 6.3.3, we find for all $E \in F$ a refutation of $EP \cup \{\Leftarrow \theta E\}$ wrt $\{\rightarrow_{ip}, \rightarrow_f\}$ and with the empty computed answer substitution. These refutations can be combined into a refutation of $EP \cup \{\Leftarrow \theta F\}$ with empty computed answer substitution. By the switching lemma for $\rightarrow_{ip}$ and $\rightarrow_f$ we find a refutation of $EP \cup \{\Leftarrow \theta F\}$ with empty computed answer substitution and via SEL. The result follows immediately by an application of the lifting lemma 6.2.6.   qed

For ground confluent equational programs we cannot prove the independence of the strong selection function. This follows immediately from the CYCLE-example in the previous section, since CYCLE is ground confluent.

In the following we concentrate on the problem that paramodulation has to be applied to variable occurrences. Recall, that in such a case not only each program clause can be used as an input clause but also each finite sequence of instantiations has to be considered.

6.4 Term Rewriting Systems

If we want to show that a ground equation is a logical E-consequence of a ground confluent equational program, we still have to use the instantiation rule. This is due to the fact that
in a program clause l→r⇐F, r and F may contain variables that do not occur in l. Hence, a
paramodulation step using such a program clause introduces new variables. As an example
consider the ground confluent equational program

GM:	a→b	(ab)
	a→c	(ac)
	b→c ⇐ EQ(g(x,c), g(b,x))	(bc)

which can be found in Giovannetti & Moiso (1987). EQ(b,c) is a logical consequence of
GM, since

⇐ EQ(b,c)	→p(bc)	⇐ EQ(c,c), EQ(g(x,c), g(b,x))
	→f	⇐ EQ(g(x,c) ,g(b,x))
	→p(ab, {x←a})	⇐ EQ(g(b,c), g(b,a))
	→p(ac)	⇐ EQ(g(b,c), g(b,c))
	→f	□.

However, to obtain this result we have to solve the problem of whether there is a substitution
θ such that θEQ(g(x,c), g(b,x)) is a logical E-consequence of GM. To avoid this equation
solving we impose a condition on the variables occurring in an equational clause (see also
Kaplan 1986).

Definition:

> An equational program EP is a **term rewriting system** iff for all l→r⇐F ∈ EP
> we have Var(F)∪Var(r) ⊆ Var(l). If all clauses in a term rewriting system EP
> have an empty body, then EP is said to be **unconditional**, otherwise it is said to
> be **conditional**. The clauses of a term rewriting system are called **rewrite rules**.

Notation:

In the sequel let **R** denote a term rewriting system.

Note, $R \cup R^{-1}$ is not necessarily a term rewriting system. As an example consider the
rewrite rule

$$f(x) \rightarrow a.$$

Clearly, f(x)→a satisfies the variable condition. However, its "inverse"

$$a \rightarrow f(x)$$

cannot be a clause in a term rewriting system, since Var(f(x)) = {x} and Var(a) = ∅.

Recall, to prove the E-unsatisfiability of a ground confluent equational program EP and an equation we need the instantiation rule and clauses form EP, but not from EP^{-1}. The following lemma shows that if EP is a term rewriting system, then the instantiation rule is not needed to show E-unsatisfiability.

Lemma 6.4.1:

> *If there exists a refutation of $R \cup \{\Leftarrow F\}$ wrt $\{\rightarrow_{ip}, \rightarrow_f\}$ and with empty computed answer substitution, then there exists a refutation of $R \cup \{\Leftarrow F\}$ wrt $\{\rightarrow_p, \rightarrow_f\}$ and with empty computed answer substitution.*

Proof:

The proof is by induction on the length n of the refutation of $R \cup \{\Leftarrow F\}$ wrt $\{\rightarrow_{ip}, \rightarrow_f\}$. The case n=0 being trivial we turn to the induction step and assume that the result holds for n-1. Suppose there exists a refutation of $R \cup \{\Leftarrow F'\}$ wrt $\{\rightarrow_{ip}, \rightarrow_f\}$ and computed answer substitution ε having length n. We distinguish two cases.

Suppose the first step is a reflection. Let EQ(s,t) be the selected equation in this step. Hence, s=t and

$$\Leftarrow F' \rightarrow_f \Leftarrow F' \backslash \{EQ(s,t)\} = \Leftarrow F.$$

From the induction hypothesis we learn, that there exists a refutation of $R \cup \{\Leftarrow F\}$ wrt $\{\rightarrow_p, \rightarrow_f\}$ and with ε as computed answer substitution. Clearly, there exists a refutation of $R \cup \{\Leftarrow F'\}$ wrt $\{\rightarrow_p, \rightarrow_f\}$ and with ε as computed answer substitution.

Now suppose the first step is an instantiation and paramodulation. Since instantiation can only be applied to a variable and in this case binds a variable occurring in F' we conclude that the first step in the refutation of $R \cup \{\Leftarrow F'\}$ must be a paramodulation step. Let P = $v \rightarrow w \Leftarrow F^*$ be the equational clause used in this step. Hence, we find an equation E' ∈ F', an occurrence $\pi \in Occ(E')$, and a substitution σ such that σ is the mgu of $E'|\pi|$ and v. Since the computed answer substitution of the refutation of $R \cup \{\Leftarrow F'\}$ wrt $\{\rightarrow_{ip}, \rightarrow_f\}$ is ε we conclude that $Dom(\sigma) \cap Var(F') = \emptyset$. Furthermore, since $E|\pi| = \sigma v$ and $v \rightarrow w \Leftarrow F^*$ is a new instance of a clause in R we find $Dom(\sigma) = Var(v)$. Let $F = F' \backslash \{E'\} \cup \{E'|\pi \leftarrow \sigma w|\} \cup \sigma F^*$. Hence, $\Leftarrow F' \rightarrow_p \Leftarrow F$ and since R is a term rewriting system we find $Var(F) \subseteq Var(F')$. By the induction hypothesis there exists a refutation of $R \cup \{\Leftarrow F\}$ wrt $\{\rightarrow_p, \rightarrow_f\}$ and with empty computed answer subsitution, which completes the proof.   qed

Since the instantiation rule is no longer needed to compute logical E-consequences from a ground confluent term rewriting system R we find that the p-success set of R is equal to the ip-success set of R.

Corollary 6.4.2:

If R is a ground confluent term rewriting system, then P-SS$_R$ = IP-SS$_R$.

Proof:

Obviously, P-SS$_R$ ⊆ IP-SS$_R$. Now if E ∈ IP-SS$_R$, then by the definition of the ip-success set we find a refutation of R∪{⇐E} wrt {→$_{ip}$, →$_f$} and with empty computed answer substitution. From lemma 6.4.1 we learn that there exists a refutation of R∪{⇐E} wrt {→$_p$, →$_f$} and with empty computed answer substitution and, thus, E ∈ P-SS$_R$.　　　qed

Notation:

A paramodulation step using a most general unifier θ and rewrite rule l→r⇐F, where Dom(θ) = Var(l), is often called a **rewriting** step, in symbols →$_R$, and θ is said to be a **(most general) matcher** for l and the respective subterm of the goal clause.

In figure 6.4.1 the rewriting rule is depicted.

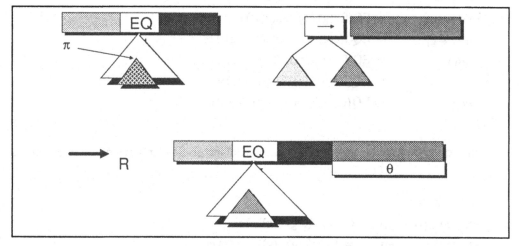

Figure 6.4.1: Rewriting

We introduced rewriting as a special form of paramodulation. Since the paramodulation rule uses the most general unifier of the selected subterm and the left-hand side of the equational clause, the rewriting rule uses the most general matcher of the selected subterm and the left-hand side of the equational clause. In the literature equational theories are sometimes handled in the opposite way by introducing at first rewriting (for arbitrary equational programs) and then generalizing rewriting to (some special form of) paramodulation (e.g. Gallier & Snyder 1987). However, to avoid the functional reflexive axioms or, equivalently, an instantiation rule, Gallier & Snyder do not require that the substitution θ used by the rewriting rule is a most general matcher of the selected subterm and the left-hand side of the rewrite rule. This was done on purpose to ensure the completeness of their calculus as can be seen in the following example. Consider the equational program

$$
\begin{array}{lll}
\textbf{GS:} & h_1 \rightarrow f(x,x) & \text{(h1)} \\
& h_2 \rightarrow d(x,x) & \text{(h2)} \\
& f(c(g),c(a)) \rightarrow d(c(g),c(a)) & \text{(f)} \\
& g \rightarrow a & \text{(g)}
\end{array}
$$

To solve the question of whether $EQ(h_1,h_2)$ is a logical E-consequence of GS we need the instantiation rule in our calculus:

$$
\begin{array}{ll}
\Leftarrow EQ(\textbf{h}_1,\textbf{h}_2) & \\
\rightarrow R(h1) & \Leftarrow EQ(f(x,x), \textbf{h}_2) \\
\rightarrow R(h2) & \Leftarrow EQ(f(x,x), d(x',x')) \\
\rightarrow i(\{x \rightarrow c(y)\}) & \Leftarrow EQ(f(c(y),c(y)), d(x',x')) \\
\rightarrow i(\{x' \rightarrow c(y')\}) & \Leftarrow EQ(f(c(y),c(y)), d(c(y'),c(y'))) \\
\rightarrow i(\{y \leftarrow g\}) & \Leftarrow EQ(f(c(g),c(g)), d(c(y'),c(y'))) \\
\rightarrow i(\{y' \leftarrow g\}) & \Leftarrow EQ(f(c(g),c(g)), d(c(g),c(g))) \\
\rightarrow R(g) & \Leftarrow EQ(f(c(g),c(a)), d(c(g),c(g))) \\
\rightarrow R(g) & \Leftarrow EQ(\textbf{f}(\textbf{c}(\textbf{g}),\textbf{c}(\textbf{a})), d(c(g),c(a))) \\
\rightarrow R(f) & \Leftarrow EQ(\textbf{d}(\textbf{c}(\textbf{g}),\textbf{c}(\textbf{a})), \textbf{d}(\textbf{c}(\textbf{g}),\textbf{c}(\textbf{a}))) \\
\rightarrow f & \quad \square
\end{array}
$$

The same question can be answered by using Gallier & Snyder's rewriting rule $\rightarrow R'$ as follows:

$$
\begin{array}{ll}
\Leftarrow EQ(\textbf{h}_1,\textbf{h}_2) & \\
\rightarrow R'((h1), \{x \leftarrow c(g)\}) & \Leftarrow EQ(f(c(g),c(g)), \textbf{h}_2) \\
\rightarrow R'((h2), \{x' \leftarrow c(g)\}) & \Leftarrow EQ(f(c(g),c(g)), d(c(g),c(g))) \\
\rightarrow R'(g) & \Leftarrow EQ(f(c(g),c(a)), d(c(g),c(g))) \\
\rightarrow R'(g) & \Leftarrow EQ(\textbf{f}(\textbf{c}(\textbf{g}),\textbf{c}(\textbf{a})), d(c(g),c(a))) \\
\rightarrow R'(f) & \Leftarrow EQ(\textbf{d}(\textbf{c}(\textbf{g}),\textbf{c}(\textbf{a})), \textbf{d}(\textbf{c}(\textbf{g}),\textbf{c}(\textbf{a}))) \\
\rightarrow f & \quad \square
\end{array}
$$

In the first as well as in the second step they have applied the matcher $\{x \leftarrow c(g)\}$ (resp. $\{x' \leftarrow c(g)\}$) which is not a most general one. Though the second refutation is shorter than the first one, it is not more efficient, since they have to guess the matcher in the same way as we have to guess the substitutions used by the instantiation rule in the first refutation. However, whereas we clearly presented the need for the instantiation rule, this fact is hidden in Gallier & Snyder's approach.

Corollary 6.4.2 ensures that logical E-consequence of a term rewriting system can be computed using rewriting and removal of trivial equations. Recall, removal of trivial equations is an inference rule (defined in section 3.4.1), which removes an equation of the form EQ(t,t) from a goal clause.

By combining the main results of sections 6.3 and 6.4 we obtain that for a ground confluent term rewriting system R the least Herbrand E-model, $M_E(R)$, the least fixpoint of T_R, and the p-success set of R are identical.

Corollary 6.4.3:

Let R be a ground confluent term rewriting system. Then
$$M_E(R) = lfp(T_R) = P\text{-}SS_R.$$

Proof:

$E \in M_E(R)$

iff $E \in lfp(T_{R \cup R\text{-}1})$ (corollaries 6.1.5 and 6.1.6)

iff $E \in lfp(T_R)$ (corollary 6.3.2)

iff $E \in IP\text{-}SS_R$ (corollaries 6.2.9(3) and 6.2.8)

iff $E \in P\text{-}SS_R$ (corollary 6.4.3)

                                                                                  qed

Figure 6.4.2 illustrates these results.

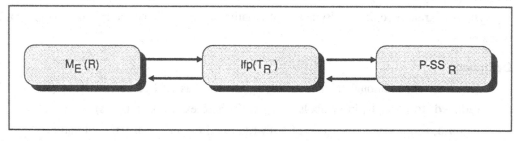

Figure 6.4.2

A rewriting step applied to an equation EQ(s,t) at an occurrence $1 \bullet \pi$ (resp. $2 \bullet \pi$) using a rewrite rule $l \to r$ and substitution θ replaces the term θl occurring in s (resp. t) at π by θr. As an example consider the term rewriting system

SUM:	sum([]) $\to$ 0	(s1)
	sum(x:y) $\to$ x+sum(y)	(s2)
	0+y $\to$ y	(+1)
	s(x)+y $\to$ s(x+y)	(+2)

which computes the sum of the elements of a list of natural numbers. To test whether the sum of the list containing the elements 3 and 5 is equal to 8 we can apply rewriting ($\to$R) and removal of trivial equations ($\to$t) to the goal clause $\Leftarrow$EQ(sum(3:5:[]),8) thus obtaining the refutation

$$\Leftarrow \text{EQ(sum(3:5:[]), 8)} \to_{R(s2)} \quad \Leftarrow \text{EQ(3+sum(5:[]), 8)}$$
$$\to_{R(s2)} \quad \Leftarrow \text{EQ(3+5+sum([]), 8)}$$
$$\to_{R(s1)} \quad \Leftarrow \text{EQ(3+5+0, 8)}$$
$$\to_{R}* \quad \Leftarrow \text{EQ(8,8)}$$
$$\to_t \quad \square.$$

In this refutation we replaced, for example, the term sum(3:5:[]) by the term 3+sum(5:[]). These two terms denote the same since they are an instance of a rewrite rule, i.e. an instance of an axiom in the equational theory defined by SUM. Furthermore, these term replacements in the left-hand (resp. right-hand) side of an equation are neither influenced nor do they affect other terms in the equation except the selected subterm. This is often called **referential transperency** and is due to the variable condition satisfied by term rewriting systems. It should be noted that only the application of removal of trivial equations terminates a derivation.

All these observations suggest to apply term rewriting only to terms. Then the test whether two terms are equal consists of finding a new term such that both terms can be rewritten to the new one. By corollary 6.4.3 such a term, however, can only be found if the term rewriting system is ground confluent. By abuse of notation we also denote the rewrite relation on terms by $\to$**R**.

Definition:

Given an unconditional term rewriting system R, s is said to be **rewritten** (or **reduced**) **to** t **wrt R**, in symbols s $\to$R t, iff there exist a $\pi \in$ Occ(s), a substitution σ, and a new variant l$\to$r of a rewrite rule in R such that s$|\pi|$ = σl and t = s$|\pi\leftarrow\sigma$r$|$.

Since R is an unconditional term rewriting system containing only finitely many rewrite rules Occ(s) is finite and, since the matching problem is decidable, it follows immediately that $\to$R is decidable.

For notational convenience, we write $\to$ instead of $\to$R if R can be determined by the context. In our example,

$$\text{sum(3:5:[])} \to \text{3+sum(5:[])} \to \text{3+5+sum([])} \to \text{3+5+0} \to* 8.$$

8 is sometimes called the **value** of sum(3:5:[]).

It is more complicated if we consider conditional term rewriting systems instead of unconditional ones. If the term rewriting system is unconditional then a rewriting applied to an equation also introduces new equations, namely the conditions of the rewrite rule used. If rewriting is applied to terms, then we have to show that these conditions are logical E-consequences of the conditional term rewriting system under consideration before the conditional rewrite rule is applied. This does not violate the refutation-completeness of rewriting and removal of trivial equations since each equation in a goal clause can be checked independently:

Corollary 6.4.4:

Let SEL be a selection function. If there exists a refutation of $R \cup \{\Leftarrow F\}$ wrt
$\{\to_R, \to_t\}$, then there exists a refutation of $R \cup \{\Leftarrow F\}$ wrt $\{\to_R, \to_t\}$ via SEL.

Proof:

If there exists a refutation of $R \cup \{\Leftarrow F\}$ wrt $\{\to_R, \to_t\}$, then for each $E \in F$ we find a refutation of $R \cup \{\Leftarrow E\}$ wrt $\{\to_R, \to_t\}$. Clearly, these refutations can be combined such that ϵ is an SEL-computed answer substitution obtained by a refutation of $R \cup \{\Leftarrow F\}$ wrt $\{\to_R, \to_t\}$.   qed

Thus, we may apply a selection function which recursively selects an equation from the conditions of the most recently used conditional rewrite rule if such conditions exist. Corollary 6.4.4 ensures the completeness of refutations with respect to rewriting and removal of trivial equations via such a selection function.

Definition:

Given a conditional term rewriting system R, s is said to be **rewritten** (or **reduced**) to t wrt **R**, in symbols $s \to_R t$, if there exist $\pi \in Occ(s)$, a substitution σ, and a new variant $l \to r \Leftarrow F$ of a rewrite rule in R such that $s|\pi| = \sigma l$, $t = s|\pi \leftarrow \sigma r|$, and each ground instance of σF is a subset of P-SS$_R$.

It was shown by Kaplan (1984) that there exists a conditional term rewriting system R such that $\to_R$ is undecidable.

There are other definitions of rewriting with respect to conditional term rewriting systems which differ in the way the conditions of a rewrite rule are treated. For an overview see (Bergstra & Klop 1986). Since we are mainly interested in equation solving in this thesis, the above definition satisfies our needs.

Definition:

A term rewriting system R is **regular** iff for all $l \to r \Leftarrow F$ in R we have $Var(l) = Var(r) \cup Var(F)$.

The term rewriting system SUM, for example, is regular.

Definition:

s is called a **redex** wrt the term rewriting system R iff there exists a new variant
$l \rightarrow r \Leftarrow F$ of a rule in R and a substitution σ such that each ground instance of σF
is a subset of P-SS$_R$ and $s = \sigma l$. $s|\pi|$ is called the **selected redex** in the reduction
from s to t iff $s \rightarrow_{(\pi)} t$ and $s|\pi|$ is called an **innermost redex** if there does not
exist a $\pi' \in Occ(s)$ such that $\pi' < \pi$ and $s|\pi'|$ is a redex.

As an example consider again the term rewriting system SUM. Then

$0+\mathbf{sum}(3:[]) \rightarrow 0+(3+\mathbf{sum}([])) \rightarrow 0+(3+0) \rightarrow^* 3.$

$0+sum(3:[])$ and $sum(3:[])$ a redeces, but only $sum(3:[])$ is an innermost redex and is also the
selected redex.

Definition:

t is in **normal form** (or **irreducible**) wrt a term rewriting system R iff s does not
contain any redex wrt R. If $s \rightarrow^* t$ and t is in normal form wrt R, then t is called
normal form of s wrt R.

We often write normal form instead of normal form with respect to R if R can be determined from the context.

In our previous example $0+sum(3:[])$ is not in normal form, However, 3 is the normal
form of $0+sum(3:[])$. There are term rewriting systems and terms such that there does not
exist a normal form of these terms. For example consider the term rewriting system R =
$\{g \rightarrow g\}$ and the term g. Also, the normal form of a term is not necessarily unique. For
example consider the term rewriting system

NC: $a \rightarrow b$

$a \rightarrow c$

and the term a. In this case b and c are normal forms of a. Note, EQ(b,c) is not an element
of the p-success set of NC and NC is not ground confluent. However, it is an immediate consequence of corollary 6.4.2 that, if a term has a normal form with respect to a ground confluent conditional term rewriting system, then this normal form is unique.

Corollary 6.4.5:

*Let R be a ground confluent term rewriting system. If there is a normal form of a
term wrt R, then it is unique.*

Proof:

Suppose by contradiction that u and v are distinct normal forms of the term t. Furthermore, suppose EQ(u,v) contains the variables $x_1, ..., x_n$. Let $a_1, ..., a_n$ be distinct constants

not appearing in $EQ(u,v)$ and R and let θ be the substitution $\{x_i \leftarrow a_i \mid 1 \leq i \leq n\}$. Clearly, $\theta EQ(u,v)$ is a logical E-consequence of R. Since $\theta EQ(u,v)$ is ground, $\theta EQ(u,v) \in M_E(R)$. From corollary 6.4.3 we learn that $\theta EQ(u,v) \in$ P-SSR since R is ground confluent. By definition, there exists a refutation of $R \cup \{ \Leftarrow \theta EQ(u,v)\}$ wrt term rewriting and removal of trivial equations. Term rewriting is not applicable since u as well as v are already in normal form and the elements of the codomain of θ are irreducible and do not occur anywhere else. Hence, we have to apply removal of trivial equations. This inference rule, however, is only applicable to trivial equations, contradicting the assumption that $u \neq v$. qed

The following technical lemma shows that whenever a term s can be reduced to a term t any instance of s can also be reduced to the respective instance of t.

Lemma 6.4.6:

   If $s \rightarrow_R^* t$ then $\sigma s \rightarrow_R^* \sigma t$.

Proof:

   The proof is by induction on the length n of the reduction sequence $s \rightarrow_R^* t$. The case $n=0$ being trivial we turn to the induction step and assume that

$$s' \rightarrow s \rightarrow^n t \tag{1}$$

Hence, there exist a $\pi \in Occ(s')$, a substitution θ, and a new instance $l \rightarrow r \Leftarrow F$ of a rewrite rule in R such that $\theta l = s'|\pi|$, each ground instance of θF is a subset of P-SSR, and $s = s'|\pi \leftarrow \theta r|$. Therefore,

$$\sigma(\theta l) = \sigma(s'|\pi|) \tag{2}$$

and

$$\sigma s = \sigma(s'|\pi \leftarrow \theta r|). \tag{3}$$

Without loss of generality we may assume that l and $\sigma s'$ have no variables in common. Applying proposition 2.2.1(2) to the left-hand side and proposition 2.2.3(2) to the right-hand side of (2) we receive

$$(\sigma\theta)l = (\sigma s')|\pi|. \tag{4}$$

Similarily, applying proposition 2.2.3(3) to the right-hand side of (3) we receive

$$\sigma s = (\sigma s')|\pi \leftarrow (\sigma\theta)r|. \tag{5}$$

Hence,

$$\sigma s' \rightarrow_{(\pi, \sigma\theta, l \rightarrow r \Leftarrow F)} \sigma s$$

and from (1) and the induction hypothesis we conclude

$$\sigma s' \rightarrow \sigma s \rightarrow^n \sigma t. \qquad \text{qed}$$

In the reduction from σs to σt rewriting is performed at the same occurrences and uses the same rewrite rules as in the reduction from s to t. It should be noted that $\sigma s \rightarrow^* \sigma t$ does not imply $s \rightarrow^* t$. As an example consider the term rewriting system $\{0+y \rightarrow y\}$, the term $s =$

x+y, and the substitution σ = {x←0}. Then, σs = 0+y → y = σt. However, x+y is in normal form. Also, if t is the normal form of s, then σt is not necessarily the normal form of σs. As an example consider again the term rewriting system {0+y→y}, the term s = x+y, and the substitution σ = {x←0}. s is in normal form whereas σs = 0+y can be reduced to y.

Remark:

Lemma 6.4.6 holds also for rewriting applied to goal clauses.

Definition:

A term rewriting system R is said to be **Noetherian** (or **terminating**) iff for no t there is an infinite sequence of reductions issuing from t.

Huet & Lankford (1978) showed that it is undecidable whether an arbitrary term rewriting system is Noetherian by reducing this problem to the Halting Problem of Turing machines. However, the problem is decidable for ground terms. For a survey on various methods to prove the termination of a term rewriting system see Huet & Oppen (1980).

The fundamental difference between equations and rewrite rules is that equations are undirected whereas rewrite rules are directed. Furthermore, the only substitutions required for term rewriting are those which substitute variables in the left-hand side of a rewrite rule in order to make it equal to a given term. These substitutions are called matchers.

From corollary 6.4.5 we conclude that a terminating conditional term rewriting system R induces a complete decision procedure for the equality of two terms under R if it is ground confluent. Let us now give the formal definition of confluence with respect to →R.

Definition:

A term rewriting system R is **confluent** (resp. **ground confluent**) iff for all terms (resp. ground terms) s, t, u such that u →* s and u →* t there exists a term v such that s →* v and t →* v. Further, R is said to be **locally confluent** iff for all s, t, u such that u → s and u → t there exists a term v such that s →* v and t →* v.

It should be noted that ground confluence implies confluence and vice versa.

Proposition 6.4.7:

Let R be a term rewriting system. R is confluent iff R is ground confluent.

Proof:

The only-if-half is trivial. The if-half is shown by contradiction. Suppose R is ground confluent and not confluent. Hence, we find terms s, u, v such that

$$s \rightarrow^* u \text{ and } s \rightarrow^* v \tag{1}$$

and there does not exist a term t such that

$$u \rightarrow^* t \text{ and } v \rightarrow^* t. \tag{2}$$

From (1) we learn that EQ(u,v) is a logical E-consequence of R. Let $Var(\{u, v, s\}) = \{x_i \mid 1 \le i \le n\}$ and $a_1, ..., a_n$ be distinct constants not appearing in R, u, v, and s. Furthermore, let $\theta = \{x_i \leftarrow a_i \mid 1 \le i \le n\}$. Clearly, $\theta EQ(u,v)$ is a logical E-consequence of R and from (1) and lemma 6.4.6 we conclude that

$$\theta s \rightarrow^* \theta u \text{ and } \theta s \rightarrow^* \theta v.$$

Since R is ground confluent we find a term t' such that

$$\theta u \rightarrow^* t' \text{ and } \theta v \rightarrow^* t'. \tag{3}$$

Since the a_i, $1 \le i \le n$, do not occur in R, s, u, and v, by textually replacing each a_i by x_i, $1 \le i \le n$, in (3) we find a term t such that $t' = \theta t$ and

$$u \rightarrow^* t \text{ and } v \rightarrow^* t,$$

which contradicts (2) and, thus, R is confluent.   qed

Proposition 6.4.7 holds only since we have made the assumption that the set of function symbols of an alphabet associated with an equational logic program ELP contains all function symbols occurring in ELP but not vice versa (see section 3.1). If we assume that each function symbol occurring in the alphabet occurs also in our program, then proposition 6.4.7 is no longer valid. The following example is due to J. Gallier and W. Snyder. Consider the terminating term rewriting system

R: $f(x) \rightarrow g(x)$
   $f(x) \rightarrow h(x)$
   $f(a) \rightarrow a$
   $g(a) \rightarrow a$
   $h(a) \rightarrow a.$

Clearly, R is ground confluent, but f(x) admits the two distinct normal forms g(x) and h(x).

Recall, if a term rewriting system is confluent then each term t has at most one normal form. If it is confluent and Noetherian, then in order to decide whether two terms s and t are equal under R simply reduce s and t to their normal forms and test whether these normal forms are literally identical. This means that for any multiset F of equations, derivations of $R \cup \{\Leftarrow F\}$ with respect to term rewriting and removal of trivial equations are always finite, if R is confluent and Noetherian.

It is undecidable whether an arbitrary unconditional term rewriting system is confluent. However, there exists a decision procedure for this problem if the term rewriting system is unconditional and terminating (Knuth & Bendix 1970), which we define in the sequel. First, we need the following theorem which establishes a relationship between confluence and local confluence.

Theorem 6.4.8 (Newman 1942):

A Noetherian unconditional term rewriting system is confluent iff it is locally confluent.

Definition:

Let l→r and l'→r' be two rewrite rules of a term rewriting system R. Assume that variables are appropriately renamed such that l and l' have no variables in common. If there exists a non-variable occurrence π in l and an mgu σ such that $\sigma l|\pi| = \sigma l'$ then the pair $<\sigma(l|\pi \leftarrow r'|), \sigma r>$ is said to be **critical** in R.

Since each term rewriting system is finite, there are only finitely many critical pairs, which can effectively be computed by using, for example, the unification algorithm presented in section 3.4.1.

As an example consider the term rewriting systems

APPEND:	append([],z) → z	(a1)
	append(x:y,z) → x:append(y,z)	(a2)

and

APPEND':	append([],z) → z	(a1)
	append(x:y,z) → x:append(y,z)	(a2)
	append(w,[]) → w	(a3)

It is easy to see that both term rewriting systems are Noetherian. APPEND does not contain a critical pair, since no substitution can make [] and x:y identical. However, in APPEND' the substitution {w←[], z←[]} (resp. {w←x:y, z←[]}) makes the left-hand sides of (a1) and (a3) (resp. (a2) and(a3)) identical. Hence, we obtain the critical pairs <[], []> and <x:y, x:append(y,[])>.

Theorem 6.4.9 (Knuth & Bendix 1970):

An unconditional term rewriting system R is locally confluent iff the normal forms of s and t are identical for every critical pair $<s,t>$ of R.

Combining theorems 6.6.8 and 6.6.9 gives a decision procedure for the property of confluency of Noetherian term rewriting systems. This procedure is often called **superposition algorithm**.

Coming back to our previous example we have to investigate the critical pairs <[], []> and <x:y, x:append(y,[])> in APPEND'. [] and x:y are in normal form and x:**append(y,[])** →(a3) x:y. An application of Theorem 6.4.9 shows that APPEND' is also confluent.

Since in this thesis we will only have to show that an unconditional term rewriting system is confluent, we do not present the details of a superposition algorithm for conditional term rewriting systems (see Bergstra & Klop 1986 and Kaplan 1986).

Definition:

> A confluent and Noetherian term rewriting system is said to be **canonical** (or a **complete set of reductions**).

Definition:

> An equational clause EQ(s,t)⇐F is a **trivial clause** iff s is a variable. An equational program is **trivial** (resp. **non-trivial**) iff it does (resp. does not) contain a trivial clause.

Observe, EP = {a→x} is non-trivial, whereas EP^{-1} = {x→a} is trivial. A rewrite rule l→r⇐F is a **trivial rule**, if l is a variable, and a term rewriting system is **trivial** iff it contains a trivial rule.

If a term rewriting system contains a trivial rule, then rewriting may be applied to variable occurrences. As an example consider the term rewriting system

> **TRIV:** x→a

and the term y. Then,

> y →R a →R a ...

is an infinite sequence, whose first reduction was applied to y. It is easy to see that if a term rewriting system is trivial then it cannot be Noetherian.

In the following proposition we show that logical E-consequence of a non-trivial and confluent term rewriting system can be proved without paying attention to variable occurrences.

Proposition 6.4.10:

> *Let R be a non-trivial and confluent term rewriting system and SEL be a selection function. If E is a logical E-consequence of R, then there exists a refutation of R∪{⇐E} wrt {→R, →t} and via SEL. Furthermore, in that refutation rewriting was never applied to a variable occurrence.*

Proof:

If E is a logical E-consequence of R, then we learn from corollaries 6.4.3 and 6.4.4 that there exists a refutation of R∪{⇐E} wrt {→R, →t} and via SEL. Now suppose that rewriting was applied to a variable occurrence in that refutation. Without loss of generality we may assume that the first step was rewriting applied to some variable occurrence $\pi \in \text{Occ}(E)$. Let $l \rightarrow r \Leftarrow F$ be a new variant of a rewrite rule and σ be the mgu used in the first step. Since the refutation computes ϵ as answer substitution we find $\text{Dom}(\sigma) \cap \text{Var}(E) = \varnothing$. Hence, $\sigma l = E|\pi|$. Therefore, l must be a variable contradicting the assumption that R is non-trivial.   qed

Proposition 6.4.10 does not hold if we drop the condition that R is non-trivial. As an example consider the term rewriting system TRIV and the equation EQ(y,a).

$$\Leftarrow EQ(y,a) \; \rightarrow_R(\{x \leftarrow y\}) \; \Leftarrow EQ(a,a) \; \rightarrow_t \; \square$$

is a refutation of $\text{TRIV} \cup \{\Leftarrow EQ(y,a)\}$ with respect to rewriting and removal of trivial equations. However, rewriting was applied to a variable occurrence.

This proposition will be important if we lift this result in section 6.5.

If a term rewriting system is non-trivial then it contains only rewrite rules of the form $f(t_1,\ldots,t_n) \rightarrow r \Leftarrow F$ and vice versa. Non-trivial term rewriting systems divide the set of function symbols in those symbols, who occur as the initial symbol of the left-hand side of the head of a rewrite rule, and other function symbols.

Definition:

> If $f(t_1,\ldots,t_n) \rightarrow r \Leftarrow F$ is a rewrite rule in R, then f is called the **name** of the rewrite rule. The set of all rewrite rules with the same name f in R is called the **definition** of f.

For example, the term rewriting system SUM contains the definition for *sum* and +.

Definition:

> Given a non-trivial term rewriting system R and a set of function symbols FS.
> The set of **defined function symbols** wrt R is defined as
> > { f ∈ FS | R contains a definition for f }
>
> and the set of **constructors** is defined as
> > { f ∈ FS | R does not contain a definition for f }

In the term rewriting system SUM we find the defined function symbols *sum* and + and the constructors :, [], *0*, and *s*. The constructors are used to build the data structures "list" and "natural numbers", whereas the defined function symbols define functions on these data structures. Clearly, each constructor is a decomposable function symbol (see section 6.2) but not vice versa.

Lemma 6.4.11:

If F contains an equation of the form $EQ(c(s_1,...,s_n), c'(t_1,...,t_n))$, where c and c'
are different constructors, then there does not exist a refutation of $R \cup \{\Leftarrow F\}$ wrt
$\{\rightarrow_p, \rightarrow_f\}$.

Proof:

The result is proved by contradiction. If F contains an equation of the form $EQ(c(s_1,...,s_n),$
$c'(t_1,...,t_n))$, where c and c' are different constructors, and if there exists a refutation of
$R \cup \{\Leftarrow F\}$ wrt $\{\rightarrow_p, \rightarrow_f\}$ and computed answer substitution σ, then $\sigma EQ(c(s_1,...,s_n),$
$c'(t_1,...,t_n))$ is a logical E-consequence of R. By corollary 6.4.3 there exists a refutation of
$R \cup \{\Leftarrow \sigma EQ(c(s_1,...,s_n), c'(t_1,...,t_n))\}$ wrt $\{\rightarrow_p, \rightarrow_f\}$ with ε as computed answer substitution.
Since c and c' are constructors paramodulation cannot be applied to $\sigma c(s_1,...,s_n)$ or
$\sigma c'(t_1,...,t_n)$ for any s_i, t_i, $1 \le i \le n$. Furthermore, since $c \ne c'$ reflection cannot be applied as the
final step of a derivation, which contradicts the assumption that there exists a refutation of
$R \cup \{\Leftarrow F\}$ wrt $\{\rightarrow_p, \rightarrow_f\}$. qed

Lemma 6.4.11 does not hold if we assume that c and c' are different decomposable function symbols. As an example consider the term rewriting system

MINUS: $-(-x) \rightarrow x$

and the equation $EQ(-(-0), 0)$. - and 0 are different decomposable function symbols (Kirch-
ner 1984). However, there exists a refutation of $MINUS \cup \{\Leftarrow EQ(-(-0), 0)\}$ wrt $\{\rightarrow_p, \rightarrow_f\}$:

$\Leftarrow EQ(-(-0), 0) \rightarrow_p \Leftarrow EQ(0,0) \rightarrow_f \square$.

Now we come back to the question of whether there exists a substitution such that the respective instance of a set of equations is a logical E-consequence of a given term rewriting
system. Recall, that for a ground confluent term rewriting systems R the least Herbrand E-
model for R, the least fixpoint of T_R, and the p-success set of R are identical (corollary
6.4.3). However, a theorem prover based on paramodulation and reflection and using clauses
from a confluent term rewriting system still generates many redundant and irrelevant derivations. This is especially the case if the "selected" occurrence is a variable occurrence. In this
case paramodulation has to be applied using as input clause each rewrite rule from the term
rewriting system and, in addition, each instantiation sequence has to be considered. Hence,
the search space would be considerably pruned if refutation completeness could be achieved
without selecting a variable occurrence. In this case the instantiation rule is no longer
needed.

6.5 Narrowing

As we demonstrated in the previous section, confluent conditional term rewriting systems have many desirable properties if we consider only ground terms and equation. In this section we investigate under which conditions we can lift these results without the need of the instantiation rule. Obviously, this rule is only needed if we apply paramodulation to a variable occurrence. But, what happens if we restrict paramodulation to be applicable only to non-variable occurrences?

Definition:

$\Leftarrow$F' is a **narrowing** from $\Leftarrow$F, in symbols $\Leftarrow$F $\rightarrow$n(E, π, P, σ) $\Leftarrow$F',

if $\Leftarrow$F $\rightarrow$p(E, π, P, σ) $\Leftarrow$F' and E|π| is not a variable.

Hence, each narrowing step is a paramodulation step, but only paramodulation steps applied to a non-variable occurrence are narrowing steps. This seems to be an unusual definition of narrowing. Narrowing was first defined by Slagle (1974) and Lankford (1975) in the context of canonical and unconditional term rewriting systems. There, narrowing was defined to be paramodulation at non-variable terms followed by a sequence of rewriting steps to normalize the clauses. A similar definition can be found by Fay (1979). Later Hullot (1980) defined narrowing to be only paramodulation at non-variable terms. Since all these papers were concerned with canonical and unconditional term rewriting systems, narrowing was always "directed" in the sense that only the left-hand side of a rewrite rule was replaced by its right-hand side. Recall, that our goal was to impose conditions one-by-one on the equational program to prune the search space generated by paramodulation, but that we want to be as general as possible. So far we considered confluent term rewriting systems. Hence, our definition of narrowing can be seen in the context of "directed" equational programs. As we will show, we do not need the termination of the term rewriting system to show the completeness of narrowing, but only the fact that each answer substitution must be normalizable.

Since instantiation can only be applied to a variable occurrence, we find that narrowing can never be preceded by a sequence of instantiation steps. In figure 6.5.1 we depicted the narrowing rule.

As an example consider the canonical term rewriting system

  IDEM: $f(x,x) \rightarrow x$

which specifies the idempotence of f. Then,

 $\Leftarrow$ EQ(f(x,y), f(a,x)) $\rightarrow$n({x$\leftarrow$y}) $\Leftarrow$ EQ(x, f(a,x)) $\rightarrow$n({x$\leftarrow$a}) $\Leftarrow$ EQ(a,a) $\rightarrow$f $\square$.

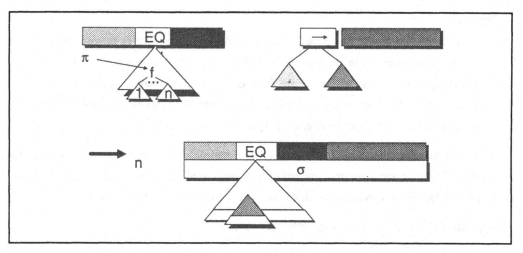

Figure 6.5.1: Narrowing

It is easy to see that narrowing and reflection is generally incomplete. As an example consider the equation EQ(x,c(x)) and the confluent term rewriting system

INFINITE: f → c(f).

{x←f} is a correct answer substitution for INFINITE∪{⇐EQ(x,c(x))}. EQ(x,c(x)) contains only two non-variable occurrences, namely Λ and 2. However, c(x) and f are not unifiable. Hence, narrowing is not applicable to ⇐EQ(x,c(x)). Furthermore, since x occurs in c(x), reflection is also not applicable. It follows that there does not exist a refutation of INFINITE∪{⇐EQ(x,c(x))} with respect to narrowing and reflection.

What condition has to be imposed on a term rewriting system such that completeness of narrowing and reflection can be obtained? From corollary 6.4.3 we learn that logical E-consequence with respect to a confluent term rewriting system R can be computed using only rewrite rules from R. Proposition 6.4.10 ensures that in a refutation of R∪{⇐σE} with respect to rewriting and removal of trivial equations, rewriting was never applied to a variable occurrence if R is non-trivial and σE is a logical E-consequence of R. Hence, by the lifting lemma for reflection, instantiation and paramodulation (lemma 6.2.6), paramodulation has to be applied to a variable occurrence in ⇐E only if rewriting was applied to ⇐σE to a term that was introduced by σ. Now, if σ does not introduce a term which can be matched by a left-hand side of a rewrite rule, we obtain a completeness result for narrowing and reflection. Before we will give a formal proof of this result, we introduce the notion of a normalized substitution.

Definition:

> Let R be a term rewriting system. A substitution θ is said to be in **normal form wrt R** iff each term t in the codomain of θ is in normal form wrt R. If θ is in normal form wrt R and was obtained from σ by rewriting some terms in the codomain of σ, then θ is said to be the **normal form of σ wrt R**. σ is said to be **normalizable wrt R** if there exists a normal form of σ wrt R.

For notational convenience we omit "wrt R" if it can be determined from the context. As an example consider again the term rewriting system IDEM. Then $\theta = \{x \leftarrow f(y,z)\}$ is not in normal form. However, θ is normalizable since $\{x \leftarrow y\}$ is the normal form of θ.

Proposition 6.5.1 states some frequently used results.

Proposition 6.5.1:

> *Let R be a term rewriting system.*
>
> *(1) If t is in normal form and $\sigma s = t$, then $\sigma|_{Var(s)}$ is in normal form.*
>
> *(2) If $\delta s = \theta t$, $Var(s) \cap Var(t) = \varnothing$, $Dom(\delta) \cap Dom(\theta) = \varnothing$, $Dom(\theta) = Var(t)$, and δ is in normal form, then there exist an mgu σ of s and t and a substitution λ such that $\lambda\sigma = \delta \cup \theta$ and λ is in normal form.*
>
> *(3) If δ is a unifier for s and t in normal form, then we find substitutions θ and λ such that θ is an mgu of s and t, $\lambda\theta = \delta$, $Dom(\lambda) \cap Dom(\theta) = \varnothing$, and θ as well as λ are in normal form.*

Proof:

(1) If $\sigma|_{Var(s)}$ is not in normal form, then we find a binding $x \leftarrow u$ in $\sigma|_{Var(s)}$ such that u is not in normal form. Since $x \in Var(s)$ we conclude that σs contains u contradicting the assumption that $\sigma s = t$ is in normal form.

(2) Suppose $\delta s = \theta t$. Since $Dom(\delta) \cap Dom(\theta) = \varnothing$ we conclude that $\delta \cup \theta$ is a unifier for s and t. By theorem 3.4.1.2 we find an mgu σ of s and t and by the definition of an mgu we find a substitution λ such that $\lambda\sigma = \delta \cup \theta$. We may assume that $Dom(\lambda) \cap Dom(\sigma) = \varnothing$. It remains to show that λ is in normal form. Let $x \in Dom(\lambda)$. We distinguish two cases:

If $x \in Dom(\delta)$, then

$$\lambda x = \lambda\sigma x = (\delta \cup \theta)x = \delta x$$

and since δ is in normal form we find that λx is in normal form.

If $x \in Dom(\theta)$, then,

$$\lambda x = \lambda\sigma x = (\delta \cup \theta)x = \theta x. \tag{*}$$

Since $\text{Dom}(\theta) = \text{Var}(t)$ and $\text{Var}(s) \cap \text{Var}(t) = \varnothing$ we find that $x \in \text{Var}(t)$ and $x \notin \text{Var}(s)$. Recall, $\text{Dom}(\sigma) \cap \text{Dom}(\lambda) = \varnothing$ implies that $x \notin \text{Dom}(\sigma)$. Furthermore, since σ is an mgu for s and t we find a variable $y \in \text{Var}(s)$ and a binding $y \leftarrow x \in \sigma$. From $\delta s = \theta t$ and (*) we conclude that

$$\lambda x = \theta x = \delta y$$

and since δ is in normal form, λx must also be in normal form.

(3)   Suppose δ is a unifier for s and t in normal form. By theorem 3.4.1.2 we find an mgu θ for s and t and by the definition of an mgu we find also a substitution λ such that $\lambda\theta$ $= \delta$. We may assume that $\text{Dom}(\theta) \cap \text{Dom}(\lambda) = \varnothing$. λ is in normal form since for all $x \in$ $\text{Dom}(\lambda)$ we find $\lambda x = \delta x$. It remains to show that θ is in normal form. Suppose θ is not in normal form. Then we find a binding $x \leftarrow u \in \theta$, an occurrence $\pi \in \text{Occ}(u)$, a new variant P of a rewrite rule in R, and a term v such that $u \rightarrow_{(P,\pi)} v$. By lemma 6.4.6 we learn that

$$\delta x = \lambda\theta x = \lambda u \rightarrow_{(P,\,\pi)} \lambda v,$$

which contradicts the assumption that δ is in normal form.   qed

Even if t and σ are not in normal form, we cannot conclude that σt is in normal form. As an example consider the term rewriting system $\{f(a) \rightarrow b\}$, the term $t = f(x)$ and the substitution $\sigma = \{x \leftarrow a\}$. Clearly, t as well as σ are in normal form, but $\sigma t = f(a)$ can be rewritten to b. Furthermore, under the conditions of proposition 6.5.1(2) we cannot conlude that σ is also in normal form. As an example consider the confluent term rewriting system

INNER: $f(x,a) \rightarrow b$ (f)

$\qquad\qquad g \rightarrow g$ (g)

the terms $s = f(g,y)$ and $t = f(x,a)$, the normalized substitution $\delta = \{y \leftarrow a\}$, and the substitution $\theta = \{x \leftarrow g\}$. Obviously, θ is not in normal form and is also not normalizable. The conditions of proposition 6.5.1(2) are fulfilled since $\delta s = f(g,a) = \theta t$. However, the most general unifier of s and t is the substitution $\sigma = \{x \leftarrow g, y \leftarrow a\} = \delta \cup \theta$, which is not in normal form and is also not normalizable.

We now give a lifting lemma for narrowing and reflection provided that R is a non-trivial term rewriting system. It should be noted that this lifting lemma is a special case of the lifting lemma 6.2.6 for reflection, instantiation and paramodulation.

Lemma 6.5.2 (Lifting Lemma for Narrowing and Reflection):

Let R be a non-trivial term rewriting system, SEL be a selection function and δ be a substitution in normal form. If $R \cup \{\Leftarrow \delta F\}$ has a refutation wrt $\{\to_R, \to_t\}$ of length n and via SEL, then $R \cup \{\Leftarrow F\}$ has a refutation wrt $\{\to_n, \to_f\}$ of length n and via SEL. Furthermore, if $\theta_1, \ldots, \theta_n$ are the substitutions used in the refutation of $R \cup \{\Leftarrow \delta F\}$ and $\sigma_1, \ldots, \sigma_n$ are the mgus used in the refutation of $R \cup \{\Leftarrow F\}$, then $\theta_n \ldots \theta_1 \delta \leq \sigma_n \ldots \sigma_1$.

Proof:

The proof is by induction on the length n of the refutation of $R \cup \{\Leftarrow \delta F\}$. The case n=0 being trivial we turn to the induction step and assume the result holds for n. Suppose that

$$\Leftarrow \delta'F' \to \; \Leftarrow \delta F \tag{1}$$

and that there exists a refutation of $R \cup \{\Leftarrow \delta F\}$ of length n and via SEL. Let F' be of the form $F^+ \cup \{E\}$ and let E = EQ(s,t) be the selected equation in (1). We distinguish two cases.

If removal of a trivial equation has been applied in (1), then δ' is a unifier for s and t. Hence, we find an mgu σ for s and t and a substitution δ such that $\delta' = \delta\sigma$, $Dom(\delta) \cap Dom(\sigma) = \varnothing$, and δ is in normal form (proposition 6.5.1(3)). Hence, $F = \sigma F^+$ and we find that

$$\Leftarrow F' \to_{f(\sigma)} \Leftarrow F.$$

From the induction hypothesis we learn that there exists a refutation of $R \cup \{\Leftarrow F\}$ wrt $\{\to_n, \to_f\}$ of length n and via SEL. Furthermore, if $\theta_1, \ldots, \theta_n$ are the substitutions used in the refutation of $R \cup \{\Leftarrow \delta F\}$ and $\sigma_1, \ldots, \sigma_n$ are the mgus used in the refutation of $R \cup \{\Leftarrow F\}$ then

$$\theta_n \ldots \theta_1 \delta \leq \sigma_n \ldots \sigma_1.$$

Clearly, there exists a refutation of $R \cup \{\Leftarrow F'\}$ wrt $\{\to_n, \to_f\}$ of length n+1 and via SEL using mgus $\sigma, \sigma_1, \ldots, \sigma_n$. Furthermore, by proposition 4.3(6),

$$\theta_n \ldots \theta_1 \varepsilon \delta' = \theta_n \ldots \theta_1 \delta\sigma \leq \sigma_n \ldots \sigma_1 \sigma.$$

If rewriting was applied to occurrence $\pi \in Occ(\delta'E)$ in (1) using $l \to r \Leftarrow F^*$, then we find a substitution θ such that $\delta'E|\pi| = \theta l$. Since δ' is in normal form $\pi \in Occ(E)$. Furthermore, since R is non-trivial, π must be a non-variable occurrence in E by proposition 6.4.10. Since $l \to r \Leftarrow F^*$ was a new variant of a rewrite rule we may assume that $Dom(\delta') \cap Dom(\theta) = \varnothing$ and $Dom(\theta) = Var(l)$. By proposition 6.5.1(2) we find an mgu σ for $E|\pi|$ and l and a substitution δ such that $\delta\sigma = \theta \cup \delta' = \theta\delta'$ and δ is in normal form. Hence, $F = \sigma(F^+ \cup \{E|\pi \leftarrow r|\} \cup F^*)$ and we conclude

$$\Leftarrow F' \to_{n(\sigma)} \Leftarrow F.$$

From the induction hypothesis we learn that there exists a refutation of $R \cup \{\Leftarrow F\}$ wrt $\{\rightarrow_n,$ $\rightarrow_f\}$ of length n and via SEL. Furthermore, if $\theta_1, \ldots, \theta_n$ are the substitutions used in the refutation of $R \cup \{\Leftarrow \delta F\}$ and $\sigma_1, \ldots, \sigma_n$ are the mgus used in the refutation of $R \cup \{\Leftarrow F\}$, then

$$\theta_n \ldots \theta_1 \delta \leq \sigma_n \ldots \sigma_1.$$

Clearly, there exists a refutation of $R \cup \{\Leftarrow F'\}$ wrt $\{\rightarrow_n, \rightarrow_f\}$ of length n+1, via SEL, and using mgus $\sigma, \sigma_1, \ldots, \sigma_n$. Furthermore, by proposition 4.3(6),

$$\theta_n \ldots \theta_1 \theta \delta' = \theta_n \ldots \theta_1 \delta \sigma \leq \sigma_n \ldots \sigma_1 \sigma. \qquad \text{qed}$$

If the i-th step in the refutation of $R \cup \{\Leftarrow \delta F\}$ wrt $\{\rightarrow_R, \rightarrow_t\}$ was a removal of a trivial equation, then the i-th step of the refutation of $R \cup \{\Leftarrow F\}$ wrt $\{\rightarrow_n, \rightarrow_f\}$ was a reflection applied to the same equation. If the i-th step in the refutation of $R \cup \{\Leftarrow \delta F\}$ wrt $\{\rightarrow_R, \rightarrow_t\}$ was a rewriting at π_i using $l_i \rightarrow r_i \Leftarrow F_i$, then the i-th step of the refutation of $R \cup \{\Leftarrow F\}$ wrt $\{\rightarrow_n, \rightarrow_f\}$ was a narrowing at the same occurrence using the same rewrite rule. In fact there is a one-to-one correspondence between the rewriting and removal of trivial equation steps applied to $\Leftarrow \delta F$ and the narrowing and reflection steps applied to $\Leftarrow F$. This follows immediately from the proof of proposition 6.2.13: If

$$\Leftarrow F' \rightarrow_{f(EQ(s,t), \sigma)} \Leftarrow F,$$

then $\sigma s = \sigma t$ and we find that

$$\Leftarrow \sigma F' \rightarrow_{t(\sigma EQ(s,t))} \Leftarrow \sigma F.$$

If

$$\Leftarrow F' \rightarrow_{n(E, \pi, l \rightarrow r \Leftarrow F^*, \sigma)} \Leftarrow F,$$

then $\sigma(E|\pi|) = \sigma l$ and with $\theta = \sigma|_{Var(l)}$ we find that

$$\Leftarrow \sigma F' \rightarrow_{R(\sigma E, \pi, l \rightarrow r \Leftarrow F^*, \theta)} \Leftarrow \sigma F.$$

It should be observed that lemma 6.5.2 does not hold if we drop the condition that R is non-trivial. As an example consider the term rewriting system $R = \{x \rightarrow c(x)\}$ and the equation $EQ(y,c(y))$. Then,

$$\Leftarrow EQ(y, c(y)) \rightarrow_{R(\{x \leftarrow y\})} \Leftarrow EQ(c(y), c(y)) \rightarrow_t \square.$$

However, there does not exist a refutation of $R \cup \{\Leftarrow EQ(y,c(y))\}$ with respect to narrowing and reflection. This case may have been overlooked by Hullot (1980), who states that the lifting lemma for narrowing and reflection holds for an arbitrary unconditional term rewriting system. (It is remarkable how many people have already used Hullot's result without discovering this gap.)

Theorem 6.5.3 (Strong Completeness of Narrowing and Reflection):

Let R be a non-trivial and confluent term rewriting system and SEL be a selection function. If θ is a normalizable correct answer substitution for R and $\Leftarrow F$, then there exists an SEL-computed answer substitution σ obtained by a refutation of $R \cup \{\Leftarrow F\}$ wrt $\{\rightarrow_n, \rightarrow_f\}$ such that $\theta \leq_R \sigma$.

Proof:

Since θ is correct, θF is a logical E-consequence of R. Let θ' be the normal form of θ. Clearly, $\theta =_R \theta'$ and $\theta'F$ is a logical E-consequence of R. Since R is confluent we find a refutation of $R \cup \{\Leftarrow E\}$ wrt $\{\to_R, \to_t\}$ for each $E \in \theta'F$. These refutations can be combined into a refutation of $R \cup \{\Leftarrow \theta'F\}$ wrt $\{\to_R, \to_t\}$ and via SEL. Let n be the length of this refutation. By the lifting lemma for $\to_n$ and $\to_f$ we find a refutation of $R \cup \{\Leftarrow F\}$ wrt $\{\to_n, \to_f\}$ of length n and via SEL. Furthermore, if $\theta_1, \ldots, \theta_n$ are the matchers used in the refutation of $R \cup \{\Leftarrow \theta'F\}$ and $\sigma_1, \ldots, \sigma_n$ are the mgus used in the refutation of $R \cup \{\Leftarrow F\}$, then $\theta_n \ldots \theta_1 \theta' \leq \sigma_n \ldots \sigma_1$. Observe, $\theta_n \ldots \theta_1 \theta'|_{\text{Var}(F)} = \theta'$. Let $\sigma = \sigma_n \ldots \sigma_1|_{\text{Var}(F)}$. As a consequence we find that $\theta' \leq \sigma$ and, by proposition 4.3(2), $\theta' \leq_R \sigma$. Finally, since $\theta =_R \theta'$, proposition 4.3(5) ensures that $\theta \leq_R \sigma$.   qed

It should be noted that if θ is already in normal form then $\theta \leq \sigma$. Furthermore, if SEL selects an equation of the form EQ(x,t), where $x \notin \text{Var}(t)$ and t does not contain a defined function symbol, then narrowing is not applicable and an application of reflection corresponds to the elimination of the variable x. Thus, variable elimination applied only to equations of the form EQ(x,t), where t does not contain a defined function symbol, can be applied as a simplification rule.

Recall, if a term rewriting system is terminating then it is non-trivial. Hence, theorem 6.5.3 generalizes a result obtained by Hullot (1980) who showed the completeness of narrowing and reflection for canonical term rewriting systems.

Kaplan (1986) demonstrated that narrowing and reflection is complete for confluent and fair conditional term rewriting systems, where **fair** means that there exists a simplification ordering > on the set of terms such that for each rewrite rule $l \to r \Leftarrow F$ and for each substitution σ we have $\sigma l > \sigma r$ and $\sigma l > \sigma s$ and $\sigma l > \sigma t$, for all EQ(s,t) $\in$ F. Note, fairness in this sense implies that the term rewriting system is non-trivial. It should be mentioned that Kaplan was mainly interested in conditional term rewriting systems R, such that $\to_R$ is decidable, and the fairness property ensures that $\to_R$ is decidable.

It is easy to see that rewriting and reflection is not complete if there exists a program clause $l \to r \Leftarrow F$, where r or F contain a variable not occurring in l. Consider, for example, the confluent equational program

FUN'':	$g \to a$	(g)
	$a \to g$	(a)
	$f(c(g),c(a)) \to d(c(g),c(a))$	(f)
	$h \to b \Leftarrow EQ(f(x,x),d(x,x))$	(h)

which contains the clauses from FUN' together with a→g. As we showed in section 6.2, ⇐EQ(h,b) can only be solved if we apply instantiation. Hence, Hussmann's (1985) completeness result for narrowing and reflection holds only if we impose the variable condition on the equational clauses and if the term rewriting system is non-trivial.

Giovannetti & Moiso (1988) have weakened the variable condition. They stated a completeness result for an extended form of narrowing (after a narrowing step the equations in the body of the rewrite rule used are unified) provided that the term rewriting system is "level-confluent" and terminating, but they allow extra variables in the body of the rewrite rule.

6.5.1 Canonical Term Rewriting Systems

In analogy to Hullot (1980) we can optimize narrowing if the term rewriting system is canonical. This optimazition is based on the observation that in order to show that a multiset of equations F is a logical E-consequence of a conditional term rewriting system R we can choose a refutation of $R \cup \{\Leftarrow F\}$ with respect to rewriting and removal of trivial equations such that each most general unifier used in this refutation is in normal form. The key to this observation is the possibility always to select an innermost redex.

Definition:

Let R be a term rewriting system. s is called a **redex wrt** $\rightarrow_R$ iff there exists a new variant $l \rightarrow r \Leftarrow F$ of a rewrite rule in R and a substitution σ such that $s = \sigma l$.

A redex with respect to $\rightarrow_R$ differs from a redex as defined in section 6.4 in that we do not impose any conditions on the equations in the body of a rewrite rule. In a rewriting step applied to a goal clause these equations are simply added to the goal clause, whereas in a rewriting step applied to a term, each ground instance of an element in σF must be an element of the success-set of R. For notational convenience we omit "wrt $\rightarrow_R$" if it can be determined by the context.

Since redexes generally are subterms of larger expressions it is sometimes necessary to consider redexes with respect to a set of occurrences.

Definition:

Let R be a term rewriting system, E be an equation, $\pi \in Occ(E)$, and O be a set of occurrences. $E|\pi|$ is said to be a **redex wrt** $\rightarrow_R$ **and O** iff $E|\pi|$ is a redex and $\pi \in O$.

Furthermore, we need the notion of an innermost redex.

Definition:

Let R be a term rewriting system, E be an equation, and $\pi \in Occ(E)$. $E|\pi|$ is said to be an **innermost redex wrt** $\rightarrow_R$ iff $E|\pi|$ is a redex and there does not exist a $\pi' \in Occ(E)$ such that $E|\pi'|$ is a redex and $\pi' < \pi$.

Definition:

Let R be a term rewriting system. A selection function is said to be **strong** iff it selects not only a subgoal E but also an occurrence $\pi \in Occ(E)$ such that $E|\pi|$ is a redex wrt $\rightarrow_R$ if such an occurrence π exists.

If a strong selection function selects the equation E and the occurrence $\pi \in Occ(E)$, then paramodulation will only be applied to $E|\pi|$. It is easy to see that refutations with respect to

rewriting and removal of trivial equations are independent of a strong selection function if
the term rewriting system is canonical.

Notation:

In the remaining part of this section we assume that R is a canonical term rewriting system
if not indicated otherwise.

Lemma 6.5.1.1:

*Let SSEL be a strong selection function. If $R \cup \{\Leftarrow F\}$ has a refutation wrt $\{\rightarrow_R,$
$\rightarrow_t\}$, then $R \cup \{\Leftarrow F\}$ has a refutation wrt $\{\rightarrow_R, \rightarrow_t\}$ and via SSEL.*

Proof:

Since R is Noetherian, each derivation wrt $\{\rightarrow_R, \rightarrow_t\}$ is finite and each term s occurring
in F has a normal form t. Because R is also confluent, this normal form is unique no matter
which redexes were selected in the reduction from s to t. Thus, we learn that there is a refutation of $R \cup \{\Leftarrow F\}$ wrt $\{\rightarrow_R, \rightarrow_t\}$ and via SSEL.   qed

We can now define innermost derivations and refutations.

Definition:

A derivation of $R \cup \{\Leftarrow F\}$ wrt $\{\rightarrow_R, \rightarrow_t\}$ is said to be **innermost** iff in each
rewriting step the selected redex is an innermost redex.

As an example consider the term rewriting system

> **BASIC:** $f(x) \rightarrow x$ (f)
>
> $g \rightarrow a$ (g)

the normalized substitution $\theta = \{y \leftarrow a\}$ and the equation $EQ(f(g), y)$. There are two possible
refutations issuing from $\Leftarrow \theta EQ(f(g), y)$:

> $\Leftarrow EQ(f(g), a) \rightarrow_{R(f, \{x \leftarrow g\})} \Leftarrow EQ(g,a) \rightarrow_{R(g)} \Leftarrow EQ(a,a) \rightarrow_t \square$ (1)

and

> $\Leftarrow EQ(f(g), a) \rightarrow_{R(g)} \Leftarrow EQ(f(a), a) \rightarrow_{R(f, \{x \leftarrow a\})} \Leftarrow EQ(a,a) \rightarrow_t \square.$ (2)

Whereas (2) is an innermost refutation, the first selected redex in (1) is not an innermost
redex. It should be observed that the substitution $\{x \leftarrow g\}$ used in (1) is not in normal form,
whereas the substitution $\{x \leftarrow a\}$ used in (2) is in normal form. Furthermore, in (1) we have
not rewritten the "a" introduced by θ, but the "g" introduced by $\{x \leftarrow g\}$.

Lemma 6.5.1.2:

> *Let SSEL be a strong selection function that selects only innermost redeces. If $R \cup \{\Leftarrow F\}$ has a refutation wrt $\{\rightarrow_R, \rightarrow_t\}$, then $R \cup \{\Leftarrow F\}$ has a refutation wrt $\{\rightarrow_R, \rightarrow_t\}$ and via SSEL. Furthermore, if $\sigma_1, ..., \sigma_n$ are the matchers used in the innermost refutation, then σ_i, $1 \leq i \leq n$, is in normal form.*

Proof:

From lemma 6.5.1.1 we learn that there is an innermost refutation of $R \cup \{\Leftarrow F\}$ wrt $\{\rightarrow_R, \rightarrow_t\}$ and via SSEL. Now, let $\Leftarrow F_i$ be the i-th goal clause in this refutation and suppose that

$$\Leftarrow F_i \rightarrow_R(E, \pi, 1 \rightarrow r \Leftarrow F, \sigma) \Leftarrow F_{i+1}.$$

Since $E|\pi|$ is an innermost redex, we find that no proper subterm of $E|\pi|$ is reducible. Furthermore, because $Dom(\sigma) = Var(1)$, $\sigma 1 = E|\pi|$, R is canonical and, hence, non-trivial, we learn that each element in the codomain of σ is a proper subterm of $E|\pi|$. Hence, σ is in normal form. Finally, if

$$\Leftarrow F_i \rightarrow_t(\sigma) \Leftarrow F_{i+1},$$

then $\sigma = \varepsilon$ and, thus, σ is in normal form.   qed

Hence, in order to show that F is a logical E-consequence of a canonical term rewriting system, it suffices to select exactly one innermost redex in each rewriting step.

Lemma 6.5.1.2 does not hold if we replace "Noetherian" by "non-trivial" in the conditions of the lemma. As an example consider again the term rewriting system

$$\textbf{INNER:} \quad f(x,a) \rightarrow b \tag{f}$$
$$g \rightarrow g \tag{g}$$

and the refutation

$$\Leftarrow EQ(f(g,a), b) \rightarrow_R(f) \Leftarrow EQ(b,b) \rightarrow \square.$$

This refutation is not an innermost one, since the only innermost redex in the initial goal clause is g. However, rewriting g yields the same goal clause again.

From lemma 6.5.1.2 we learn that each innermost refutation with respect to rewriting and removal of trivial equations uses only normalized substitutions. Hence, the occurrences to which rewriting is applied are either non-variable occurrences in the initial goal clause or are constructed by concatenating the selected occurrence in a rewriting step with the non-variable occurrences of the right-hand side of the rewrite rule used in this rewriting step. These occurrences were called "basic" in Hullot (1980) and subsequent papers. Furthermore, derivations in which only "basic" occurrences are selected are also called "basic". As an example recall the term rewrite system

BASIC: $f(x) \rightarrow x$ (f)

$g \rightarrow a$ (g)

and the innermost refutation

$$\Leftarrow EQ(f(g), a) \rightarrow_{R(g)} \Leftarrow EQ(f(a), a) \rightarrow_{R(f, \{x \leftarrow a\})} \Leftarrow EQ(a,a) \rightarrow_t \square.$$

The non-variable occurrences of the equation $EQ(f(g), a)$ are Λ, 1, 1•1, and 2. The "basic" occurrences of the equation $EQ(f(a), a)$ are again Λ, 1, 1•1, and 2, whereas the "basic" occurrences in the equation $EQ(a,a)$ are Λ and 2. Hence, the refutation is "basic". However, there are "non-basic" refutations as well. For example, the refutation

$$\Leftarrow EQ(f(g), a) \rightarrow_{R(f, \{x \leftarrow g\})} \Leftarrow EQ(g,a) \rightarrow_{R(g)} \Leftarrow EQ(a,a) \rightarrow_t \square$$

is not "basic", since in the only "basic" occurrences in the second equation $EQ(g,a)$ are Λ and 2. However, rewriting was applied to 1. This refutation contradicts lemma 3 in Hullot (1980). As a consequence Hullot's theorem 3 is also not valid. However, his main result, the completeness of basic narrowing, holds as we show in the following.

The question is whether "basic" innermost refutations with respect to rewriting and removal of trivial equations can be lifted to "basic" refutations with respect to narrowing and reflection. Before turning to the answer of this question we define the notion of a redex with respect to narrowing.

Definition:

Let R be a term rewriting system. s is called a **redex wrt** $\rightarrow_n$ iff there exists a new variant $l \rightarrow r \Leftarrow F$ of a rule in R and a substitution σ such that $\sigma s = \sigma l$.

For notational convenience we often omit "wrt $\rightarrow_n$" if it can be determined from the context. The definition of an innermost redex with respect to $\rightarrow_R$ and a set of occurrences carries over to redexes with respect to $\rightarrow_n$ in the obvious way.

We now come back to the lifting problem for basic innermost rewriting and removal of trivial equations. A difficulty arises since an innermost redex with respect to $\rightarrow_n$ in a goal clause $\Leftarrow F$ must not correspond to an innermost redex with respect to $\rightarrow_R$ in $\Leftarrow \theta F$, where θ is assumed to be in normal form. As an example consider the term rewriting system

INN: $f(a) \rightarrow b$ (f)

$g(x) \rightarrow c$ (g)

the substitution $\theta = \{y \leftarrow c\}$ and the equation $E = EQ(g(f(y)), c)$. $f(y)$ is the innermost redex with respect to narrowing in $EQ(g(f(y)), c)$. However, $\theta f(y) = f(c)$ is not even a redex with respect to rewriting in θE and $g(f(c))$ is the innermost redex with respect to rewriting. Thus, if we select an innermost redex t in a derivation with respect to to narrowing and reflection, we do not know whether narrowing should be applied to t or whether narrowing should be applied to a redex "above" t. Furthermore, how can we represent our goal clauses such that it can easily be decided whether a redex is a "basic" one, i.e. was not introduced by a substitution, and should not be kept invariant?

It should be noted that we have not formally defined the notion of a "basic" occurrence (resp. redex). It seems to us that the definition fomulated by Hullot (1980) is very clumsy. In fact we show that the notion of a "basic" occurrence can completely be avoided if we represent goal clauses by a **skeleton** and an **environment part** (Boyer & Moore 1972). We now formally define this representation.

Definition:

Let R be a conditional term rewriting system and $\Leftarrow F_0$ be a goal clause. The **representation of a derivation** of $R \cup \{\Leftarrow F_0\}$ is inductively defined as follows:

(0)   The initial goal clause $\Leftarrow F_0$ is represented by $\Leftarrow F_0, \varepsilon$.

Let $\Leftarrow F_i, \sigma_i$ be the i-th goal clause in the derivation, $E = EQ(s,t) \in F_i$ be the selected subgoal, $F_i' = F_i \setminus \{E\}$, and O be the set of non-variable occurrences in E.

(1)   If $\sigma_i s$ and $\sigma_i t$ are unifiable with mgu θ, then

$$\Leftarrow F_i, \sigma_i \to_r \Leftarrow F_i', \theta\sigma_i.$$

(2)   If $\pi \in Occ(E)$, $\sigma_i(E|\pi|)$ is an innermost redex wrt $\to_n$ and O, $l \to r \Leftarrow F$ is a new variant of a rewrite rule in R, and l and $\sigma_i(E|\pi|)$ are unifiable with mgu θ, then

$$\Leftarrow F_i, \sigma_i \to_{in} \Leftarrow F_i' \cup F \cup \{E|\pi \leftarrow r|\}, \theta\sigma_i.$$

(3)   If $\pi \in Occ(E)$, $\sigma_i(E|\pi|)$ is an innermost redex wrt $\to_n$ and O, x is a new variable, and $\theta = \{x \leftarrow \sigma_i(E|\pi|)\}$, then

$$\Leftarrow F_i, \sigma_i \to_{if} \Leftarrow F_i' \cup \{E|\pi \leftarrow x\}, \theta\sigma_i.$$

Part (1) represents a reflection. $\to_{in}$ represents a narrowing and is called **innermost narrowing**. $\to_{if}$ represents the elimination of an innermost redex wrt $\to_n$ from the set of redexes in $\Leftarrow F_i$ and is called **innermost reflection**.

It should be noted that due to our chosen representation $\Leftarrow F,\sigma$ instead of $\Leftarrow \sigma F$, the "basic" occurrences (in the sense of Hullot (1980)) in $\Leftarrow \sigma F$ are all in $\Leftarrow F$, whereas the "non-basic" occurrences are all in the codomain of σ.

Corollary 6.5.1.3 (Soundness of $\to_f$, $\to_{in}$, and $\to_{if}$):

If there exists a refutation of $R \cup \{\Leftarrow F, \sigma\}$ wrt $\{\to_f, \to_{in}, \to_{if}\}$ and with comput-
ed answer substitution θ, then θ is a correct answer substitution for R and $\Leftarrow \sigma F$.

Proof:

We show that for each refutation of $R \cup \{\Leftarrow F, \sigma\}$ wrt $\{\to_f, \to_{in}, \to_{if}\}$ and with computed
answer substitution θ there exists a refutation of $R \cup \{\Leftarrow \sigma F\}$ wrt $\{\to_f, \to_n\}$ and with computed answer substitution θ. The soundness follows immediately from the soundness of para-
modulation and reflection (theorem 6.2.1).

The proof of the claim is by induction on the length n of the refutation of $R \cup \{\Leftarrow F, \sigma\}$ wrt
$\{\to_f, \to_{in}, \to_{if}\}$. The case n=0 being trivial we turn to the induction step and assume that the
result holds for n. Suppose that

$$\Leftarrow F', \sigma' \to_{(E, \lambda)} \Leftarrow F, \sigma \qquad (1)$$

and that there exists a refutation of $R \cup \{\Leftarrow F, \sigma\}$ wrt $\{\to_f, \to_{in}, \to_{if}\}$ and with computed
answer substitution θ. Hence, $\sigma = \lambda\sigma'$ and $\theta' = \theta\lambda|_{Var(\sigma'F')}$ is the computed answer substi-
tution of the refutation of $R \cup \{\Leftarrow F', \sigma'\}$. Let E = EQ(s,t). We distinguish three cases wrt the
inference rule applied in (1).

If reflection was applied in (1), then λ is the mgu of σs and σt and $F = F' \setminus \{E\}$. It follows
immediately that

$$\Leftarrow \sigma'F' \to_{f(E, \lambda)} \Leftarrow \sigma F. \qquad (2)$$

If innermost narrowing was applied in (1), then we find $\pi \in Occ(E)$ and a new variant
$l \to r \Leftarrow F^*$ of a rewrite rule in R such that $\sigma'(E|\pi|)$ and l are unifiable with mgu λ. Further-
more, $F = (F' \setminus \{E\}) \cup \{E|\pi \leftarrow r|\} \cup F^*$ and it follows immediately that

$$\Leftarrow \sigma'F' \to_{n(E, \lambda)} \Leftarrow \sigma F. \qquad (3)$$

Finally, if innermost reflection was applied in (1), then

$$\Leftarrow \sigma'F = \Leftarrow \sigma F. \qquad (4)$$

In any case, by the induction hypothesis we find a refutation of $R \cup \{\Leftarrow \sigma F\}$ wrt $\{\to_f, \to_n\}$.
Furthermore, if θ is the computed answer substitution of the refutation of $R \cup \{\Leftarrow F, \sigma\}$ wrt
$\{\to_f, \to_{in}, \to_{if}\}$, then θ is the computed answer substitution of the refutation of $R \cup \{\Leftarrow \sigma F\}$.
The result follows immediately with (2), (3), and (4).   qed

The following technical lemma shows that the main effect of an application of the innermost reflection rule is that an innermost redex with respect to narrowing is moved from the
skeleton to the environment part of a goal clause.

Lemma 6.5.1.4:

Let R be a conditional term rewriting system, $\Leftarrow F \cup \{E\}$, μ be a goal clause, and $\pi \in Occ(E)$. If $\mu E|\pi|$ is a redex wrt $\to_n$, then there exists a derivation from $\Leftarrow F \cup \{E\}$, μ to $\Leftarrow F \cup \{E^*\}$, $\lambda\mu$ wrt $\{\to_{if}\}$ such that $Dom(\lambda)$ contains only new variables, $\lambda\mu E^* = \mu E$, and $\mu E|\pi|$ is an innermost redex wrt $\to_n$ and the non-variable occurrences in E^*.

Proof:

The proof is by induction on the number k of redexes wrt $\to_n$ and $Occ(E)$ that are "below" $\mu E|\pi|$. The case k=0 being trivial we turn to the induction step and assume that the result holds for k. If there are k+1 redeces below $\mu'E'|\pi|$, then we find a $\pi' \in Occ(E')$ such that $\pi' < \pi$ and $\mu'E'|\pi'|$ is an innermost redex wrt $\to_n$ and the non-variable occurrences in E'. Now let x be a new variable, θ be the substitution $\{x \leftarrow \mu'E'|\pi'|\}$, $E = E'|\pi' \leftarrow x|$ and $\mu = \theta\mu'$. Then,

$$\Leftarrow F \cup \{E'\}, \mu' \to_{if} \Leftarrow F \cup \{E\}, \mu. \tag{*}$$

Clearly, there are only k redeces below $\mu E|\pi|$. By an application of the induction hypothesis we find a derivation from $\Leftarrow F \cup \{E\}$, μ to $\Leftarrow F \cup \{E^*\}$, $\lambda\mu$ wrt $\{\to_{if}\}$ such that $Dom(\lambda)$ contains only new variables, $\lambda\mu E^* = \mu E$ and $\mu E|\pi|$ is an innermost redex wrt $\to_n$ and the non-variable occurrences in E^*. The result follows immediately with (*) and $\lambda' = \lambda\theta$.   qed

To prove that our representation is complete we need a lifting lemma.

Lemma 6.5.1.5 (Lifting Lemma for $\to_f$, $\to_{in}$, and $\to_{if}$):

Let R be a non-trivial term rewriting system and $\delta\mu$ be a substitution in normal form. If $R \cup \{\Leftarrow \delta\mu F\}$ has an innermost refutation wrt $\{\to_R, \to_t\}$, then $R \cup \{\Leftarrow F, \mu\}$ has a refutation wrt $\{\to_f, \to_{in}, \to_{if}\}$. Furthermore, if $\theta_1, ..., \theta_n$ are the matchers used in the refutation of $R \cup \{\Leftarrow \delta\mu F\}$ and $\sigma_1, ..., \sigma_m$ are the unifiers used in the refutation of $R \cup \{\Leftarrow F, \mu\}$, then $\theta_n...\theta_1\delta \leq \sigma_m...\sigma_1$.

Proof:

The proof is by induction on the length n of the innermost refutation of $R \cup \{\Leftarrow \delta\mu F\}$ wrt $\{\to_R, \to_t\}$. The case n=0 being trivial we turn to the induction step and assume that the result holds for n. Suppose that $\delta'\mu'$ is in normal form,

$$\Leftarrow \delta'\mu'F' \to \Leftarrow \delta\mu F, \tag{1}$$

and that there exists an innermost refutation of $R \cup \{\Leftarrow \delta\mu F\}$ of length n. Let F' be of the form $F^+ \cup \{E\}$ and $E = EQ(s,t)$ be the selected equation in the first step. We distinguish two cases:

If removal of a trivial equation was applied in (1), then δ' is a unifier for μ's and μ't. Hence, we find an mgu σ for μ's and μ't and a substitution δ such that $\delta' = \delta\sigma$,

$Dom(\delta) \cap Dom(\lambda) = \varnothing$, and δ as well as σ are in normal form (proposition 6.5.1(3)). Now let $\mu = \sigma\mu'$ and $F = F^+$. Hence,

$$\Leftarrow F', \mu' \rightarrow_f \Leftarrow F, \mu.$$

From the induction hypothesis we learn that there exists a refutation of $R \cup \{\Leftarrow F, \mu\}$ wrt $\{\rightarrow_f, \rightarrow_{in}, \rightarrow_{if}\}$. Furthermore, if $\theta_1, ..., \theta_n$ are the matchers used in the refutation of $R \cup \{\Leftarrow \delta\mu F\}$ and $\sigma_1, ..., \sigma_m$ are the unifiers used in the refutation of $R \cup \{\Leftarrow F, \mu\}$ then

$$\theta_n...\theta_1\delta \leq \sigma_m...\sigma_1.$$

Clearly, there exists a refutation of $R \cup \{\Leftarrow F', \mu'\}$ wrt $\{\rightarrow_f, \rightarrow_{in}, \rightarrow_{if}\}$ using unifiers $\sigma, \sigma_1, ..., \sigma_m$. Furthermore, by proposition 4.3(6),

$$\theta_n...\theta_1\varepsilon\delta' = \theta_n...\theta_1\delta\sigma \leq \sigma_m...\sigma_1\sigma.$$

Now, if in (1) innermost rewriting was applied to the occurrence $\pi \in Occ(\delta'\mu'E)$ using the rewrite rule $l \rightarrow r \Leftarrow F^*$, then we find a substitution θ such that $\delta'\mu'E|\pi| = \theta l$. Since $\delta'\mu'$ is in normal form $\pi \in Occ(E)$. Furthermore, since R is non-trivial π must be a non-variable occurrence in E by proposition 6.4.10. Because $(\delta'\mu'E)|\pi|$ is an innermost redex, we find that θ is also in normal form. Since $l \rightarrow r \Leftarrow F^*$ was a new variant of a rewrite rule in R we may assume that $Dom(\delta') \cap Dom(\theta) = \varnothing$ and $Dom(\theta) = Var(l)$. Thus, $\delta' \cup \theta = \theta\delta'$ is a unifier for $\mu'E|\pi|$ and l in normal form. By proposition 6.5.1(3) we find an mgu σ for $\mu'E|\pi|$ and l and a substitution δ such that $\delta\sigma = \theta\delta'$ and δ as well as σ are in normal form. Now let $\mu = \sigma\mu'$ and $F = F^+ \cup \{E|\pi \leftarrow r]\} \cup F^*$. We distinguish two cases:

If $\mu'E|\pi|$ is an innermost redex wrt $\rightarrow_n$ and the non-variable occurrences in E, then

$$\Leftarrow F', \mu' \rightarrow_{in(\sigma)} \Leftarrow F, \mu.$$

From the induction hypothesis we learn that there exists a refutation of $R \cup \{\Leftarrow F, \mu\}$ wrt $\{\rightarrow_f, \rightarrow_{in}, \rightarrow_{if}\}$. Furthermore, if $\theta_1, ..., \theta_n$ are the matchers used in the refutation of $R \cup \{\Leftarrow \delta\mu F\}$ and $\sigma_1, ..., \sigma_m$ are the unifiers used in the refutation of $R \cup \{\Leftarrow F, \mu\}$ then

$$\theta_n...\theta_1\delta \leq \sigma_m...\sigma_1.$$

Clearly, there exists a refutation of $R \cup \{\Leftarrow F', \mu'\}$ wrt $\{\rightarrow_f, \rightarrow_{in}, \rightarrow_{if}\}$ using unifiers $\sigma, \sigma_1, ..., \sigma_m$. Furthermore,

$$\theta_n...\theta_1\theta\delta' = \theta_n...\theta_1\delta\sigma \leq \sigma_m...\sigma_1\sigma.$$

Otherwise, if $\mu'E|\pi|$ is not an innermost redex wrt $\rightarrow_n$ and the non-variable occurrences in E, then, by lemma 6.5.1.4, we find a derivation from $\Leftarrow F', \mu' = \Leftarrow F^+ \cup \{E\}, \mu'$ to $\Leftarrow F^+ \cup \{E'\}, \lambda\mu'$ wrt $\{\rightarrow_{if}\}$ such that $Dom(\lambda)$ contains only new variables, $\lambda\mu'E = \mu'E$, and $\lambda\mu'E'|\pi|$ is an innermost redex wrt $\rightarrow_n$ and the occurrences in E'. Since $\delta'\mu'F' = \delta'\mu'(F^+ \cup \{E\}) = \delta'\lambda\mu'(F^+ \cup \{E'\})$ the lemma follows in analogy to the previous case.   qed

We now turn to the proof that reflection, innermost narrowing, and innermost reflection is complete.

Theorem 6.5.1.6 (Completeness of $\rightarrow_f$, $\rightarrow_{in}$, and $\rightarrow_{if}$):

If θ is a correct answer substitution for R and $\Leftarrow F$, then there exists a computed answer substitution σ obtained by a refutation of $R \cup \{\Leftarrow F, \varepsilon\}$ wrt $\{\rightarrow_f, \rightarrow_{in}, \rightarrow_{if}\}$ such that $\theta \leq_R \sigma$.

Proof:

Since θ is correct θF is a logical E-consequence of R. Because R is canonical θ is normalizable. Let θ' be the normal form of θ. Clearly $\theta =_R \theta'$ and $\theta'F$ is a logical E-consequence of R. Since R is confluent we find a refutation of $R \cup \{\Leftarrow E\}$ wrt $\{\rightarrow_R, \rightarrow_t\}$ for each $E \in \theta'F$. These refutations can be combined into a refutation of $R \cup \{\Leftarrow \theta'F\}$ wrt $\{\rightarrow_R, \rightarrow_t\}$. By lemma 6.5.1.2 there exists an innermost refutation of $R \cup \{\Leftarrow \theta'F\}$ wrt $\{\rightarrow_R, \rightarrow_t\}$ and by the lifting lemma 6.5.1.5 there exists a refutation of $R \cup \{\Leftarrow F, \varepsilon\}$ wrt $\{\rightarrow_f, \rightarrow_{in}, \rightarrow_{if}\}$. Furthermore, if $\theta_1, ..., \theta_n$ are the matchers used in the refutation of $R \cup \{\Leftarrow \theta'F\}$ and $\sigma_1, ..., \sigma_m$ are the unifiers used in the refutation of $R \cup \{\Leftarrow F, \varepsilon\}$, then $\theta_n...\theta_1\theta' \leq \sigma_m...\sigma_1$. Observe, $\theta_n...\theta_1\theta'|_{Var(F')} = \theta'$. Let $\sigma = \sigma_m...\sigma_1|_{Var(F)}$. Then $\theta' \leq \sigma$ and, by proposition 4.3(2), $\theta' \leq_R \sigma$. Finally, since $\theta =_R \theta'$ proposition 4.3(5) ensures that $\theta \leq_R \sigma$.   qed

As we demonstrated in section 6.2, paramodulation, instantiation, and reflection are independent of a selection function if instantiations are only applied before a paramodulation step. The independence was proved by showing that refutations computing the empty answer substitution are independent of a selection function and by applying the lifting lemma which preserves the selection function. It is easy to see that an even stronger result can be proved for refutations with respect to reflection, innermost narrowing, and innermost reflection. From lemma 6.5.1.2 we learn that rewriting and removal of trivial equations are independent of a strong selection function which selects not only equations but also an innermost redex in this equation if rewriting is to be applied. By the proof of the lifting lemma 6.5.1.5 we find that innermost reflection is only applied before an innermost narrowing if an innermost redex with respect to $\rightarrow_R$ in $\delta\mu F$ does not correspond to an innermost redex wrt $\rightarrow_n$ in μF. If we comprise these innermost reflection steps with the following innermost narrowing step, then the lifting lemma preserves the strong selection function and, in analogy to the proof of theorem 6.5.1.6, we obtain a strong completeness result for reflection, innermost reflection and narrowing.

Hullot (1980) proved that if a term rewriting system is unconditional, canonical, and any "basic" derivation (or, as we would call it, derivation with respect to innermost narrowing, innermost reflection, and reflection) issuing from the right-hand side of a rewrite rule is terminating, then any "basic" derivation is terminating. His proof is based on two observations. A non-variable occurrence in the initial goal clause is selected at most once in a "basic" derivation and there is an upper bound for the length of "basic" derivations issuing from occurrences in the skeleton part of a goal clause that were introduced by the right-hand side of a used rewrite rule. It is easy to see that this result can be extended to hold also for conditional term rewriting systems.

In the following sections we show two refinements for reflection and narrowing: First, we prove that rewriting can be applied as a simplification rule if the term rewriting system is canonical and, second, we give a condition such that innermost reflection need not be applied.

6.5.2 Narrowing and Rewriting

As we already mentioned in the introduction, rewriting a goal clause may cut down an infinite search space to a finite one. As an example consider the term rewriting system

$$\textbf{MAP-ADD1:} \quad \text{append}([],z) \rightarrow z \qquad\qquad\qquad\qquad\qquad\qquad (a1)$$

$$\text{append}(x{:}y,z) \rightarrow x{:}\text{append}(y,z) \qquad\qquad\qquad (a2)$$

$$\text{map-add1}([]) \rightarrow [] \qquad\qquad\qquad\qquad\qquad\qquad (m1)$$

$$\text{map-add1}(x{:}y) \rightarrow s(x){:}\text{map-add1}(y) \qquad\qquad\quad (m2)$$

Informally, the function map-add1 applied to a list of natural numbers adds 1 to each element of this list. It is easy to see that there exists an infinite derivation from

$$\Leftarrow \text{EQ}(\text{map-add1}(0{:}\text{append}(x,y)), 0{:}z), \varepsilon$$

wrt $\{\rightarrow_f, \rightarrow_{in}, \rightarrow_{if}\}$ by repeatedly applying innermost narrowing and using (a2):

$$\Leftarrow \text{EQ}(\text{map-add1}(0{:}\textbf{append(y,z)}), 0{:}x), \varepsilon$$

$$\rightarrow_{in} \qquad \Leftarrow \text{EQ}(\text{map-add1}(0{:}x'{:}\textbf{append(y',z')}), 0{:}x), \{y \leftarrow x'{:}y', z \leftarrow z'\}$$

... .

But,

$$\Leftarrow \text{EQ}(\textbf{map-add1(0:append(x,y))}, 0{:}z), \varepsilon$$

$$\rightarrow_{R(m2)} \quad \Leftarrow \text{EQ}(s(0){:}\text{map-add1}(\text{append}(x,y)),0{:}z), \varepsilon.$$

We can now apply the simplification rule "term decomposition" since "$:$" is a constructor obtaining

$$\Leftarrow \text{EQ}(s(0), 0), \text{EQ}(\text{map-add1}(\text{append}(x,y)), z), \varepsilon.$$

This goal clause, however, can easily be recognized as a failure by lemma 6.4.11, since "s" and "0" are different constructors.

But how can rewriting be combined with $\{\rightarrow_f, \rightarrow_{in}, \rightarrow_{if}\}$ such that the system remains complete? Obviously, we would like to treat rewriting as a simplification rule. To get the idea of our solution take again a close look at the one-to-one correspondence between refutations of $R \cup \{\Leftarrow \theta F\}$ with respect to rewriting and removal of trivial equations and refutations of $R \cup \{\Leftarrow F\}$ with respect to narrowing and reflection. Rewriting applied to $\Leftarrow F$ corresponds to a rewriting applied to $\Leftarrow \theta F$. However, this rewriting must not be an innermost one. As an example consider again the term rewriting system

$$\textbf{BASIC:} \quad f(x) \rightarrow x \qquad\qquad\qquad\qquad\qquad\qquad\qquad (f)$$

$$g \rightarrow a \qquad\qquad\qquad\qquad\qquad\qquad\qquad\qquad (g)$$

the substitution $\theta = \{y\leftarrow a\}$, and the equation $EQ(f(g), y)$. $EQ(f(g), y)$ can be rewritten to $EQ(g,y)$ upon occurrence 1 and using rule (f). Clearly, this is not an innermost rewriting step. As a consequence, the substitution used in a non-innermost rewriting step need not be in normal form. This means that if we define a rewriting step for goal clauses which are represented by a skeleton and an environment part we cannot simply compose the substitution used in this rewriting step with the environment part but we have to keep the substitution in the skeleton part.

Definition:

> Let R be a term rewriting system, $\Leftarrow F\cup\{E\}$, σ be a goal clause, $P = l\rightarrow r\Leftarrow F^*$ be a new variant of a rewrite rule, and $\pi \in Occ(E)$. If there exists a substitution θ such that $\theta l = \sigma E|\pi|$, then
>
> $$\Leftarrow F\cup\{E\}, \sigma \rightarrow_{R}(E, \pi, P, \theta) \Leftarrow F\cup\theta F^*\cup\{E|\pi\leftarrow\theta r|\}, \sigma.$$

We now show that rewriting as defined above can be applied as a simplification rule to derivations with respect to reflection, innermost narrowing, and innermost reflection. At first we prove that a rewriting applied to $\Leftarrow\mu F$ corresponds precisely to a rewriting applied to $\Leftarrow F$, μ if μ is in normal form.

Lemma 6.5.2.1:

> *Let R be a conditional term rewriting system and μ be a substitution in normal form. If $\Leftarrow\mu F \rightarrow_R \Leftarrow F'$, then there exists an F'' such that $F' = \mu F''$ and $\Leftarrow F$, μ $\rightarrow_R \Leftarrow F''$, μ.*

Proof:

Let $E \in F$, $F^+ = F\setminus\{E\}$, and P be a new variant of a rewrite rule in R. If

$$\Leftarrow \mu F \rightarrow_{R}(\mu E, \pi, P, \sigma) \Leftarrow F',$$

then

$$F' = \mu F^+\cup\sigma F^*\cup\{(\mu E)|\pi\leftarrow\sigma r|\}.$$

Since μ is in normal form, $\pi \in Occ(E)$, and, hence,

$$F' = \mu F^+\cup\sigma F^*\cup\{\mu(E|\pi\leftarrow\sigma r|)\}.$$

Because P is a new variant of a rewrite rule in R we may assume that $Dom(\sigma)\cap Dom(\mu) = \emptyset$ and $Dom(\sigma)\cap VCod(\mu) = \emptyset$. Hence, $(\mu\cup\sigma)F^* = \mu\sigma F^* = \sigma F$. Now let $F'' = F^+\cup\sigma F^*\cup\{E|\pi\leftarrow\sigma r|\}$ and we obtain

$$F' = \mu F''.$$

Furthermore, by the definition of rewriting applied to goal clauses that are represented as a skeleton and an environment part we learn that

$$\Leftarrow F, \mu \rightarrow_{R}(E, \pi, P, \sigma) \Leftarrow F'', \mu. \qquad \text{qed}$$

A drawback of our definition of the rewriting rule is the fact that terms from the environment part may be moved back into the skeleton part of the goal clause and, thus, become again available as redexes for narrowing steps. As an example consider the rewrite rule $f(c(x),z) \rightarrow g(x,z)$, the terms s, t, u, and the substitution $\sigma = \{x \leftarrow s, z \leftarrow u\}$. Then

$$\Leftarrow EQ(f(y,u), t), \{y \leftarrow c(s)\} \rightarrow R(\sigma) \Leftarrow EQ(g(s,u), t), \{y \leftarrow c(s)\} \tag{1}$$

and the term s occurs in the skeleton part of the goal clause. This problem was first observed by Nutt et al. (1987) and they propose a method to transfer the term s back to the environment part: First, an application of their "unfolding rule" to (1) yields

$$\Leftarrow EQ(g(z',u), t), EQ(z',s), \{y \leftarrow c(s)\}, \tag{2}$$

where z' is a new variable. Then, an application of their "safe blocking rule 1" to (2) yields

$$\Leftarrow EQ(g(z',u), t), \{z' \leftarrow s, y \leftarrow c(s)\}.$$

The "safe blocking rule 1" is applicable since the term s occurs already in the codomain of $\{y \leftarrow c(s)\}$. Though Nutt et al. proved that the "unfolding rule" and the "safe blocking rule 1" can be used as simplification rules, it is not immediately clear how these rules should be applied in practice. The "unfoldung rule" requires the identification of a certain subterm in the skeleton part, whereas the "safe blocking rule 1" has to check whether this subterm occurs already in the codomain of the environment part of the goal clause. Would it not be better to modify the rewriting rule such that a term - like the "s" in the above example - is not moved from the skeleton to the environment part? In our example, we could split the substitution $\sigma = \{x \leftarrow s, z \leftarrow u\}$ into the parts $\sigma_e = \{x \leftarrow s\}$ and $\sigma_s = \{z \leftarrow u\}$ and in the rewriting step σ_e is composed with the environment part whereas σ_s is applied to the skeleton part. Thus we would achieve the same effect as Nutt et al. in their approach. But how can we determine the substitutions σ_e and σ_s?

We now prove a lifting lemma for reflection, innermost narrowing and innermost reflection, where rewriting is applied as a simplification rule.

Lemma 6.5.2.2 (Lifting Lemma for $\rightarrow_f$, $\rightarrow_{in}$, $\rightarrow_{if}$, and $\rightarrow_R$):

Let R be a canonical term rewriting system and $\delta\mu$ be a substitution in normal form. If $R \cup \{\Leftarrow \delta\mu F\}$ has a refutation wrt $\{\rightarrow_R, \rightarrow_f\}$, then $R \cup \{\Leftarrow F, \mu\}$ has a refutation wrt $\{\rightarrow_f, \rightarrow_{in}, \rightarrow_{if}, \rightarrow_R\}$, such that $\rightarrow_f$, $\rightarrow_{in}$, and $\rightarrow_{if}$ are only applied to goal clauses in normal form. Furthermore, if $\theta_1, ..., \theta_n$ are the matchers used in the refutation of $R \cup \{\Leftarrow \delta\mu F\}$ and $\sigma_1, ..., \sigma_m$ are the unifiers used in the refutation of $R \cup \{\Leftarrow F, \mu\}$, then $\theta_n...\theta_1\delta \leq \sigma_m...\sigma_1$.

Proof:

The proof is by induction on the length n of the refutation of $R \cup \{\Leftarrow \delta\mu F\}$ wrt $\{\rightarrow_R, \rightarrow_t\}$. The case n=0 being trivial we turn to the induction step and assume that the result holds for n. Suppose that $\delta'\mu'$ is in normalform,

$$\Leftarrow \delta'\mu'F' \;\rightarrow\; \Leftarrow \delta\mu F, \tag{1}$$

and that there exists a refutation of $R\cup\{\Leftarrow\delta\mu F\}$ of length n. Let F' be of the form $F^+\cup\{E\}$ and $E = EQ(s,t)$ be the selected equation in the first step. We distinguish two cases:

If $\mu'F'$ is in normal form, then $\Leftarrow F',\mu'$ is also in normal form. Since refutations wrt $\{\rightarrow_R, \rightarrow_t\}$ are independent of a strong selection function (lemma 6.5.1.1) we may assume that in (1) either removal of trivial equations was applied or rewriting was applied to an innermost redex. In this case the result follows in analogy to lemma 6.5.1.5.

Suppose now that $\mu'F'$ is not in normal form. Since refutations wrt $\{\rightarrow_R, \rightarrow_t\}$ are independent of a strong selection function (lemma 6.5.1.1) we may assume that $\mu'F'$ was rewritten in (1), i.e. we find an occurrence $\pi \in Occ(\mu'E)$, a rewrite rule $P = 1\rightarrow r\Leftarrow F^*$, a substitution θ', and a multiset of equations F" such that $(\delta'\mu'E)|\pi| = \theta'1$ and

$$\Leftarrow \mu'F' \;\rightarrow_R(\mu'E, \pi, P, \theta')\; \Leftarrow F". \tag{2}$$

By lemma 6.5.2.1 we find an F such that

$$\Leftarrow \mu'F' \;\rightarrow_R(\mu'E, \pi, P, \theta')\; \Leftarrow \mu'F. \tag{3}$$

Now let $\delta = \delta'$ and $\mu = \mu'$. By an application of lemma 6.4.6 we find a substitution $\theta = \delta'\theta'|Dom(\theta')$ such that

$$\Leftarrow \delta'\mu'F' \;\rightarrow_R(\delta'\mu'E, \pi, P, \theta)\; \Leftarrow \delta\mu F.$$

Since μ' is in normal form an application of lemma 6.5.2.1 to (3) ensures that

$$\Leftarrow F', \mu' \;\rightarrow_R\; \Leftarrow F, \mu' = \Leftarrow F, \mu.$$

From the induction hypothesis we learn that there exists a refutation of $R\cup\{\Leftarrow F, \mu\}$ wrt $\{\rightarrow_f, \rightarrow_{in}, \rightarrow_{if}, \rightarrow_R\}$ such that $\rightarrow_f$, $\rightarrow_{in}$, and $\rightarrow_{if}$ are only applied to goal clauses in normal form. Furthermore, if $\theta_1, ..., \theta_n$ are the matchers used in the refutation of $R\cup\{\Leftarrow\delta\mu F\}$ and $\sigma_1, ..., \sigma_m$ are the unifiers used in the refutation of $R\cup\{\Leftarrow F, \mu\}$, then

$$\theta_n...\theta_1\delta \le \sigma_m...\sigma_1.$$

Clearly, there exists a refutation of $R\cup\{\Leftarrow F', \mu'\}$ wrt $\{\rightarrow_f, \rightarrow_{in}, \rightarrow_{if}, \rightarrow_R\}$ using unifiers θ, $\sigma_1, ..., \sigma_n$ such that $\rightarrow_f$, $\rightarrow_{in}$, and $\rightarrow_{if}$ are only applied to goal clauses in normal form. Furthermore, by proposition 4.3(6),

$$\theta_n...\theta_1\theta\delta' = \theta_n...\theta_1\theta\delta \le \sigma_m...\sigma_1\theta. \qquad\qquad \text{qed}$$

With the help of this lifting lemma we can now show that reflection, innermost narrowing, and innermost reflection are complete even if rewriting is applied as a simplification rule.

Theorem 6.5.2.3 (Completeness of $\rightarrow_f$, $\rightarrow_{in}$, $\rightarrow_{if}$, and $\rightarrow_R$):

Let R be a canonical term rewriting system. If θ be a correct answer substitution for R and $\Leftarrow F$, then exists a computed answer substitution σ obtained by a refutation of $R\cup\{\Leftarrow F, \varepsilon\}$ wrt $\{\rightarrow_f, \rightarrow_{in}, \rightarrow_{if}, \rightarrow_R\}$ such that $\rightarrow_f$, $\rightarrow_{in}$, and $\rightarrow_{if}$ are only applied to goal clauses in normal form and $\theta \le_R \sigma$.

Proof:

The proof can be obtained in analogy to the proof of theorem 6.5.1.6; just replace lemma 6.5.1.5 by lemma 6.5.2.2.   qed

In analogy to the previous section it is easy to see that refutations with respect to reflection, innermost reflection, innermost narrowing, and rewriting are independent of a strong selection function which selects only innermost redexes if innermost reflection steps are only applied before an innermost narrowing step.

6.5.3 Completely Defined Term Rewriting Systems

In section 6.4 we showed that a term rewriting systems R devides the set of function symbols into the disjoint sets of defined function symbols and constructors, where f is said to be a defined function symbol iff R contains a definition of f.

Definition:

Let R be a conditional term rewriting system and f be a defined function symbol. f is said to be **completely defined** iff it does not occur in any ground term in normal form. R is said to be **completely defined** iff each defined function symbol is completely defined.

For completely defined and canonical term rewriting systems we can show that reflection and innermost narrowing are complete, if we are only interested in ground substitutions, i.e. substitutions whose codomain only contains ground terms. The reason for such a completeness result follows immediately from the lifting lemma for reflection, innermost narrowing, and innermost reflection. The innermost reflection rule is only needed if an innermost redex with respect to $\to_R$ in $\Leftarrow\delta\mu F$ does not correspond to an innermost redex with respect to $\to_n$ in $\Leftarrow F$, μ. However, if the term rewriting system is completely defined and $\delta\mu$ is a ground normalized substitution, then s being an innermost redex with respect to $\to_R$ in $\Leftarrow\delta\mu F$ implies that s does not contain any defined function symbol. Hence, the corresponding term occurring in $\Leftarrow F$, μ must be an innermost redex with respect to $\to_n$. As an immediate consequence we obtain

Theorem 6.5.3.1:

Let R be a completely defined and canonical term rewriting system. If θ is a ground and correct answer substitution for R and $\Leftarrow F$, then there exists a computed answer substitution σ obtained by a refutation of $R\cup\{\Leftarrow F, \varepsilon\}$ wrt $\{\to_f, \to_{in}\}$ such that $\theta \leq_R \sigma$.

In analogy to theorem 6.5.2.3 we can strengthen theorem 6.5.3.1 by allowing to normalize goal clauses in a refutation with respect to reflection and innermost narrowing. Recall that the lifting lemma for reflection, innermost reflection, and innermost narrowing was applied to an innermost refutation with respect to rewriting and removal of trivial equations. From lemma 6.5.1.2 we learn that such an innermost refutation is independent of a strong selection function. Since R is completely defined, innermost reflection need not be applied and, hence, the lifting lemma preserves the selection function. As a consequence, for a completely defined and canonical term rewriting system we learn that refutations with respect to reflection and innermost narrowing are independent of a strong selection function which selects only innermost redexes. This corresponds to the result obtained by Fribourg (1985).

It should be observed that in untyped theories - as we consider them within this thesis - completely defined functions occur only rarely. However, in typed theories a result corresponding to theorem 6.5.3.1 will often be applicable.

We showed that refutations with respect to reflection and innermost narrowing are independent of a strong selection function as long as the selection functions always selects an innermost redex, if such a redex exists. This result cannot be extended to arbitrarily strong selection functions as the following example shows (see Echahed 1988): Consider the rewrite rules

$$f(0,0) \rightarrow 0 \qquad\qquad\qquad\qquad\qquad\qquad (f1)$$
$$f(s(x),0) \rightarrow 1 \qquad\qquad\qquad\qquad\qquad\qquad (f2)$$
$$f(x,s(y)) \rightarrow 2 \qquad\qquad\qquad\qquad\qquad\qquad (f3)$$

and the equation $EQ(f(f(x,y), z),0)$. If we select an outermost redex, then

$$\Leftarrow EQ(f(f(x,y),z), 0) \rightarrow_{n(f3)} \Leftarrow EQ(2,0)$$

and the derivation fails since $2 \neq 0$. However,

$$\Leftarrow EQ(f(f(x,y),z), 0) \rightarrow_{n(f1)} \Leftarrow EQ(f(0,z), 0) \rightarrow_{n(f1)} \Leftarrow EQ(0,0) \rightarrow_t \Box$$

and, thus, outermost narrowing is incomplete. As Echahed showed completeness of an arbitrarily strong selection function can be achieved if we assume that the left-hand sides of the rewrite rules are pairwise "not strictly subunifiable", i.e. for two left-hand sides l_1 and l_2 there does not exist an occurrence $\pi \in Occ(l_1) \cap Occ(l_2)$ such that $l_1|\pi|$ and $l_2|\pi|$ are unifiable (with a substitution that is not the identity or a variable renaming) and for all $\pi' > \pi$ we find that the initial symbols of $l_1|\pi'|$ and $l_2|\pi'|$ are identical. For example, $f(0,0)$ and $f(x,s(y))$ are strictly subunifiable at 1 with $\{x \leftarrow 0\}$, whereas $f(0,0)$ and $f(s(x),0)$ are not strictly subunifiable. A similar condition called "uniformity" was defined by Padawitz (1987).

We finish this chapter by demonstrating that the universal unification and matching problem for canonical theories is undecidable.

6.6 The Unification and Matching Problem for Canonical Theories

In this section we investigate the problem whether two terms s and t are unifiable under a canonical and conditional term rewriting system R. Hence, we have to solve the problem of whether there exists a substitution σ such that $\sigma s =_R \sigma t$ or, equivalently, whether $\sigma EQ(s,t)$ is a logical E-consequence of R or, equivalently, whether σs and σt have the same normal form with respect to R.

Moreover we are interested in the matching problem for canonical theories.

Definition:

An **EP-matching problem** $<s \leq t>_{EP}$ consists of an equation $EQ(s,t)$ and an equational program EP. The problem has a solution, if there exists a substitution σ such that $s =_{EP} \sigma t$. A **universal matching problem** for a given class C of equational programs consists of finding an algorithm which for all EP $\in$ C and equations $EQ(s,t)$ decides whether $<s \leq t>_{EP}$ has a solution.

As with the unification problem we find that the EP-matching problem is equivalent to the problem whether s and σt have the same normal form if EP is a canonical term rewriting system.

6.6.1 A Decidability Metatheorem

To prove that the universal unification problem for canonical theories is undecidable we use a metatheorem introduced by Heilbrunner (1983). The universal unification problem will be reduced to the problem of whether the languages generated by two simple grammars are disjoint. Hence, we need some definitions concerning language theory which are borrowed from Harrison (1978).

Definition:

A **context-free grammar (CFG)** is a 4-tuple $G = (N, T, P, S)$ where
(1) N is a finite set of **nonterminal symbols.**
(2) T is a finite set of **terminal symbols,** disjoint from N.
(3) P is a finite subset of $Nx(N \cup T)^*$. An element (A,β) in P will be written $A \Rightarrow \beta$ and called a **production.**
(4) S is a distinguished symbol in N called the **sentence (or start) symbol.**

When talking about G in the remaining parts of this section we mean a context free grammer $G = (N, T, P, S)$. $V = N \cup T$. The notational conventions are laid down in the following table. All symbols are possibly indexed. Further, $|u|$ denotes the length of the string u.

Symbol	A,B,...	a,b,...	u,v,...	ε	$\alpha,\beta,...$
Element of	N	T	T^*	V^0	V^*

Definition:

Let G be a CFG. α **directly generates (or derives)** β, in symbols $\alpha \Rightarrow \beta$, if there exist α_1, α_2, A, and γ, such that $\alpha = \alpha_1 A \alpha_2$, $\beta = \alpha_1 \gamma \alpha_2$, and $A \Rightarrow \gamma$ is in P. If $\alpha_1 \in T^*$, then $\alpha \Rightarrow \beta$ is a **leftmost generation (derivation).**

Since we consider only leftmost generations we omit the index L generally used to denote leftmost generations.

Definition:

$\Rightarrow^*$ denotes the transitive and reflexive closure of $\Rightarrow$.

Definition:

Let G be a CFG. The **language generated by** G, denoted L(G), is the set
$$L(G) = \{ u \in T^* \mid S \Rightarrow^* u \}.$$

Definition:

> A grammar G is said to be an s- (or **simple**) **grammar in Greibach Normal Form** (GNF), if
>
> (1) $P \subseteq N \times TN^*$,
>
> (2) $\forall A \, \forall a \, \forall \beta, \gamma \colon A \Rightarrow a\beta \in P \wedge A \Rightarrow a\gamma \in P \Rightarrow \beta = \gamma$.

There is a straightforward algorithm which establishes property (1) for a grammar which satisfies (2). To each terminal symbol $a \in T$ introduce a new nonterminal $[a]$ and a production rule $[a] \Rightarrow a$. In addition, define $[B]$ by $[B] = B$ for all nonterminals $B \in N$ and replace all rules $A \Rightarrow aX_1 \ldots X_n$ by $A \Rightarrow a[X_1] \ldots [X_n]$.

Definition:

> For arbitrary sets X, Y the **relative decision problem for X and Y** is the following: Given x in X, is x in Y? We say that the problem is **undecidable** if there is no Turing machine which halts for all members of X and accepts some $x \in X$ iff $x \in Y$.

The following theorem is a simplified version of theorem 2.1 of Heilbrunner (1983). Essentially the same proposition is contained in Korenjak & Hopcroft (1966).

Theorem 6.6.1.1:

> Let X, Y, and Z be sets with $Y \cap Z = \emptyset$ and let θ be a computable function such that for every pair (G_1, G_2) of s-grammars in GNF
>
> (1) $\theta(G_1, G_2) \in X$,
>
> (2) $L(G_1) \cap L(G_2) = \emptyset \Rightarrow \theta(G_1, G_2) \in Y$, and
>
> (3) $L(G_1) \cap L(G_2) \neq \emptyset \Rightarrow \theta(G_1, G_2) \in Z$.
>
> Then the relative decision problems for X, Y and for X, Z are undecidable.

Proof:

We use theorem 2.1 of Heilbrunner (1983). Let T be the straightforward transformation which converts an s-grammar into GNF and define θ by

$$\Phi(G_1, G_2) = \theta(T(G_1), T(G_2)).$$

Then $\Phi(G_1, G_2) \in X$ is immediate. If $G_1 \cup G_2$ is an LL grammar, then $L(T(G_1)) \cap L(T(G_2)) = \emptyset$ and $\Phi(G_1, G_2) = \theta(T(G_1), T(G_2)) \in Y$ by (2). Likewise, $|L(G_1) \cap L(G_2)| = 1$ implies $L(T(G_1)) \cap L(T(G_2)) \neq \emptyset$ so that $\Phi(G_1, G_2) = \theta(T(G_1), T(G_2)) \in Z$ by (1). An application of theorem 2.1 in Heilbrunner (1983) completes the proof.   qed

Figure 6.6.1 illustrates this theorem.

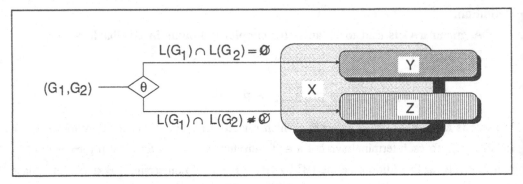

Figure 6.6.1

6.6.2 The Undecidability of the Unification and Matching Problem

In this section we prove the undecidability of the universal unification problem for canonical theories, i.e. the undecidability of the relative decision problem X, Z, where

$$X = \{ (R, <s=t>_R) \mid R \text{ is canonical and } s, t \text{ are terms} \}$$

and

$$Z = \{ (R, <s=t>_R) \in X \mid \exists \sigma: \exists r: \sigma s \rightarrow^* r \wedge \sigma t \rightarrow^* r \}.$$

We prepare for an application of theorem 6.6.1. and let $Y = X \backslash Z$. For the definition of $\theta(G_1, G_2)$ we assume $G_i = (N_i, T, P_i, S_i)$, $N_1 \cap N_2 = \emptyset$, and define a term rewriting system scheme **RS** as follows. Let

x, y, z	be variables,
$\{\$\} \cup N_1 \cup N_2 \cup T$	be the set of constants,
$\bullet$	be a 2-ary constructor, and
f	be a 3-ary defined function symbol.

Using infix notation for "$\bullet$" we abbreviate $(X_1 \bullet (X_2 \bullet \ldots \bullet (X_n \bullet \alpha) \ldots))$ to $[X_1 \ldots X_n] \bullet \alpha$, where X_1, ..., X_n are constants.

We define

$$\mathbf{RS} = \{ f(A \bullet x, B \bullet y, a \bullet z) \rightarrow f([X_1 \ldots X_n] \bullet x, [Y_1 \ldots Y_m] \bullet y, z) \mid$$
$$A \Rightarrow aX_1 \ldots X_n \in P_1 \text{ and } B \Rightarrow aY_1 \ldots Y_m \in P_2\}.$$

Note the correspondence between the function definition for f and a top down parser $\vdash$ for an s-grammar G in GNF defined by

$$(Ax, az) \vdash (X_1 \ldots X_n x, z) \text{ iff } A \Rightarrow aX_1 \ldots X_n \in P.$$

At first we prove some properties of **RS**. Recall that Con(X) denotes the set of constructions occurring in X (p. 19).

Lemma 6.6.2.1:

If u_1, v_1, and w_1 are in normal form, then
$$f(u_1, v_1, w_1) \rightarrow^k f(u_2, v_2, w_2) \text{ implies } |Con(w_1)| = |Con(w_2)| + k.$$

Proof:

The proof is by an induction on k. The case k=0 being trivial we turn to the induction step and assume that

$$f(u, v, w) \rightarrow f(u_1, v_1, w_1) \tag{1}$$

and

$$f(u_1, v_1, w_1) \rightarrow^k f(u_2, v_2, w_2) \tag{2}$$

where u, v, and w are in normal form. Hence, rewriting is performed at occurrence Λ of $f(u,v,w)$ in (1). Therefore, we find a new variant

$$f(A \cdot x, B \cdot y, a \cdot z) \rightarrow f([X_1 \ldots X_n] \cdot x, [Y_1 \ldots Y_m] \cdot y, z) \tag{3}$$

of some rule in **RS** and a substitution σ such that

$$f(u,v,w) = f(A \cdot \sigma x, B \cdot \sigma y, a \cdot \sigma z) \tag{4}$$

and

$$f(u_1,v_1,w_1) = f([X_1 \ldots X_n] \cdot \sigma x, [Y_1 \ldots Y_m] \cdot \sigma y, \sigma z). \tag{5}$$

By comparing the third arguments of f in (4) we find some w' such that

$$w = a \cdot w' = a \cdot \sigma z. \tag{6}$$

Obviously,

$$|Con(w)| = |Con(a \cdot w')| = |Con(w')| + 1. \tag{7}$$

We insert (6) into (5) and use (2) to obtain

$$f([X_1 \ldots X_n] \cdot \sigma x, [Y_1 \ldots Y_m] \cdot \sigma y, w') \rightarrow^k f(u_2, v_2, w_2). \tag{8}$$

An application of the induction hypothesis to (8) shows that

$$|Con(w')| = |Con(w_2)| + k \tag{9}$$

and together with (7) we obtain

$$|Con(w)| = |Con(w_2)| + k + 1. \qquad \text{qed}$$

Observe that in the previous lemma u_2, v_2, and w_2 are also in normal form.

Lemma 6.2.2:

RS is terminating.

Proof:

The proof is by induction on the structure of terms. If t is a constant or a variable, then t is in normal form. Now let $t = g(t_1,\ldots,t_m)$ and assume that there exist $n_i \in N$ such that t_i reduces in n_i steps to its normal form s_i, $1 \leq i \leq m$. Then, obviously,

$$t \rightarrow^n g(s_1,\ldots,s_m) = t', \quad \text{where } n = \Sigma_i n_i.$$

We distinguish two cases:

If t' is not a redex, then t' is in normal form.

If t' is a redex, then t' matches a left-hand side of a rewrite rule in **RS** only if $m = 3$ and $|Con(s_3)| > 0$. According to lemma 6.6.2.1 each reduction step reduces the number of constants occurring in s_3 by 1 and hence the reduction issuing from t' terminates after k steps for some $k \in N_0$.   qed

Lemma 6.6.2.3:

RS is confluent.

Proof:

We prove the lemma by applying the superposition algorithm to **RS**. From the definition of **RS** follows that a critical pair may only be obtained if two left-hand sides l and l' of rewrite rules in **RS** are unifiable. In this case l and l' must both be of the form

$f(A \bullet x, B \bullet y, a \bullet z)$.

Since G_1 and G_2 are s-grammars in GNF it follows that the respective right-hand sides r and r' must both be of the form

$f([X_1...X_n] \bullet x, [Y_1...Y_m] \bullet y, z)$.

Hence, $l \to r$ and $l' \to r'$ are identical. It follows that there does not exist a critical pair and theorems 6.4.8 and 6.4.9 ensure that **RS** is confluent.   qed

The following technical lemma states that during the reduction of s the number of functional expressions occurring in s, Fun(s), remains unchanged.

Lemma 6.6.2.4:

If $s \to^* t$ then $|Fun(s)| = |Fun(t)|$.

Proof:

The proof is by induction on the length of the reduction sequence. The case k=0 being trivial we turn to the induction step and assume that

$$s' \to s \tag{1}$$

and

$$s \to^k t. \tag{2}$$

Hence, we find an occurrence π of s', a new variant

$$f(A \bullet x, B \bullet y, a \bullet z) \to f([X_1...X_n] \bullet x, [Y_1...Y_m] \bullet y, z) \tag{3}$$

of some rule in **RS**, and a substitution σ such that

$$s'|\pi| = \sigma f(A \bullet x, B \bullet y, a \bullet z) \tag{4}$$

and

$$s = s'|\pi \leftarrow \sigma f([X_1...X_n] \bullet x, [Y_1...Y_m] \bullet y, z)|. \tag{5}$$

From (4) and (5) follows immediately that

$$|Fun(s')| = |Fun(s)|. \tag{6}$$

By an application of the induction hypothesis to (5) and (2) we obtain together with (6) that

$$|Fun(s')| = |Fun(s)| = |Fun(t)|$$

which completes the proof.   qed

An immediate consequence of lemma 6.6.2.4 is

Corollary 6.6.2.5:

If $f(t_1, t_2, t_3) \to^* f(\$, \$, \$)$ then t_1, t_2, and t_3 do not contain any redex.

The unification problem **U** for a given pair of s-grammars can now be defined as

$$U = <f(S_1 \bullet \$, S_2 \bullet \$, z) = f(\$, \$, \$)>RS.$$

Lemma 6.6.2.6:

U has a solution iff $L(G_1) \cap L(G_2) \neq \emptyset$.

Proof:

We have to show

$$\exists \sigma: \exists r: \sigma f(S_1 \bullet \$, S_2 \bullet \$, z) \rightarrow^* r \wedge \sigma f(\$, \$, \$) \rightarrow^* r \text{ iff } L(G_1) \cap L(G_2) \neq \emptyset.$$

Since $f(\$, \$, \$)$ is not changed under any substitution and cannot be rewritten under **RS**, an application of the definitions reduces the claim to

$$\exists \sigma: f(S_1 \bullet \$, S_2 \bullet \$, \sigma z) \rightarrow^* f(\$, \$, \$) \text{ iff } \exists u: S_1 \Rightarrow^* u \wedge S_2 \Rightarrow^* u.$$

We now turn to the proof of this claim.

To prove the if-half we start with showing by induction on the length k of u that

$$S_1 \Rightarrow^* u\alpha \wedge S_2 \Rightarrow^* u\beta \wedge \alpha \in N_1^* \wedge \beta \in N_2^*$$

implies

$$f(S_1 \bullet \$, S_2 \bullet \$, [u] \bullet z) \rightarrow^* f([\alpha] \bullet \$, [\beta] \bullet \$, z).$$

The case k=0 implies $\alpha = S_1$ and $\beta = S_2$ and, hence, is trivial. In the induction step we may assume

$$S_1 \Rightarrow^* u\alpha = uA\alpha' \Rightarrow uaX_1...X_n\alpha',$$
$$S_2 \Rightarrow^* u\beta = uB\beta' \Rightarrow uaY_1...Y_m\beta',$$
$$|u| = k,$$

and

$$n, m \geq 0.$$

The induction hypothesis ensures

$$
\begin{aligned}
f(S_1 \bullet \$, S_2 \bullet \$, [ua] \bullet z) \quad &= \quad f(S_1 \bullet \$, S_2 \bullet \$, [u] \bullet (a \bullet z)) \\
&\rightarrow^* \quad f([\alpha] \bullet \$), [\beta] \bullet \$, a \bullet z) \\
&= \quad f([A\alpha'] \bullet \$, [B\beta'] \bullet \$, a \bullet z).
\end{aligned}
$$

Since $A \Rightarrow aX_1...X_n \in P_1$ and $B \Rightarrow aY_1...Y_m \in P_2$, we find

$$f(A \bullet x, B \bullet y, a \bullet z) \rightarrow f([X_1...X_n] \bullet x, [Y_1...Y_m] \bullet y, z) \in RS.$$

Therefore,

$$f([A\alpha'] \bullet \$, [B\beta'] \bullet \$, a \bullet z) \rightarrow f([X_1...X_n\alpha'] \bullet \$, [Y_1...Y_m\beta'] \bullet \$, z).$$

We turn to the proof of the claim and assume that $u \in L(G_1) \cap L(G_2)$, i.e. $S_1 \Rightarrow^* u$ and $S_2 \Rightarrow^* u$. Define a substitution σ by

$$\sigma = \{z <- [u] \bullet \$\}.$$

Using the above property we conclude

$$f(S_1 \bullet \$, S_2 \bullet \$, \sigma z) = f(S_1 \bullet \$, S_2 \bullet \$, [u] \bullet \$) \rightarrow^* f(\$, \$, \$).$$

To prove the only-if-half we shall prove by induction on k that

$$f([\alpha]\bullet\$,[\beta]\bullet\$,t) \to^k f(\$,\$,\$)$$

implies

$$\exists u: t = [u]\bullet\$ \wedge \alpha \Rightarrow^* u \wedge \beta \Rightarrow^* u.$$

The case k=0 being trivial we turn to the induction step and assume

$$f([\gamma]\bullet\$,[\delta]\bullet\$,s) \to f(t_1,t_2,t) \tag{1}$$

and

$$f(t_1,t_2,t) \to^k f(\$,\$,\$). \tag{2}$$

Because of $|Fun(s)| = 0$ (lemma 6.6.2.5) rewriting is performed at occurrence Λ of $f([\gamma]\bullet\$,[\delta]\bullet\$,s)$ at (1). Hence, we find a new variant

$$f(A\bullet x,B\bullet y,a\bullet z) \to f([X_1...X_n]\bullet x,[Y_1...Y_m]\bullet y,z) \tag{3}$$

of some rule in **RS** and a substitution σ such that

$$f([\gamma]\bullet\$,[\delta]\bullet\$,s) = \sigma f(A\bullet x,B\bullet y,a\bullet z) = f(A\bullet\sigma x,B\bullet\sigma y,a\bullet\sigma z) \tag{4}$$

and

$$
\begin{aligned}
f(t_1,t_2,t) \quad &= \quad \sigma f([X_1...X_n]\bullet x,[Y_1...Y_m]\bullet y,z) \\
&= \quad f([X_1...X_n]\bullet\sigma x,[Y_1...Y_m]\bullet\sigma y,\sigma z)
\end{aligned}
\tag{5}
$$

By comparing corresponding arguments of (4) we find some α_1, β_1 such that

$$\sigma x = [\alpha_1]\bullet\$ \text{ and } \gamma = A\alpha_1 \tag{6}$$

and

$$\sigma y = [\beta_1]\bullet\$ \text{ and } \delta = B\beta_1. \tag{7}$$

We insert (6) and (7) into (5) and use (2) to obtain

$$f([X_1...X_n\alpha_1]\bullet\$,[Y_1...Y_m\beta_1]\bullet\$,t) \to^k f(\$,\$,\$). \tag{8}$$

An application of the induction hypothesis to (8) yields some u such that

$$t = [u]\bullet\$ \wedge X_1...X_n\alpha_1 \Rightarrow^* u \wedge Y_1...Y_m\beta_1 \Rightarrow^* u. \tag{9}$$

Using $t = [u]\bullet\$$ and comparing again corresponding arguments in (4) and (5) we obtain

$$t = \sigma z, \; \sigma z = [u]\bullet\$, \; s = a\bullet\sigma z, \text{ and } s = [au]\bullet\$. \tag{10}$$

From (3) we learn

$$A\Rightarrow aX_1...X_n \in P_1 \wedge B\Rightarrow aY_1...Y_m \in P_2. \tag{11}$$

We conclude

$$
\begin{array}{llll}
\gamma & = & A\alpha_1 & \text{by (6)} \\
 & \Rightarrow & aX_1...X_n\alpha_1 & \text{by (11)} \\
 & \Rightarrow^* & au & \text{by (9)}
\end{array}
$$

and, likewise,

$$\delta \Rightarrow^* au,$$

so that $s = [au]\bullet\$$ from (10) completes the induction step.

Turning to the proof of the claim, we may assume

$$f(S_1 \bullet \$, S_2 \bullet \$, \sigma z) \to^* f(\$,\$,\$)$$

and conclude

$$\exists u: \sigma z = [u] \bullet \$ \wedge S_1 \Rightarrow^* u \wedge S_2 \Rightarrow^* u.$$

Therefore, $L(G_1) \cap L(G_2) \neq \emptyset$.   qed

As an example consider the s-grammars G_1 and G_2 where

$$N_1 = \{ S_1, B_1, C_1 \},$$
$$N_2 = \{ S_2, B_2, C_2 \},$$
$$T = \{ a, b, c \},$$
$$P_1 = \{ S_1 \Rightarrow aB_1C_1, B_1 \Rightarrow b, C_1 \Rightarrow c \},$$

and

$$P_2 = \{ S_2 \Rightarrow aB_2, B_2 \Rightarrow bC_2, B_2 \Rightarrow a, C_2 \Rightarrow c \}.$$

Hence, **RS** is instantiated to

$$f(S_1 \bullet x, B_2 \bullet y, a \bullet z) \to f([B_1C_1] \bullet x, y, z) \tag{f0}$$
$$f(S_1 \bullet x, S_2 \bullet y, a \bullet z) \to f([B_1C_1] \bullet x, B_2 \bullet y, z) \tag{f1}$$
$$f(B_1 \bullet x, B_2 \bullet y, b \bullet z) \to f(x, C_2 \bullet y, z) \tag{f2}$$
$$f(C_1 \bullet x, C_2 \bullet y, c \bullet z) \to f(x, y, z). \tag{f3}$$

Obviously, $L(G_1) = \{abc\}$ and $L(G_2) = \{abc, aa\}$ and

$$\begin{aligned}
f(S_1 \bullet \$, S_2 \bullet \$, [abc] \bullet \$) \quad &\to_{(f1)} \quad & f([B_1C_1] \bullet \$, B_2 \bullet \$, [bc] \bullet \$) \\
&\to_{(f2)} \quad & f(C_1 \bullet \$, C_2 \bullet \$, c \bullet \$) \\
&\to_{(f3)} \quad & f(\$,\$,\$).
\end{aligned}$$

The normal form of $f(S_1 \bullet \$, S_2 \bullet \$, [aa] \bullet \$)$ is $f([B_1C_1] \bullet \$, B_2 \bullet \$, [a] \bullet \$)$.

Theorem 6.6.2.7:

The universal unification problem for the class of canonical theories is undecidable.

Proof:

Referring to the preceding discussion we define

$$\theta(G_1, G_2) = (\textbf{RS}, \textbf{U}),$$

Note that θ is computable. Conditions (2) and (3) of theorem 6.6.1.1 are guaranteed by lemma 6.6.2.6. An application of theorem 6.6.1.1 completes the proof.   qed

However, as we showed in theorem 6.5.3 the universal unification problem for canonical theories is semidecidable.

Let us again take a look at the unification problem

$$U = <f(S_1 \bullet \$, S_2 \bullet \$, z) = f(\$,\$,\$)>_{\textbf{RS}}$$

we considered in the previous proof. Observe that no variable occurs in the term $f(\$,\$,\$)$. Hence, $\sigma f(\$,\$,\$) = f(\$,\$,\$)$ for all substitutions σ and, therefore, U is equivalent to the matching problem

$$M = <f(S_1{\cdot}\$,S_2{\cdot}\$,z){\geq}f(\$,\$,\$)>_{RS}.$$

Theorem 6.6.2.8:

The universal matching problem for class of canonical theories is undecidable.

Proof:

The proof is in analogy to the proof of theorem 6.6.2.7: just replace U by M, $<s{=}t>_{RS}$ by $<s{\geq}t>_{RS}$, $\sigma t \to^* r$ by $t \to^* r$, and unification by matching.   qed

Definition:

A term rewriting system R is said to be **admissible** iff the R-matching problem is decidable.

An immediate consequence of theorem 6.6.2.8 is that **RS** is not admissible.

Corollary 6.6.2.9:

The class of admissible canonical theories is a proper subset of the class of canonical theories.

Proof:

Let **RS** be defined as above. By lemmas 6.6.2.2 and 6.6.2.3, **RS** is canonical. However, the matching problem $<s{\geq}t>_{RS}$ is undecidable (theorem 6.6.2.8) and therefore **RS** is not admissible.   qed

Corollary 6.6.2.9 solves a problem posed by Szabo (1982, III.3.1.P.1) and Siekmann (1984, P9): there exists a canonical term rewriting system for which the matching problem is undecidable. Furthermore, since **RS** is regular, there exists also a regular term rewriting system for which the matching problem is undecidable.

Recently, Bockmayr (1987) showed that the unification and matching problem for canonical theories can be reduced to Hilbert's Tenth Problem. His proof does not seem to be simpler, in fact he uses the same steps as we did: First a term rewriting system (for integers) is given and it is shown that the term rewriting system in confluent. Finally, it is proved that, if the unification (resp. matching) problem is decidable, then for any term t it is decidable whether there exists a substitution μ such that μt is equal to 0. The latter problem is Hilbert's Tenth problem, which is known to be undecidable.

6.7 Summary

Let us briefly summarize the results that we obtained in this chapter (see also figure 6.7.1). We showed in the first two sections that paramodulation and reflection is complete for equational programs EP if an instantiation rule was added and if clauses from EP^{-1} were used. The result was proved by defining a monotonic and continuous function T_{EP} for EP and showing that the least Herbrand E-model of EP is equal to the least fixpoint of $T_{EP\cup EP^{-1}}$. Furthermore, since each step from an argument to a value of T_{EP} corresponds to a instantiation and paramodulation (resp. reflection) step, the least fixpoint of $T_{EP\cup EP^{-1}}$ is also equal to the success set of $EP\cup EP^{-1}$ with respect to reflection, instantiation and paramodulation. We demonstrated in detail the need for the instantiation rule or, equivalently, the functional reflexive axioms. Furthermore, we proved that refutations with respect to reflection, instantiation and paramodulation are independent of a selection function.

In the following sections we were concerned with the problem of how to prune the search space generated by paramodulation. In section 6.3 we showed that clauses from EP^{-1} can be omitted if the equational program is ground confluent. In addition, if the equational program is a term rewriting system, then the instantiation rule is not needed as long as we only consider ground goal clauses (section 6.4). This result can be lifted if the equational program is a non-trivial and confluent term rewriting system and answer substitutions are normalizable (section 6.5). In section 6.5.1 we demonstrated that for canonical term rewriting systems reflection, innermost reflection, and innermost narrowing are complete and that rewriting can be applied as a simplification rule (section 6.5.2). This result was obtained by applying Boyer & Moore's (1972) technique of structure sharing to refutations with respect to reflection and narrowing. We showed that each "basic" term (Hullot 1980) occurred in the skeleton and each "non-basic" term occurred in the environment part of a goal clause. As a consequence we gave a completeness result for "basic" narrowing without introducing the somewhat "clumsy" notion of a "basic" occurrence. Finally, if the canonical term rewriting system is completely defined and all answer substitutions are ground, then reflection and innermost narrowing are complete.

Thus, we defined a framework for universal unification procedures based on paramodulation and showed how various results from the literature can be mapped into this framework.

In the final section 6.6 we solved the problem of whether there exists a canonical term rewriting system for which the matching problem is undecidable by reducing it to the problem of whether the intersection of the languages generated by two context-free grammars is disjoint.

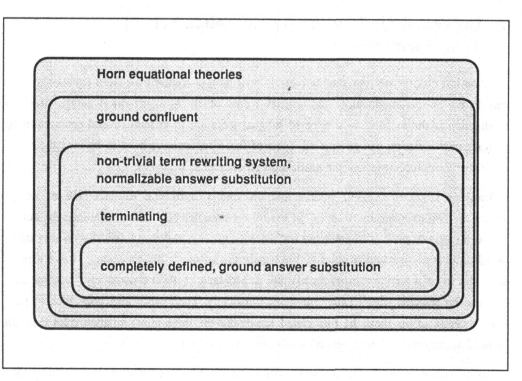

Figure 6.7.1

7 Universal Unification by Complete Sets of Transformations

In the last chapter we presented universal unification procedures for Horn equational theories based on paramodulation and special forms of it. A major disadvantage of paramodulation is the fact that in a selected subgoal there are in general several occurrences to which paramodulation can be applied. Most of these occurrences have to be investigated to guarentee the completeness of the unification procedure.

Similarly, Digricoli's (1979) "RUE-resolution" rule is based on a "disagreement set" analysis for the two expressions to unify. To ensure the completeness of his technique the author has to investigate each "disagreement set" "don't know" non-deterministically. In the traditional unification problem (Robinson 1965) only the leftmost "disagreement" of two expressions has to be solved at a time. As Martelli & Montanari (1982) showed any "disagreement set" can be selected "don't care" non-deterministically. Their basic idea goes back to Herbrand (1930). In his thesis he formulated essentially the three transformation rules that can be used to compute the most general unifier of two terms (see section 3.4.1).

Let us look at a small example which demonstrates the use of these transformation rules. Suppose we want to unify the terms $f(x,g(x))$ and $f(a,g(a))$. Since both terms have the same initial symbol "f" we can decompose these terms. It remains to be shown that x and a as well as $g(x)$ and $g(a)$ can simultaneously be made equal. If we select the first two terms then, since x is a variable, the substitution $\{x \leftarrow a\}$ solves this problem. Applying $\{x \leftarrow a\}$ to $g(x)$ yields $g(a)$ and, thus, we obtain the trivial problem $<g(a)=g(a)>$. Therefore, always the initial symbols of the two terms which are to be unified determine which rule has to be applied to them.

This idea was generalized to higher order unification by G. Huet (1972). Recently, several authors have proposed to extend Herbrand's and Martelli & Montanari's transformations respectively in order to compute complete sets of unifiers under unconditional equational theories (Kirchner 1984, Martelli et al. 1986, Gallier & Snyder 1987a,b, Hölldobler 1987a).

In this chapter we define a framework for universal unification procedures for Horn equational theories based on sets of transformations. To show that our set of transformations is complete we give a procedure that transforms a refutation with respect to paramodulation into a refutation with respect to the transformation rules. This technique allows to refine our set of transformations if the equational program is confluent or canonical in much the same way as paramodulation can be restricted under the respective conditions.

The transformation rules are generally applicable with respect to the form of the elements of the selected equation. However, the order of the elements is not important. For example, consider the "variable elimination" rule, which is applicable to equations of the form $EQ(x,t)$ as well as $EQ(t,x)$. What really matters is the question of whether the selected equation consists of a term and a variable which does not occur in the term. Since we introduce several new inference rules which take into account the form of the elements of an equation we no longer distinguish between the equations $EQ(s,t)$ and $EQ(t,s)$.

7.1 The Transformation Rules

The set of transformations is an extension of the set of transformations used to compute the most general unifier of two terms. Therefore, we briefly repeat these rules.

The **term decomposition rule** ($\rightarrow_d$) decomposes an equation of the form EQ($f(s_1,...,s_n)$, $f(t_1,...,t_n)$) into the set of its corresponding arguments, i.e. into {EQ(s_i,t_i) | $1 \leq i \leq n$}. In section 6.2 we demonstrated that decomposable equations, that is equations of the form EQ($f(s_1,...,s_n)$, $f(t_1,...,t_n)$), where f is a decomposable function symbol, should be decomposed as early as possible. We show that such a simplification is also applicable to refutations with respect to the set of transformations we define in this section. Therefore, later on we split the term decomposition rule into the rules **decomposition of decomposable equations** ($\rightarrow_{dd}$) and **decomposition of non-decomposable equations** ($\rightarrow_{dn}$).

The **variable elimination rule** ($\rightarrow_v$) applied to a set of equations F containing EQ(x,t) (or EQ(t,x)) replaces each occurrence of x in F by t and removes the trivial equation EQ(t,t) from F if x does not occur in t. In section 6.5 we demonstrated that the variable elimination rule can be applied to an equation EQ(x,t) (or EQ(t,x)) as a simplification rule in refutations with respect to narrowing and reflection if t is only built by constructors and variables. We show that such a simplification is also applicable to refutations with respect to the set of transformations we define in this section. Therefore, later on we split the variable elimination rule into the rules **variable elimination on equations that contain only variables and constructors** ($\rightarrow_{vc}$) and **variable elimination on equations that contain a defined function symbol** ($\rightarrow_{vf}$).

Finally, the rule **removal of trivial equations** ($\rightarrow_t$) simply removes a trivial equation from a set of equations. Obviously, the rule removal of trivial equations can be replaced by a simpler rule which replaces a trivial equation only if its constituent is a variable. We call this simpler rule **removal of trivial variable-equations** ($\rightarrow_{tv}$). All other applications of removal of trivial equations can be replaced by the term decomposition rule. As an example consider the trivial equation EQ($f(a,x)$, $f(a,x)$), then

$$\Leftarrow \text{EQ}(f(a,x), f(a,x)) \rightarrow_d \Leftarrow \text{EQ}(a,a), \text{EQ}(x,x) \rightarrow_d \Leftarrow \text{EQ}(x,x) \rightarrow_{tv} \square.$$

The transformation rules introduced so far do not take the equational program into account. The following rule is only applicable with respect to a given equational program EP and if the selected equation contains a non-variable term. It corresponds to a narrowing step in the same sense as a lazy resolution step corresponds to a resolution step.

Definition (Lazy Narrowing →ln):

Let $f(t_1,...,t_n) \to t_{n+1} \Leftarrow F^*$ be a new variant of an equational clause in EP. Then,

$$\Leftarrow F \cup \{EQ(f(s_1,...,s_n), s_{n+1})\} \to_{ln} \Leftarrow F \cup F^* \cup \{EQ(s_i,t_i) \mid 1 \leq i \leq n+1\}.$$

The lazy narrowing rule compares the initial symbol of an element of the selected equation with the initial symbol of the equational clause and forces the comparison of corresponding arguments and the respective right-hand sides. In figure 7.1.1 we depict the lazy narrowing rule.

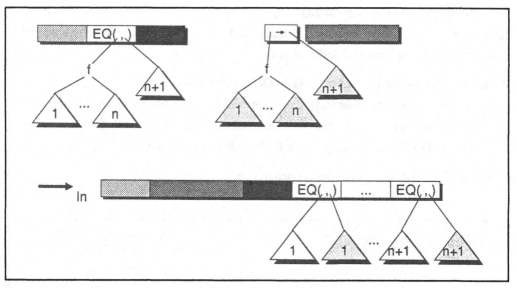

Figure 7.1.1: Lazy Narrowing

As an example consider the term rewriting system

CON: $f(x) \to a$

which defines a constant function f mapping each argument to a. Then,

$$\Leftarrow EQ(a, f(c(y))) \qquad \to_{ln} \qquad \Leftarrow EQ(c(y), x), EQ(a,a)$$
$$\to_t \qquad \Leftarrow EQ(c(y), x)$$
$$\to_{v(\{x \leftarrow c(y)\})} \qquad \square.$$

Lazy narrowing is only applicable to an equation containing a non-variable term whose initial symbol is equal to the initial symbol of the non-trivial equational clause. This corresponds to the non-variable subterm narrowed upon in an inference system based on the narrowing relation.

In section 6.2 we showed that the completeness of paramodulation and reflection also requires paramodulation at variable occurrences even if the equational program is ground confluent. As an example consider the term rewriting system

INFINITE: $f \to c(f)$

Since INFINITE is confluent we want to use the rules from left-to-right only. Hence, to solve the question of whether there exists a substitution σ such that $\sigma EQ(c(x),x)$ is a logical consequence of INFINITE, we have to apply paramodulation to x:

$$\Leftarrow EQ(c(x), x) \to_{p(\{x \leftarrow f\})} \Leftarrow EQ(c(f), c(f)) \to_t \Box.$$

Such an application cannot be modelled using the lazy narrowing rule. Therefore, we introduce a new transformation rule designed to cope with this case:

Definition (Paramodulation at a Variable Occurrence $\to_{pv}$):

Let s be a non-variable term, $f(t_1,...,t_n) \to r \Leftarrow F^* $ be a new variant of an equational clause in EP, $x_1, ..., x_n$ be new variables, and $\sigma = \{x \leftarrow f(x_1,...,x_n)\}$). Then,

$$\Leftarrow F \cup \{EQ(x,s)\} \to_{pv(\sigma)} \Leftarrow \sigma(F \cup F^* \cup \{EQ(x_i,t_i) \mid 1 \leq i \leq n\} \cup \{EQ(s,r)\}).$$

In figure 7.1.2 we depict this transformation rule.

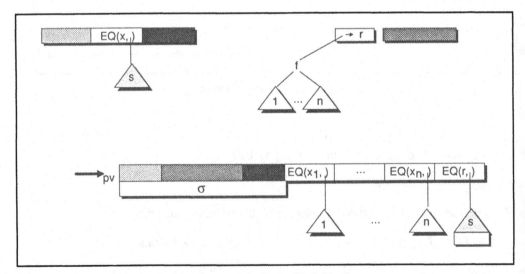

Figure 7.1.2: Paramodulation at Variable Occurrences

In our example,

$$\Leftarrow EQ(c(x), x) \to_{pv(\{x \leftarrow f\})} \Leftarrow EQ(c(f),c(f)) \to_t \Box.$$

However, our equational program may also contain trivial clauses, i.e clauses of the form $x{\rightarrow}r{\Leftarrow}F^*$. Since x is unifiable with every term not containing x such a clause can be used as an input clause everywhere. This is mirrored by the following transformation rule.

Definition (Application of a Trivial Clause $\rightarrow_{tc}$):

Let $x{\rightarrow}r{\Leftarrow}F^*$ be a new variant of a trivial clause in EP. Then,

$$\Leftarrow F{\cup}\{EQ(s,t)\} \rightarrow_{tc} \Leftarrow F{\cup}F^*{\cup}\{EQ(s,x), EQ(r,t)\}$$

and neither $\rightarrow_{ln}$, nor $\rightarrow_{pv}$, nor $\rightarrow_{tc}$ will be applied to EQ(s,x) anymore.

In figure 7.1.3 we depict the application of a trivial clause.

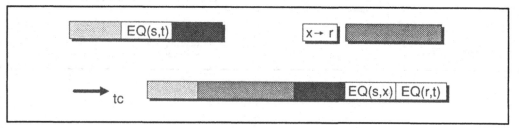

Figure 7.1.3: Application of a Trivial Clause

As an example consider the term rewriting system

TRIV: $x \rightarrow a$

which states that each term denotes the same as a. Then,

$$\Leftarrow EQ(a,t) \rightarrow_{tc} \Leftarrow EQ(t,x), EQ(a,a) \rightarrow_t \Leftarrow EQ(t,x) \rightarrow_v \square.$$

Due to the lazy nature of the transformation rules introduced so far, lazy narrowing can only be applied to the elements of an equation but not to proper subterms of these elements. This would lead to an incompleteness of our set of transformation rules as the following example shows. Consider again the term rewriting system

CON: $f(x) \rightarrow a.$

To find a solution for the unification problem $<c(f(y))=y>_{CON}$ we have to narrow upon the term f(y) replacing it by "a". However, this is not possible with the lazy narrowing rule, since f(y) does not occur in an outermost position. Therefore, we have to "strip" the c surrounding f(y). This will be done by the transformation rule **imitation**:

Definition (Imitation $\rightarrow_{im}$):

Let $x_1, ..., x_n$ be new variables and $\sigma = \{x{\leftarrow}f(x_1,...,x_n)\}$. Then

$$\Leftarrow F{\cup}\{EQ(x, f(t_1,...,t_n))\} \rightarrow_{im(\sigma)} \Leftarrow \sigma(F{\cup}\{EQ(x_i,t_i) \mid 1{\leq}i{\leq}n\}).$$

In figure 7.1.4 we depict an imitation step.

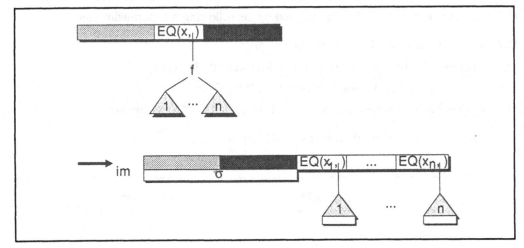

Figure 7.1.4: Imitation

We can now solve the unification problem $<c(f(y))=y>_{CON}$ by applying the transformation rules:

$\Leftarrow EQ(y, c(f(y)))$ $\quad \rightarrow_{im}(\{y \leftarrow c(z)\}) \quad \Leftarrow EQ(f(c(z)), z)$

$\rightarrow_{ln} \quad \Leftarrow EQ(c(z), x), EQ(z,a)$

$\rightarrow_{v}(\{z \leftarrow a\}) \quad \Leftarrow EQ(c(a), x)$

$\rightarrow_{v}(\{x \leftarrow c(a)\}) \quad \square$

with computed answer substitution $\{y \leftarrow c(a)\}$.

Notation:

In the sequel we assume that $\mathbf{TRANS} = \{\rightarrow_d, \rightarrow_v, \rightarrow_t, \rightarrow_{ln}, \rightarrow_{pv}, \rightarrow_{tc}, \rightarrow_{im}\}$.

The transformation rules in TRANS can be roughly divided into three groups:

-   The **unification rules** term decomposition, variable elimination, and removal of trivial equations,

-   the **lazy paramodulation rules** lazy narrowing, application of a trivial clause, and paramodulation at a variable occurrence, and

-   the **imitation rule**.

Gallier & Snyder (1987b) defined similar rules for unconditional equational programs. These rules differ from ours as follows. Gallier & Snyder need a rule which, applied to an equation of the form $EQ(x,y)$, instantiates the goal clause by $\{x \leftarrow f(x_1,...,x_n)\}$, where f is an n-ary function symbol and x_i, $1 \leq i \leq n$, are new variables. As we will see this rule is unnecessary if we apply the strategy developed at the end of section 6.2 (never select an equation of the form $EQ(x,y)$ if you have another choice and if the goal clause contains only equations of this form, then apply only reflection) to refutations with respect to our transformation rules. Furthermore, if the selected equation is of the form $EQ(x,t)$ and t is not a variable, then Gallier & Snyder apply lazy paramodulation rules only to the term t. As an example consider again the term rewriting system

INFINITE: $f \rightarrow c(f)$ (f).

Let (f^1) be the rule $c(f) \rightarrow f \in \text{INFINITE}^{-1}$. Then,

$$\Leftarrow EQ(x,c(x)) \rightarrow_{In(f\text{-}1)} \Leftarrow EQ(x,f), EQ(x,f) \rightarrow_{v(\{x\leftarrow f\})} \Leftarrow EQ(f,f) \rightarrow_t \square$$

and this is the only way to solve the unification problem $<x=c(x)>_{\text{INFINITE}}$ since $\rightarrow_{pv}$ cannot be applied due to the chosen restriction, variable elimination cannot be applied since the occur check fails, and an imitation yieds a variant of $\Leftarrow EQ(x,c(x))$. This restriction reduces the search space generated by the transformation rules applied to (unrestricted) equational programs. However, if the equational program is ground confluent, then - due to their restriction - Gallier & Snyder have to use program clauses in both directions, whereas we find without the restriction that

$$\Leftarrow EQ(x, c(x)) \rightarrow_{pv(f, \{x\leftarrow f\})} \Leftarrow EQ(c(f), c(f)) \rightarrow_t \square.$$

As we will see in section 7.3 we can refine our transformation rules step-by-step if we impose the same conditions on an equational program as in chapter 6. Since the completeness of the transformation rules will be proved by transforming refutations with respect to instantiation, paramodulation, and reflection into refutations with respect to TRANS, the completeness of the refined set of transformations can easily be obtained, whereas Gallier & Snyder give a second completeness proof if their refined rules are applied to canonical and unconditional theories.

We shall show in the following sections that TRANS is a sound and complete basis for computing correct answers to arbitrary equational programs and goal clauses and, hence, TRANS is a correct and complete universal unification procedure for Horn equational theories.

7.2 Soundness of the Transformation Rules

We prove that the rules in TRANS are correct by giving sequences of resolution steps using clauses from $EP^+ = EP \cup EAX(EP)$ that simulate the transformation rules introduced in the previous section. In other words, we show that each computed answer substitution of an equational program EP and a goal clause $\Leftarrow F$ with respect to the transformation rules is also a computed answer substitution of $EP^+ \cup \{\Leftarrow F\}$ with respect to SLD-resolution. The soundness of the transformation rules is an immediate consequence of the soundness of SLD-resolution (theorem 3.4.2.4).

First we demonstrate that each derivation step using a transformation rule can be simulated by a sequence of resolution steps taking into account the axioms of equality for a given equational program EP

Lemma 7.2.1:

Let $\rightarrow \in TRANS$. If $\Leftarrow F' \rightarrow_{(\sigma)} \Leftarrow F$, then there exists an SLD-derivation from $\Leftarrow F'$ to $\Leftarrow F$ wrt EP^+. Furthermore, if $\sigma_1, \ldots, \sigma_n$ are the mgus used in the SLD-derivation, then $\sigma|_{Var(F')} = \sigma_n \ldots \sigma_1|_{Var(F')}$

Proof:

The proof is by case analysis with respect to the transformation rule applied to obtain $\Leftarrow F$ from $\Leftarrow F'$.

1. If term decomposition was applied, we find F^+, $EQ(f(s_1,\ldots,s_m), f(t_1,\ldots,t_m))$, and σ such that

    $F' = F^+ \cup \{EQ(f(s_1,\ldots,s_m), f(t_1,\ldots,t_m))\}$, $\sigma = \varepsilon$,
    and $F = F^+ \cup \{EQ(s_i,t_i) \mid 1 \le i \le m\}$.

    Since f is an m-ary function symbol we find a new variant

    $EQ(f(x_1,\ldots,x_m), f(y_1,\ldots,y_m)) \Leftarrow \{EQ(x_i,y_i) \mid 1 \le i \le m\}$

    of an f-substitutivity axiom in EAX(EP). Obviously, $EQ(f(s_1,\ldots,s_m), f(t_1,\ldots,t_m))$ and $EQ(f(x_1,\ldots,x_m), f(y_1,\ldots,y_m))$ are unifiable with mgu

    $\sigma_1 = \{x_i \leftarrow s_i \mid 1 \le i \le m\} \cup \{y_i \leftarrow t_i \mid 1 \le i \le m\}$.

    Hence,

    $\Leftarrow F' \rightarrow_{rr(\sigma_1)} \Leftarrow F$ and $\sigma|_{Var(F')} = \varepsilon = \sigma_1|_{Var(F')}$.

2. If variable elimination was applied, we find F^+, $EQ(x,t)$, and σ such that
    $F' = F^+ \cup \{EQ(x,t)\}$, $x \notin Var(t)$, $\sigma = \{x \leftarrow t\}$, and $F = \sigma F^+$.

    Obviously, we find a new variant

    $EQ(y,y) \Leftarrow$

of the axiom of reflexivity in EAX(EP). Obviously, $EQ(x,t)$ and $EQ(y,y)$ are unifiable with mgu

$$\sigma_1 = \{x\leftarrow t, y\leftarrow t\}$$

and it follows immediately that

$$\Leftarrow F' \to_{rr(\sigma_1)} \Leftarrow F \text{ and } \sigma|Var(F') = \{x\leftarrow t\} = \sigma_1|Var(F').$$

3.   If a trivial equation was removed, we find F^+, $EQ(t,t)$, and σ such that

$$F' = F^+\cup\{EQ(t,t)\}, \sigma = \varepsilon, \text{ and } F = F^+.$$

Obviously, we find a new variant

$$EQ(y,y) \Leftarrow$$

of the axiom of reflexivity in EAX(EP). $EQ(t,t)$ and $EQ(y,y)$ are unifiable with mgu

$$\sigma_1 = \{y\leftarrow t\}.$$

Hence,

$$\Leftarrow F' \to_{rr(\sigma_1)} \Leftarrow F \text{ and } \sigma|Var(F') = \varepsilon = \sigma_1|Var(F').$$

4.   If lazy narrowing was applied, we find F^+, σ, $EQ(f(s_1,...,s_m), s_{m+1})$, and a new variant $P = f(t_1,...,t_m)\to t_{m+1}\Leftarrow F^*$ of an equational clause in EP such that

$$F' = F^+\cup\{EQ(f(s_1,...,s_m), s_{m+1})\}, \sigma = \varepsilon,$$
$$\text{and } F = F^+\cup F^*\cup\{EQ(s_i,t_i) \mid 1\leq i\leq m+1\}.$$

Let x, y, and z (possibly indexed) be new variables. Then,

$$\Leftarrow F = \Leftarrow F^+ \cup \{EQ(f(s_1,...,s_m), s_{m+1})\}$$

$$\to_{rr(t, \sigma_1)} \Leftarrow F^+ \cup \{EQ(f(s_1,...,s_m), y_1), EQ(y_1,s_{m+1})\}$$
$$\text{where } \sigma_1 = \{x_1\leftarrow f(s_1,...,s_m), z_1\leftarrow s_{m+1}\}$$

$$\to_{rr(t, \sigma_2)} \Leftarrow F^+ \cup \{EQ(f(s_1,...,s_m), y_2), EQ(y_2,y_1), EQ(y_1,s_{m+1})\}$$
$$\text{where } \sigma_2 = \{x_2\leftarrow f(s_1,...,s_m), z_2\leftarrow y_1\}$$

$$\to_{rr(P, \sigma_3)} \Leftarrow F^+ \cup F^* \cup \{EQ(f(s_1,...,s_m), f(t_1,...,t_m)), EQ(t_{m+1},s_{m+1})\}$$
$$\text{where } \sigma_3 = \{y_2\leftarrow f(t_1,...,t_m), y_1\leftarrow t_{m+1}\}$$

$$\to_{rr(sf, \sigma_4)} \Leftarrow F$$
$$\text{where } \sigma_4 = \{x_i'\leftarrow s_i \mid 1\leq i\leq m\} \cup \{y_i'\leftarrow t_i \mid 1\leq i\leq m\}$$

and $\sigma|Var(F') = \varepsilon = \sigma_4\sigma_3\sigma_2\sigma_1|Var(F')$.

5.   If paramodulation was applied to a variable occurrence, we find F^+, σ, $EQ(x,s)$, and a new variant $P = f(t_1,...,t_n)\to r\Leftarrow F^*$ of an equational clause in EP such that

$$F' = F^+\cup\{EQ(x,s)\}, \sigma = \{x\leftarrow f(x_1,...,x_n)\},$$
$$\text{and } F = \sigma(F^+\cup F^*\cup\{EQ(x_i,t_i) \mid 1\leq i\leq n\}\cup\{EQ(s,r)\}).$$

Let x, y, and z (possibly indexed) be new variables. Then,

$$\Leftarrow F' = \qquad \Leftarrow F^+ \cup \{EQ(x,s)\}$$

$$\rightarrow_{rr(t,\,\sigma 1)} \;\Leftarrow F^+ \cup \{EQ(x,y_1'),\, EQ(y_1',s)\}$$

$$\text{where } \sigma_1 = \{x_1' \leftarrow x,\, z_1' \leftarrow s\}$$

$$\rightarrow_{rr(t,\,\sigma 2)} \;\Leftarrow F^+ \cup \{EQ(x,y_2'),\, \mathbf{EQ(y_2',y_1')},\, EQ(y_1',s)\}$$

$$\text{where } \sigma_2 = \{x_2' \leftarrow x,\, z_2' \leftarrow y_1'\}$$

$$\rightarrow_{rr(P,\,\sigma 3)} \;\Leftarrow F^+ \cup F^* \cup \{EQ(x,f(t_1,\ldots,t_n)), EQ(r,s)\}$$

$$\text{where } \sigma_3 = \{y_2' \leftarrow f(t_1,\ldots,t_n),\, y_1' \leftarrow r\}$$

$$\rightarrow_{rr(sf,\,\sigma 4)} \;\Leftarrow F$$

$$\text{where } \sigma_4 = \{x \leftarrow f(x_1,\ldots,x_n)\} \cup \{y_i \leftarrow t_i \mid 1 \leq i \leq n\}$$

and $\sigma|_{Var(F')} = \{x \leftarrow f(x_1,\ldots,x_n)\} = \sigma_4\sigma_3\sigma_2\sigma_1|_{Var(F')}$.

6. If a trivial clause was applied, we find F^+, $EQ(s,t)$, σ, and a new variant $P = x \rightarrow r \Leftarrow F^*$ of a clause in EP such that

$$F' = F^+ \cup \{EQ(s,t)\}, \; \sigma = \varepsilon, \text{ and } F = F^+ \cup F^* \cup \{EQ(s,x),\, EQ(r,t)\}.$$

Let x, y, and z (possibly indexed) be new variables. Then,

$$\Leftarrow F' = \qquad \Leftarrow F^+ \cup \{\mathbf{EQ(s,t)}\}$$

$$\rightarrow_{rr(t,\,\sigma 1)} \;\Leftarrow F^+ \cup \{EQ(s,y),\, EQ(y,t)\}$$

$$\text{where } \sigma_1 = \{x \leftarrow s,\, z \leftarrow t\}$$

$$\rightarrow_{rr(t,\,\sigma 2)} \;\Leftarrow F^+ \cup \{EQ(s,y'),\, \mathbf{EQ(y',y)},\, EQ(y,t)\}$$

$$\text{where } \sigma_2 = \{x' \leftarrow s,\, z' \leftarrow y\}$$

$$\rightarrow_{rr(P,\,\sigma 3)} \;\Leftarrow F \qquad \text{where } \sigma_3 = \{x \leftarrow y',\, y \leftarrow r\}$$

and $\sigma|_{Var(F')} = \varepsilon = \sigma_3\sigma_2\sigma_1|_{Var(F')}$.

7. If imitation was applied, we find F^+, $EQ(x, f(t_1,\ldots,t_n))$, new variables $x_1, \ldots, x_n$, and σ such that

$$F' = F^+ \cup \{EQ(x, f(t_1,\ldots,t_n))\}, \; \sigma = \{x \leftarrow f(x_1,\ldots,x_n)\},$$

$$\text{and } F = \sigma(F^+ \cup \{EQ(x_i,t_i) \mid 1 \leq i \leq n\}.$$

Let x_i and y_i, $1 \leq i \leq n$, be new variables. Then,

$$\Leftarrow F' = \Leftarrow F^+ \cup \{EQ(x, f(t_1,\ldots,t_n))\} \rightarrow_{rr(sf,\,\sigma 1)} \Leftarrow F$$

$$\text{where } \sigma_1 = \{x \leftarrow f(x_1,\ldots,x_n)\} \cup \{y_i \leftarrow t_i \mid 1 \leq i \leq n\}$$

and $\sigma|_{Var(F')} = \{x \leftarrow f(x_1,\ldots,x_n)\} = \sigma_1|_{Var(F')}$. \hfill qed

From the previous proof we learn that term decomposition corresponds to SLD-resolution using an f-substitutivity axiom, variable elimination, and removal of trivial equations, imitation corresponds to SLD-resolution using the axiom of reflexivity, lazy narrowing corresponds to four SLD-resolution steps twice using the axiom of transitivity, the respective equational clause, and the substitutivity axiom, paramodulation at a variable occurrence corresponds to four SLD-resolution steps twice using the axiom of transitivity, the respective equational clause, and the axiom of reflexivity, and, finally, the application of a trivial clause corresponds to three SLD-resolution steps twice using the axiom of transitivity and the respective trivial clause.

It should be noted that in cases 2 and 4-7 we assumed that the respective transformation was applied to the "right-hand side" of the selected equation. For example, lazy narrowing was applied to an equation of the form $EQ(f(s_1,...,s_n), s_{n+1})$. As we said at the beginning of this chapter we do not distinguish between equations of the form $EQ(s,t)$ and $EQ(t,s)$. This is perfectly safe as long as we apply our transformations. In the proof of lemma 7.2.1, however, we have to include an SLD-resolution step using the axiom of symmetry if, for example, lazy narrowing was applied to an equation of the form $EQ(s_{n+1}, f(s_1,...,s_n))$, i.e.

$$\Leftarrow F^+\cup\{EQ(s_{n+1}, f(s_1,...,s_n))\} \rightarrow_{rr(s)} \Leftarrow F^+\cup\{EQ(f(s_1,...,s_n), s_{n+1})\}.$$

Then we can proceed as in case 4.

As an example consider again the term rewriting system TRIV $\cup$ CON which consists of the rules $x \rightarrow a$ and $f(x) \rightarrow a$ (see section 7.1). Then,

$\Leftarrow EQ(y, c(f(y)))$	$\rightarrow_{im(\{y \leftarrow c(y')\})}$	$\Leftarrow EQ(y', f(c(y')))$
	$\rightarrow_{tc}$	$\Leftarrow EQ(y',x), EQ(a, f(c(y')))$
	$\rightarrow_{v(\{x \leftarrow y'\})}$	$\Leftarrow EQ(a, f(c(y')))$
	$\rightarrow_{ln}$	$\Leftarrow EQ(c(y'), x'), EQ(a,a)$
	$\rightarrow_{t}$	$\Leftarrow EQ(c(y'), x')$
	$\rightarrow_{v(\{x' \leftarrow c(y')\})}$	$\square$

with computed answer substitution $\{y \leftarrow c(y')\}$. This refutation can be modelled by SLD-resolution using clauses from $(TRIV \cup CON)^+$:

$\Leftarrow EQ(y, c(f(y)))$	$\rightarrow_{rr(sf, \{y \leftarrow c(y')\})}$	$\Leftarrow EQ(y', f(c(y')))$
	$\rightarrow_{rr(t)}$	$\Leftarrow EQ(y',y_1), EQ(y_1, f(c(y')))$
	$\rightarrow_{rr(t)}$	$\Leftarrow EQ(y',y_2), EQ(y_2,y_1), EQ(y_1, f(c(y')))$
	$\rightarrow_{rr(x \rightarrow a)}$	$\Leftarrow EQ(y',x), EQ(a, f(c(y')))$
	$\rightarrow_{rr(r)}$	$\Leftarrow EQ(a, f(c(y')))$
	$\rightarrow_{rr(s)}$	$\Leftarrow EQ(f(c(y')), a)$
	$\rightarrow_{rr(t)}$	$\Leftarrow EQ(f(c(y')), y_3), EQ(y_3,a)$
	$\rightarrow_{rr(t)}$	$\Leftarrow EQ(f(c(y')), y_4), EQ(y_4,y_3), EQ(y_3,a)$
	$\rightarrow_{rr(f(x') \rightarrow a)}$	$\Leftarrow EQ(f(c(y')), f(x')), EQ(a,a)$
	$\rightarrow_{rr(sf)}$	$\Leftarrow EQ(c(y'), x'), EQ(a,a)$
	$\rightarrow_{rr(r)}$	$\Leftarrow EQ(c(y'), x')$
	$\rightarrow_{rr(r)}$	$\square$

with computed answer substitution $\{y \leftarrow c(y')\}$.

In lemma 7.2.2 we give a formal proof of the result obtained in the previous example.

Lemma 7.2.2:

> *If there exists a refutation of $EP \cup \{\Leftarrow F\}$ wrt TRANS and computed answer substitution θ, then there exists an SLD-refutation of $EP^+ \cup \{\Leftarrow F\}$ and computed answer substitution θ.*

Proof:

The proof is by induction on the length n of the refutation of $EP \cup \{\Leftarrow F\}$ wrt TRANS. The case $n=0$ being trivial we turn to the induction step and assume that the result holds for n. Suppose there exists a refutation of $EP \cup \{\Leftarrow F'\}$ wrt TRANS, computed answer substitution θ', and of length $n+1$. Let $\rightarrow \in$ TRANS and suppose that $\Leftarrow F' \rightarrow_{(\sigma)} \Leftarrow F$ is the first step of that refutation. By lemma 7.2.1 we find an SLD-derivation from $\Leftarrow F'$ to $\Leftarrow F$. Furthermore, if $\sigma_1, \ldots, \sigma_n$ are the mgus used in the SLD-derivation, then $\sigma|_{Var(F')} = \sigma_n...\sigma_1|_{Var(F')}$. Since there exists a refutation of $EP \cup \{\Leftarrow F\}$ wrt TRANS, computed answer substitution, and of length n the induction hypothesis ensures that we find an SLD-refutation of $EP^+ \cup \{\Leftarrow F\}$ with computed answer substitution θ. Clearly, there exists an SLD-refutation of $EP^+ \cup \{\Leftarrow F'\}$ with computed answer substitution $\theta' = \theta\gamma|_{Var(F')}$.   qed

It is an immediate consequence of lemma 7.2.2 and the soundness of SLD-resolution (theorem 3.4.2.4) that each computed answer substitution for EP and $\Leftarrow F$ with respect to TRANS is a correct answer substitution for EP and $\Leftarrow F$.

Theorem 7.2.3 (Soundness of the Transformation Rules):

> *Every computed answer substitution of a refutation of $EP \cup \{\Leftarrow F\}$ wrt TRANS is a correct answer substitution of EP and $\Leftarrow F$.*

Proof:

Suppose θ is a computed answer substitution of $EP \cup \{\Leftarrow F\}$ wrt TRANS. By lemma 7.2.2, θ is a computed answer substitution obtained by an SLD-refutation of $EP^+ \cup \{\Leftarrow F\}$. From theorem 3.4.2.4 we learn that θ is a correct answer substitution for EP and $\Leftarrow F$.   qed

Now we turn to the completeness of the transformation rules and show that, whenever there exists a refutation of $EP \cup EP^{-1} \cup \{\Leftarrow F\}$ with respect to paramodulation, instantiation, and reflection, then there exists also a refutation of $EP \cup EP^{-1} \cup \{\Leftarrow F\}$ with respect to TRANS.

7.3 Completeness of the Transformation Rules

In this section we show that the transformation rules are complete for arbitrary Horn equational theories. To obtain this result we prove that each refutation with respect to paramodulation, instantiation, and reflection can be modelled by the transformations introduced in section 7.1. The completeness of the transformations follows immediately from the completeness of paramodulation, instantiation, and reflection.

Before we turn to the completeness proof itself we need some definitions and technical propositions.

Definition:

Suppose $\Leftarrow F'$ was obtained from $\Leftarrow F$ by reflection or instantiation and paramodulation using substitution σ.

(1)   If $E \in F$ was not the selected subgoal, then $\sigma E \in F'$ is the **immediate descendant** of E.

(2)   If $E \in F$ was the selected subgoal and instantiation and paramodulation was applied transforming E into E', then $E' \in F'$ is the **immediate descendant** of E.

E' is a **descendant** of E iff E' is in the transitive and reflexive closure of the "immediate descendant relation".

As an example recall the equational program

$$\textbf{FUN:} \qquad f(c(g),c(a)) \rightarrow d(c(g),c(a)) \qquad\qquad (f)$$
$$g \rightarrow a \qquad\qquad (g)$$

and the refutation

$$\Leftarrow EQ(f(x,x), d(x,x)) \quad \rightarrow_{ip(g, \{x\leftarrow c(y)\})} \quad \Leftarrow EQ(f(c(g),c(a)), d(c(g),c(g)))$$
$$\rightarrow_{p(f, \varepsilon)} \quad \Leftarrow EQ(d(c(g),c(a)), d(c(g),c(g)))$$
$$\rightarrow_{p(g, \varepsilon)} \quad \Leftarrow EQ(d(c(g),c(a)), d(c(g),c(a)))$$
$$\rightarrow_{f(\varepsilon)} \qquad \square$$

with computed answer substitution $\{x\leftarrow c(g)\}$. The equations in the first four goal clauses of this refutations are descendants of $EQ(f(x,x), d(x,x))$.

Definition:

The **depth** of a term is inductively defined as follows:

$depth(x) = 1$

$depth(f(t_1,\ldots,t_n)) = 1 + \max\{depth(t_i) \mid 1 \leq i \leq n\}$

As an example consider the terms c(a) and a; the depth of c(a) is 2, whereas the depth of a is 1.

Definition:

For each substitution θ the complexity measure $D(\theta)$ is defined as the multiset $\{depth(t) \mid x \leftarrow t \in \theta\}$.

As an example consider the substitutions $\theta = \{x \leftarrow c(a)\}$ and $\sigma = \{y \leftarrow a\}$; then $D(\theta) = \{2\}$ and $D(\sigma) = \{1\}$. It should be noted that $D(\gamma) \neq \{depth(t) \mid t \in Cod(\gamma)\}$. This can be exemplified by the substitution $\gamma = \{x \leftarrow c(a), y \leftarrow c(a)\}$, where $D(\gamma) = \{2, 2\} \neq \{2\} = \{depth(c(a))\}$.

Dershowitz & Manna (1979) showed that a well-founded ordering over a set S induces a well-founded ordering over multisets whose elements are taken from S.

Definition:

Suppose S is a well-founded set with ordering < and M and M' are two finite multisets over S. M' << M iff M' can be obtained from M by replacing one or more elements in M by any finite number of elements taken from S, each of which is smaller than one of the replaced elements.

For example, let $\theta = \{x \leftarrow f(t_1, \ldots, t_n)\}$ and $\theta' = \{x_i \leftarrow t_i \mid 1 \leq i \leq n\}$. Then $D(\theta') << D(\theta)$ since $depth(f(t_1, \ldots, t_n)) > max\{depth(t_i) \mid 1 \leq i \leq n\}$.

Theorem 7.3.1 (Dershowitz & Manna 1979):

For a given partially-ordered set $(S,<)$, let $M(S)$ be the set of all finite multisets with elements taken from the set S and let $<<$ be the ordering on $M(S)$ induced by the ordering $<$ on S. $(M(S), <<)$ is well-founded iff $(S, <)$ is well-founded.

We now define a measure of complexity for refutations with respect to paramodulation, instantiation, and reflection. Recall, that a reflection step is nothing else but a sequence of $\rightarrow_{tv}$, $\rightarrow_d$, and $\rightarrow_v$ steps (theorem 3.4.1.2).

Definition:

The **complexity** of a refutation of $EP \cup \{\Leftarrow F\}$ wrt $\{\rightarrow_{ip}, \rightarrow_f\}$ and computed answer substitution θ is $<\#p, D(\theta), \#s, \#e>$, where

#p   is the number of applications of paramodulation in the refutation of $EP \cup \{\Leftarrow F\}$,

#s   is the number of occurrences of function symbols and variables in F, and

#e   is the number of equations occurring in F.

#s can be viewed as a function as follows:

$\#s(x) = 1$,

$\#s(f(t_1,\ldots,t_n)) = 1 + \Sigma_i \ \#s(t_i)$

$\#s(EQ(s,t)) = \#s(s) + \#s(t)$

$\#s(F) = \Sigma_{i \in \#F} \ i$, where $\#F = \{\#s(E) \mid E \in F\}$.

In the refutation of $FUN \cup \{\Leftarrow EQ(f(x,x), \ d(x,x))\}$ with respect to $\{\rightarrow_{ip}, \ \rightarrow_f\}$ para-modulation was applied three times. Since $\{x \leftarrow c(g)\}$ is the computed answer substitution of this refutation, we find that its complexity is $<3, \{2\}, 6, 1>$.

Definition:

The ordering « on complexities of refutations is defined to be the lexicographic ordering of the < ordering on natural numbers, the << ordering on multisets of natural numbers, the < ordering on natural numbers, and again the < ordering on natural numbers.

Clearly, « is well-founded. For example,

$<0, \emptyset, 0, 0> « <2, \emptyset, 14, 2> « <2, \{2\}, 14, 3> « <3, \{2\}, 6, 1>$.

The following corollary shows that the choice of a selection function in a refutation with respect to paramodulation, instantiation, and reflection has no effect on the complexity of the refutation.

Corollary 7.3.2:

Let SEL be a selection function. If there exists a refutation of $EP \cup \{\Leftarrow F\}$ wrt $\{\rightarrow_{ip}, \ \rightarrow_f\}$, computed answer substitution θ, and complexity M, then there exists a refutation of $EP \cup \{\Leftarrow F\}$ wrt $\{\rightarrow_{ip}, \ \rightarrow_f\}$ and via SEL. Furthermore, if σ is the computed answer substitution and N is the complexity of the refutation via SEL, then σ and θ are variants and M = N.

Proof:

Suppose θ was computed via the selection function SEL'. The soundness of $\rightarrow_{ip}$ and $\rightarrow_f$ (theorem 6.2.1) ensures that θ is a correct answer substitution for EP and $\Leftarrow F$. By the strong completeness of $\rightarrow_{ip}$ and $\rightarrow_f$ (theorem 6.2.16) we find an SEL-computed answer substitution σ for $EP \cup \{\Leftarrow F\}$ wrt $\{\rightarrow_{ip}, \ \rightarrow_f\}$ such that $\theta \leq \sigma$. Analogously, σ is a correct answer substitution and we find an SEL'-computed answer substitution θ' for $EP \cup \{\Leftarrow F\}$ wrt $\{\rightarrow_{ip}, \ \rightarrow_f\}$ such that $\sigma \leq \theta'$. However, since $\theta' = \theta$ we find that $\theta \leq \sigma$ and $\sigma \leq \theta$. By definition θ and σ are variants. It follows immediately, that $D(\theta) = D(\sigma)$. Furthermore, from the proofs of lemmas 6.2.15 and 6.2.6 we learn that the number of applications of paramodulation in the refutations via SEL' and SEL is the same. Hence, the refutations must also have the same complexity.   qed

Proposition 7.3.3:

Let $E = EQ(f(s_1,...,s_m), f(t_1,...,t_m))$. If there exists a refutation of $EP \cup \{ \Leftarrow F \cup \{E\}\}$ wrt $\{\rightarrow_f, \rightarrow_{ip}\}$, computed answer substitution θ, and complexity $M = <\#p, D(\theta), \#s, \#e>$, where paramodulation was never applied to an element of a descendant of E, then there exists a refutation of $EP \cup \{\Leftarrow F \cup \{EQ(s_i,t_i) \mid 1 \leq i \leq m\}\}$ wrt $\{\rightarrow_f, \rightarrow_{ip}\}$, computed answer substitution θ, and complexity $<\#p, D(\theta), \#s-2, e+m-1> \ll M$.

For example, consider the refutation

$\Leftarrow F \cup \{EQ(f(s_1,...,s_m), f(t_1,...,t_m))\}$
$\rightarrow^n \Leftarrow F' \cup \{EQ(f(s_1',...,s_m'), f(t_1',...,t_m'))\}$
$\rightarrow_d \Leftarrow F' \cup \{EQ(s_i',t_i') \mid 1 \leq i \leq m\}$
$\rightarrow^* \quad \square$

with computed answer substitution θ and complexity $<\#p, D(\theta), \#s, \#e>$. Since paramodulation was never applied to an element of a descendant of $EQ(f(s_1,...,s_m), f(t_1,...,t_m))$, we conclude that in the first n steps of this refutation reflection or instantiation and paramodulation was applied either to descendants of elements of F or to ("descendants" of the) subterms of s_i, t_i, $1 \leq i \leq n$. Hence, it is easy to see that

$\Leftarrow F \cup \{EQ(s_i,t_i) \mid 1 \leq i \leq m\} \rightarrow^n \Leftarrow F' \cup \{EQ(s_i',t_i') \mid 1 \leq i \leq m\} \rightarrow^* \square$

with computed answer substitution θ and complexity $<\#p, D(\theta), \#s-2, \#e+m-1>$.

Proposition 7.3.4:

Suppose there exists a refutation of $EP \cup \{\Leftarrow F \cup \{EQ(s,t)\}\}$ wrt $\{\rightarrow_f, \rightarrow_{ip}\}$, computed answer substitution θ, and complexity $M = <\#p, D(\theta), \#s, \#e>$, where paramodulation was applied to an element, say s', of a descendant $EQ(s',t')$ of $EQ(s,t)$. Let $P = l \rightarrow r \Leftarrow F^*$ be the program clause used in the first of these applications. Then there exists a refutation of $EP \cup \{\Leftarrow F \cup F^* \cup \{EQ(s,l), EQ(r,t)\}\}$ wrt $\{\rightarrow_f, \rightarrow_{ip}\}$, computed answer substitution θ' and complexity $<\#p-1, D(\theta'), \#s', \#e'> \ll M$ such that $\theta'|_{Var(F \cup \{EQ(s,t)\})} = \theta$.

For example consider the refutation

$\Leftarrow F \cup \{EQ(s,t)\} \rightarrow^n \Leftarrow F' \cup \{EQ(s',t')\}$
$\rightarrow_p \Leftarrow \mu(F' \cup F^* \cup \{EQ(r,t')\})$
$\rightarrow^* \quad \square$

with computed answer substitution θ and complexity $M = <\#p, D(\theta), \#s, \#e>$. Since in the first n steps paramodulation was not applied to a descendant of $EQ(s,t)$ we find, in analogy to the example following proposition 7.3.3, that

$$\Leftarrow F\cup\{EQ(s,l), EQ(r,t)\} \quad \rightarrow^n \quad \Leftarrow F'\cup F^*\cup\{EQ(s',l), EQ(r,t')\}$$
$$\rightarrow_{f(\mu)} \quad \Leftarrow \mu(F'\cup F^*\cup\{EQ(r,t')\})$$
$$\rightarrow^* \quad \square$$

with computed answer substitution σ and complexity M such that $\theta = \sigma|_{Var(F\cup\{EQ(s,t)\})}$. Furthermore, in the refutation of $EP\cup\{\Leftarrow F\cup\{EQ(s,l), EQ(r,t)\}\}$ paramodulation was never applied to an element of a descendant of $EQ(s,l)$.

Corollary 7.3.5:

Suppose there exists a refutation of $EP\cup\{\Leftarrow F\}$ wrt $\{\rightarrow_{ip}, \rightarrow_f\}$, computed answer substitution θ and complexity M. Suppose $x\leftarrow f(t_1,...,t_n) \in \theta$. Let x_i, $1\leq i\leq n$, be new variables and $\gamma = \{x\leftarrow f(x_1,...,x_n)\}$. Then there exists a refutation of $EP\cup\{\Leftarrow\gamma F\}$ wrt $\{\rightarrow_{ip}, \rightarrow_f\}$. Furthermore, if σ is the computed answer substitution and N the complexity of the refutation of $EP\cup\{\Leftarrow\gamma F\}$, then $\theta \leq \sigma\gamma$ $[Dom(\theta)]$ and $N \ll M$.

Proof:

Let $\#p$ be the number of paramodulation steps in the refutation of $EP\cup\{\Leftarrow F\}$ and
$$\sigma' = (\theta\backslash\{x\leftarrow f(t_1,...,t_n)\})\cup\{x_i\leftarrow t_i|1\leq i\leq n\}.$$
Hence, $\theta = \sigma'\gamma|_{Dom(\theta)}$, $\theta < \sigma'$ and $D(\sigma') \ll D(\theta)$. By proposition 6.2.13 we find a refutation of $EP\cup\{\Leftarrow\sigma'\gamma F\}$ wrt $\{\rightarrow_{ip}, \rightarrow_f\}$, computed answer substitution ε, and $\#p$ applications of paramodulation. An application of the lifting lemma 6.2.6 for $\rightarrow_{ip}$ and $\rightarrow_f$ yields a refutation of $EP\cup\{\Leftarrow\gamma F\}$ wrt $\{\rightarrow_{ip}, \rightarrow_f\}$ and $\#p$ applications of paramodulation. Furthermore, if σ is the computed answer substitution of the refutation of $EP\cup\{\Leftarrow\gamma F\}$, then $\sigma' \leq \sigma$. Since $\theta = \sigma'\gamma|_{Dom(\theta)}$ we find $\theta \leq \sigma\gamma$ $[Dom(\theta)]$. Hence, $D(\sigma) \ll D(\theta)$ and, if N is the complexity of the refutation of $EP\cup\{\Leftarrow\gamma F\}$, then $N \ll M$.   qed

As an example consider the equational program

CON: $f(x) \rightarrow a$

and the refutation

$\Leftarrow EQ(y, c(f(y))) \rightarrow_{p(\{x\leftarrow y\})} \Leftarrow EQ(y, c(a)) \rightarrow_{v\{y\leftarrow c(a)\}} \square.$

Clearly, $\{y\leftarrow c(a)\}$ is the computed answer substitution and $<1, \{2\}, 4, 1>$ the complexity of this refutation. Now, let $\gamma = \{y\leftarrow c(z)\}$. Then

$$\Leftarrow \gamma EQ(y,c(f(y))) = \qquad\qquad \Leftarrow EQ(c(z), c(f(c(z))))$$
$$\rightarrow_p(\{x \leftarrow c(z)\}) \quad \Leftarrow EQ(c(z), c(a))$$
$$\rightarrow_f(\{z \leftarrow a\}) \qquad \square$$

with computed answer substitution $\{z \leftarrow a\}$ and complexity $<1, \{1\}, 6, 1> \ll <1, \{2\}, 4, 1>$.

It should be observed that, if in the refutation of $EP \cup \{\Leftarrow F\}$ paramodulation was never applied to an element of a descendant of $E \in F$, then paramodulation was never applied to an element of a descendant of $\gamma E \in \gamma F$ in the refutation of $EP \cup \{\Leftarrow \gamma F\}$.

We can now prove that for each refutation with respect to paramodulation, instantiation, and reflection there exists a corresponding one with respect to TRANS yielding a more general computed answer substitution. Recall, at the end of section 6.2 we made the assumption that a selection function applied to a derivation with respect to reflection, instantiation and paramodulation selects an equation of the form $EQ(x,y)$ only if it has no other choice and, if such an equation is selected, then only reflection is to be applied. It should be observed that for each refutation of $EP \cup \{\Leftarrow F\}$ wrt $\{\rightarrow_f, \rightarrow_{ip}\}$, computed answer substitution θ, and complexity M, there exists a refutation of $EP \cup \{\Leftarrow F\}$ wrt $\{\rightarrow_f, \rightarrow_{ip}\}$ obeying this strategy. Furthermore if σ (resp. N) is the computed answer substitution (resp. complexity) of the latter refutation, then $\theta \leq_{EP} \sigma$ and $N \ll M$ or $N = M$. $\theta \leq_{EP} \sigma$ follows immediately from proposition 6.2.19 and the strong completeness of reflection, instantiation and paramodulation. Now let

$$\Leftarrow F \rightarrow^* \Leftarrow F' \rightarrow^* \square \qquad\qquad\qquad\qquad\qquad (*)$$

be a refutation of $EP \cup \{\Leftarrow F\}$ wrt $\{\rightarrow_f, \rightarrow_{ip}\}$ such that F' contains only equations of the form $EQ(x,y)$ and that in the derivation from $\Leftarrow F$ to $\Leftarrow F'$ no selected subgoal is of the form $EQ(x,y)$, $x \neq y$. From lemma 7.3.2 we learn that M is also the complexity of (*). Let

$$\Leftarrow F' \rightarrow_f^* \square \qquad\qquad\qquad\qquad\qquad\qquad\qquad (**)$$

be the refutation of $EP \cup \{\Leftarrow F'\}$ with respect to reflection. If in (*) paramodulation is applied at least once in the refutation of $EP \cup \{\Leftarrow F'\}$, then, obviously, $N \ll M$; otherwise $N = M$.

Notation:

Let **SEL$^+$** be a selection function that never selects an equation of the form $EQ(x,y)$ if it has another choice.

Theorem 7.3.6:

> *If there exists a refutation of $EP \cup \{\Leftarrow F\}$ wrt $\{\rightarrow_{ip}, \rightarrow_f\}$ and computed answer substitution θ, then there exists a refutation of $EP \cup \{\Leftarrow F\}$ wrt TRANS and via SEL$^+$. Furthermore, if σ is the computed answer substitution of the refutation wrt TRANS, then $\theta \leq_{EP} \sigma$.*

Proof:

The proof is by transfinite induction on the complexity M of the refutation of $EP\cup\{\Leftarrow F\}$ wrt $\{\rightarrow_{ip}, \rightarrow_f\}$. We assume that the result holds for all $M \ll M'$. Suppose

$$\Leftarrow F'\cup\{EQ(s,t)\} \rightarrow^* \square \qquad (1)$$

wrt $\{\rightarrow_f, \rightarrow_{ip}\}$, computed answer substitution θ', and complexity $M' = <\#p', D(\theta'), \#s',$ $\#e'>$. Let $EQ(s,t)$ be the first selected equation by SEL^+. By corollary 7.3.2 and by the above remarks we may assume that $EQ(s,t)$ is the first selected equation in (1). We distinguish three cases:

1. If s and t are variables, then F' contains only equations of the form $EQ(x,y)$ and we may assume that in (1) only reflection is applied. Since reflection can be modelled by the rules $\rightarrow_t$, $\rightarrow_v$, $\rightarrow_d$, the theorem follows immediately.

In the remaining cases we assume that either s or t is a non-variable term.

2. Suppose that in (1) paramodulation is applied to an element, say s', of a descendant $EQ(s',t')$ of $EQ(s,t)$. Let $P = l\rightarrow r\Leftarrow F^*$ be the equational clause used in the first such application. By proposition 7.3.4 we find

    $$\Leftarrow F'\cup\{EQ(s,l), EQ(r,t)\}\cup F^* \rightarrow^* \square \qquad (2)$$

    wrt $\{\rightarrow_f, \rightarrow_{ip}\}$, computed answer substitution θ^*, and complexity M^* such that $\theta^*|_{Var(F'\cup\{EQ(s,t)\})} = \theta'$ and $M^* \ll M'$. Recall, in (2) paramodulation need not be applied to an element of a descendant of $EQ(s,l)$.

2.1 Suppose P is a trivial clause. Let $F = F'\cup F^*\cup\{EQ(s,l), EQ(r,t)\}$. Then,

    $$\Leftarrow F'\cup\{EQ(s,t)\} \rightarrow_{tc} \Leftarrow F$$

    and (2) ensures that there exists a refutation of $EP\cup\{\Leftarrow F\}$ wrt $\{\rightarrow_{ip}, \rightarrow_f\}$, computed answer substitution $\theta = \theta^*$, and complexity $M = M^*$. The result follows by an application of the induction hypothesis.

In the remaining two cases we assume that P is of the form $f(l_1,...,l_m)\rightarrow r\Leftarrow F^*$.

2.2 Suppose s is of the form $f(s_1,...,s_m)$. Let $F = F'\cup F^*\cup\{EQ(s_i,l_i) \mid 1\leq i\leq m\}\cup\{EQ(r,t)\}$. Then

    $$\Leftarrow F'\cup\{EQ(s,t) \rightarrow_{ln} \Leftarrow F.$$

    By an application of proposition 7.3.3 to (2) we find a refutation of $EP\cup\{\Leftarrow F\}$ wrt $\{\rightarrow_f, \rightarrow_{ip}\}$, computed answer substitution $\theta = \theta^*$, and complexity $M \ll M^* \ll M'$. The result follows by an application of the induction hypothesis.

2.3 Suppose s is a variable. Hence, t must be a non-variable term. Let x_i, $1\leq i\leq m$, be new variables, $\gamma = \{s\leftarrow f(x_1,...,x_m)\}$, and $F = \gamma(F'\cup F^*\cup\{EQ(x_i,l_i) \mid 1\leq i\leq m\}\cup\{EQ(r,t)\})$. Then,

$\Leftarrow F' \cup \{EQ(s,t)\} \rightarrow_{pv} \Leftarrow F.$

By an application of proposition 7.3.5 to (2) we find

$\Leftarrow \gamma(F' \cup F^* \cup \{EQ(s,l), EQ(r,t)\})$

$= \quad \Leftarrow \gamma F' \cup F^* \cup \{EQ(f(x_1,...,x_m), f(l_1,...,l_m)), EQ(r,\gamma t)\}$

$\rightarrow^* \quad \square$ (3)

wrt $\{\rightarrow_f, \rightarrow_{ip}\}$, computed answer substitution θ^+, and complexity M^+ such that $\theta^* \leq \theta^+ \gamma|_{Var(\gamma(F' \cup F^* \cup \{EQ(s,l), EQ(r,t)\}))}$ and $M^+ \ll M^* \ll M'$. Note, in (3) paramodulation need not be applied to an element of a descendent of $EQ(f(x_1,...,x_m), f(l_1,...,l_m))$. Hence, by application of proposition 7.3.3 to (3) we find a refutation of $EP \cup \{\Leftarrow F\}$ wrt $\{\rightarrow_{ip}, \rightarrow_f\}$, computed answer substitution $\theta = \theta''$, and complexity $M \ll M^+ \ll M^* \ll M'$. The result follows by an application of the induction hypothesis.

3.   Suppose that in (1) paramodulation is never applied to an element of a descendant of $EQ(s,t)$. We distinguish three cases:

3.1   If reflection is applied in the first step of (1), then the result follows by the induction hypothesis since each reflection step in (1) can be replaced by a sequence of $\rightarrow_t$, $\rightarrow_d$, and $\rightarrow_v$ steps (theorem 3.4.1.2) and each application of $\rightarrow_t$, $\rightarrow_d$, or $\rightarrow_v$ decreases M'.

In the remaining two cases we assume that instantiation or paramodulation (using $P = l \rightarrow r \Leftarrow F^*$) is applied in the first step of (1). Recall, s and t cannot both be variables.

3.2   Suppose s (resp. t) is of the form $f(s_1,...,s_m)$ (resp. $g(t_1,...,t_n)$). Since in (1) paramodulation is never applied to an element of a descendant of $EQ(s,t)$ we find that $f = g$, $n = m$. Let $F = F' \cup \{EQ(s_i,t_i) \mid 1 \leq i \leq m\}$. Then

$\Leftarrow F' \cup \{EQ(s,t)\} \rightarrow_d \Leftarrow F$

and by an application of proposition 7.3.3 to (1) we find a refutation of $EP \cup \{\Leftarrow F\}$ wrt $\{\rightarrow_{ip}, \rightarrow_f\}$, computed answer substitution $\theta = \theta'$, and complexity $M \ll M'$. The result follows by an application of the induction hypothesis.

3.3   Finally, suppose that s is a variable and t is a term of the form $f(t_1,...,t_m)$. Since in (1) paramodulation is never applied to an element of a descendant of $EQ(s,t)$ we find a binding $s \leftarrow f(s_1,...,s_m)$ in θ'. Now let x_i, $1 \leq i \leq m$, be new variables, $\gamma = \{x \leftarrow f(x_1,...,x_m)\}$, and $F = \gamma(F' \cup \{EQ(x_i,t_i) \mid 1 \leq i \leq m\})$. Then,

$\Leftarrow F' \cup \{EQ(s,t)\} \text{ im} \Leftarrow F.$

By an application of proposition 7.3.5 to (1) we find a refutation of $EP \cup \{\Leftarrow F\}$ wrt $\{\rightarrow_{ip}, \rightarrow_f\}$, computed answer substitution θ, and complexity M such that $\theta' \leq \theta \gamma|_{Var(F' \cup \{EQ(s,t)\})}$ and $M \ll M'$. The result follows by an application of the induction hypothesis.   qed

To examplify the proof of theorem 7.3.6 we consider again the equational program

FUN: $f(c(g),c(a)) \rightarrow d(c(g),c(a))$ (f)

$g \rightarrow a$ (g)

and the refutation

$\Leftarrow EQ(f(x,x), d(x,x))$		(1)
$\rightarrow ip(g, \{x\leftarrow c(g)\}$	$\Leftarrow EQ(f(c(g),c(a)), d(c(g),c(g)))$	(2)
$\rightarrow p(f, \varepsilon)$	$\Leftarrow EQ(d(c(g),c(a)), d(c(g),c(g)))$	(3)
$\rightarrow p(g, \varepsilon)$	$\Leftarrow EQ(d(c(g),c(a)), d(c(g),c(a)))$	(4)
$\rightarrow f(\varepsilon)$	$\square$	(5)

with computed answer substitution $\{x\leftarrow c(g)\}$ and complexity $<3, \{2\}, 6, 1>$. Since in (3) paramodulation is for the first time applied to an element of a descendant of $EQ(f(x,x), d(x,x))$ we find with case 2.2 that

$\Leftarrow EQ(f(x,x), d(x,x))$		(i)
$\rightarrow ln(f)$	$\Leftarrow EQ(x, c(g)), EQ(x, c(a)), EQ(d(x,x), d(c(g),c(a)))$.	(ii)

Furthermore,

$\Leftarrow EQ(x, c(g)), EQ(x, c(a)), EQ(d(x,x), d(c(g),c(a)))$		(6)
$\rightarrow v(\{x\leftarrow c(g)\}$	$\Leftarrow EQ(c(g), c(a)), EQ(d(c(g),c(g)), d(c(g),c(a)))$	(7)
$\rightarrow p(g)$	$\Leftarrow EQ(c(a), c(a)), EQ(d(c(g),c(g)), d(c(g),c(a)))$	(8)
$\rightarrow f$	$\Leftarrow EQ(d(c(g),c(g)), d(c(g),c(a)))$	(9)
$\rightarrow p(g)$	$\Leftarrow EQ(d(c(g),c(a)), d(c(g),c(a)))$	(10)
$\rightarrow f$	$\square$	(11)

with computed answer substitution $\{x\leftarrow c(g)\}$ and complexity $<2, \{2\}, 14, 3> \ll <3, \{2\}, 6, 1>$. The first step of the refutation (6) - (11) was a variable elimination and since $\rightarrow_v \in$ TRANS we can simulate this step according to case 3.1:

$\Leftarrow EQ(x, c(g)), EQ(x, c(a)), EQ(d(x,x), d(c(g),c(a)))$		(ii)
$\rightarrow v(\{x\leftarrow c(g)\}$	$\Leftarrow EQ(c(g), c(a)), EQ(d(c(g),c(g)), d(c(g),c(a)))$.	(iii)

Observe, the complexity of the refutation (7) - (11) is $<2, \emptyset, 14, 2>$. Since in the refutation (7) - (11) paramodulation is never applied to an element of a descendant of $EQ(c(g), c(a))$ or $EQ(d(c(g),c(g)), d(c(g),c(a)))$ we find with case 3.2 that

$\Leftarrow EQ(c(g), c(a)), EQ(d(c(g),c(g)), d(c(g),c(a)))$		(iii)
$\rightarrow d$	$\Leftarrow EQ(g,a), EQ(d(c(g),c(g)), d(c(g),c(a)))$	(iv)
$\rightarrow d$	$\Leftarrow EQ(g,a), EQ(c(g), c(g)), EQ(c(g), c(a))$.	(v)

Furthermore,

$$\Leftarrow EQ(g,a), \ \mathbf{EQ(c(g), \ c(g))}, \ EQ(c(g), \ c(a)) \tag{12}$$

$\rightarrow_f \qquad\qquad \Leftarrow EQ(g,a), \ EQ(c(g), \ c(a)) \tag{13}$

$\rightarrow_{p(g)} \qquad\qquad \Leftarrow EQ(a,a), \ EQ(c(g), \ c(a)) \tag{14}$

$\rightarrow_{p(g)} \qquad\qquad \Leftarrow \mathbf{EQ(a,a)}, \ EQ(c(a), \ c(a)) \tag{15}$

$\rightarrow_f \qquad\qquad \Leftarrow EQ(c(a), \ c(a)) \tag{16}$

$\rightarrow_f \qquad\qquad \square \tag{17}$

with computed answer substitution ε and complexity $<2, \varnothing, 10, 3> \ll <2, \varnothing, 14, 2>$. It is easy to see that the refutation (12) - (17) can also be modelled by

$$\Leftarrow EQ(g,a), \ \mathbf{EQ(c(g), \ c(g))}, \ EQ(c(g), \ c(a)) \tag{v}$$

$\rightarrow_t \qquad\qquad \Leftarrow EQ(g,a), \ \mathbf{EQ(c(g), \ c(a))} \tag{vi}$

$\rightarrow_d \qquad\qquad \Leftarrow EQ(g,a), \ EQ(g,a) \tag{vii}$

$\rightarrow_{p(g)} \qquad\qquad \Leftarrow \mathbf{EQ(a,a)}, \ EQ(g,a) \tag{viii}$

$\rightarrow_t \qquad\qquad \Leftarrow EQ(g,a) \tag{ix}$

$\rightarrow_{p(g)} \qquad\qquad \Leftarrow EQ(a,a) \tag{x}$

$\rightarrow_t \qquad\qquad \square \tag{xi}$

and, thus, we find that by the proof of theorem 7.3.6 the refutation (1) - (5) was transformed into the refutation (i) - (xi). Furthermore, the answer substitution computed by both refutations is $\{x \leftarrow c(g)\}$.

It should be observed that the empty clause was derived in the refutation (i) - (xi) by applying only lazy narrowing, term decomposition, variable elimination, and removal of trivial equations. This is remarkable, since in section 6.2 the FUN-example served to show that paramodulation and reflection are complete only if the functional reflexive axioms or, equivalently, the instantiation rule was added. Since lazy narrowing was applied to f(x,x) using the clause f(c(g),c(a))→d(c(g),c(a)), the uninformed use of the instantiation rule in the refutation of FUN∪{⇐EQ(f(x,x), d(x,x))} with respect to reflection, instantiation and paramodulation to instantiate the x was replaced by an informed application of the term decomposition rule in the corresponding refutation of FUN∪{⇐EQ(f(x,x), d(x,x))} with respect to TRANS.

This example also shows why we called the rule $\rightarrow_{ln}$ lazy narrowing. In a narrowing step the corresponding arguments have to be unified before narrowing can be applied, whereas in a lazy narrowing step only the initial function symbols of the corresponding terms must be identical and the requirement that the corresponding arguments have to be equal is added as a "constraint" (see Huet 1972) to the new goal clause.

We can now show that the transformations introduced in section 7.1 are complete.

Theorem 7.3.7 (Strong Completeness of the Transformation Rules):

For every correct answer substitution θ for EP and $\Leftarrow F$ there exists an SEL^+-computed answer substitution σ obtained by a refutation of $EP \cup EP^{-1} \cup \{\Leftarrow F\}$ wrt TRANS such that $\theta \leq_{EP} \sigma$.

Proof:

Suppose θ is a correct answer substitution for EP and $\Leftarrow F$. By the completeness of para-modulation, instantiation, and reflection (theorem 6.2.12) we find a computed answer substitution γ obtained by a refutation of $EP \cup EP^{-1} \cup \{\Leftarrow F\}$ wrt $\{\rightarrow_{ip}, \rightarrow_f\}$ such that $\theta \leq \gamma$. The theorem follows immediately by an application of theorem 7.3.6.   qed

In chapter 6 we defined refinements of paramodulation if the equational program satisfies certain conditions. We show that most of these refinements carry over to derivations with respect to TRANS. This is done by a close examination of the proof of theorem 7.3.6. In this theorem we demonstrated that for each refutation

$$\Leftarrow F \rightarrow^* \square \quad \text{wrt } \{\rightarrow_{ip}, \rightarrow_f\} \tag{*}$$

and computed answer substitution θ we can find a refutation

$$\Leftarrow F \rightarrow^* \square \quad \text{wrt TRANS} \tag{**}$$

yielding a more general computed answer substitution. If we take a close look at the proof of theorem 7.3.6 we can make the following three observations:

1. An equational clause P is used in an $\rightarrow_{ln}$, $\rightarrow_{pv}$, or $\rightarrow_{tc}$ step in (**) only if the same clause is used in a paramodulation step in (*). Moreover, in both refutations P is used in the same direction. Hence, by theorem 6.3.4 clauses from EP^{-1} are no longer needed if EP is ground confluent.

Corollary 7.3.8:

Let EP be a ground confluent equational program. For every correct answer substitution θ for EP and $\Leftarrow F$ there exists an SEL^+-computed answer substitution σ obtained by a refutation of $EP \cup \{\Leftarrow F\}$ wrt TRANS such that $\theta \leq_{EP} \sigma$.

2. If paramodulation at a variable occurrence is applied in (**), then the computed answer substitution is not in normalform. As an example consider the term rewriting system

    CON: $f(x) \rightarrow b$

and the equation $EQ(y,b)$. Then

$$\Leftarrow EQ(y,b) \rightarrow_{pv(\{y \leftarrow f(z)\})} \Leftarrow EQ(z,x), EQ(b,b) \rightarrow_t \Leftarrow EQ(z,x) \rightarrow_{v(\{z \leftarrow y\})} \square$$

with computed answer substitution $\{y \leftarrow f(x)\}$.

A trivial clause is applied in (**) only if a trivial clause is applied in (*). Hence, if $EP \cup EP^{-1}$ is non-trivial the rule $\to_{tc}$ is no longer needed to ensure the completeness of TRANS.

Now, since we know that narrowing and reflection is complete for collapse free and confluent term rewriting systems as long as we consider only normalizable answer substitutions (theorem 6.5.3) we conclude that in this case $\to_{pv}$ and $\to_{tc}$ are no longer needed. Furthermore, if an equation of the form EQ(x,y) is selected, then only reflection can be applied in a refutation with respect to reflection, instantiation and paramodulation. Hence, we need not restrict our selection function.

Corollary 7.3.9:

Let SEL be a selection function and R be a collapse free and confluent term rewriting system. For every normalizable correct answer substitution θ for EP and $\Leftarrow F$ there exists an SEL-computed answer substitution σ obtained by a refutation of $R \cup \{\Leftarrow F\}$ wrt $\{\to_t, \to_v, \to_d, \to_{ln}, \to_{im}\}$ such that $\theta \leq_R \sigma$.

3.   In section 6.2 we showed that for arbitrary equational programs removal of trivial equations and the decomposition of decomposable equations can be applied as simplification rules in derivations with respect to paramodulation, instantiation, and reflection (lemmas 6.2.17 and 6.2.18). From theorem 6.5.3 we learned that variable elimination applied to equations of the form EQ(x,t), where $x \notin Var(t)$ and t does not contain a defined function symbol, can be applied as a simplification rule to refutations with respect to narrowing and reflection. Finally, from theorem 6.5.2.3 follows immediately that rewriting can be applied as a simplification rule to refutations with respect to narrowing and reflection if the equational program in consideration is a canonical term rewriting system.

We now show that removal of trivial equations ($\to_t$), decomposition of decomposable equations ($\to_{dd}$), elimination of variables applied to equations of the form EQ(s,t), where t does not contain a defined function symbol, ($\to_{vc}$), and rewriting ($\to_R$) can be applied as simplification rules to derivations with respect to TRANS if we consider canonical term rewriting systems only. In lemma 6.4.11 we proved that there does not exist a refutation of $EP \cup \{\Leftarrow F\}$ with respect to paramodulation and reflection if F contains an equation of the form EQ(c(s₁,...,sₙ), d(t₁,...,tₘ)), where c and d are different constructors. Observe, no transformation rule in TRANS is applicable to an equation of this form.

Definition:

> The function **simplify** applied to a goal clause $\Leftarrow F$ yields $\Leftarrow F'$ which is obtained
> from $\Leftarrow F$ by applying $\rightarrow_t$, $\rightarrow_{dd}$, $\rightarrow_{vc}$, and $\rightarrow_R$ as long as possible and by testing
> that it is not a failure.

Definition:

> An **s-derivation** is a derivation where each goal clause is simplified.

Lemma 7.3.10:

> *Let SEL be a selection function and R be a canonical term rewriting system. If*
> *there exists a refutation of $R \cup \{\Leftarrow F\}$ wrt $\{\rightarrow_n, \rightarrow_f\}$ and computed answer substi-*
> *tution θ in normalform, then there exists an s-refutation of $R \cup \{\Leftarrow F\}$ wrt $\{\rightarrow_{dn},$*
> *$\rightarrow_{vf}, \rightarrow_{ln}, \rightarrow_{im}\}$ and via SEL. Furthermore, if σ is the computed answer substi-*
> *tution of the refutation wrt TRANS, then $\theta \leq_R \sigma$.*

Proof:

The proof is in analogy to the proof of theorem 7.3.6. However, we have to change the
complexity assigned to a refutation wrt $\{\rightarrow_n, \rightarrow_f\}$: Let #p be the maximum number of applications of $\rightarrow_R$ in a derivation issuing from $\Leftarrow \theta F$ wrt R and $\{\rightarrow_R, \rightarrow_t\}$. The other parts of
the complexity remain unchanged. The proof is by transfinite induction on the complexity M
of the refutation of $R \cup \{\Leftarrow F\}$ wrt $\{\rightarrow_n, \rightarrow_f\}$. We assume that the result holds for all M « M'.
Suppose there exists a refutation of $R \cup \{\Leftarrow F'\}$ wrt $\{\rightarrow_n, \rightarrow_f\}$, computed answer substitution
θ, and complexity M' = <#p', D(θ'), #s', #e'>. We distinguish two cases:

If F' cannot be further simplified, then the result follows in analogy to the proof of
theorem 7.3.6.

If F' can be simplified, then SEL selects an equation E to which $\rightarrow_t$, $\rightarrow_{dd}$, $\rightarrow_{vc}$, or $\rightarrow_R$
can be applied. By theorem 7.3.2 we may assume that E is also the first selected equation in
the refutation of $R \cup \{\Leftarrow F'\}$ wrt $\{\rightarrow_n, \rightarrow_f\}$ and since $\rightarrow_t$, $\rightarrow_{dd}$, and $\rightarrow_{vc}$ are simplification rules for refutations wrt $\{\rightarrow_n, \rightarrow_f\}$ we may assume that one of these rules was applied
to E. An application of $\rightarrow_t$ decreases #e' and does not increase #p', D(θ'), and #s', an application of $\rightarrow_{dd}$ decreases #s' and does not increase #p' and D(θ'), an application of $\rightarrow_{vc}$ decreases D(θ') and does not increase #p', and an application of $\rightarrow_R$ decreases #p'. In any
case, the lemma holds by the induction hypothesis   qed

Theorem 7.3.11:

> Let *SEL* be a selection function and *R* be a canonical term rewriting system. If θ
> is a normalized correct answer substitution for *R* and $\Leftarrow F$, then there exists an
> *SEL*-computed answer substitution obtained by an s-refutation of $R \cup \{\Leftarrow F\}$ wrt
> $\{\rightarrow_{dn}, \rightarrow_{vf}, \rightarrow_{ln}, \rightarrow_{im}\}$ such that $\theta \leq_R \sigma$.

Proof:

The proof follows in analogy to the proof of theorem 7.3.7, but apply lemma 7.3.10 instead of theorem 7.3.6.   qed

The imitation rule is needed to ensure theorem 7.3.11. This fact is demonstrated by the following example. Let

    CON: $f(x) \rightarrow a$

be the canonical term rewriting system. Then

$$\Leftarrow EQ(y, c(f(y))) \qquad \rightarrow_{im}(\{y \leftarrow c(z)\}) \qquad \Leftarrow EQ(z, f(c(z)))$$
$$\rightarrow_{ln} \qquad \Leftarrow EQ(z,a), EQ(c(z), x)$$
$$\rightarrow_v(\{z \leftarrow a\}) \qquad \Leftarrow EQ(c(a), x)$$
$$\rightarrow_v(\{x \leftarrow c(a)\}) \qquad \square$$

with computed answer substitution $\{y \leftarrow c(a)\}$. Imitation is the only transformation rule that is applicable to $EQ(y, c(f(y)))$. We are unaware of an example where imitation has to be applied to an equation of the form $EQ(x,t)$, where $x \notin Var(t)$, but we cannot give a completeness result for such a restricted use of the imitation rule. In other words, it is an open problem, whether variable elimination can generally be applied eagerly.

To sum up, we generalized the results obtained by Gallier & Snyder (1987a,b) and Martelli et al. (1986) to hold for arbitrary equational programs (resp. conditional term rewriting systems). Moreover, we refined their results: To ensure the completeness of their sets of transformations for canonical term rewriting system, Gallier & Snyder as well as Martelli et al. have modified the lazy narrowing rule to be applicable also to arbitrarily proper subterms of an equation. This does not only violate the demand-driven nature of the transformation rules but also expands the search space since, in general, there is more than one subterm of an equation to which their lazy narrowing rule can be applied. We ensure the completeness by repeated applications of the imitation rule as shown in the last example.

Gallier & Snyder (1987a,b) have pointed out that successive applications of the imitation rule to an equation of the form $EQ(x,t)$, where x occurs in t, generate an instance of the equation and, thus, lead to a cycle. However, they also showed that in case of unconditional equational theories these cycles can be avoided. We believe that this result holds also for Horn equational theories.

8 Lazy Resolution and Complete Sets of Inference Rules for Horn Equational Theories

In chapters 6 and 7 we developed universal unification procedures for Horn equational theories, which were based on paramodulation and complete sets of transformations respectively. These unification procedures can be built into EP-resolution and by theorems 5.2 and 5.5 we obtain a sound and strongly complete system.

However, the use of EP-resolution together with the various techniques developed for solving sets of equations inherit a principal problem. As G. D. Plotkin (1972) showed, a complete and even independent set of EP-unifiers may be infinite or may not even exist. Moreover, the EP-unification problem is in general undecidable (see theorem 6.6.2.7) even if the equational program is a canonical and unconditional term rewriting system. Hence, the search space may not only be infinite in its depth but may also be infinite in its breadth and, whenever we call the EP-unification procedure, we cannot be sure that it will terminate even if it does not produce a single substitution. These problems can be avoided by using the lazy resolution rule and applying the inference rules used to solve the EP-unification problem.

In this chapter we prove the strong completeness of lazy resolution and complete sets of inference rules for Horn equational theories. As a consequence, lazy resolution steps and inference steps to compute solutions for unification problems under Horn equational theories can be mixed freely by defining an appropriate selection function. Thus, costly computations of EP-unifiers can be delayed until eventually more information becomes available which leads to a reduction of the search space.

The idea to consider unification problems as "constraints" can already be found in G. Huet's (1972) thesis, where he develops a complete method to mechanize higher order logic. As an example consider again the equational logic program

P-ASSOC:	$P(x',f(x',g(a,b))) \Leftarrow$	(p)
	$EQ(f(x,f(y,z)), f(f(x,y),z)) \Leftarrow$	(a)

from chapter 5. Suppose we want to find a refutation of P-ASSOC and

$$\Leftarrow P(x,f(g(y,b),x)), EQ(x, g(a,b))$$

with respect to EP-resolution. If for some reason the selection function selects $P(x,f(g(y,b),x))$ in the first place, then we have to solve the problem of whether $f(x,g(a,b))$ and $f(g(y,b),x)$ are unifiable under associativity. The set of solutions is the infinite set

$\{x \leftarrow g(a,b), y \leftarrow a\},$

$\{x \leftarrow f(g(a,b),g(a,b)), y \leftarrow a\},$

$\{x \leftarrow f(g(a,b),f(g(a,b),g(a,b))), y \leftarrow a\}$

... .

Consequently, we then apply each of these substitutions to $EQ(x,g(a,b))$ and "test" whether x was instantiated to $g(a,b)$. This test will be successful in the first place but afterwards it will fail infinitely many times. However, applying lazy resolution to $P(x,f(g(y,b),x)$ using $P(x',f(x',g(a,b))) \Leftarrow$ yields the new goal clause

$\Leftarrow EQ(x,x'), EQ(f(g(y,b),x), f(x',g(a,b))), EQ(x, g(a,b)).$

Eliminating the variable x' yields

$\Leftarrow EQ(f(g(y,b),x), f(x,g(a,b))), EQ(x, g(a,b)).$

If in the following step the selection function selects the equation $EQ(x,g(a,b))$, then x is bound to $g(a,b)$ and the goal becomes

$\Leftarrow EQ(f(g(y,b),g(a,b)), f(g(a,b),g(a,b))$

which can immediately be solved binding y to a.

Now, let EP be an equational program, F be a multiset of equations, and SEL be a selection function. We assume to have a set of inference rules RULES satisfying the following conditions:

A. *Soundness*: Every computed answer substitution of $EP \cup \{\Leftarrow F\}$ with respect to RULES is correct, and

B. *Strong Completeness*: For every correct answer θ for EP and $\Leftarrow F$ there exists a computed answer substitution σ obtained by an SEL-refutation of $EP \cup \{\Leftarrow F\}$ with respect to RULES such that $\theta \leq_{EP} \sigma$.

In this thesis we have presented several sets of inference rules that satisfy these conditions, for example

(1) the inference rules reflection, instantiation and paramodulation for arbitrary equational programs, or

(2) the transformation rules variable elimination, term decomposition, removal of trivial equations, lazy narrowing, and imitation for canonical term rewriting systems.

In the proof of the strong completeness of RULES a measure of complexity for refutations and a well-founded ordering over sets of complexities are generally used. Furthermore, the complexity can always be defined, such that it is independent of the selection function. For example, in (1) the complexity is the length of the refutation of $EP \cup \{\Leftarrow F\}$ or, equivalently, the number of reflection, instantiation and paramodulation steps, whereas in (2) the complexity is a quadruple $\langle \#p, D(\theta), \#s, \#e \rangle$ assigned to the refutation of $R \cup \{\Leftarrow F\}$, where $D(\theta)$ is the depth of the computed answer substitution θ, $\#p$ is the maximimum length of reductions issuing from $\Leftarrow \theta F$, $\#s$ is the number of occurrences of function symbols and variables in F, and $\#e$ is the number of equations in F. These measures of complexity are used to show that each application of an inference rule decreases the complexity of the refutation.

Let S be a set of complexities assigned with refutations of $EP \cup \{\Leftarrow F\}$ wrt RULES and $<$ be a well-founded ordering over S such that

C.   the complexity assigned to a refutation is independent of the selection function.

We now extend the well-founded ordering $(S,<)$ assigned to refutations with respect to RULES to refutations with respect to RULES and the lazy resolution rule. Therefore, let

    $RULES^+ = RULES \cup \{\rightarrow_{lr}\}$,

    $S' = \{ \langle n,M \rangle \mid n \text{ is a natural number and } M \in S \}$,

and let « be defined as follows:

    $\langle n',M' \rangle$ « $\langle n,M \rangle$ iff $n' < n$ or if $n = m$ then $M' < M$.

Clearly, « is well-founded over S'. With refutations of $\langle EP,LP \rangle \cup \{\Leftarrow D\}$ with respect to $RULES^+$ we assign the complexity

    $\langle \#r,M \rangle$,

where $\#r$ is the number of lazy resolution steps in the refutation and M is the complexity assigned to the "equational part" of the refutation.

As an example consider the equational logic program

    PALINDROM: Palindrom(x) $\Leftarrow$ EQ(x, reverse(x))   (P)

                length([]) $\rightarrow$ 0   (l1)

                length(x:y) $\rightarrow$ s(length(y)   (l2)

                reverse(x) $\rightarrow$ rev(x,[])   (r1)

                rev([],z) $\rightarrow$ z   (r2)

                rev(x:y,z) $\rightarrow$ rev(y,x:z)   (r3)

which states that the list x can be regarded as a palindrom if x and its reversed form are equal. We may obtain the s-refutation (see section 7.3)

$\Leftarrow$ **Palindrom(a:b:x)**, EQ(length(x), 2)

$\rightarrow$lr(P) $\Leftarrow$ EQ(a:b:x, **reverse(a:b:x)**), EQ(length(x), 2)

$\rightarrow$ln(r1) $\Leftarrow$ EQ(a:b:x, **rev(a:b:x,[])**), EQ(length(x), 2)

$\rightarrow$ln(r3) $\Leftarrow$ EQ(a:b:x, **rev(b:x,a:[])**), EQ(length(x), 2)

$\rightarrow$ln(r3) $\Leftarrow$ EQ(a:b:x, rev(x,b:a:[])), EQ(**length(x)**, 2)

$\rightarrow$ln(l2) $\Leftarrow$ EQ(a:b:x3:y3, rev(x3:y3,b:a:[]), EQ(**length(y3)**, 1)

$\rightarrow$ln(l2) $\Leftarrow$ EQ(a:b:x3:x4:y4, rev(x3:x4:y4,b:a:[]), EQ(**length(y4)**, 0)

$\rightarrow$ln(l1) $\Leftarrow$ EQ(a:b:x3:x4:[], **rev(x3:x4:[],b:a:[])**)

$\rightarrow$ln(r3) $\Leftarrow$ EQ(a:b:x3:x4:[], **rev(x4:[],x3:b:a:[])**)

$\rightarrow$ln(r3) $\Leftarrow$ EQ(a:b:x3:x4:[], **rev([],x4:x3:b:a:[])**)

$\rightarrow$ln(r2) $\square$

with respect to $\{\rightarrow$lr, $\rightarrow$ln, $\rightarrow$im, $\rightarrow$v, $\rightarrow$d, $\rightarrow$t$\}$ and computed answer substitution $\theta = \{x\leftarrow b:a:[]\}$. In this refutation we applied lazy resolution once, the longest reduction issuing from $\Leftarrow\theta F$ is

length(b:a:[]) $\rightarrow$R s(length(a:[])) $\rightarrow$R s(s(**length(0)**)) $\rightarrow$R s(s(0)),

the number of occurrences of function symbols and variables in EQ(length(x), s(s(0))) is 5 and EQ(length(x), s(s(0))) is the only equation in the initial goal clause. Hence, the refutation has complexity <1, <3, {3}, 5, 1>>.

The following three propositions show that we may swap two inference steps if lazy resolution is one of the inference rules applied. Therefore assume that $\rightarrow$ is an inference rule from RULES and recall that A denotes an atom, E denotes an equation, D denotes a multiset of atoms and equations, and F denotes a multiset of equations.

Proposition 8.1:

    If $\Leftarrow D\cup\{A_1, A_2\}$ $\rightarrow$lr $\Leftarrow D\cup D_1\cup\{A_2\}$ $\rightarrow$lr $\Leftarrow D\cup D_1\cup D_2$

    then $\Leftarrow D\cup\{A_1, A_2\}$ $\rightarrow$lr $\Leftarrow D\cup D_2\cup\{A_1\}$ $\rightarrow$lr $\Leftarrow D\cup D_1\cup D_2$.

Proposition 8.2:

    If $\Leftarrow D\cup\{A, E\}$ $\rightarrow$lr $\Leftarrow D\cup D'\cup\{E\}$ $\rightarrow$(σ) $\Leftarrow \sigma(D\cup D'\cup F)$

    then $\Leftarrow D\cup\{A, E\}$ $\rightarrow$(σ) $\Leftarrow \sigma(D\cup F\cup\{A\})$ $\rightarrow$lr $\Leftarrow \sigma(D\cup D'\cup F)$.

Proposition 8.3:

    If $\Leftarrow D\cup\{A, E\}$ $\rightarrow$(σ) $\Leftarrow \sigma(D\cup F\cup\{A\})$ $\rightarrow$lr $\Leftarrow \sigma(D\cup D'\cup F)$

    then $\Leftarrow D\cup\{A, E\}$ $\rightarrow$lr $\Leftarrow D\cup D'\cup\{E\}$ $\rightarrow$(σ) $\Leftarrow \sigma(D\cup D'\cup F)$.

With the help of these propositions we can now prove the independence of the selection function for refutations with respect to RULES and lazy resolution.

Theorem 8.4 (Indepedence of the Selection Function for RULES$^+$):

> Let SEL and SEL' be two selection functions. If there exists a refutation of
> $<EP,LP>\cup\{\Leftarrow D\}$ wrt RULES$^+$ and via SEL, then there exists a refutation of
> $<EP,LP>\cup\{\Leftarrow D\}$ wrt RULES$^+$ and via SEL'. Furthermore, if θ and σ are the
> respective computed answer substitutions and M and N are the respective com-
> plexities, then θ and σ are EP-variants and M = N.

Proof:

The proof is by transfinite induction on the complexity M of the refutation of
$<EP,LP>\cup\{\Leftarrow D\}$ wrt RULES$^+$ via SEL. We assume that the result holds for all M « M'.
Suppose there exists a refutation of $<EP,LP>\cup\{\Leftarrow D'\}$ wrt RULES$^+$, computed answer substitution θ', complexity M', and via SEL. Let $C_1 \in D'$ (resp. $C_2 \in D'$) be the first selected
subgoal of SEL (resp. SEL'). If $C_1 = C_2$, then the theorem follows immediately by an application of the induction hypothesis. Now suppose that $C_1 \neq C_2$. We distinguish three cases.

If D' does not contain an atom, then no goal clause in the refutation of $<EP,LP>\cup\{\Leftarrow D'\}$
contains an atom. By property A, θ' is a correct answer substitution for EP and $\Leftarrow D'$ and, by
property B, we find an SEL'-computed answer substitution σ' for EP and $\Leftarrow D'$ such that θ'
$\leq_{EP} \sigma'$. Reversing the arguments we find that $\sigma' \leq_{EP} \theta'$ and, hence, σ' and θ' are EP-variants. Furthermore, if N' is the complexity of the refutation of $<EP,LP>\cup\{\Leftarrow D'\}$ via SEL',
then, by property C, N = M.

Suppose C_1 or C_2 is an atom. Let $V = Var(D')$, $\to \in$ RULES$^+$, and assume that

$$\Leftarrow D' \to (C_1, \theta_1) \Leftarrow D.$$

Clearly, there exists a refutation of $<EP,LP>\cup\{\Leftarrow D\}$ wrt RULES$^+$ and via SEL and, if θ is
the computed answer substitution and M is the complexity of this refutation, then $\theta' = \theta\theta_1|v$
and M « M'. By an application of the induction hypothesis we find a refutation of
$<EP,LP>\cup\{\Leftarrow D\}$ wrt RULES$^+$ such that $\theta_1 C_2$ is the first selected subgoal and, if γ is the
computed answer substitution and N the complexity of this refutation, then γ and θ are EP-
variants and N = M. Hence, we find a refutation of $<EP,LP>\cup\{\Leftarrow D'\}$ wrt RULES$^+$ with
computed answer substitution $\gamma' = \gamma\theta_1|v$ and complexity N', where C_1 (resp. $\theta_1 C_2$) is the
first (resp. second) selected subgoal. By proposition 4.3(7), γ' is an EP-variant of θ' and N' =
M'. Since C_1 or C_2 is an atom propositions 8.1 - 8.3 ensure that there exists a refutation of
$<EP,LP>\cup\{\Leftarrow D'\}$ wrt RULES$^+$, where C_2 (resp. C_1) is the first (resp. second) selected
subgoal. Furthermore, if γ'' is the computed answer substitution and N'' the compexity of
this refutation, then γ'' and γ' (resp. θ') are EP-variants and N'' = N' = M'. An application of
the induction hypothesis completes the proof in this case.

Finally, suppose that both, C_1 and C_2, are equations and that D' contains at least one atom, say A. Let $\rightarrow \in RULES^+$ and assume that

$$\Leftarrow D' \rightarrow (C_1, \theta_1) \Leftarrow D.$$

Clearly, there exists a refutation of $<EP,LP> \cup \{\Leftarrow D\}$ wrt $RULES^+$ via SEL and, if θ is the computed answer substitution and M is the complexity of this refutation, then $\theta' = \theta\theta_1|_V$ and M « M'. By an application of the induction hypothesis we find a refutation of $<EP,LP> \cup \{\Leftarrow D\}$ wrt $RULES^+$ such that $\theta_1 A$ is the first selected subgoal and, if γ is the computed answer substitution and N the complexity of this refutation, then γ and θ are EP-variants and N = M. Hence, we find a refutation of $<EP,LP> \cup \{\Leftarrow D'\}$ wrt $RULES^+$ with computed answer substitution $\gamma' = \gamma\theta_1|_V$ and complexity N', where C_1 (resp. $\theta_1 A$) is the first (resp. second) selected subgoal. By proposition 4,3(7), γ' is a variant of θ' and N' = M'. By proposition 8.3 there exists a refutation of $<EP,LP> \cup \{\Leftarrow D'\}$ wrt $RULES^+$ where A (resp. C_1) is the first (resp. second) selected subgoal. Furthermore, if γ'' is the computed answer substitution and N'' the compexity of this refutation, then γ'' and γ' (resp. θ') are EP-variants and N'' = N' = M'. The result follows in analogy to the previous case.   qed

We can now show the strong completeness of refutations with respect to RULES and lazy resolution.

Theorem 8.5 (Strong Completeness of $RULES^+$):

Let SEL be a selection function. For every correct answer substitution θ for $<EP,LP>$ and $\Leftarrow D$ there exists an SEL-computed answer substitution σ obtained by a refutation of $<EP,LP> \cup \{\Leftarrow D\}$ wrt $RULES^+$ such that $\theta \leq_{EP} \sigma$.

Proof:

Let UP_{EP} be a complete EP-unification procedure. From theorem 5.5 we learn that for every correct answer substitution θ for $<EP,LP>$ and $\Leftarrow D$ there exists a computed answer substitution γ obtained by a refutation of $LP \cup \{\Leftarrow D\}$ wrt EP-resolution such that $\theta \leq_{EP} \gamma$. By property B RULES define a complete EP-unification procedure. Hence, there exists a refutation of $<EP,LP> \cup \{\Leftarrow D\}$ wrt $RULES^+$ and computed answer substitution γ and the result follows immediately by an application of theorem 8.4.   qed

From this theorem we learn that we need not compute the set of EP-unifiers of a set of equations completely, rather we may compute only a partial unifier and, then, add the yet unsolved equations, sometimes called residuum, to the goal clause. The result is completely general in that we only assume to have a set of inference rules for the equality theory enjoying properties A - C. Hence, we may instantiate theorem 8.5, for example, by the inference rules reflection, paramodulation, and instantiation for arbitrary equational programs, or by the transformations variable elimination, term decomposition, removal of trivial equations, lazy narrowing, and imitation for canonical term rewriting systems.

Theorem 8.5 shows also the strong completeness of Bürckert's (1986, 1987) strategy to compute only a unitary partial EP-unifier for a set of equations, to delay the remaining equations until all other subgoals are solved, and then to submit the delayed subgoals to a complete EP-unification procedure.

Another equational logic programming language that can be based on theorem 8.5 is LeFun (Ait Kaci et al. 1986, 1987). In LeFun, functional expressions are reduced before they are submitted to the unification algorithm. If two reduced expressions cannot be unified, then they are recorded as "residuations" and delayed until a variable occurring in these expressions is bound. In this case it is checked, whether the expressions reduce to the same value. Obviously, LeFun is incomplete, but could easily be turned into a complete language if a complete EP-unification procedure took care of the remaining residuations.

Instantiated with the inference rules narrowing and reflection, theorem 8.5 defines an operational semantics for EQLOG (Goguen & Meseguer 1984, 1986).

Similarly, Yamamoto's (1987) strong completeness result for SLD-resolution and narrowing (for unconditional equational theories) is just an instance of theorem 8.5.

Another good candidate for an application of theorem 8.5 would be narrowing modulo equality (Jouannaud et al. 1983, Bockmayr 1988). In this approach troublesome axioms such as associativity and commutativity axioms are built into the unification algorithm used within narrowing. More formally, if an unconditional equational theory can be split into a set of rewrite rules R and a set of equations E, then narrowing modulo equality is complete if $R \cup E$ is "confluent modulo E", "E-terminating", and E has a finite and complete E-unification algorithm. (Let an E,R-rewriting step be a rewriting step with respect to R, where a matcher modulo E has been used. Then, "confluency modulo E" and "E-termination" are defined as confluency and termination, but with respect to E,R-rewriting.) Jouannaud et al. proved the completeness of narrowing modulo equality and A. Bockmayr showed that this technique may prune the search space considerably. But to instantiate theorem 8.5 we also need the independence of a selection function.

9 Conclusion

In this thesis we investigated equational logic programs, i.e. logic programs which are augmented with a Horn equational theory. We proved rigorously that many results known to hold for unconditional equational theories can be generalized to hold also for conditional equational theories. In this chapter we summarize our results and we compare our approaches to other techniques. Finally we point out some open problems and further developments.

9.1 Summary

In recent years many proposals were made to integrate functional and logic programming. Among them equational logic programs were of special interest since the main semantic properties of logic programs hold also for equational logic programs. As the equational part of such a program is a set of Horn clauses, it admits a finest congruence relation $\equiv$ on the set of ground terms. The Herbrand $\equiv$-universe was defined as the quotient of the set of ground terms modulo $\equiv$ and the Herbrand $\equiv$-base was defined as the set of atoms that can be built from the predicate symbols occurring in LP and the elements of the Herbrand $\equiv$-universe. A Herbrand $\equiv$-model of <EP,LP> is a subset of the Herbrand $\equiv$-base which E-satisfies <EP,LP>. As the model intersection property holds also for Herbrand $\equiv$-models, the semantics of an equational logic program was given by the least Herbrand $\equiv$-model. Moreover, a declarative meaning of a correct answer to a query posed to an equational logic program was defined as a substitution for the variables occurring in the query such that the instantiated subgoals of the query are logical E-consequences of the equational logic program.

We then turned our interest to the question of how queries to an equational logic program can be answered or, more formally, how answer substitutions for the variables occurring in the query can be computed. Starting from the well-known result that resolution can be used to compute the E-unsatisfiability of a set of clauses if the axioms of equality were included in this set of clauses, we extended the SLD-resolution rule to SLDE-resolution and EP-resolution. SLDE-resolution differs from SLD-resolution in that the notion of a most general unifier of two expressions was replaced by the notion of an EP-unifier of these expressions. However, EP-unifiers are only defined declaratively as correct answer substitutions to Horn equational theories EP and goal clauses that contain only equations. In order to mechanize SLDE-resolution we generalized the notion of a complete set of unifiers under an unconditional equational theory (e.g. Siekmann 1984, 1986, 1989) to a complete set of unifiers under a Horn equational theory. Similarly, an EP-unification procedure was defined for Horn equational theory as a procedure that enumerates a set of EP-unifiers for a given EP-unification problem. Consequently, EP-resolution differs from SLD-resolution in that the traditional unification algorithm used to compute the most general unifier of two terms was replaced by a sound and complete EP-unification procedure. Both, SLDE-resolution and EP-resolution, were shown to be sound, complete, and independent of a selection function. Thus we generalized results obtained by Gallier & Raatz (1986, 1989), who proved the completeness of EP-resolution (there called "SLDE[†]-resolution") for logic programs augmented with an unconditional equational theory. It seems to us that Gallier & Raatz restricted their SLDE[†]-resolution rule to unconditional equational theories EP since they did not realize that the notion of a complete set of unifiers under an unconditional equational theory can be generalized to the notion of a complete set of unifiers under a Horn equational theory and that the latter set is recursively enumerable.

Having obtained the strong completeness of EP-resolution we concentrated on the problem to define sound, complete, and universal EP-unification procedures for equational programs EP. These procedures were based on (linear) paramodulation and complete sets of transformations.

We demonstrated that paramodulation and reflection is complete only if the instantiation rule or, equivalently, the functional reflexive axioms, is (resp. are) added. The completeness was proved by showing that the least fixpoint of an appropriate function T_{EP} is equal to the least model of an equational program EP and to the success set of reflection, instantiation and paramodulation. A similar technique was used by Gallier & Raatz (1989). However, they distinguish between implicational and equational reasoning and, therefore, use a congruence closure construction, where successively the computation of the implicational closure of a set of equations is followed by the computation of the equational closure. We claim that our fixpoint construction is much more elegant and corresponds directly to paramodulation.

Since paramodulation generates far too many redundant and irrelevant clauses we investigated how certain restrictions imposed one-by-one on the equational program can cut the search space.

If the equational program is ground confluent, then the equational clauses have to be used only in one direction.

If, in addition, answer substitutions are normalizable and the equational program is a nontrivial term rewriting system, then paramodulation need no longer be applied to variable occurrences. This restricted form of paramodulation is called narrowing. As a consequence the instantiation rule can be omitted. Recall, that a term rewriting system generally contains conditional rules. Thus, we generalized a result obtained by Hullot (1980), who showed the completeness of narrowing for unconditional canonical term rewriting systems. We also corrected a result by Hussmann (1985), who stated a completeness result for confluent equational programs if answer substitutions are normalizable but allowed extra variables in the right-hand sides of the heads and in the bodies of the equational clauses. We showed in section 6.5 that these extra variables lead to an incompleteness of narrowing and reflection.

If the equational program is a canonical term rewriting system, then innermost narrowing, innermost reflection, and reflection is complete and the search space can be further reduced by applying Boyer & Moore's (1972) technique of structure sharing to split clauses into a skeleton and an environment part. Thus we again generalized a result obtained by Hullot

(1980) for unconditional term rewriting systems. Moreover, we achieved the same effect as Hullot's "basic" narrowing without introducing the clumsy notion of a "basic" occurrence. (It should also be noted that Hullot's proof of the completeness of narrowing and "basic narrowing" contains several flaws which were corrected in this thesis.) A further advantage of canonical term rewriting systems is the fact that rewriting can be applied as a simplification rule, which may cut an infinite search space to a finite one. This was an open problem for a long time and was only recently solved by Réty (1987) for unconditional term rewriting systems. But Réty had to introduce several complicated technical notions, whereas our solution comes almost immediately with the adaptation of Boyer and Moore's technique. It should be noted that Nutt et al. (1987) achieved a similar result for unconditional term rewriting systems, but in their proofs they use a different technique.

Finally, if the term rewriting system is, in addition, completely defined and we are interested only in ground substitutions, then we could easily derive the completeness of innermost narrowing and reflection, a result that was shown by Fribourg (1985).

It should be observed that we always proved the strong completeness of the respective set of inference rules, i.e. a computation rule may select an arbitrary subgoal from a goal clause and it suffices to apply the inference rules to this subgoal in order to compute a complete set of answers. Moreover, if the equational program is a canonical and completely defined term rewriting system, the answer substitution is ground, and narrowing is to be applied, then it suffices to select a single innermost redex from the selected subgoal. To the best of our knowledge only Nutt et al. (1987) also showed the strong completeness of their system, whereas all other authors gave only completeness proofs (e.g. Hullot 1980, Hussmann 1985). As a consequence, they cannot select a subgoal "don't care" non-deterministically from a goal clause. It should be noted that if an inference system based on paramodulation (or special forms of it) is strongly complete, then Morris' (1969) and Anderson's (1970) technique of applying paramodulation subsequently to a subgoal until it can be solved is just the application of a special selection function.

Altogether we defined a single uniform framework for universal unification procedures, that compute solutions for unification problems under Horn equational theories and are based on (linear) paramodulation. We demonstrated how certain restrictions imposed one-by-one on the equational program reduce the search space and lead to special forms of paramodulation.

In chapter 7 we defined certain transformations which extend the rules that were formulated by Herbrand (1930) and later used by Martelli & Montanari (1982) to compute the most general unifier of two expressions. Our transformations can be seen as extensions of the rules given by Gallier & Snyder (1987, 1988) to Horn equational theories. But they also refine Gallier & Snyder's transformations in that we do not include a rule that corresponds to an instantiation step. To prove the strong completeness of our set of transformations we showed how each refutation with respect to paramodulation, instantiation, and reflection can be transformed into a refutation with respect to the transformation rules. Moreover, the simple proof allows to carry over the restrictions of paramodulation if certain conditions are imposed on the equational program. This successively leads to refined sets of transformations if the equational program is confluent, if it is a non-trivial term rewriting system and the answer substitution is normalizable, and if it is a canonical term rewriting system. Recall again, that we considered conditional term rewriting systems. Thus we generalized results by Gallier & Snyder (1987, 1988) and Martelli et al. (1986) who have given complete sets of transformations for canonical and unconditional term rewriting systems. Moreover, we showed rigorously that rewriting can be applied as a simplification rule if the equational program is a canonical term rewriting system.

Again we provided a single uniform framework for universal unification procedures, that compute solutions for unification problems under Horn equational theories and are based on complete sets of transformations, and we showed how certain restrictions imposed one-by-one on the equational program reduce the search space and lead to refined sets of transformations.

Using the universal unification procedures for Horn equational theories based on paramodulation or complete sets of transformations, we can instantiate our EP-resolution rule to compute answers to queries posed to equational logic programs. However, the use of EP-resolution inherits a principal problem. As G. D. Plotkin (1972) showed, a complete and even independent set of EP-unifiers may be infinite or may not even exist. Moreover, the EP-unification problem is generally undecidable even if the equational program is a canonical and unconditional term rewriting system (see section 6.6). Hence, the search space may not only be infinite in its depth but may also be infinite in its breadth and, whenever we call the EP-unification procedure, we cannot be sure that it will terminate even if it does not produce a single unifier after some time.

To overcome these problems we introduced the lazy resolution rule. This rule has the advantage that a unification problem must not be solved before the rule can be applied but the unification problem is added as a "constraint" to the derived goal clause (Huet 1972). If the universal unification procedure is defined by a sound and strongly complete set of inference rules, then these inference rules can be used to solve these "constraints". But since refutations with respect to lazy resolution and this set of inference rules are independent of a selection function (see section 8), the user can control at what time the "constraint solving" will take place. (This application shows again the need to prove strong completeness results.) Yamamoto's (1987) strong completeness result for SLD-resolution and narrowing is just a special case of our result, where narrowing is used to solve the "constraints" for given unconditional equational theories. Our result provides also an operational semantics for EQLOG (Goguen & Meseguer 1984, 1986): any complete set of inference rules for the equational part of an EQLOG-program (e.g. narrowing) combined with the lazy resolution rule is strongly complete.

9.2 Discussion

Let us now compare our approaches to handle equational logic programs with others.

E-resolution

E-resolution was introduced by Morris (1969) as a restricted form of paramodulation to compute the unsatisfiability of sets of arbitrary clauses: Two clauses are selected and a literal is selected from each clause as possible literals to be resolved upon. Then paramodulation is applied to these literals until they become syntactically unifiable. Analogously, if an equation in a clause was selected, then paramodulation is applied to this equation until the elements become syntactically unifiable. Thus, the only paramodulation which is done is paramodulation to the selected literal(s). The basic idea is to restrict paramodulation to those applications which are immediately relevant. Anderson (1970) showed that E-resolution is complete and, recently, Gallier & Raatz (1986, 1989) adopted E-resolution for sets of Horn clauses.

Due to our strong completeness results for paramodulation, reflection, and lazy resolution (theorems 6.2.17, 8.5), E-resolution is just the application of a certain selection function. Moreover, this selection function has the disadvantage that there may be infinitely many different ways to apply E-resolution to two expressions. Even worse, since the E-unification problem is in general undecidable (see theorem 6.6.2.7), there is no procedure to decide whether two expressions are E-unifiable and, hence, a single E-resolution step may run forever without producing any output.

E-resolution was generalized by Harrison & Rubin (1978) to "generalized resolution" in that they are not devoted to paramodulation as an inference rule to compute the E-unifier of two expressions. Generalized resolution can also be seen in the application of a certain selection function in refutations with respect to lazy resolution and some complete set of inference rules (theorem 8.5).

Resolution by Unification and Equality

The inference rules RUE (resolution by unification and equality) and NRF (negative reflexive function rule) were introduced by Digricoly (1979) to compute the E-unsatisfiability of a set of arbitrary clauses containing neither the equality nor the functional reflexive axioms. They are sound and complete and are based on a disagreement set analysis. In Digricoly & Harrison (1986) it was shown that for each E-unsatisfiable set of Horn clauses there exists a positive unit RUE-NRF-refutation. Due to the close relationship between unit and input refutations (e.g. Chang & Lee 1973) such a unit RUE-NRF-refutation can easily be transformed into a RUE-NRF-refutation.

Let <EP,LP> be an equational logic program, X be an n-ary predicate symbol or "EQ", G = ⇐D∪{X(s₁,...,sₙ)} be a goal clause, and P = X(t₁,...,tₙ)⇐D* be a new variant of a clause in <EP,LP>. Then ⇐σD∪σD*∪F is called **RUE-resolvent** of G and P, where σ is an arbitrary substitution and F is an arbitrary disagreement set of σX(s₁,...,sₙ) and σX(t₁,...,tₙ).

Let G = ⇐D∪{EQ(s,t)} be a goal clause. Then ⇐σD∪F is called **NRF-resolvent** of G, where σ is an arbitrary substitution and F is an arbitrary disagreement set of σs and σt.

Since RUE-NRF-derivations are based on a disagreement set analysis we have to investigate all possible **disagreement sets** for two expressions:
(1)   If the terms s and t are identical, then ∅ is the only disagreement set.
(2)   If the terms s and t are not identical, then {EQ(s,t)} is a disagreement set.
(3)   If the term s (resp. t) is of the form $f(s_1,...,s_n)$ (resp. $f(t_1,...,t_n)$), then the set of all EQ(sᵢ,tᵢ) such that $s_i \neq t_i$, $1 \leq i \leq n$, is a disagreement set.
(4)   If F is a disagreement set, then F' formed by replacing any member of F by elements of its disagreement set is also a disagreement set.
(5)   If X(s₁,...,sₙ) and X(t₁,...,tₙ) are two atoms or equations, then
          F = { Dᵢ | Dᵢ is a disagreement set of sᵢ and tᵢ, $1 \leq i \leq n$ }
       is a disagreement set.

As an example consider the atoms P(h(x),i(y)) and P(h(b),i(b)). The disagreement sets for these atoms are

      { EQ(h(x),h(b)), EQ(i(y),i(b)) },
      { EQ(x,b), EQ(i(y),i(b)) },
      { EQ(h(x),h(b)), EQ(y,b) },
      { EQ(x,b), EQ(y,b) }.

It should be observed that any one of these disagreement sets can be obtained by repeated applications of the term decomposition rule if lazy resolution was applied to the atom P(h(x),i(y)) using a program clause whose head is P(h(b),i(b)).

In order to apply resolution by unification and equality or the negative reflexive function rule one has to make two decisions: Firstly, a substitution has to be selected and, secondly, a disgreement set has to be chosen.

To show the completeness of RUE-NRF-resolution Digricoli needs arbitrary substitutions, however, for practical purposes he suggests to use substitutions "between" the empty substitution and the so-called most general partial unifier. The **most general partial unifier** (mpgu) of two expressions can be obtained by unifiying the expressions from left-to-right and skipping over irreducible disagreements. For example, the mpgu of P(a,f(b,c),y) and P(x,f(x,c),e) is $\{x \leftarrow a, y \leftarrow e\}$. It is easy to see that we can simulate each RUE- or NRF-step using a unifier "between" ε and the mpgu by repeated applications of lazy resolution, term decomposition, variable elimination, paramodulation at variable occurrences, and imitation: Consider the program clause P(x,f(x,c),e)⇐. By applying RUE-resolution to

$\quad$ ⇐ P(a,f(b,c),y)

using the substitution $\{x \leftarrow a, y \leftarrow e\}$ we obtain

$\quad$ ⇐ EQ(f(b,c), f(a,c)),

whereas

$\quad$ ⇐ P(a,f(b,c),y) $\rightarrow_{lr}$ $\qquad$ ⇐ EQ(a,x), EQ(f(b,c), f(x,c)), EQ(y,e)

$\qquad\qquad\qquad$ $\rightarrow_{v}(\{x \leftarrow a\})$ ⇐ EQ(f(b,c), f(a,c)), EQ(y,e)

$\qquad\qquad\qquad$ $\rightarrow_{v}(\{y \leftarrow e\})$ ⇐ EQ(f(b,c), f(a,c)).

Unfortunately, as Digricoli (1979) demonstrated, using only the mgpu is not complete.

It should be noted that we cannot simulate each RUE-NRF-refutation by applying lazy resolution and the transformations from RULES. For example,

$\quad$ ⇐ EQ(g(b), h(a))

is a NRF-resolvent of

$\quad$ ⇐ EQ(f(g(x)), f(h(a)))

using $\{x \leftarrow b\}$ but we can only apply term decomposition to ⇐EQ(f(g(x)),f(h(a))) yielding ⇐EQ(g(x),h(a)) and there is no possibility to instantiate the x to b.

To restrict the number of disagreement sets that can be used in a RUE- or NRF-step Digricoli specified certain conditions that are necessary such that a certain disagreement set may participate in a refutation. The viability condition is a generalization of our failure rule for term rewriting systems. Consider the equational program

$\quad$ { f(x)→g, g→c(b) }

and the disagreement set {EQ(f(a), c(a))}. Though f(a) can be replaced by c(b), this set is not viable since a and b are different constructors. Of course, using our transformations and our failure rule we will recognize the failure after a lazy narrowing and a term decomposition step:

$\quad$ ⇐ EQ(f(a), c(a)) $\rightarrow_{ln}$ ⇐ EQ(c(b), c(a)), EQ(a,x) $\rightarrow_{d}$ ⇐ EQ(b,a), EQ(a,x).

It is not immediately obvious whether a viability test or the application of some transformations is more expensive.

Digricoli also defined equality restrictions for RUE-NRF-refutations. These restrictions corresponds to our lazy narrowing rule as it requires that the initial symbols of an element of an equation and the head of an equational clause must be identical.

In conclusion, using lazy resolution and the transformations in RULES generates less derivations than using the negative reflexive function rule and resolution by unification and equality due to the fact that in the latter case we have to consider arbitrary substitutions. Our technique abstracts from the notion of a disagreement set in much the same way as Martelli & Montanari's (1982) transformation rules compute the most general unifier of two expressions without explicitly investigating disagreement sets.

Equality Graphs

Based on Kowalski's (1975) proof procedure for connection graphs and its extension to paramodulated connection graphs (Siekmann & Wrightson 1980), Bläsius (1987) and Siekmann & Bläsius (1988) developed a partial unification procedure for graph based equational reasoning. To examplify the method consider the equational theory

EP:	$EQ(g(x,x), h(x,b))$	(g)
	$EQ(h(u,v), h(v,u))$	(h1)
	$EQ(h(b,a), f(b))$	(h2)
	$EQ(b,c)$	(b)
	$EQ(c,e)$	(c)

and the problem $<g(a,y)=f(e)>$EP. The main discrepancies are the different initial symbols g and f. The equations (g) and (h1) can be combined to form a "chain", which can be used to remove this discepancy. In our notation, from

$$\Leftarrow EQ(g(a,y), f(e)) \tag{*}$$

we can deduce

$$\Leftarrow EQ(g(a,y), g(x,x)), EQ(h(x,b), h(b,a)), EQ(f(b), f(e))$$

using (g) and (h2). Applying term decomposition to all three equations yields

$$\Leftarrow EQ(a,x), EQ(y,x), EQ(x,b), EQ(b,a), EQ(b,e).$$

Some of the equations, like $EQ(a,x)$, can now be solved using variable elimination. However, the equation $EQ(b,a)$ cannot be solved, because there is no "chain" of equations from EP to connect a and b. Backtracking to our original problem (*) we notice that there is a second "chain" formed by (g), (h1), and (h2), that can be used to remove the difference between the symbols f and g. Using these equations we obtain from (*) the problem

$$\Leftarrow EQ(g(a,y), g(x,x), EQ(h(x,b), h(u,v)), EQ(h(v,u), h(b,a)), EQ(f(b), f(e)).$$

Decomposing each equation yields

$\Leftarrow$ EQ(a,x), EQ(y,x), EQ(x,u), EQ(b,v), EQ(v,b), EQ(u,a), EQ(b,e)

which can be solved with "computed answer substitution"

{ x$\leftarrow$a, y$\leftarrow$a, u$\leftarrow$a, v$\leftarrow$b }.

We did not use the graphical notation invented by Bläsius and Siekmann to show the relationship of this method to our set of transformations defined in chapter 7. Using our transformations the original problem (*) can be solved as follows:

$\Leftarrow$ **EQ(g(a,y), f(e))**	
$\rightarrow$ln(g)	$\Leftarrow$ **EQ(a,x), EQ(y,x), EQ(h(x,b), f(e))**
$\rightarrow$v({x$\leftarrow$a})	$\Leftarrow$ **EQ(y,a), EQ(h(a,b), f(e))**
$\rightarrow$v({y$\leftarrow$a})	$\Leftarrow$ **EQ(h(a,b), f(e))**
$\rightarrow$ln(h1)	$\Leftarrow$ **EQ(a,u), EQ(b,v), EQ(h(v,u), f(e))**
$\rightarrow$v({u$\leftarrow$a})	$\Leftarrow$ **EQ(b,v), EQ(h(v,a), f(e))**
$\rightarrow$v({v$\leftarrow$b})	$\Leftarrow$ **EQ(h(b,a), f(e))**
$\rightarrow$ln(h2)	$\Leftarrow$ **EQ(b,b), EQ(a,a), EQ(f(b), f(e))**
$\rightarrow$t	$\Leftarrow$ **EQ(a,a), EQ(f(b), f(e))**
$\rightarrow$t	$\Leftarrow$ **EQ(f(b), f(e))**
$\rightarrow$d	$\Leftarrow$ **EQ(b,e)**
$\rightarrow$ln(b)	$\Leftarrow$ **EQ(c,e)**
$\rightarrow$ln(c)	$\Leftarrow$ **EQ(e,e)**
$\rightarrow$t	□.

Using Bläsius and Siekmann's technique we should define another failure rule for refutations with respect to our sets of transformations. Recall, that the problem <a=b>EP could not be solved as there was no "chain" of equations from EP such that the difference between the symbols a and b could be removed. Since each equational program is finite, the existence of such a "chain" can easily be checked. Consequently, a derivation should be terminated with failure if such a "chain" does not exist.

Special Predicates

Many researchers proposed to enrich PROLOG with some special predicates in order to include equality.

In Kornfeld's (1983) PROLOG-with-equality the user is encouraged to specify that two terms are equal by means of a special predicate "Equals". For example, two rational numbers - given as terms made up of the constructor "rat" with two arguments nominator and denominator - are equal if the products of their respective nominator and denominator are equal:

Equals(rat(n1,d1), rat(n2,d2)) $\Leftarrow$ Times(n1,d2,i), Times(n2,d1,i).

The unification algorithm is altered such that, if two terms s and t do not unify syntactically, an attempt is made to prove that Equals(s,t) holds. In our example rat(2,3) and rat(x,3) unify with {x←2}, whereas rat(2,3) and rat(x,6) can be proved equal with {x←4}. In order to avoid cycles the initial symbol of the first argument of an Equals predicate must always be a function symbol and - due to standard PROLOG - unification in PROLOG-with-equality succeeds at most once. Kornfeld's aim was not to design a complete system, rather he wanted to show that by a slight modification of the PROLOG interpreter certain nice properties become available such as automatic type conversion, generic operations, class structuring, or partially instantiated objects. For example, an integer n can be unified with a term rat(x,y) yielding the substitution {x←n, y←1}.

Tamaki (1984) suggested a "reducibility predicate" instead of the equality sign. Similar to the "→" we used in the head of an equational clause, the reducibility predicate makes explicit, semantically as well as syntactically, that left-hand sides can be replaced by right-hand sides but not vice versa. To define the semantics of logic programs with a reducibility predicate the reducibility axioms - these are the axioms of equality except the axiom of symmetry and the p-substitutivity axioms for the reducibility predicate - are added to the program. It is, of course, infeasible to apply SLD-resolution to the reducibility axioms. To overcome these combinatorial problems Tamaki imposed two restrictions on his language: the left-hand side of a reduction atom must be of the form $f(t_1,...,t_n)$ such that the t_i do not contain a defined function symbol and the program has to be confluent. As we showed in section 6.3, the confluency guarantees that completeness can be achieved also if reduction atoms are only used from left-to-right. Finally, program and goal clause are flattened and, thus, the transitivity and substitutivity axioms can be dropped. The flattened clauses can now be submitted to an SLD-refutation procedure.

Unfortunately, Tamaki did not specify a computation rule for the flattened clauses and, hence, it is not obvious, in which order terms are reduced. A similar technique to implement reductions was used by van Emden & Yukawe (1987). In their interpretational approach terms are reduced with respect to a Noetherian term rewriting system by a logic program that essentially controls the use of the equality axioms, whereas in their compilational approach the term rewriting system is transformed into a logic program in much the same way as Tamaki flattens his programs. Van Emden & Yukawa were mainly interested in correct implementations of the reduction relation for Noetherian term rewriting systems and, hence, they show how the PROLOG strategy of selecting almost the leftmost subgoal can be applied to compute the normal form of a ground term. They did not address the problem of solving equations under equational theories nor the problem of combining logic and equational programming.

Flattening

The homogeneous form of a logic program was introduced by van Emden & Lloyd (1974) to show that Colmerauer's (1982) Prolog II can be viewed as a logic programming language augmented with a some equational theory. As an example consider the clauses

Append([],z,z) ⇐   (a1),

Append(x:y,z,z') → Append(y,z,z') ⇐   (a2),

whose homogeneous forms are

Append(x,z,z) ⇐ EQ(x,[])   (a1'),

Append(v,z,w) ⇐ EQ(v,x:y), EQ(w,x:z'), Append(y,z,z')   (a2').

Later, Hoddinott & Elcock (1986) showed that the homogeneous form of an equational logic program <EP,LP> subsumes the p-substitutivity axioms (theorem 3.4.2.2). Furthermore, if we consider also the homogeneous form of EP, the axiom of transitivity is subsumed. If, in addition, nested terms occurring in goal as well as in program clauses are "flattened", then the f-substitutivity axioms are subsumed as well (Cox, Pietrzykowski 1985, 1986). For example, the goal clause

⇐ Append(a:[],b:[],z)

can be flattened to

⇐ Append(x,y,z), EQ(x,v:w), EQ(v,a), EQ(w,[]), EQ(y,v':w), EQ(v',b).

Formally, a clause is said to be **flat** iff every atom has the form $P(x_1,...,x_n)$, every equation has the form $EQ(x,f(x_1,...,x_n))$ or $EQ(x,y)$, and if an equation of the form $EQ(x,y)$ occurs in a clause, then y occurs only as right-hand side of an equation in that clause.

To be able to remove the axiom of reflexivity, Cox & Pietrzykowski introduced two new inference rules, surface factoring and compression. The goal clause σG is a **surface factor** of the goal clause G on equalities E_1 and E_2 occurring in G iff E_1 (resp. E_2) is of the form $EQ(x,s)$ (resp. $EQ(x,t)$) and s and t are unifiable with mgu σ. The goal clause ⇐D\{EQ(x,t)} is a **compression** of the goal clause ⇐D iff $EQ(x,t) \in D$ and x has only one occurrence in D.

It should be noted that each clause can be transformed into a flat clause and the application of resolution, surface factoring, or compression to flat clauses yields again a flat clause.

As Cox & Pietrzykowski demonstrated, the remaining equality axiom - the symmetry - can be subsumed by adding the clauses from EP^{-1} to the clauses of an equational logic program <EP,LP>: <EP,LP> and the goal clause G are E-unsatisfiable iff there exists a refutation for every flattening of $<EP \cup EP^{-1}, LP \backslash \{EQ(x,x) \Leftarrow\} > \cup \{G\}$ with respect to resolution, surface factoring, and compression.

Various modifications of the technique to apply SLD-resolution to flattened clauses were proposed: We already mentioned Tamaki's (1984) reducibility predicate, which is implemented this way, except that he did not use the axiom of symmetry - or, equivalently clauses from EP^{-1} - since his programs are confluent. Similarly, Bosco et al. (1987) defined a sound and complete unification procedure for canonical conditional theories. This procedure corresponds roughly to the technique of applying innermost narrowing, innermost reflection, and reflection to equational goal clauses which was developed in section 6.5.1. Brand (1975) showed that the flattening - or as he called it, the "modification" - of an E-unsatisfiable set of clauses with equality yields an unsatisfiable set of clauses and as a consequence that unrestricted paramodulation is complete even without the functional reflexive axioms.

The principal disadvantage of flattening clauses is the lost possibility to reduce terms. As an example consider the rewrite rules

$$f(a) \rightarrow a \qquad\qquad\qquad (f1)$$
$$f(c(x)) \rightarrow c(f(x)) \qquad\qquad\qquad (f2)$$

and the goal clause

$\Leftarrow EQ(f(c(f(y))), a).$

$f(c(f(y)))$ can be rewritten to $c(f(f(y)))$ using (f2) and a failure can immediately be recognized since a and c are different constructors. Flattening the rewrite rules yields the conditional clauses

$$x \rightarrow a \Leftarrow EQ(x,f(y)), EQ(y,a) \qquad\qquad (f1')$$
$$z \rightarrow c(y) \Leftarrow EQ(z,f(v)), EQ(v,c(x)), EQ(y,c(x)) \qquad\qquad (f2')$$

and the goal clause

$\Leftarrow EQ(x,a), \mathbf{EQ(x,f(z)), EQ(z,c(v)), EQ(v,f(y))}$

and its surface factor

$\Leftarrow EQ(x,a), EQ(x,f(y)), \mathbf{EQ(y,c(x))}.$

By applying resolution using (f2') we obtain

$\Leftarrow EQ(x,a), EQ(x,f(y)), \mathbf{EQ(y,f(v_1)), EQ(v_1,c(x_1)), EQ(x,c(x_1))}$

which can successively be factored to

$\Leftarrow EQ(x,a), \mathbf{EQ(x,f(y)), EQ(y,f(x))}, EQ(x,c(x_1))$

and

$\Leftarrow EQ(x,a), \mathbf{EQ(x,f(x))}, EQ(x,c(x_1)).$

Now, applying resolution again and again to the last equation leads to an infinite derivation.

To overcome this problem in LEAF, Barbuti et al. (1986) imposed an annotation on variables, i.e. variables may be in input or output mode. They also designed a complex selection function and added a new rule to terminate computations.

Flattening clauses can be seen as the application of the substitutivity axioms at compile time whereas the axioms are applied implicitly at runtime if we use, for example, the transformation rules introduced in chapter 7. The transformation rules are applied by demand and we can apply rewriting as a simplification rule.

EQLOG

Goguen & Meseguer (1984, 1986) developed EQLOG, an equational logic programming language comprising logic programming, equational reasoning, term rewriting, order-sorted typing, and generic modules. The authors define an initial model semantics for EQLOG-programs, but fail to give a refutation-complete proof procedure for EQLOG. They give *in words* a semidecision procedure to answer questions posed to EQLOG-programs which consist of a logic program and an unconditional equational theory. The EP-resolution rule defined in this thesis can be seen as a rigorous formalization of Goguen's & Meseguer's description. Though the authors refer lateron to narrowing in order to compute a complete set of unifiers under an unconditional equational theory, we showed in chapter 8 that any complete set of inference rules for Horn equational theories together with the lazy resolution rule can be used to define a proof theoretic semantics for EQLOG.

Constraint Logic Programming

So far we have computed answers to queries posed to an equational logic program over the Herbrand universe only. For example, to be able to express predicates over natural numbers we have to map the natural numbers 0, 1, 2, ... onto the Herbrand terms 0, s(0), s(s(0)), ... and in order to add 1 and 2 we have to solve the goal $\Leftarrow$EQ(s(0)+s(s(0)),x) with respect to the rewrite rules $0+y \rightarrow y$ and $s(x)+y \rightarrow s(x+y)$. In such a refutation the variable x was eventually bound to s(s(s(0))) by the unification algorithm.

The basic idea of constraint logic programming is to replace the unification algorithm which operates on the Herbrand universe by a *constraint solver* which operates directly on the intended domain. As an example consider the following program which can be used to order a light meal (Colmerauer 1987):

Light-Meal(a,m,d) ⇐ Appetizer(a,i), Main(m,j), Dessert(d,k),

$$\{i \geq 0, j \geq 0, k \geq 0, i+j+k \leq 10\}$$

Main(m,i) ⇐ Meat(m,i)

Main(m,i) ⇐ Fish(m,i)

Appetizer(radishes,1) ⇐

Appetizer(paté,6) ⇐

Meat(beef,5) ⇐

Meat(pork,7) ⇐

Fish(sole,2) ⇐

Fish(tuna,4) ⇐

Dessert(fruit,2) ⇐

Dessert(icecream,6) ⇐

In general a constraint program clause is of the form

$P(s_1,...,s_n) \Leftarrow D, S,$

where D is a set of atoms and S is a set of constraints. Similarly, a constraint goal clause is of the form

$\Leftarrow D', S'.$

Suppose D' contains an atom of the form $P(t_1,...,t_n)$. Instead of unifying $P(s_1,...,s_n)$ and $P(t_1,...,t_n)$ a constraint solver will add the constraints $\{s_i = t_i \mid 1 \leq i \leq n\}$ to $S \cup S'$ and, thus, resolves the two clauses to

$\Leftarrow (D' \setminus \{P(t_1,...,t_n)\}) \cup D, S \cup S' \cup \{s_i = t_i \mid 1 \leq i \leq n\}$

if the newly generated set of constraints is solvable.

For example, to order a light meal we pose the query

$\Leftarrow$ Light-Meal(x,y,z).

By applying the program clause

Light-Meal(a,m,d) ⇐ Appetizer(a,i), Main(m,j), Dessert(d,k),

$$\{i \geq 0, j \geq 0, k \geq 0, i+j+k \leq 10\}$$

we obtain

$\Leftarrow$ Appetizer(a,i), Main(m,j), Dessert(d,k),

$$\{i \geq 0, j \geq 0, k \geq 0, i+j+k \leq 10, x=a, y=m, z=d\}.$$

The newly generated constraints may be simplified to

$\Leftarrow$ Appetizer(x,i), Main(y,j), Dessert(z,k), $\{i \geq 0, j \geq 0, k \geq 0, i+j+k \leq 10\}$.

By applying the rule

$\Leftarrow$ Appetizer(paté,6)

we obtain

$\Leftarrow$ Main(y,j), Dessert(z,k), $\{i \geq 0, j \geq 0, k \geq 0, i+j+k \leq 10, x=paté, i=6\}$

which may be simplified to

    $\Leftarrow$ Main(y,j), Dessert(z,k), {j$\geq$0, k$\geq$0, j+k$\leq$4, x=paté}.

Finally, we may obtain the goal clause

    $\Leftarrow$ {x=paté, y=sole, z=fruit},

whose constraints can be regarded as the answer substitution.

As we examplified, a constraint solver does not only check whether a set of constraints is solvable but also simplifies the constraints.

Jaffar & Lassez (1987) devised a "constraint logic programming scheme", "CLP(X)", where X may be instantiated to a theory over an arbitrary domain. They showed that the principal semantic properties of logic programs,

-   the existence of a canonical domain of computation,
-   the existence of a least and greatest model semantics,
-   the existence of a least and greatest fixpoint semantics,
-   soundness and completeness results for successful or finitely failed derivations of the underlying implementation model, and
-   soundness and completeness results for negation-as-failure,

hold also for constraint logic programming languages. Heintze et al. (1987) instantiated CLP(X) to CLP(R), where a simplex algorithm is used to solve constraints over real arithmetic expressions. On the other hand, Colmerauer's (1987) PROLOG III is intended to operate on rational trees, boolean expressions, and rational numbers.

CHIP - Constraint Handling in PROLOG

Another approach to constraint logic programming was developed by van Hentenryck & Dincbas (1986). Their basis is a domain concept which specifies the range of variables. For example, a variable may range over the Herbrand universe, over a finite set {a_1, ..., a_n} of values, or an interval [n,m] of natural numbers. In other words, variables are typed. When unifying a domain-variable with a constant, it has to be checked whether the constant is in the domain of the variable. When unifying two domain-variables, their domain intersection has to be computed and must be non-empty.

This method allows to handle inequalities even if one element of the inequality is a variable. For example, consider the inequality x$\neq$e, where x is a domain variable ranging over domain D and e is an element of D. Let D' be D\{e}. If D' is a singleton, then x is bound to the singleton, otherwise x is bound to a new variable y ranging over D'.

Recently, van Hentenryck (1988) showed that the domain concept and the eager treatment of not completely instantiated inequalities greatly improves the efficiency of generate-and-test programs.

Based on these techniques the programming language CHIP (Constraint Handling In PROLOG) was developed. The expressiveness, efficiency, and flexibility of CHIP was shown by solving several difficult combinatorial problems in operations reasearch (Dincbas et al. 1988a,b).

Order-Sorted Horn Logic

Throughout this thesis we only considered unsorted (or one-sorted) theories. In recent years order-sorted Horn logic has attracted many researchers because it supports data abstraction, inheritance, readability, and early error detection. Furthermore, its enhanced expressiveness leads to shorter programs. C. Walther (1983, 1987) set up an order-sorted calculus based on resolution and unrestricted paramodulation. Based on his work EPOS (Huber & Varsek 1987), an order-sorted logic programming language, was developed. The semantics of EPOS was captured by expressing sorted terms in the unsorted calculus, whereas the proof theory was given with respect to order-sorted SLD-resolution. Whereas EPOS does not include equality, G. Smolka's (1986) calculus comprises logic programming, equational reasoning, and order-sorted logic. Programs are given an initial algebra semantics and deductions are based on order-sorted equational unification and resolution. TEL (Smolka 1987) is a programming language built on these ideas which combines types, equations, and logic. Order-sorted equational unification was studied by Meseguer et al. (1987) and Smolka et al. (1987). Whereas in these approaches order-sorted unification problems are solved by first solving the unsorted instance of the problem and, then, testing the well-sortedness of the solutions, C. Kirchner (1988) developed a unification procedure in which the sort information is used as soon as possible to discard failures quickly and to direct the unification process more efficiently.

LIFE

The programming language LIFE (Ait-Kaci & Lincoln 1988) was developed to explore whether the advantages of functional, logic, and object-oriented programming can be combined. Accordingly, LIFE consists of a functional, a relational, and an object-oriented component (see figure 9.2.1). The functional part is based on λ-calculus programming, the relation part is based on programming in a first order calculus restricted to Horn clauses, and object-oriented programming is based on Ait-Kaci's (1984) ψ-calculus. The language of the ψ-calculus consists of structured types (called ψ-terms), subtyping, and type-intersection operations. ψ-terms can be used to represent record-like data structures in functional and logic programming languages. Two ψ-terms s and t are "unified" in the sense that a new ψ-term is constructed which inherits the common properties of s and t, if they have any. (ψ-term unification was recasted within the framework of order-sorted equational unification by Smolka & Ait-Kaci (1987)).

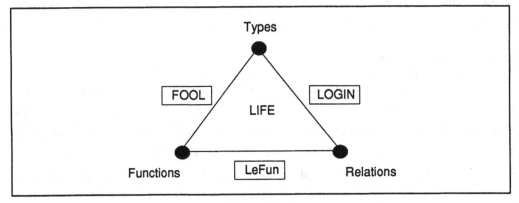

Figure 9.2.1

The components of LIFE were pairwise integerated. LOGIN (Ait-Kaci & Nasr 1986) is a logic programming language, where the traditional first-order terms were replaced by ψ-terms. Similarly, FOOL is a functional programming language, where the first-order constructor terms were replaced by ψ-terms. In chapter 8 we already mentioned LeFun (Ait-Kaci et al. 1987), which is a relational and logic programming language. In LeFun, functional expressions are reduced before they are submitted to the unification algorithm. If two reduced expressions cannot be unified, then they are recorded as "residuations" and delayed until variables occurring in the "residuations" become instantiated.

Finally, LIFE is the combination of LOGIN, FOOL, and LeFun. In LIFE the user can specify types, functions, and relations. ψ-terms are used within functions and relations to specify types, subtypes, and inheritance. On the hand, functional and relational constraints can be specified on ψ-terms.

Theory Resolution

In this thesis we augmented logic programs with Horn equality theories. This can be seen as a special form of Stickel's (1985) approach to add arbitrary theories to sets of clauses and to apply theory resolution, i.e. the selected literals are unified under the given theory.

9.3 Open Problems

At the end of this thesis we point out some problems and we give a brief outlook on future work.

Virtually all PROLOG systems avoid the occur check, since it is very time consuming. (As Cox & Pietrzykowski (1985) remarked, to perform the occur check but to allow cycles in logic programming seems to be an arbitrary decision, since after flattening the clauses, the two problems are almost identical.) To give a semantics for those PROLOG systems, Colmerauer (1983, 1983, 1984) interpreted PROLOG over the domain of rational trees. This technique should be applied to equational logic programming as well to compute EP-unifiers over the domain of rational trees.

It seems to us that a major open problem is the question of eager variable elimation or, more precisely, the question for which equational theory and for which set of inference rules can variables be eliminated eagerly without violating completeness. Many authors proposed that variables can be eliminated as early as possible (e.g. Martelli et al 1986, Gallier & Snyder 1987a, Hölldobler 1987a) but failed to give a rigorous proof for their claim or overlooked a case in their proof. In a subsequent paper Gallier & Snyder (1987b) expressed their belief that variables cannot be eliminated eagerly, yet they were unable to give an example for it. Only recently, Hsiang & Jouannaud (1988) announced a proof for this problem if the equational theory is unconditional and canonical.

Just to give the reader an idea what effect an eager variable elimination might have we recall the transformation rules introduced in chapter 7. If variables can be eliminated as early as possible, then

a) lazy narrowing need only be applied to equations of the form $EQ(f(s_1,...,s_n),t)$, where t is either non-variable or t occurs in $f(s_1,...,s_n)$,

b) paramodulation at variable occurrences need only be applied to equations of the form $EQ(x,t)$, where x occurs in t,

c) a trivial clause need only be applied to equations of the form $EQ(s,t)$, where s is either non-variable or occurs in t, and

d) imitation need only be applied to equations of the form $EQ(x,f(s_1,...,s_n))$, where x occurs in $f(s_1,...,s_n)$.

As a consequence we would be able to handle infinite objects as the following example demonstrates. Consider the term rewriting system

INTEGERS: int(w) → x:int(s(w))   (i)

                       first(0,y) → []   (f1)

                       first(s(x),y:z) → y:first(x,z)   (f2)

which can be used to compute the first n elements of an infinite list of integers. Suppose we have to answer the request of computing the first element of a list of integers and comparing it with a partially instantiated list. In figure 9.3.1 we depict the derivation tree generated by the transformation rules term decomposition, variable elimination, elimination of trivial

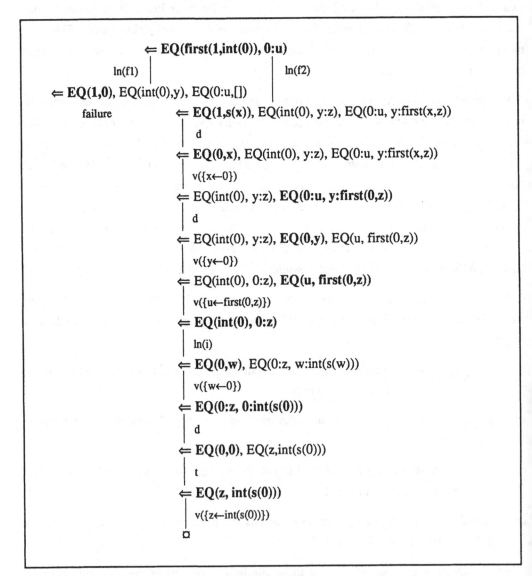

Figure 9.3.1

equations, lazy narrowing, and imitation, where variables are eliminated eagerly. The derivation tree is finite and we obtain the answer substitution {u←first(0,int(s(0)))}. It should be
noted that the answer is not in normal form and that there has never been a request to
evaluate the term int(s(0)).

The eager variable elimination problem also shows why it is interesting to investigate EP-
unifiers over the domain of rational trees. A set of transformations to compute such EP-unifiers does not have to consider the cases b) and d) and lazy narrowing need only be applied
if the "t" in a) is non-variable.

In recent years many proposals have been made to handle equations in logic languages.
Each of these proposals seems to be superior to another one in some aspect. However, we
need a general setting to compare the various techniques. In this thesis a first attempt is
made by transforming refutations with respect to paramodulation, instantiation, and reflection
into refutations with respect to the transformations in TRANS. By looking at examples like
the question of whether f(g(a)) and b are equal under the term rewriting system

R:	f(x) → x	(f)
	g(x) → h(x)	(g)
	h(x) → b	(h)

we have the impression that the search space generated with respect to our transformation
rules (figure 9.3.3) is smaller than the corresponding one generated by paramodulation and
reflection (figure 9.3.2). In the example each of the three possible refutations with respect to
paramodulation and reflection was transformed into the same refutation with respect to our
transformation rules. However, we were unable to give a rigorous proof for this impression.

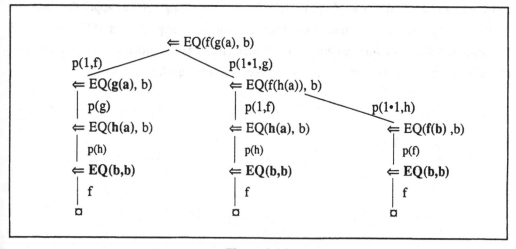

Figure 9.3.2

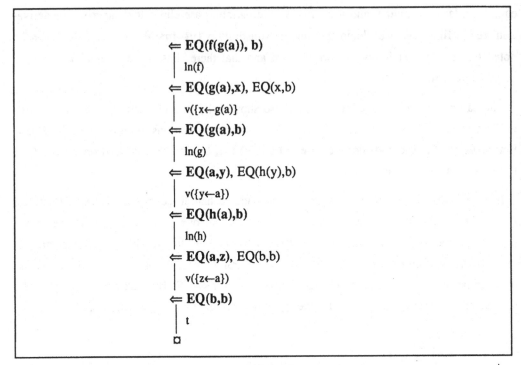

Figure 9.3.3

Another attempt is the work of Nutt et al. (1987), in which in one system flattening and narrowing steps can be mixed freely. But again the authors give no statement concerning the problem under which conditions flattening is superior to narrowing or vice versa.

In this thesis we were interested in soundness and strong completeness properties of first-order theories with equality. Except for "basic" narrowing we did not consider representation and implementation problems of our calculi. We feel the strong need to apply the most advanced implementation techniques from logic programming (e.g. Warren 1983), functional programming (e.g. Fairbairn & Wray 1987), automatic theorem proving, and combinations thereof (e.g. Jamsek et al. 1988) to first-order theories with equality.

References

We use the following abbreviations for technical reports, proceedings, journals, etc.:

ACM	Association for Computing Machinery
CAAP	Proceedings of the Colloquium on Trees in Algebra and Programming
CACM	Communications of the ACM
CADE	Proceedings of the Conference on Automated Deduction
CRIN	Centre de Recherche en Informatique de Nancy, Campus Scientifique, B.P.239, 54506 Vandoeuvre Les Nancy Cedex
ECAI	Proceedings of the European Conference on Artificial Intelligence
FGCS	Proceedings of the International Conference on Fifth Generation Computer Systems
GWAI	Proceedings of the German Workshop on Artificial Intelligence
ICALP	Proceedings of the International Colloquium on Automata, Languages, and Programming
ICLP	Proceedings of the International Conference on Logic Programming
IEEE	The Institute of Electrical and Electronics Engineers
IFB	Informatik-Fachberichte, Springer
IFIP	Proceedings of the World Computer Congress of the International Federation of Information Processing Societies
IJCAI	Proceedings of the International Joint Conference on Artificial Intelligence
IRIA	Institute de Recherche d'Informatique et d'Automatique, Domaine de Voluceau, Rocquencourt, B.P.10578150, Le Chesnay, France
JACM	Journal of the ACM
JAR	Journal of Automated Reasoning
JLP	Journal of Logic Programming
JSC	Journal of Symbolic Computation
LNCS	Lecture Notes in Computer Science, Springer
MCC	Microelectronics and Computer Technology Corporation, 3500 West Balcones Center Drive, Austin, TX 78759
POPL	Proceedings of the Annual ACM Symposium on Principles of Programming Languages
RTA	Proceedings of the International Conference on Rewriting Techniques and Applications
SIAM	Society for Industrial and Applied Mathematics
SLP	Proceedings of the Symposium on Logic Programming
TCS	Journal of Theoretical Computer Science

H. Ait-Kaci: A Lattice-Theoretic Approach to Computation Based on a Calculus of Partially-Ordered Type Structures. Ph.D. Thesis. Department of Computer and Information Science, University of Pennsylvania, Philadelphia, 1984

H. Ait-Kaci, P. Lincoln: LIFE: A Natural Language for Natural Language. MCC Technical Report ACA-ST-074-88, 1988

H. Ait-Kaci, P. Lincoln, R. Nasr: Le Fun: Logic, Equations, and Functions. SLP '87, 17-23, 1987

H. Ait-Kaci, R. Nasr: Residuation: A Paradigm for Integrating Logic and Functional Programming. MCC Technical Report AI-359-86, 1986a

H. Ait-Kaci, R.Nasr: LOGIN: A Logic Programming Language with Built-in Inheritance. JLP 3, 187-215, 1986b

H. Ait-Kaci, G. Smolka: Inheritance Hierarchies: Semantics and Unification. MCC Technical Report AI-057-87, 1987

R. Anderson: Completeness Results for E-Resolution. Proceedings of the AFIPS (American Federation of Information Processing Societies) Spring Joint Computer Conference, 36, 653-656, 1970

K. R. Apt, M. H. van Emden: Contributions to the Theory of Logic Programming. JACM 29, 841 - 862, 1982

R. Barbuti, M. Bellia, G. Levi, M. Martelli: LEAF: A Language which Integrates Logic, Equations and Functions. In: Logic Programming (DeGroot, Lindstrom eds.), Prentice Hall, 201-238, 1986

C. Beierle, U. Pletat: On the Integration of Equality, Sorts, and Logic Programming. Proceedings Österreichische AI-Tagung (ÖGAI), IFB 151, 133-144, 1987

J. A. Bergstra, J. W. Klop: Conditional Rewrite Rules: Confluence and Termination. Journal of Computer and System Sciences 32, 323-362, 1986

K. H. Bläsius: Equality Reasoning Based on Graphs. Universität Kaiserslautern, SEKI-Report SR-87-01, 1987

K. H. Bläsius, J. Siekmann: Partial Unification for Graph Based Equational Reasoning. CADE '88, LNCS 310, 397-414, 1988

D. G. Bobrow: If PROLOG is the Answer, What is the Question? FGCS '84, 138-145, 1984

A. Bockmayr: A Note on a Canonical Theory with Undecidable Unification and Matching Problem. JAR 3, 379-381, 1987

A. Bockmayr: Narrowing with Built-in Theories. Proceedings of the First International Workshop on Algebraic and Logic Programming (Grabowski, Lescanne, Wechler, eds.), Akademie-Verlag, Berlin, 83-92, 1988

P. G. Bosco, E. Giovanetti, C. Moiso: Refined Strategies for Semantic Unification. Proceedings of the Conference on Theory and Practice of Software Development (TAPSOFT), LNCS 250, 276-290, 1987

R. S. Boyer, J. S. Moore: The Sharing of Structure in Theorem-Proving Programs. Machine Intelligence 7 (Meltzer, Michie, eds.) Edinburgh University Press, 1972

D. Brand: Proving Theorems with the Modification Method. SIAM Journal of Computing 4, 412-430, 1975

H-J. Bürckert: Lazy Theory Unification in PROLOG: An Extension of the Warran Abstract Machine. GWAI '86, IFB 124, 277-288, 1986

H-J. Bürckert: Lazy E-Unification - A Method to Delay Alternative Solutions. First Workshop on Unification, University Nancy, Rapport Interne no 87 R 34 (C. Kirchner ed.), 1987

W. Büttner, H. Simonis: Embedding Boolean Expressions into Logic Programming. JSC 4, 191-205, 1987

R. M. Burstall, D. B. MacQueen, D.T. Sanella: HOPE: An Experimental Applicative Language. Internal Report, University of Edinburgh, 1980

C. L. Chang, R. C. T. Lee: Symbolic Logic and Mechanical Theorem Proving. Academic Press, 1973

A. Church: The Calculi of Lambda-Conversion. Princeton University Press, 1941

K. L. Clark: Negation as Failure. Proceedings of the Workshop on Logic and Databases (Gallaire, Nicolas, eds.), Toulouse, France, 1977

K. L. Clark: Predicate Logic as a Computational Formalism. Research Report DOC 79/59, Department of Computing, Imperial College, 1979

K. L. Clark, S. Gregory: A Relational Language for Parallel Programming. Proceedings of the ACM Conference on Functional Programming Languages and Computer Architecture, 171-178, 1981

W. F. Clocksin, C. S. Mellish: Programming in Prolog. Springer, 1981, 3rd ed. 1987

J. Cohen: A View of the Origins and Development of PROLOG. CACM 31, 26-23, 1988

S. Cohen: The APPLOG Language. In: Logic Programming (DeGroot, Lindstrom, eds.), Prentice Hall, 239 - 276, 1986

A. Colmerauer: Prolog and Infinite Trees. In: Logic Programming (Clark, Tarnlund, eds.), Academic Press, 231-251, 1982

A. Colmerauer: Prolog in 10 Figures. IJCAI '83, 487-499, 1983

A. Colmerauer: Equations and Inequations on Finite and Infinite Trees. FGCS '84, 85-99, 1984

A. Colmerauer: Opening the PROLOG III Universe. Technical Report, University of Aix-Marseille II, 1987

J. Corbin, M. Bidoit: A Rehabilitation of Robinson's Unification Algorithm. IFIP '83, 909-914, 1983

P. T. Cox, T. Pietrzykowski: Surface Deduction: A Uniform Mechanism for Logic Programming. SLP '85, 220-227, 1985

P. T. Cox, T. Pietrzykowski: Incorporating Equality into Logic Programming via Surface Deduction. Annals of Pure and Applied Logic 31, 177-189, 1986

J. Darlington, A. J. Field, H. Pull: The Unification of Functional and Logic Languages. Logic Programming (DeGroot, Lindstrom, eds), Prentice Hall, 37-70, 1986

M. Davis: The Prehistory and Early History of Automated Deduction. In: Automation of Reasoning; Classical Papers on Computational Logic 1957-1966 (Siekmann, Wrightson, eds.), Springer, 1-28, 1983

N. Dershowitz, Z. Manna: Proving Termination with Multiset Orderings. CACM 22, 465-475, 1979

N. Dershowitz, D. A. Plaisted: Logic Programming cum Applicative Programming. SLP '85, 54-66, 1985

V. J. Digricoli: Resolution by Unification and Equality. CADE '79, 43-52, 1979

V. J. Digricoli, M. C. Harrison: Equality-Based Binary Resolution. JACM 33, 253-289, 1986

M. Dincbas, H. Simonis, P. van Hentenryck: Solving the Car-Sequencing Problem in Constraint Logic Programming. ECAI '88, 290-295, 1988a

M. Dincbas, H. Simonis, P. van Hentenryck: Solving a Cutting Stock Problem in Constraint Logic Programming: ICLP/SLP '88, 42-58, 1988b

R. Echahed: On Completeness of Narrowing Strategies. CAAP '88, LNCS 299, 89-101, 1988

F. Fages, G. Huet: Complete Sets of Unifiers and Matchers in Equational Theories. LNCS 159, 205-220, 1983

F. Fages, G. Huet: Complete Sets of Unifiers and Matchers in Equational Theories. TCS 43, 189-200, 1986

J. Fairbairn, S. Wray: TIM: A Simple Lazy Abstract Machine to Execute Supercombinators. Proceedings of the Functional Languages and Computer Architecture Conference, 1987

M. Fay: First-Order Unification in an Equational Theory. CADE '79, 161-167, 1979

G. Frege: Begriffsschrift, a Formal Language, Modelled upon that of Arithmetic, for Pure Thought. In: From Frege to Gödel (Heijenoort ed.) Harvard University Press, 1971

L. Fribourg: Oriented Equational Clauses as a Programming Language. JLP 1, 165-177, 1984

L. Fribourg: SLOG: A Logic Programming Language Interpreter Based on Clausal Superposition and Rewriting. SLP '85, 172-185, 1985

U. Furbach: Oldy but Goody: Paramodulation Revisited. GWAI '87, IFB 152, 195-200, 1987

U. Furbach, S. Hölldobler: Modelling the Combination of Functional and Logic Programming Languages. JSC 2, 123-138, 1986

U. Furbach, S. Hölldobler: FHCL - Functions in Horn Clause Logic: Report FKI-66-88, Technische Universität München, 1988

U. Furbach, S. Hölldobler, J. Schreiber: Horn Equality Theories and Paramodulation. Technical Report 8801, UniBwM, *to appear in:* JAR, 1989

H. Gallaire: Logic Programming: Further Developments. SLP '85, 88-96, 1985

J. H. Gallier, S. Raatz: SLD-Resolution Methods for Horn Clauses with Equality Based on E-Unification. SLP '86, 168-179, 1986

J. H. Gallier, S. Raatz: Extending SLD-Resolution to Equational Horn Clauses using E-Unification. JLP 6, 3-43 1989

J. H. Gallier, W. Snyder: A General Complete E-Unification Procedure. RTA '87, LNCS 256, 1987a

J. H. Gallier, W. Snyder: Complete Sets of Transformations for General E-Unification. Department of Computer and Information Science, University of Pennsylvania, Philadelphia, 1987b

E. Giovannetti, C. Moiso: A Completeness Result for E-Unification Algorithms based on Conditional Narrowing. LNCS 308, 1988

J. A. Goguen, J. Meseguer: Equality, Types, and Generics for Logic Programming. JLP 1, 179-210, 1984

J. A. Goguen, J. Meseguer: EQLOG: Equality, Types, and Generic Modules for Logic Programming. In: Logic Programming (DeGroot, Lindstrom, eds.), Prentice Hall, 295-363, 1986

J. A. Goguen, J. W. Thatcher, E. G. Wagner, J. B. Wright: Initial Algebra Semantics and Continuous Algebras. JACM 24, 68-95, 1977

F. Goldfarb: The Undecidability of the Second-Order Unification Problem. TCS 13, 225-230, 1981

K. J. Greene: A Fully Lazy Higher Order Purely Functional Programming Language with Reduction Semantics. Syracuse University, CASE Center Technical Report No. 8503, 1985

M. A. Harrison: Introduction to Formal Language Theory. Addison-Wesley, 1978

M. A. Harrison, N. Rubin: Another Generalization of Resolution. JACM 25, 341-351, 1978

S. Heilbrunner: A Metatheorem for Undecidable Properties of Formal Languages and its Application to LRR and URR Grammars and Languages. TCS 23, 49-68, 1983

S. Heilbrunner, S. Hölldobler: The Undecidability of the Unification and Matching Problem for Canonical Theories. Acta Informatica 24, 157-171, 1987

N. Heinze, J. Jaffar, S. Michaylov, P. Stuckey, R. Yap: The CLP(R) Programmer's Manual. Deptartment of Computer Science, Monash University, Clayton, Australia, 1987

P. Henderson: Functional Programming. Prentice Hall, 1980

L. Henschen, L. Wos: Unit Refutations and Horn Sets. JACM 21, 590-605, 1974

J. Herbrand: Sur la Théorie de la Démonstration. Logical Writings (W. Goldfarb, ed.), Cambridge, 1971

A. Herold: Some Basic Notions of First-Order Unification Theory. Bericht Nr. 15/83, Fakultät für Informatik, Universität Karlsruhe, 1983

R. Hill: LUSH-Resolution and Its Completeness. DCI Memo 78, Department of Artificial Intelligence, University of Edinburgh, 1974

P. Hoddinott, E. W. Elcock: PROLOG: Subsumption of Equality Axioms by the Homogeneous Form. SLP '86, 115-126, 1986

S. Hölldobler, U. Furbach, T. Laußermair: Extended Unification and its Implementation. GWAI '85, IFB 118, 176-185, 1985

S. Hölldobler: A Unification Algorithm for Confluent Theories. ICALP '87, LNCS 267, 31-41, 1987a

S. Hölldobler: Equational Logic Programming. SLP '87, 335-346, 1987b

S. Hölldobler: From Paramodulation to Narrowing. ICLP/SLP '88, 327-342, 1988a

S. Hölldobler: Horn Equational Theories and Complete Sets of Transformations. FGCS '88, 405-412, 1988b

J. Hsiang, J. P. Jouannaud: General E-Unification Revisited. Second International Workshop on Unification, Val d'Ajol, France, 1988

J. Hsiang, M. Rusinowitch: On Word Problems in Equational Theories. ICALP '87, LNCS 267, 54-71, 1987

M. Huber, I. Varsek: Extended Prolog for Order-Sorted Resolution. SLP '87, 34-43, 1987

G. Huet: Constrained Resolution: A Complete Method for Higher-Order Logic. Ph.D. Thesis, Case Western Reserve University, Department of Computing and Information Science, Report 1117, 1972

G. Huet: The Undecidability of Unification in Third Order Logic. Information and Control 22, 257-267, 1973

G. Huet: A Unification Algorithm for Typed Lambda Calculus. TCS 1, 27-57, 1975

G. Huet: Confluent Reductions: Abstract Properties and Applications to Term Rewriting Systems. JACM 27, 797-821, 1980

G. Huet, D. Lankford: On the Uniform Halting Problem For Term Rewriting Systems. Rapport de Recherche No 283, IRIA, 1978

G. Huet, D. C. Oppen: Equations and Rewrite Rules. In: Formal Languages: Perspectives and Open Problems (Book, ed.), Academic Press, 1980

J. M. Hullot: Canonical Forms and Unification. CADE '80, 318-334, 1980

H. Hussmann: Unification in Conditional-Equational Theories. Proceedings of the European Conference on Computer Algebra (EUROCAL), LNCS 204, 543-553, 1985

J. Jaffar, J.-L. Lassez: Constraint Logic Programming. POPL '87, 111-119, 1987

J. Jaffar, J.-L. Lassez, M. J. Maher: A Theory of Complete Logic Programs with Equality. FGCS '84, 175-184, 1984

J. Jaffar, J.-L. Lassez, M. J. Maher: Prolog-II as an Instance of the Logic Programming Language Scheme. Technical Report, IBM T.J.Watson Lab., 1985

J. Jaffar, J.-L. Lassez, M. J. Maher: A Logic Programming Language Scheme. In: Logic Programming (DeGroot, Lindstrom eds.), Prentice Hall, 441-467, 1986

D. A. Jamsek, K. J. Greene, S.-K. Chin, P. R. Humenn: WINTER: An Architecture Supporting a Purely Declarative Language. Syracuse University, 1988

J. P. Jouannaud, C. Kirchner, H. Kirchner: Incremental Construction of Unification Algorithms in Equational Theories. ICALP '83, LNCS 154, 361-373, 1983

S. Kaplan: Conditional Rewrite Rules. TCS 33, 175-193, 1984

S. Kaplan: Fair Conditional Term Rewriting Systems: Unification, Termination, and Confluence. Recent Trends in Data Type Specification (Kreowski, ed.), IFB 116, 136-155, 1986

C. Kirchner: A New Equational Unification Method: A Generalization of Martelli-Montanari's Algorithm. CADE '84, 224-247, 1984

C. Kirchner: Order-Sorted Equational Unification. ICLP/SLP '88, 1988

D. E. Knuth, P. B. Bendix: Simple Word Problems in Universal Algebras. In: Computational Problems in Abstract Algebra (Leech ed.), Pergamon Press, 1970

A. J. Korenjak, J. E. Hopcroft: Simple Deterministic Languages. Annual Symposium on Switching and Automata Theory 7, 36-46, 1966

W. A. Kornfeld: Equality for Prolog. IJCAI '83, 514-519, 1983

R. A. Kowalski: Predicate Logic as Programming Language. IFIP '74, 570-574, 1974

R. A. Kowalski: A Proof Procedure Using Connection Graphs. JACM 22, 572-595, 1975

R. A. Kowalski: Algorithm = Logic + Control. CACM 22, 424-436, 1979a

R. A. Kowalski: Logic for Problem Solving. North-Holland, 1979b

R. A. Kowalski: Logic Programming. IFIP '83, 133-145, 1983

R. A. Kowalski: The Early Years of Logic Programming. CACM 31, 38-43:,1988

R. A. Kowalski, D. Kuehner: Linear Resolution with Selection Function. Artificial Intelligence 2, 227-260, 1971

D. S. Lankford: Canonical Inference. Technical Report, Department of Mathematics, Southwestern University, Georgetown, Texas, 1975

G. Lindstrom: Functional Programming and the Logical Variable. POPL '85, 1985

J. W. Lloyd: Foundations of Logic Programming. Springer, 1984, 2nd ed. 1987

J. W. Lloyd, R. W. Topor: Making Prolog more Expressive. JLP 1, 225-240, 1984

J. W. Lloyd, R. W. Topor: A Basis for Deductive Database Systems. JLP 2, 93-110, 1985

J. W. Lloyd, R. W.Topor: A Basis for Deductive Database Systens II. JLP 3, 55-68, 1986

D. W. Loveland: Automated Theorem Proving: A Logical Basis. Fundamental Studies in Computer Science 6, North-Holland,1978

B. Mahr, J. A. Makowsky: Characterizing Specification Languages Which Admit Initial Semantics. CAAP '83, LNCS 159, 300-316, 1983

Z. Manna: Mathematical Theory of Computation. McGraw-Hill, 1974

A. Martelli, U. Montanari: An Efficient Unification Algorithm. ACM Transactions on Programming Languages and Systems (TOPLAS) 4, 258-282, 1982

A. Martelli, C. Moiso, C. F. Rossi: An Algorithm for Unification in Equational Theories. SLP '86, 180-186, 1986

J. McCarthy, P. W. Abrahams, D. J. Edwards, T. P. Hart, M. I. Levin: The LISP 1.5 Programmer's Manual. MIT Press, 1965

E. Mendelson: Introduction to Mathematical Logic. van Nostrand Company, 1979

J. Meseguer, J. A. Goguen, G. Smolka: Order-Sorted Unification. Center for the Study of Language and Information Report No. CSLI-87-86, 1987

D. Miller, G. Nadathur: A Logic Programming Approach to Manipulating Formulas and Programs. SLP '87, 379-388, 1987

J. Morris: E-resolution: An Extension of Resolution to Include the Equality Relation. IJCAI '69, 287-294, 1969

M. H. A. Newman: On Theories with a Combinatorical Definition of "Equivalence". Annals of Mathematics 43, 223-243, 1942

T. Nipkow: Unification in Primal Algebras. Technical Report, Department of Computer Science, University of Manchester, 1987

W. Nutt, P. Réty, G. Smolka: Basic Narrowing Revisited. SEKI Report SR-87-07, Universität Kaiserslautern, 1987

P. Padawitz: Strategy-Controlled Reduction and Narrowing. RTA '87, LNCS 256, 242-255, 1987

P. Padawitz: Foundations of Specification and Programming with Horn Clauses. EATCS Monograph on Theoretical Computer Science 16, Springer, 1988

M. S. Paterson, M. N. Wegman: Linear Unification. Journal of Computer Systems and Sciences 16, 158-167, 1978

G. Peterson: A Technique for Establishing Completeness Results in Theorem Proving with Equality. SIAM Journal of Computing 12, 82-100, 1983

G. D. Plotkin: Building-In Equational Theories. In: Machine Intelligence 7 (Meltzer, Michie, eds.), 73-90, 1972

U. S. Reddy: Narrowing as the Operational Semantics of Functional Languages. SLP '85, 138-151, 1985

R. Reiter: On Closed World Data Bases. Proceedings of the Workshop on Logic and Databases (Gallaire, Nicolas, eds.), Toulouse, France, 1977

P. Réty: Improving Basic Narrowing Techniques and Commutation Properties. Technical Report, CRIN, 1987

P. Réty, C. Kirchner, H. Kirchner, P. Lescanne: NARROWER: A New Algorithm for Unification and its Application to Logic Programming. LNCS 202, 141-155, 1985

J. Reynolds: Transformational Systems and the Algebraic Structure of Atomic Formulas. Machine Intelligence 5 (Meltzer, Michie, eds.), American Elsevier, 135-152, 1970

G. A. Ringwood: SLD: A Folk Acronym? Logic Programming Newsletter 2/1, 5-7, 1988

G. A. Robinson, L. Wos: Paramodulation and Theorem Proving in First Order Theories with Equality. Machine Intelligence 4 (Meltzer, Michie, eds.), 1969

J. A. Robinson: A Machine-Oriented Logic based on the Resolution Principle. JACM 12, 23-41, 1965

J. A. Robinson: A Review on Automatic Theorem Proving. Annual Symposia in Applied Mathematics 19, 1-18, 1967

J. A. Robinson: Computational Logic: The Unification Computation. Machine Intelligence 6 (Meltzer, Michie, eds), Edinburgh University Press, 63-72, 1971

J. A. Robinson: LOGIC: Form and Function. North-Holland, 1979

J. A. Robinson: Logic Programming - Past, Present and Future. New Generation Computing 1, 107-124, 1983

J. A. Robinson, K. J. Greene: New Generation Knowledge Processing: Final Report on the SUPER System. CASE Center Technical Report 8707, Syracuse University, 1987

J. A. Robinson, E. E. Sibert: LOGLISP: An Alternative to PROLOG. Machine Intelligence 10 (Hayes, Michie, eds.), 399-419, 1982

M. Sato, T. Sakurai: QUTE: A PROLOG/LISP Type Language for Logic Programming. IJCAI '83, 507-513, 1983

M. Schmidt-Schauss: Unification in a Combination of Arbitrary Disjoint Equational Theories. CADE '88, LNCS 310, 378-396, 1988

M. Schönfinkel: Über die Bausteine der Mathematischen Logik. Mathematische Annalen 82, 305-316, 1924

D. Scott: Outline of a Mathematical Theory of Computation. Technical Monograph PRG-2, Oxford University Computing Laboratory, Programming Research Group, 1970

J. C. Sheperdson: Negation as Failure: A Comparison of Clark's Completed Data Base and Reiter's Closed World Assumption. JLP 1, 51-79, 1984

J. H. Siekmann: Universal Unification. LNCS 170, 1-42, 1984

J. H. Siekmann: Unification Theory. ECAI '88, 365-400, 1986

J. H. Siekmann: Geschichte und Anwendungen. In: Deduktionssysteme (Bläsius, Bürckert, eds.), Oldenbourg, 3-21, 1987

J. H. Siekmann: Unification Theory. *To appear in:* JSC, 1989

J. H. Siekmann, P. Szabo: The Undecidability of the DA-Unification Problem. *To appear in:* Journal of Symbolic Logic, 1989

J. H. Siekmann, G. Wrightson: Paramodulated Connectiongraphs. Acta Informatica 13, 67-86, 1980

J. R. Slagle: Automatic Theorem Proving with Built-in Theories Including Equality, Partial Orderings, and Sets. JACM 19, 120-135, 1972

J. R. Slagle: Automatic Theorem Proving in Theories with Simplifiers, Commutativity and Associativity. JACM 21, 622-642, 1974

G. Smolka: Order-Sorted Horn Logic: Semantics and Deduction. Universität Kaiserslautern, SEKI-Report SR-86-17, 1986

G. Smolka: TEL (Version 0.9) Report and User Manual. Universität Kaiserslautern, SEKI-Report SR-87-11, 1987

G. Smolka, W. Nutt, J. A. Goguen, J. Meseguer: Order-Sorted Equational Computation. Universität Kaiserslautern, SEKI-Report SR-87-14, 1987

M. E. Stickel: Automated Deduction by Theory Resolution. JAR 1, 333-356, 1985

J. E. Stoy: Denotational Semantics. MIT Press, 1977

P. A. Subrahmanyam, J.-H. You: Conceptual Basis and Evaluation Strategies for Integrating Functional and Logic Programming. SLP '84, 144-153, 1984

P. A. Subrahmanyam, J.-H. You: FUNLOG: A Computational Model Integrating Logic Programming and Functional Programming. Logic Programming (DeGroot, Lindstrom, eds.), Prentice Hall, 157-198, 1986.

P. Szabo: Unifikationstheorie erster Ordnung. Dissertation, Fakultät für Informatik, Universität Karlsruhe, 1982

H. Tamaki: Semantics of a Logic Programming Language with a Reducibility Predicate. SLP '84: 259-264, 1984

A. Tarski: A Lattice Theoretic Fixpoint Theorem and its Applications. Pacific Journal of Mathematics 5, 285-309, 1955

A. Togushi, S. Noguchi: A Program Transformation from Equational into Logic Programs. JLP 4, 85-103, 1987

D. A. Turner: The Semantic Elegance of Applicative Languages. Symposium on Functional Languages and their Implications for Computer Architecture, 85-92, 1981

M. H. van Emden, R. A. Kowalski: The Semantics of Predicate Logic as a Programming Language. JACM 23, 733-742, 1976

M. H. van Emden, J. W. Lloyd: A Logical Reconstruction of Prolog II. JLP 1, 143-149, 1984

M. H. van Emden, K. Yukawe: Logic Programming with Equations. JLP 4, 265-288, 1987

P. van Hentenryck, M. Dincbas: Domains in Logic Programming. Proceedings of the AAAI '86, 759-765, 1986

P. van Hentenryck: A Constraint Approach to Mastermind in Logic Programming. ACM Special Interest Group on Artificial Intelligence (SIGART) Newsletter 103, 31-35, 1988

C. Walther: A Many-Sorted Calculus Based on Resolution and Paramodulation. IJCAI '83, 882-891, 1983

C. Walther: A Many-Sorted Calculus Based on Resolution and Paramodulation. In: Research Notes in Artificial Intelligence, Morgan Kaufmann, 1987

D. H. D. Warren: An Abstract PROLOG Instruction Set. SRI International, Technical Note 306, 1983

A. Yamamoto: A Theoretical Combination of SLD-Resolution and Narrowing. ICLP'87, 470-487, 1987

Index

The Inference Rules

Examples

Notations

π	occurrence	*18*
$\sigma, \theta, \ldots$	substitutions	*16*
$\sigma\|_V$	restriction of σ to V	*20*
$\sigma =_{EP} \theta [V]$	for all x in V we find $\sigma x =_{EP} \theta x$	*68*
$\sigma \sim_{EP} \theta [V]$	EP-variants with respect to V	*68*
ω	first infinite ordinal	*41*
$\neg$	not	*15*
$\wedge$	and	*15*
$\vee$	or	*15*
$\Rightarrow$	implication	*15*
$\Leftrightarrow$	equivalence	*15*
$\exists$	existential quantifier	*15*
$\forall$	universal quantifier	*15*
$\bullet$	concatenation	*18*
$=$	(multiset) equality	*16*
$\cup$	(multiset) union	*16*
$\setminus$	(multiset) difference	*16*
$\equiv$	congruence relation on the set of ground terms generated by EP	*30*
$\equiv_{EP}$	finest congruence relation on the set of ground terms generated by EP	*35*
$\square$	empty clause	*26*
$\leq_{EP}$	instantiation preorder	*67,68*
$\sim_{EP}$	EP-variants	*68*
$<<$	multiset ordering induced by $<$	*188*
$\ll$	ordering on complexities of refutations	*189*
#e	number of equations occurring in a goal clause	*188*
#p	number of applications of paramodulation in a derivation	*188*
#r	number of lazy resolution steps in a derivation	*203*
#s	number of symbols occurring in a goal clause	*188*

Lecture Notes in Computer Science

This subseries of the Lecture Notes in Computer Science reports new developments in Artificial Intelligence research and teaching – quickly, informally and at a high level. The type of material considered for publication includes preliminary drafts of original papers and monographs, technical reports of high quality and broad interest, advanced level lectures, reports of meetings, provided they are of exceptional interest and focused on a single topic. The timeliness of a manuscript is more important than its form which may be unfinished or tentative. If possible, a subject index should be included. Publication of Lecture Notes is intended as a service to the international computer science community, in that a commercial publisher, Springer-Verlag, can offer a wide distribution of documents which would otherwise have a restricted readership. Once published and copyrighted, they can be referred to in the scientific literature.

Manuscripts

Manuscripts should be no less than 100 and preferably no more than 500 pages in length.

They are reproduced by a photographic process and therefore must be prepared with extreme care according to the instructions available from the publisher. Proceedings' editors and authors of monographs receive 75 free copies. Authors of contributions to proceedings are free to use the material in other publications upon notification to the publisher. The typescript is reduced slightly in size during reproduction; best results will not be obtained unless the text on any one page is kept within the overall limit of 18 × 26,5 cm (7 × 10½ inches). On request, the publisher will supply special paper with the typing area outlined.

Manuscripts should be sent to Prof. J. Siekmann, Institut für Informatik, Universität Kaiserslautern, Postfach 30 49, D-6750 Kaiserslautern, FRG, or directly to Springer-Verlag Heidelberg.

Springer-Verlag, Heidelberger Platz 3, D-1000 Berlin 33
Springer-Verlag, Tiergartenstraße 17, D-6900 Heidelberg 1
Springer-Verlag, 175 Fifth Avenue, New York, NY 10010/USA
Springer-Verlag, 37-3, Hongo 3-chome, Bunkyo-ku, Tokyo 113, Japan

---

ISBN 3-540-51533-X
ISBN 0-387-51533-X